Travel in England

in the Seventeenth Century

THE TITLE-PAGE OF OGILBY'S *BRITANNIA*, 1675

Travel in England

in the Seventeenth Century

By

JOAN PARKES

GREENWOOD PRESS, PUBLISHERS
WESTPORT, CONNECTICUT

Originally published in 1925
by Oxford University Press, London

First Greenwood Reprinting 1970

Library of Congress Catalogue Card Number 70-109817

SBN 8371-4308-X

Printed in the United States of America

NOTE

I wish to express my gratitude to Mr. William Hoar who so kindly read my MS. and who gave me much helpful advice ; to Mr. Laurence Binyon, deputy Keeper of Prints, British Museum, for suggestions regarding the choice of engravings for illustration, to the Society of Antiquaries and to the proprietors of the *Connoisseur Magazine* for permission to reproduce prints and woodcuts in their possession ; and to the London Library, without the use of which this book could never have been written.

CONTENTS

III

THE WATCH

IV

CARRIAGE BY LAND AND WATER

V

INNS, ALEHOUSES, AND OTHER LODGING

VI

HIGHWAYMEN

VII

TRIALS AND TRIBULATIONS

VIII

ON THE ROAD

IX

TRAVELLERS AND TRAVELLING

LIST OF ILLUSTRATIONS

INTRODUCTION

TRAVEL ! How much is included in the word; what various sensations it imparts, and has imparted to generations of English men and women since it became detached in meaning from the old Norman-French *Travail*—work, labour !

Travail it was in the days of old, when the saddle, the pillion, and ' Shanks's mare ' were the only means of progress. Travail it was too, though less of labour than of spirit, when the waggon and the coach jolted through lanes such as we no longer know in England, toiling from early morn until nightfall to cover thirty or forty miles, or, when the days were short, and the rain-soused roads deep in adhesive, all-pervading mud, no more, perhaps, than would to-day be accomplished in a two or three hours' walk.

So passed one hundred and fifty years and more, with little change to mark their course. Then came the mail-coach and improved roads to ease travel of its greatest rigours. Edinburgh was brought as near London as Newark had been in earlier days of coaching. Travel became, if not an experience to be enjoyed for its own sake, at least a tolerable means of seeking enjoyment far from home. The word gained in value; adventure, allurement, came within its compass. Ere long the railways banished all that had gone before. Travelling became in the course of a few decades a thing of ease, to be as lightly undertaken as a hackney coach-ride in the days of Pepys. All trace of the original meaning of the word had gone. Its scope extended, its value still increased. Foreign lands, wide oceans, were brought more readily into view, until it seems to-day a word fraught with too large a significance for the short, uneventful trips, familiar or readily imagined, to which we are restricted in this small, sea-girt country.

It is in wanderings afar that we now visualize the word ; swift smooth-running trains or the slower but less trammelled motors ; palatial floating hotels, carrying us to scenes and climes alien enough to our own to give us pleasurable sensations of novelty and such adventures great or small as, according to the intrepidity of our natures, may lure us from our fireside. A few years, may-be, and we shall fly to the uttermost ends of the earth, and Yokohama will be no farther than were Launceston or Bodmin to the weary traveller of three centuries ago. Men travel at divers paces in divers ages—to adapt a line of Shakespeare. Time and space are relative in this world, whatever they may be in the greater universe around us.

Gradually the word will become limited to smaller, less attractive proportions. The allurement of the unknown will be succeeded by the known and the commonplace : a result alike of the ease and familiarity of travel and of the levelling effect of intercourse upon the habits and customs of different races. The spell that the little word casts upon the spirits of men will have faded away. Travel will mean no more than the definition it receives in a modern dictionary : ' the act of travelling or journeying from place to place '.

No more ? Perhaps not for some who are weighed down with the dross of civilization. But while love of Mother Earth is implanted in the souls of men, there will ever be those whom the manifold beauties of earth and sky will tempt, over the hills and far away, in search of that sudden uprushing and all-pervading emotion that comes to him who gazes upon the grandeurs of nature ; that sensation, half rapture, half longing, so typical of this pleasant but transient world of imperfect joys and nebulous desires.

ENGLAND IN THE SEVENTEENTH CENTURY

SEVENTEENTH-CENTURY England was not, as to-day, a land of fields and meadows girt with hedge-rows ; with rivers and streams that flow in orderly fashion through clear-cut channels and chequer the flat low-lands with the precision of a chess-board ; a land thick traced with roads and railways, and scarred with the bricks, stone, cement, and smoke-belching chimneys of great cities and agglomerations of cities.

It was a rural nation of perhaps three millions at the beginning of the century, and somewhat over five at its termination.[1] Half, or more than half, of the country was wilderness, heath, moor, hill, and common, supporting besides indigenous fauna no more than a sparse and scattered population of ' heathers ', or squatters, and here and there the lean, starveling cattle of labouring folk.

Of the residue, wide stretches were unfenced plough lands, more than half the total acreage under cultiva-

---

[1] These figures are only approximate, for no exact census of the population of England and Wales was ever taken. Estimates were made towards the end of the century by several publicists from the parish registers and from the records of the Hearth Tax, but as there is nearly three millions difference between the highest and the lowest figures no reliance can be placed on any one estimate. An eminent actuary of the reign of William IV placed the population, at the close of the seventeenth century, at five million two hundred thousand. See W. C. Sydney's *Social Life in England from the Restoration to the Revolution*, pp. 39–40. J. E. Thorold Rogers estimated the population to be about five and a half millions at the end of the period, and not more than half that number at the close of the sixteenth century. This great increase he considered to be due partly to immigration from the Continent and partly to the settlement and growing prosperity of the North as a result of the Union of England and Scotland. See *History of Agriculture and Prices*, vol. v, pp. 782 and 798, ed. 1887.

tion being worked on the old common field system of the long defunct feudal era ; and this, in spite of the newer economy of pasture-farming that had caused since the fifteenth century, and was still causing, the enclosure of more and more farm land, arable as well as pasture.

Nevertheless the garden of England was already sufficiently in the making to call forth comment by observant travellers, in Leicestershire, Warwickshire, Lancashire, Devon, Somerset, and elsewhere, and as well in the county which was to become the pre-eminent exemplar of English scenery : Kent. 'Almost throughout England,' writes M. Jorevin, a visitor here during the reign of Charles II, 'the fields are encompassed by hedges . . . insomuch that one may sometimes travel half a day's journey between two hedges, or in an avenue of trees.' This was little pleasing to the solitary traveller, for it signified, in some cases at least, a depopulated countryside, with few or none to direct him on his way. Sparsely populated too were the water-logged and uncultivable fenlands. Efforts were made (chiefly during the earlier part of the century) to redeem the better parts for agriculture, but the process was slow and not always successful, a consequence not only of the primitive mechanism employed, but also of the hostility of the wild, untutored folk to whom their bird life afforded a precarious living.

If the aspect of the country was different from that which we know, so also were the towns and cities. The streets were narrow ; the houses, for the most part, of irregular design, built of half-timber and plaster-work ; the poorer dwellings and those in some of the lesser towns, wholly of timber, of clay, or of mud mixed with straw. No public services cleansed the streets—such efforts as were made in London were quite inadequate—or brought sanitation into the home ; nor, save in London and a few other cities, was water supplied to the houses.

London with its adjunct Westminster was indeed a great city : five hundred thousand persons or one-tenth of the total population of England and Wales were, during the latter part of the century, concentrated within the area covered by the Bills of Mortality. No other centre of population reached our modern conception of a city. Norwich and Bristol, or Bristow as it was more usually called, the two chief cities of the provinces, each numbered at this period about twenty-eight thousand souls ; this was, in respect of Bristol, an increase of almost eighteen thousand persons since the commencement of the reign of James I. Of all cities and market towns, excluding the capital, the total number of inhabitants at the end of the century fell short of nine hundred thousand.

England was then in transition from the primitive industrial state of handicraft production of the Middle Ages to the more complex manufacturing era of the eighteenth century. A slow but persistent migration from the country to the town was beginning. South, East, and West gathered the prosperity and intelligence of the kingdom. In Sussex iron-ore was smelted. In East Anglia and the West were the ancient, closely settled, and, in the main, prosperous regions of the clothing industry. The Midlands possessed rich farming lands, some woollen manufactures, and a small and immature mining industry was concentrated in the Derbyshire Peak district. The North, far from the heart of things, sparsely populated for the most part, with wide stretches of waste, lay half, but only half, dormant. In the coal mines of Newcastle, the fustians, cottons, and linens of the petty Lancashire towns, and in the old-established and vigorous woollen manu-factories of the Yorkshire wolds were centred the nuclei of an industrial expansion that was soon to threaten and ultimately destroy the trading supremacy of the South.

That the industries to which allusion has just been made had, with few exceptions, easy access to the coasts was no fortuitous coincidence. Rather was it a determining factor in their rise to prosperity, for the sea and tidal rivers gave ready to hand a means of transport surer and less costly than that to be obtained by land carriage. But for a description of the roads, those bugbears of Kings and Legislators, Justices, Surveyors, Ratepayers, Travellers, and of all who used them, a whole chapter is needed.

ROADS AND BRIDGES

BEGETTERS of civilization, of communication between man and man, community and community, roads were for long ages the Cinderella of all the concerns of man. No godmothers had they in England, fairy or human, to render them capable of bearing their proper part in the development of the nation.

An inheritance from the dim past, stamped out for the most part by foot and hoof as necessity dictated, they suffered neglect at the hands of man largely by reason of the haphazard nature of their origin. Had man but known it the neglect recoiled on his own head, for their influence on his doings has been all-important and pervasive. Hence, no true comprehension of the history of English travel—nor of English history in its larger sphere—can be obtained without consideration of the history, method of upkeep, and condition, of the roads of the nation.

In the Dark and Middle Ages the system of road maintenance was sufficient for the character and extent of the traffic using it. Kings and barons with their retinues, migrating from one manor to another, armies on the march, moved with a rapidity that was rarely possible in later days. It was in the fifteenth century, with Henry V pursuing his exhausting French Wars, with the manorial system breaking up and leaving a derelict society, with tillage on the decline owing to the high price of wool, and with agricultural labour deficient in the years succeeding the Black Death—it was then that the roads first suffered neglect, and that there began the steady decay which once started, nothing but the genius of a Metcalf, a McAdam, or

a Telford could positively arrest.   In the following
century the final dissolution of the monasteries took
away almost the last friends of the highway ; almost
but not quite.   There were always a few public-
spirited persons to bequeath money for the repair of
specific, and probably notorious, portions of local
highway.

The advent of the seventeenth century found national
consciousness fully awake.   Trade and commerce
were rapidly expanding.   Through traffic was no longer
restricted, as in earlier ages, to pilgrims, great landowners, and the frequenters of fairs.   The condition
of the highways was by now deplorable in the extreme,
and, for such as are used only to the ways of highly
organized States, difficult to realize.   The only roads
with any pretensions to good foundations were those
made by the engineering skill of Rome more than
fourteen centuries earlier.   This state of affairs would
have been of less serious consequence had it not been
for the fact that a new method of progression was being
employed in all practicable districts ; that of wheeled
traffic.   Hitherto, the riding horse, the pillion-saddle,
the litter, the pack-horse, and the plough [1] had
sufficed for the needs of man and his burdens, save,
perhaps, rude agricultural carts, and the jolting
waggons known variously by the names of cars, chares,
charettes, chariots, and whirlicotes, used by persons
of royal and noble birth for the transport of themselves
and their household goods.   Moreover, the strings
of pack-horses, droves of cattle, and other four-footed

[1] It was customary to use ploughs, with some box attachment we may
suppose, for purposes of transport, and, in particular for the carriage of
stones with which to repair the highways.   That their presence on the
roads was deprecated by the authorities except for the benefit of road
repair, is suggested by the orders given at Ilchester and at Bridgwater
Sessions (1614 and 1622) prohibiting the passage of laden ploughs on certain
newly repaired highways, with penalties of six shillings and eightpence and
five shillings respectively.   *Somersetshire Record Soc.*, No. 23, pp. 110
and 320.

beasts, which by the nature of their going helped to keep the roads in a perpetual slough, relished the yielding surface of unmade roads. Already the four-wheeled waggon [1] with its great draught of ten or twelve horses or oxen was ploughing its way through the heavy clays and loams of the home counties. The coach, an introduction from the continent during the reign of Elizabeth, was becoming more and more popular. The stage-waggon, a slow and uncomfortable but convenient method of travel for the poor and sickly, had been lumbering its way from town to town on the great highways for half a century or more. The stage-coach only was unknown. Its first certain appearance dates from the inauspicious period that ushered in the great Civil War.

That the problem of road maintenance had made itself felt before the final disappearance of the monasteries, is suggested by the passing of two Acts during the reign of Henry VIII,[2] whereby it was permitted for roads in Kent and Sussex that were ' depe and noyous by wearyng and Course of water ', and, therefore, full of ' great paynes, Perils and Jeopardie ' to travellers, to be diverted by landowners through whose estates they lay. During the reigns of Mary and Elizabeth a large number of Highway Acts testified to the growing needs of the kingdom and the increasing decay of the means of internal communication. On four of these Acts [3] depended the general highway administration during the first half of the century.

---

[1] The intrusion of the Dutch form ' waggon ' (English wain) into the English language during the sixteenth century suggests that the four-wheeled waggon was probably introduced from the Low Countries at this period, the new word being borrowed to differentiate it from the ruder two-wheeled wain hitherto employed. For history of the word waggon, see Skeat's *Principles of English Etymology*, 1st Series, note to p. 416.

[2] 14–15 Hen. VIII, c. 6 (1523) ; 26 Hen. VIII, c. 7 (1533–4).

[3] 2–3 Phil. & Mar. c. 8 (1555) ; 5 Eliz. c. 13 (1562–3) ; 18 Eliz. c. 10 (1575–6). These Acts made perpetual 29 Eliz. c. 5 (1586–7) ; repealed 7 Geo. III, c. 42.

Liability for highway maintenance was placed on the parishes ; the by-roads continued, as from the days of Offa, to be the care of individual landowners. Each parish delegated its authority to two surveyors, elected yearly, whose duty it was to appoint certain days before the feast of St. John the Baptist (24th June) for remaking the highways within the parish. Refusal to act or neglect to carry out any detail of the statutes subjected the delinquent surveyor to presentment and a fine. All men who possessed land in tillage or pasture, and all who kept a plough and draught were to send ' one Wayne or Carte furnished after the costume of the Cuntrey, withe Oxen, Horses, or other Cattell, . . . & also twoo hable men . . . upon payne of every Draught making defaults x s.' Other parishioners were to bring their spades, picks, and mattocks, and to give their labour for six days, or, on default, lose 12*d*. for every day's absence. Neglect to keep the roads in good condition rendered the inhabitants liable to be presented at Quarter Sessions by the High Constable of their Hundred, the local Justices, or any informer—that well-known member of seventeenth-century society—who for a gratuity cared to undertake the unkindly task. A parish when summoned was sometimes given a further period of grace, but if the work was still neglected a fine was levied on some one inhabitant of the parish, and the money handed over to the surveyors, or to delegates appointed to superintend the repair of the highway in question. Should the unfortunate person mulcted for the fine be unable to regain his money from his fellow parishioners, he could appeal for redress to Quarter Sessions. Sometimes, when the fine was paid the inhabitants set about repairing their roads and so got the penalty remitted.

Though an elaborate system, it neither sought to introduce any effective method of repair nor took heed of the frailty of human nature. Not only was it

PIAZZA in Coventgarden.

THE PIAZZA, COVENT GARDEN. From an engraving by Hollar

based upon forced labour, but this labour was exacted, if the statute was obeyed, at one of the busiest seasons of the year. The labourers—often poor men who could ill afford wageless days—would spend 'most of their time in standing still and prating', or asking for largesse of the passers-by—Pepys, we know, gave generously on occasions [1]—so that they became known as 'The King's Loiterers', in derision of their earlier title, 'The King's Highwaymen'. If they worked, they would lay '*one load here* and then another quite cross *five or six Cart-wayes* aside, and in a contrary *Tract*'. Sometimes they would send their children as substitutes ; but if they were present neither in person nor by proxy their absence might well pass unnoticed by the surveyors, who were not only aware of the unfair incidence of the law, but would themselves be liable for statute labour as soon as their term of office ended. A day-labourer hired 'will do more work . . . in one Day than is done by six or seven of others that come . . . as cottagers or that are sent in by them', says a critic of road administration towards the end of the century. But, except for the customary, though illegal, fixed payments for defaults, the only means of raising revenue was by fines exacted at Quarter Sessions for non-fulfilment of statute labour. It is not surprising, therefore, to learn from a sixteenth-century writer that, during all the six days set apart, scarcely two good days' work were well performed ; and those likely enough were devoted

[1] The Lady Arabella gave more generously still, as befitted her rank. The following items appear in an account of her expenses for her northern progress, 1609 :
'To those that mended the highway betwixt Melwood and Stockwith 13s.'
'Given to certen laborers mended the wayes that day on the mores, 5s.' (near Buxton).
'To 3 men that mended the ways for the coach short of Stockwith half a mile, 2s. 6d.' (near Bawtrey). See *Life of the Lady Arabella Stuart*, by E. T. Bradley, vol. ii.

to roads leading to fields and pastures of surveyors and influential parishioners, work more profitable to the individual or the parish than to the country at large. If a presentment were made, the piece of road indicated would most likely be patched with an ill grace and be of doubtful permanent value. Sometimes two neighbouring parishes would both disavow responsibility for the upkeep of a highway. Then, until a ruling was made by the Justices, the road in question would lie neglected, perhaps for several years ; unless an order was made for repair without prejudice to the disputants. In favoured districts, however, especially where there were few or no persons solely dependent on wages— and therefore few who were likely to come on the rates—the roads were maintained to the low standard prescribed without recourse to legal proceedings. So thankless a task was that of surveyor, supervisor, or waywarden, as the officer was variously designated, that the position was frequently thrust upon an unpopular member of the community, as at Sennen, Cornwall, where one of that much-hated sect, the Quakers, was elected ' out of envy '. He had his revenge, for he took two granite crosses wherewith to mend the road, to the annoyance of the parishioners, who, in his absence, took one of them back whence it came. This was mild vengeance, as befitted a member of that long-suffering brotherhood. Others of more vindictive temperament would block up the waggon way of some unfortunate farmer against whom they had a grudge, dig for stone on his choicest land, or indict him at Quarter Sessions for failure to perform statute labour, or for neglect to repair a by-road for maintenance of which he was liable.

Ditching and scouring, as necessary as repair to proper road-maintenance, were often neglected, though but a yearly task. Trees and shrubs were allowed to wander at will, shrouding the roads from the

beneficial effects of sun and wind and giving useful
cover to members of the highway fraternity.   As
a consequence it was no uncommon custom in the
more rural parts of the country to send a footman
with an axe ahead of a journeying coach.   Where the
soil was rich, encroachments would be made by
covetous landowners, rendering nugatory that excellent
thirteenth-century statute [1] which enjoined the maintenance of an open space of two hundred feet on either
side of the highway.

It was in the richer counties that the problem of
road repair was most pressing and most difficult to
solve.   Cotton, in his continuation of *The Compleat
Angler*, quotes a proverb, ' There is good land where
there is foul way ' : an axiom which was taken for
granted by all contemporary writers.   Not only was
hard stone far to seek where it was most needed, but
the very fact that the roads were in such a bad state
made the transport of stone from distant quarries
impossible, except where there was good river communication.   One Somersetshire parish complained
at Quarter Sessions—in addition to the usual moan
about recalcitrant outdwellers and the decrease in
the number of ploughs—that they had to go at least
two miles for stones ! Prehistoric monuments,
shrines, monastic ruins, all were grist to surveyors
whose parish contained no quarry.   More usual
substitutes were loose stones, pebbles, flint, chalk,
lime, slag, and cinders.   Cart ruts were seldom or
never properly levelled but were beaten down and
sprinkled with gravel, stones, or ' base ill-favour'd
Rubbish ' : within a couple of days of mending
waggon wheels would again have deeply scored the
surface.   In many parts of the country waggons with a
wheel base broader or narrower than the local variety
could not move without danger of overturning, while

[1] 13 Edw. I, Stat. Winchester (1285).

in Sussex it was often impossible ' to go double with
horses or beasts ' in waggons or coaches, for the ruts
were ' so deep and the hills so steep '.[1] Occasionally,
when ruts became too deep cut, bundles of heather
or faggots were thrown between the ridges. A futile—
and forbidden—practice was that of throwing the
mud from the ditches on to the road. In the weald
of Kent it was customary, as soon as summer had fairly
set in, to plough up the roads and lay the surface soil
in a half-circle to dry. Except in the towns—where
the process of road-making appears to have been
lengthy [2]—no attempt was made to bind the surface.
As a country tanner aptly complained, whose breeches
had been caught by a dog in East Cheap : ' here the
stones are fast in the streets, and the Dogs are loose,
but in the Country, the dogs are fast tied, and the
stones are loose to throw at them.'

Sometimes the highway consisted of a narrow
raised track, flanked on each side by a quagmire of
mud into which unfortunate riders had to venture
when meeting waggons or strings of pack-horses ;
a constant hindrance to safe and speedy travel in the
neighbourhood of market-towns, and one giving rise
to frequent disputes. Where the land was enclosed
the roads were frequently worn into hollow lanes,
which were so narrow that the wheels had ' worn
a diversity of tracts, which were either deep, or rough,
or stony, or high or low, as mother nature had placed
the materials upon the face of the ground ', the space
between ' being frequently furzy hillocks of thorny
brakes '. Each season of the year gave to the roads

---

[1] Mr. Garroway in a debate on the repair of highways, 1669. *Debates of
the House of Commons, 1667–1694,* collected by the Hon. Anchitell Grey, Esq.

[2] An Oxford highway (St. Clement's Street) took between three and four
months to pitch, for two carts abreast, with a central causeway of pebbles
and two flankers of hard white stone, a fund for its execution being raised
by town and gown. See *Life and Times of Anthony Wood,* vol. iii, p. 25,
under 1682.

a different and unenviable character. In summer there was a smothering, suffocating dust ; in spring and autumn the ruts filled with water, leaving hard dry ridges, enough to overturn a coach ; in winter the mud levelled road and ditch to a quagmire, except during periods of hard frost, when it turned into slippery ice until a thaw brought its own peculiar dangers. Of all dangers, however, floods were by far the most serious. Even summer showers would raise the waters in places above road and meadow, hindering traffic for hours. In winter it might be days before coach or waggon could complete its journey. Riders often deserted the road for higher ground, to the advantage, near the great highways, of canny landowners who sometimes made them pay for the privilege. Boats were frequently used in winter ; horses were swum across swollen streams, and many a traveller ended his travels in a watery grave, especially he who had already drowned his sorrows in liberal potations. Sometimes a rider would be up to the saddle-girths in mud ; the humble wayfarer and the foot-soldier would think it no uncommon hardship to walk in mud to the ankles. It is said that after a skirmish in Northamptonshire during the Civil War a troop of horse stuck in the mud and could not escape.

In open country—known by the name of champaign or champion country—there was not always a settled track, and each traveller went the way which seemed to him best. Strangers were frequently at a loss to find their way and wandered about down or meadow until they found some one to direct them. Others who were familiar with the roads they were traversing not only crossed fields to avoid bad places but made short cuts when it suited their convenience.[1] This was not the lack of respect for private property it

[1] See Appendix I.

would seem ; though doubtless in the second instance travellers were committing trespass. By ancient custom the public had no right to any definite road but only to ' good passage ' from village to village. Consequently, if the beaten track became founderous travellers might diverge from it, even to the extent of ' going upon the corn '.

With such roads as have been described it is no wonder that accidents occurred. Riders fell from their horses with alarming frequency ; coaches overturned, were left stranded amid quicksand, and lost in flood waters. The wonder is that any persons escaped. But clergymen, doctors, travellers of pleasure, and others who have written of their wanderings, show us that it was possible to travel hundreds and even thousands of miles without hurt. George Fox, the Quaker, who spent something like a quarter of a century perambulating England, speaks of few hindrances to his labours other than human.

The roads, of course, varied in the degree of their vileness. The Dover road, it has been said, was the best in England during the period immediately preceding the Civil Wars. If this were true its upkeep was a notable achievement, considering the great continental traffic it had to bear. The foreign visitors who have written of their English travels certainly make no complaints as to its condition.

Norfolk roads too were well thought of, at least by the merry and witty Monarch, who suggested that the county should be cut up to provide roads for the rest of the kingdom. Evils are apt to overshadow excellence. Therefore we hear more of the counties with notorious and unenviable reputations, and in particular of Sussex and some of the Midland shires. But if the ways of these localities were bad they had great excuse. Their very geographical positions, the one close to the metropolis, the others in the heart of the kingdom invited criticism. Moreover, they had more than their quota of traffic. Sussex was the outlet to several Channel ports ; it was also the forge and timber yard of the nation.[1] On the Midland roads fell the chief burden of increasing trade. The records of Sussex, however, so well illustrate the difficulties of communication in heavy country that a few facts relating to that county may be taken, as showing the condition of all deep and water-logged districts. There, when the autumn rains commenced, timber in transport to London was left stranded by the roadside, until spring had reduced the adhesive qualities of the surface; unless, indeed, hard frost restored for a season passable conditions. Travelling was well-nigh abandoned during the winter. Even the Circuit visited Horsham, in the heart of the Weald, only for the summer assizes. The Duke of Somerset whose estate, Petworth Park, lay on one of the worst roads of the kingdom, found it necessary to keep a house at Guildford, at which to lie whenever he made the journey to London. So dreadful was the way that Prince George of Denmark, when, in December 1703, he travelled there from Windsor to greet the so-called King Charles of Spain [2] to these shores, spent fourteen hours in his coach, which had to be prevented at intervals from sinking into quagmires by the ' nimble boors ' of Sussex who accompanied its painful progress. The last nine miles took them six hours to cover. On the return journey several of the attendant coaches overturned once or twice. Strange as it may seem to us, many of the Sussex gentry looked upon the backward state of their road system—for roads were few as well as bad—as a merciful dispensation of providence ; an impediment

[1] Statutes 27 Eliz. c. 19 (1584–5) and 39 Eliz. c. 19 (1597–8) had put a special onus on the Sussex ironmasters for the upkeep of the Sussex roads, on the ground that their heavy traffic spoiled them.

[2] The Archduke Charles whose (unsuccessful) claim to the throne caused the War of the Spanish Succession.

to foreign invasion, alike from enemies beyond seas
and from the evil ways and dubious characters of the
metropolis. This attitude can hardly have been
shared by the farmers who had to content themselves
with the prices of the local markets, and who at times
found themselves entirely cut off from the possibility
of disposing of their wares.

The three great highways leading north each had
their 'lacunae'. The most notorious part of the North
Road was that known as Baldock Lane, leading to
Biggleswade. Always in bad condition during the
winter—Pepys notes, as early as 7th October, that it
was getting bad—it was often quite impassable. Once,
at least, a traveller, a poor higgler, fell a victim to its
waters. Farther north the danger zones were at
Newark and Doncaster, where the Trent and the Don
were liable at small provocation to overflow their
banks. On the eastern branch of the great highway—
leading also to Cambridge and the fens—the two first
stages, to Ware and Puckeridge, seem to have been
most difficult to traverse in wet weather. On the
Chester road the way from Dunstable to Fenny Stratford was as founderous as any in the country—to use
the expressive term of Quarter Session Records. Here
was 'Hockley in the Hole', with a most unenviable
reputation amongst travellers. Somewhat farther, on
the alternative route through Northampton, Middleton
Keynes, near Newport Pagnell, could lay claim to one
victim, at least, in the person of Dr. Atterbury, brother
to the bishop of that name. Somersetshire roads had
also a poor reputation. ' 'Tis a Country ', says Blome,
the topographer, ' of much pleasure in *Sommer*, and
as bad in the *Winter* ; occasioned by its being *wet*
and *moorish*, especially in the midst of the County,
which is a great trouble to *Travellers* ; but this inconvenience they may well pass over, knowing the
ensuing profits and pleasures that the *Sommer season*

In perpetuam Memoriam celeberrima Vrbs flamms prope desolate N.prodigioso 1666. Columna baec ex Basi 27 ped in altitudinem 202 ped sublime caput elevat fundata Richardo Ford eq Pretore Lond 1671 finita Josepho Sheldon eq Pret 1670.

A VIEW OF THE MONUMENT, WITH TYPES OF WAYFARERS

From an engraving of about 1676

IN the time of King *Charles* the Second, Sir *John Robinson* being Lieutenant of the *Tower*, used to go hunt often into *Epping-Forest*, but the Ways without *White-Chappell* were very bad and troublesome to him, upon which he was resolved to have them mended, either by Indictment or other Way: Upon this (as I have been informed) were laid cross the Ways, Trees, Earth, and then Gravel, and Ditches were made, which made it good for the present; and to keep it so every Year, in the middle is laid a high Row of large Gravel, which is force'd-in, and keeps that Part highest to throw off the Water, and the Dirt is press'd or cast into the Ditches, which are every Year cleansed, and thus it's likely to last for ever. Indeed by reason of it's being a *Flat*, in the Winter 'tis pochy, but it's generally without Holes and even

Sir Christopher Wren, the King's Surveyer General told me, that when he came first into his Place, he found the Way by the Privy Garden, between the 2 Gates at *White-hall*, to be extreme bad, and it had baffled all his Predecessors by means of being and ill Earth; upon this he dug it down (I think) 2 Feet, and there pitch'd and ramm'd it well: upon that he threw what came out, and pitch'd it again substantially, and it remains firm to this Day, only must be mended what the Coaches wear out.

To add to my Proposal of mending the High-ways, and the History how some have been mended, I must tell you that one Dr *Harvey* (the Inventour of the *Harvey-Apple*, Master of *Trinity Hall* in *Cambridge*) about 60 Years since, left an Estate to mend the Roads *versus Londinum* (towards *London*) and 'tis as well mended as any in *England* to *Fulmer*, 6 Miles. *Vide Fuller's History of Cambridge*.

From Houghton's *Collection*

(539)

Advertisements.

WE are desired to give notice that the Old Road from *London* to *York*, *Newcastle*, and all the Northern parts (which of late years hath been gulled and not passable for Horse or Coach) is now so well mended, from *Ware* to *Puckeridge*, *Buntingford*, *Rayston*, *Huntingdon*, and so downwards, that Horse, Coach, or Waggon may more easily pass and have as good if not better accommendation, then any other By-Roads lately used, whereof upon tryal any man may had the benefit.

From *The Kingdoms Intelligencer*, No. 32, Aug. 11-18, 1662

affordeth them, insomuch that they have this *Proverb,
That what is worse for the rider, is best for the abider* '—
a variant of the proverb quoted in a preceding page.

In Devon and Cornwall, in the Peak district, in
Wales, and in the border counties of the North, the
problem was somewhat different to that which con-
fronted the authorities of the more central regions.
There the obstacles to proper road maintenance were
in great part the steep gradients and the consequent
effect of rushing water.   In Devon and Cornwall the
extreme narrowness of the ways, frequently hollowed
below the level of their surroundings, and the sticky
nature of the soil, made it especially difficult to maintain
the road surface.   But in all these distant counties—save
a small slice of Devon—the populations were scanty
and primitive in their requirements, wheels were rarely
used, through traffic was negligible, and the condition
of the roads therefore attracted less attention.   Furthermore, in some of these districts, there was the coasting
trade to lighten the burden of land transport.

Some of the worst roads in the kingdom were those
in the neighbourhood of London.   The constant
passage of traffic kept churning the mud which was
mixed with age-long accumulations of extraneous
filth, disturbing even to the well-hardened senses of
seventeenth-century travellers who were sometimes
' forced to stop their noses to avoid the ill smell
occasioned by it '.   No mere ceremonial was it to mend
the highway in anticipation of a royal progress.
Charles II, in his speech to Parliament, 1662, had to
request that the ways into Westminster might be
mended before the arrival of his bride so that she
might not find Whitehall surrounded by water ; yet
some of the streets of the city of Westminster were
paved, as appears from the records of the Burgess
Court.

London itself was in little better plight.   True,

most of the main streets had been paved in the previous
century, and so saved Londoners the risk of being
pinned waist deep in mud. M. Misson, a foreign
writer of the second half of the century, observed
notwithstanding, that the women there were ' forc'd
to raise themselves upon Pattins or Goloshoes of Iron,
to keep themselves out of the Dirt and Wet ' ; doubtless in bad weather. The paved ways, solid though
they were beneath the outer covering of mud, were
rough in the extreme. Sir Ralph Verney, who, living
as he did on Buckinghamshire clay, had ample warranty
for his assertion, wrote in May 1685 that his coach
was more prejudiced by one day in London than
probably by ten in the country ' the Stones being ready
to shake it in pieces '. The streets were narrow, so
narrow that in some cases vehicular traffic was prohibited, if not impossible, while in others coaches
made their way with difficulty. As a consequence
' stops ', as they were called, were frequent ; at times
they blocked the traffic so effectually that coach-
passengers had to return the way they had come, or,
if they happened to be in the Strand, proceed by water.
These hindrances always led to wordy disputes between
coachmen and carmen, sometimes between passengers,
so that the drawing of blood was not an infrequent
accompaniment, and murder on occasions ensued.
Fogs caused, then as now, a great dislocation of traffic ;
and, in the suburbs, encouraged the assaults of thieves.
As unpleasant as fogs must have been the heavy
rainstorms which for a time turned streets like Dowgate
and Snowhill into rushing streams. For the pedestrians there were other disagreeables ; the refuse
thrown without doors, which accumulated in street
channels and vacant spaces ; the pit-falls after dark
caused by new dug vaults and open-flapped cellars
where lived the poorest of city dwellers—indictable
offences it is true, but tolerated for the most part by

the lax administration of the law, and therefore all too prevalent ; [1] the splashes from coaches and carts in the narrow ways which led to frequent, and sometimes fatal, disputes between passers-by for the privilege of ' taking the wall '.

London surpassed other towns only in its size, the volume of its traffic, and the measures taken for its cleansing. Every provincial corporation was faced with the twofold difficulty of keeping the town scavenger to his weekly or bi-weekly task of sweeping the market square and other vacant spaces, and of checking inconsiderate citizens from raising dunghills before their neighbours' doors, and from setting up shop-bulks and stone washing-stools in front of their dwellings ' to the hurt of the King's subjects ' and the obstruction of the highway. In some towns there were further problems to be ignored. Thus at Oxford the highways were so waterlogged, after heavy showers, that all traffic was stopped until the waters had subsided. At Bristol the extreme narrowness of the streets would not admit the use of coaches : a deprivation surely to the rich merchants of the second city of the kingdom, disguise it though they might by ostentatious display of gold chains and richly clad attendants. In this and in many other towns, sledges

---

[1] For a short season during the last year of the reign of Charles II and first of James II much energy was shown by the Justices of Westminster in indicting householders for leaving cellar-flaps open. This appears to have been occasioned by John Young, carver, and Thomas Streeter, painter, having dug a pit in Gerrard Street, ten yards broad and eleven feet deep, into which Thomas Whitehead fell on the night of 21 June 1684, so that his right arm ' became broake '. For this the culprits, who confessed the indictment, were fined the small sums of three shillings and fourpence each. There followed one hundred and sixty-five indictments for leaving cellar doors open, one of these in consequence of another accident. On this occasion it was Sir Robert Clarke, who, walking on 1 January 1684–5, between 6 and 7 p.m. along Holborn, fell through a cellar door belonging to Benjamin Poole, Yeoman, and was thereby shaken and bruised. For thus ' unlawfully and wittingly ' allowing the door of his cellar, six feet long and two feet wide, to be open, Poole forfeited twelve shillings. *Middlesex County Records*, vol. iv, Introduction, p. lv et seq.

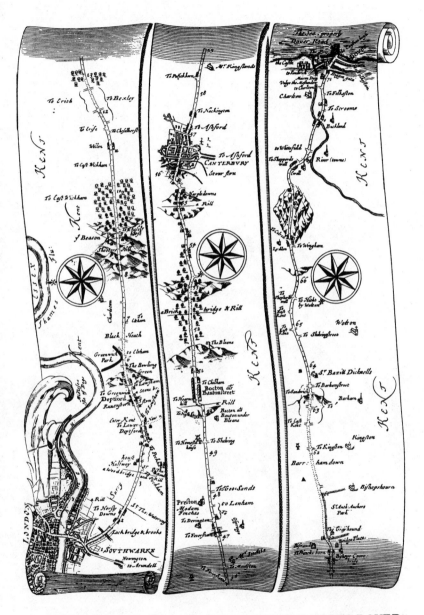

THREE SECTIONS OF THE ROAD FROM SOUTHWARK TO DOVER

From Ogilby's *Britannia*

were used in lieu of waggons to preserve the pitching
of the streets, and, in Bristol, at least, were drawn by
dogs, possibly owing to the strain felt by horses on
smooth, worn, and slippery pavements. In better
posture were Norwich, Gloucester, and Newcastle
with broad, well-paved streets, and Salisbury with its
peculiar but excellent arrangement of watercourses
flowing down the channels of its principal streets.
For real cleanliness Leicester and Barnstaple seem to
have excelled all other towns. Indeed, in regard to
Barnstaple, two very dissimilar writers, at dissimilar
periods, have declared that it was possible to walk
its streets in the foulest weather without soiling boots
or slippers. Commendation could go no farther.
Very different was Darlington, where, one November
day of 1678, the Captain of a company of Dragoons,
bound for Scotland, made his men kneel ' in mire of
great depth ' to pledge the healths of the King and
Duke of York—an incident which ended, as not
infrequently happened, in a drunken brawl and
' slashing one another '.

Just as the rapid expansion of heavy motor traffic
after the Great War (1914–18) disclosed the inade-
quacy of modern roads, so it was in the districts where
the pack-saddle was giving way to the waggon, and
the riding horse to the coach, that the unsound nature
of the seventeenth-century road surface was most
apparent. All through the century Statutes and
Proclamations betray the concern of the authorities
for the terrible condition of the roads ; an attitude
so much at variance with that of the population in
general that most schemes for improving or saving
the roads came to naught, for the superiority of
the constructive method over that of the passive was
grasped by few until the latter part of the century.
There was, it is true, a small select band of publicists
who had no doubt about the seriousness of the problem

—and no doubt about the excellence of their own remedial measures. As early as 1610 Thomas Proctor came forward with a proposal to make foundations with timber frames filled with stones, sand, or faggots ; but, as if to deprecate his own argument, he offered, in a final paragraph, not to remake the roads in the manner suggested, but to canalize streams linking navigable rivers. The next writer to concern himself with the question, sixty-three years later, advocated straight roads, parallel tracks with a space between, and a rule of the road, as a means of circumventing the difficulty. He offered to assist in the making of an experimental five hundred miles. In the last decade of the century three separate pamphlets testify to the growing interest that was being taken in a problem that was becoming more and more pressing. Defoe, with his usual vigour and fertility of brain, published a most carefully worked out scheme for the constant upkeep of the roads, with a piquant suggestion that highwaymen and other malefactors should be put to work upon them. More directly practical were the inventors, one of whom in 1619 patented ' strong engines for making and repairing of roads '. Another, in the last year of the century, devised a scheme for throwing ' all the rising ridges into the ruts '. Not one of these reformers, pamphleteers, or patentees met with any reward for his exertions.

Government, for the most part, sought the millennium by restricting the use of carriages and limiting the size of draughts. A proclamation of 1618 ascribed the decay of highways and bridges to the new use by carriers of four-wheeled waggons, drawn by eight, nine, and ten horses, carrying sixty or seventy hundred-weight ; it therefore limited draughts to five horses, on pain of Star Chamber proceedings.[1]   Four years

---

[1] Busino, Chaplain to the Venetian Embassy, describes the London carts in this very year of 1618, as being for the most part ' on two broad and high

later the new-fashioned waggons were themselves included in the prohibition ; an order which was no doubt evaded, for two further proclamations of similar strain appeared in the course of the next thirteen years. These were followed, in 1654, by a clause in the Highway Act of that year limiting draughts to five horses, or six oxen and one horse. In 1662 an increase to seven ' horse-beasts ' or eight oxen was allowed with a burden of not more than thirty hundredweight in summer and twenty in winter. A further allowance of one ' extra ' horse was granted in the Act of 1696, despite the evasion therein described which enabled waggoners, while observing the letter of the law, to employ draughts in excess of the authorized number. In fact the very nature of the roads made employment of heavy draughts necessary, if commodities were to be carried in bulk ; a principle so well understood by the purblind authorities, that they excluded numerous classes of vehicles from the scope of the various enactments. The relief to the roads, when one considers exemptions and infractions, must therefore have been of the slightest.

Another attempt to solve this most obstinate problem was by deepening the rivers, so as to increase their barge-carrying capacity. It was with this express motive—to preserve the highways about Oxford which by continual passage of wains were so worn and broken as hardly to be travelled in the winter season—that the Thames was made more easily navigable from Burcott to Oxford. But Government had no love for works of so costly and difficult a nature, however beneficial to trade, when, as they fondly hoped, they could accomplish the miracle with small trouble to themselves, and none to the national purse, by sump-

wheels like those of Rome ', although some had four wheels. Carts, he tells us, were very numerous in London, including manure carts, the drivers of which were ' the most insolent fellows in the world '. *Venetian State Papers,* 1617-19.

tuary regulations. More in keeping with their point
of view was the regulation enjoining the use of waggon
wheels broad enough to act the part of the modern
steam-roller ; but this fruitful source of contention
between waggoners and constables did not become
a regular feature of legislation until the following
century.[1]

Patentees, naturally, sought the improvement of
carriages and not their restriction. There were
devices to prevent coaches from overturning ; to
keep coach-bodies upright under all circumstances ;
and to give greater freedom of movement so as to
enable vehicles to approach or avoid each other
' where the narrowness of the way may require '.
All were unsuccessful.

During the second half of the century a dawning
perception of the true solution of the problem broke
upon official intelligence. The Civil Wars had been
for the roads an unmitigated evil. They had been
subjected to hard usage, and had received less than
the modicum of attention previously bestowed.
Parishes had neglected to appoint surveyors : parishioners had refused to perform statute duty, and had
sometimes beaten the surveyor who had attempted to
enforce obedience. With the restoration of stable
government, lawlessness gradually passed away ; a
rapid extension of the stage-coach services took place ;
trade and commerce made sudden growth ; the
population prospered, causing inevitably a vast increase
of road traffic. Already, in 1654, the Commonwealth
had shown concern at the evil fruits of hostilities by

[1] 14 Car. II, c. 6 (1662) directed that all wheels must have four-inch
tyres, but complaints being made ' that the ruts will not receive such a
tyre, that new wheels for the whole country cannot be made at once, and
that traffic will be stopped ' (Proclamation 14 October 1662), the Act
was suspended and was ultimately repealed (22 Car. II, c. 12, 1670). The
use of iron-shod wheels was forbidden by the Corporation of the City of
London, the Burgesses of Westminster, and the parish of St. Giles, on the
score that they destroyed the pavement.

MODES OF TRAVEL

From Loggan's *Cantabrigia Illustrata*

passing a new general Highway Act, and, three years later, by projecting a further Bill which was apparently dropped upon the dissolution of the House by Cromwell, although a Surveyor-General had already been appointed. Under the Act of 1654[1] a practice had been regularized to which the Justices in Quarter Sessions had resorted for at least thirty years ;[2] that of raising revenue to be expended on the roads by means of a tax on the annual value of land. By this Act a maximum of one shilling in the pound was allowed. Where this proved insufficient the Justices could rate-in-aid other parishes the rates of which were less than that amount. An attempt was at the same time made to secure surveyors of a better class than had hitherto been obtained, by attaching a considerable property qualification to the appointment ; but it does not appear that many of the gentry took upon themselves the burden of office. The first two Highway Acts subsequent to the Restoration allowed a rate of sixpence in the pound, but only for specific periods. Nor was it to be levied until statute labour had been performed and proved insufficient. With the funds thus raised persons liable to labour were to be remunerated for extra work. In 1691 the measure became permanent. Yet the parishes, with the conservatism inherent in the nation, persisted in the use of the wasteful, unpopular, unfair, and almost valueless statute labour and its concomitant of raising money by fines and commutations. No appreciable number of parishes availed themselves of the highway rate until the eighteenth century was well on its way.

In 1663 an experiment of medieval origin was resuscitated. The Southern portion of the North Road had become ' very ruinous ' and ' almost impassable ',

---

[1] Ordinance, 31 March 1654.

[2] See *Somerset Record Society*, no. 28, p. 149, where mention is made of a rule which had been framed for this purpose ' in the one and Twenth yeare of the Rayne of James late Kinge of England '.

owing to the great trade in barley and malt and other traffic thereabouts. More than one Hertfordshire parish had petitioned the Justices in Quarter Sessions to be eased of a burden beyond its resources. Thus, as early as 1646 or 1647 the inhabitants of Standon (North of Ware) had petitioned that, despite all efforts to keep their portion of the London road in order, two-thirds were exceedingly bad and very dangerous to travel upon by reason of the many springs of water which arose in the 'swallowinge clay' and sandy places. Without stones, gravel, or other material they had spent £100 on one 'causy' not above eighty poles in length, but owing to the number of waggons having seven, eight, and sometimes nine horses each, it was again in decay. Another of their highways, that leading to Hertford, had become so impassable that they had had to buy 'a new way' out of adjoining ground—since decayed—at a cost of £10, while for the repair of a third highway, three miles long, they were in debt. Ware, making representations at the same time, had spoken of the unreasonable loads of malt from remote parts and the excessive weekly loads from Norwich, Bury, and Cambridge. Nine or ten years later Radwell, near Baldock, had petitioned for relief, owing to the soil 'being such as the winter devours whatsoever they are able to lay on in summer', and the parish so small that it had only two teams. The Justices were at length aroused and made representation to Parliament. The outcome was the passing of the first Turnpike Act.[1] By this Act the Justices responsible for the counties of Hertford, Cambridge, and Huntingdon, within whose jurisdiction the ruinous portions lay, were directed to appoint surveyors with powers to require the services of all persons liable to statute labour living within three miles of the road, and to

[1] 15 Car. II, c. 1 (1663).

pay them according to the usual rate of the county. Funds for the purpose were to be raised by the levying of certain tolls by means of toll bars or turnpikes, as they were variously called, which might be mortgaged for a period not exceeding nine years. If the tolls failed to yield a sum sufficient for all purposes, recourse could be had to the Highway Acts and rates levied upon adjacent parishes. Of the three gates erected in pursuance of the Act only one was effective, that at Wadesmill near Ware ; one was never set up ; and one was so easily evaded that it was removed to another locality. Whether the new economy had any effect or not—it may have stayed the canker—it certainly pointed the way to a new, profitable, and just means of raising revenue. No extension of the system took place, however, until the last decade of the century. Then, authorities and instructed opinion having awakened to the necessity of a progressive road policy, four new Turnpike Acts and three general Highway Acts were placed upon the statute book.[1] Provision was made for enlarging all cartways to a breadth of eight yards ; for the setting up of directing stones wherever two or more highways crossed one another—an order that had not by 1713 been ' duly observed ' in many parts of Devon—and for the transference of the power of nominating surveyors from the parishioners to the Justices. The last innovation might well have brought the roads to a standard of excellence more in harmony with the cultural state of the nation had the zeal of the Justices been as considerable as their duties were multifarious. The gradual amelioration of the great highways of the home and adjacent counties may rather be ascribed to the institution, in the following century, of Turnpike

---

[1] 7 & 8 Gul. III, c. 9 (1695-6); 7 & 8 Gul. III, c. 26; 8 & 9 Gul. III, c. 15 (1696-7); 9 Gul. III, c. 18 (1697-8); 3 Gul. & Mar. c. 12 (1691); 7 & 8 Gul. III, c. 29 (1696-7); 8 & 9 Gul. III, c. 16.

Trusts, to whom were delegated the duties of road maintenance and the levying of tolls for their upkeep. Defoe, writing in 1724, is agreeably impressed with the improvement already achieved by the system, and full of optimism for the future. ' It 's more than probable ', he says, ' that our Posterity may see the Roads all over *England* restor'd in their Time to such Perfection, that Travelling and Carriage of Goods will be much more easy both to Man and Horse, than ever it was since the *Romans* lost this Island.' A cautious prophecy giving no date for fulfilment ; and no wonder, considering what a disgrace throughout the eighteenth century were the by-roads and highways far distant from the metropolis. But the prophecy was fulfilled, though not until a hundred years were past.

Bridges like roads suffered from the unbusinesslike sluggish methods of the age, from lack of skill, and, to a less extent, from actual neglect. By an Act of Henry VIII [1] the general maintenance of bridges had been placed in the hands of the Justices, who were empowered to act, both as judicial tribunals to determine causes, and as administrative officials to oversee the work of surveyors and collectors. These officers were appointed by them to report on defects, superintend repairs, and collect rates, the levying of which was prescribed by law for the maintenance of the more important bridges, known as County and Hundred bridges from the fact that these administrative areas were responsible for their upkeep. In practice the Justices not infrequently dispensed with surveyors, preferring to work more directly through their other subordinates, the constables. In addition to these two categories of bridges there were parish bridges, usually situated on by-roads and supported by the parishes, and bridges where liability for

[1] 22 Hen. VIII, c. 5 (1530–1).

repair lay by tenure or prescription on certain properties. To avoid the difficulties inherent in such a system, the statute directed that where obligation was unknown, or could not be proved, the bridge in question should be repaired at the charge of the county or borough within whose area it lay. It did nothing, however, to dispatch quickly cases of disavowed or disputed liability on the part of those indicted or presented for failure to maintain bridges for which they were held responsible. Thus Justices in Quarter Session adjourned disputed cases again and again, in attempts to reach a correct legal decision, the while the bridges in question were suffered to fall into increasing decay ; until suddenly realizing the danger to the community, they ordered the necessary repairs to be done without prejudice to the disputants.

Thus Mark Bridge in Somersetshire was found to be in decay in 1621–2, and the liability being in dispute between the Lords and inhabitants of four neighbouring manors, and the inhabitants of Mark, it was referred to certain of the Justices for examination. The matter was again before the first two Sessions of the following year, and again in 1624–5, but, though the bridge was presumably mended, the question was not even then determined, for it was once more before the Justices in 1630. Twenty years later amercements for non-repair of the bridge were under consideration ; it is probable, however, that this concerned further repairs, for the wooden bridges that were usual in all the country South of the Trent needed repeated restoration. An instance of this may be seen in the records of Stanmore Bridge in the same county. Orders for its repair came before the Sessions in 1613, 1624–5, 1634, and 1648–9, ten separate parishes being chargeable for its maintenance. On the last occasion dilapidation had probably resulted from rough usage during the Civil War. Many bridges in the county between 1646 and 1649 were found to be defective and out of repair, travellers being 'many tymes . . . much obstructed in their Journeyes and passages, and many of them forced to the hazard of theire lives'; a condition of affairs that led the Justices to order, in 1649, the raising of two hundred pounds for the repair of the county bridges. Even so late as 1670 an Act was placed on the Statute Book requiring that all bridges in Cheshire demolished in the late wars were to be repaired.

That new bridges were but seldom constructed may be ascribed, we believe, to the fact that bridge-building had been a lost art since the days when the Brethren of the Bridge had exercised their function. The only mode of securing foundations seems to have been 'the clumsy one of throwing loose stones promiscuously into the bed of the river, so as to find their own bearing, and then, on top of these loose stones, to erect the stonework [or brickwork] of the starlings'. We can therefore scarcely be surprised that some of these bridges went by the name of quaking or shaking bridges.

The history of Wadesmill Bridge, on the eastern branch of the North Road, near Ware, demonstrates, very forcibly, the expense and trouble incurred in the maintenance of a bridge improperly secured. In 1609–10 it was in such a state of disrepair that passengers could not pass. In 1644, 1662, and 1666 its defective condition was again matter for regulation at Quarter Sessions. In 1674–5 the rebuilding of 'Wardsmill Bridge', by two carpenters, was estimated at one hundred and forty-seven pounds, twelve shillings, and fourpence, the old bridge being valued at ten pounds. By 1680 the bridge was once more found to be in decay; 'it is supposed by the defect of the building thereof'. To John Crofts, one of

the two aforementioned carpenters, was assigned the
job of examining its condition. Not unnaturally he
certified that ' the brickwork was sound with well-
burned bricks and good mortar, and joyned with
tarrice, well wrought '. Its decay he ascribed to the
' fierceness of two waters which meet at the point of
one peire with such violence that it forced up the
ground so deep till it had quite undermind the foundation that one part sank right about a foot, and caused
two of the arches to crack and sink '. He estimated
the cost of repair at twenty pounds ; and, as is evident
from his receipt, performed the work he deemed
necessary. His appeal to the ' gentlemen of this
honourable bench ' who knew the violence of the
waters ' and that such exigencies many times fall out
where worke is very well done ', had had the desired
effect. Nevertheless, building operations were again
undertaken in 1685 and in 1687. In the latter year
three arches had to be renewed at a charge of fifty-six
pounds. A twelvemonth later the brickwork was
found to be falling down. Payment for its amendment,
and for the setting up of a new spur-post came to
a total of three pounds, three shillings, and tenpence.
In 1693 and 1695 further repairs were made, in the
first instance at a cost of thirteen pounds. Further
records pertaining to its upkeep belong to the following
century, and have no place here.

Neglect and insecure foundations accounted only
in part for the hazards run by travellers in the crossing
of bridges. Many of the structures were so narrow
as to admit the passage of vehicles with difficulty.
In some, wheel traffic was entirely precluded. Many
were without rails.

The Bow Bridge near York on the North Road
appears to have lacked these desirable adjuncts. As the
Edinburgh stage-coach with five passengers was crossing it, the postillion by careless driving let both wheels

on one side slip over the edge ; happily the side with
the lesser weight. The coachman flinging himself from
his box in a panic, the whole coach would have tipped
into the stream below, had not ' some good angell '
seen the danger, and held it up all the way until the
farther bank was reached. No wonder that passengers
sometimes fell from bridges in the dark. Indeed, it
must have been a fair test of sobriety to cross a narrow
packhorse bridge in safety after a night's potations.

Even in London in 1677 it was possible for a
hackney-coach to fall into Fleet ditch—there were no
rails, says our informant—the occupant being either
drowned or smothered in mud. How the accident
occurred it is difficult to imagine ; the four bridges
which spanned the Fleet ditch had just been rebuilt
of Portland and Burbeck stone, and the stream had
been cleaned and made navigable as far as Holborn
bridge, with rails of oak breast high on either side.
Possibly the rails had already suffered damage and
neglect ; or it may be that the work of construction—
the total cost of which was over twenty-seven thousand
pounds—was still going on, though it is said to have
been completed by 1673–4.

Here and there during the second half of the
century bridges were being widened to admit the new
traffic ; it is probable that this was only done where
absolute necessity dictated the measure. In some
parts of the country, such as Lancashire and Cheshire,
bridges were few and far between ; rivers and streams
—often swift and always ill-regulated—had to be
forded, or crossed by ferry boat. Even London,
busy, traffic-laden London, had but one bridge, and,
though it was wide enough to permit the passage of
two coaches side by side, it was all too narrow for its
heavy burden of traffic ; no bridge linked the Surrey
and Middlesex banks between this and Kingston.
It was moreover as little pleasing to the eye as it was

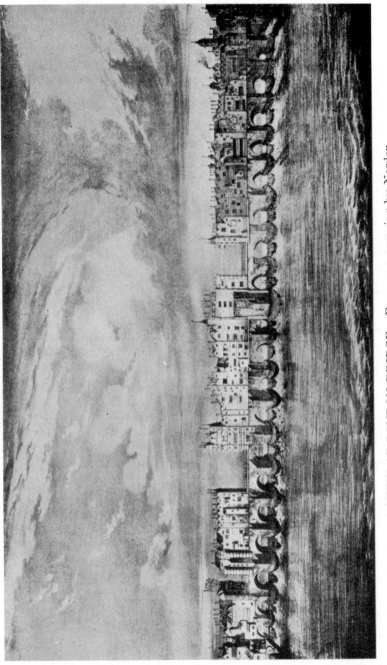

A VIEW OF LONDON BRIDGE. From an engraving by Norden

safe to the person. The Southern portion was darkened by the bordering houses ; the North end, after the destructive fire of 1632–3, was boarded with deal pales, many of which blew down in gales, leaving gaps, dangerous enough to travellers at night, in spite of the lanthorns hung upon the cross beams which held the pales together. Its state of disrepair was proverbial —' women and bridges always lack mending ' says Middleton in referring to it. To this Pepys bears testimony. In crossing the bridge one dark night he put his leg in a hole and would have fallen, had not the constable, standing there to keep people from it, caught him up. Another time he found the pales gone from both sides and had to stoop low for fear of being blown off. Yet the bridge was maintained. then as now, by a special trust. This was a usual method of dealing with bridges of great importance ; the far-famed Rochester Bridge was maintained in this way.

Whether or no Derbyshire, like other remote and somewhat inaccessible counties, was inadequately supplied with bridges, it is evident that the bridges which did cross its hill streams were of untrustworthy appearance and singularly narrow. Southerners, used though they were to narrow and rickety bridges, looked askance at the rude structures of the dale folk. Thus the young Brownes, sons to Sir Thomas Browne, the author of *Religio Medici*, debated at Ashford in that county whether they would swim their horses through an ' overflown ditch ' or ride the bridge. Finally, having heard ' that elephants had danc'd upon roapes ', they adventured themselves upon the latter. ' Viator,' an Essex gentleman, riding across the Derbyshire hill-country with ' Piscator Junior ' (Charles Cotton) and his servant, and walking warily down the hills with ' Piscator's ' helping hand, came to a bridge of such slender proportions that, but for the ridicule he feared from his dalesmen companions, he would, as he declares, have gone over on all fours. Happily he was near the end of his uncomfortable journey, and had 'no more of these Alps [or bridges] to pass over '.

It will be readily understood that bridges, so frail and jerry-built, not infrequently tumbled into swollen streams, carrying with them any unwary passengers who had ventured upon them. In time of great flood they were swept away in wholesale fashion, leaving unlucky, or perhaps we should say lucky, travellers stranded on either bank, to await with what patience they could muster the subsiding of the waters and the feasibility of crossing by ford or ferry. If in the diaries and autobiographies of the day we read of many fatal accidents, we also read of one or two singular escapes. Parson Cheldrey and a boy, while crossing Harewood Bridge in Yorkshire, fell over in the dark, but ' were wonderfully preserved upon the piers that the bridge is built upon, till help got to their relief '. More extraordinary still, during the summer flood at Northampton in 1663, when bridges were borne away, and men, horses, and cattle drowned, was the escape of two riders who were actually on the crown of a bridge when the arches before and behind were carried away, and they left stranded between.

Of floods, and their dire effect upon travelling and travellers, much yet remains to be said ; but as this concerns not ' Roads and Bridges ' but ' Trials and Tribulations ', it may be more fittingly dealt with under that heading.

A CITIZEN AND HIS WIFE, *c.* 1623

THE BEGGAR'S BRIDGE

III

THE WATCH

The necessity of delegating highway maintenance to paid officials was, as we have seen, slowly but surely obtaining public recognition. Yet the advisability of delegating the maintenance of law and order to a paid police was, in the main, beyond the comprehension of seventeenth-century intelligence. Strange paradox, for, slow as were the authorities to understand the needs of improved land communication, they were fully alive to the importance of keeping the public, and especially the travelling public, under observation.

Since the time of Edward I nightly watch had been maintained in all towns and villages from Ascension Day to Michaelmas by two, three, four, or more able-bodied householders, as the size of the community warranted.[1] Called upon in rotation to serve under the orders of the constable—an unpaid official like his subordinates—they were required to stand in some convenient place, and there stop all strangers travelling the road, examine them, and, if found to be suspicious persons, detain them until morning, when they were to be delivered to the constable and carried to a Justice who could dismiss, bind over, or commit the suspects to Quarter Sessions, there to be tried according to law. Should travellers refuse to stop, or should they break away from their interrogators the Watch was entitled to raise hue and cry to capture them,[2] beat them, and set them in the stocks until morning, when, if no suspicion was found to be attached to

[1] 13 Edw. I (Stat. Winchester), c. 4 (1285).
[2] See Chap. VI, pp. 152-3.

them, they could depart their ways. Those considered suspicious persons were rogues, vagabonds, night-walkers, eavesdroppers, scouts, roberdsmen, draw-latches, wasters, and such ' as to goe or ride armed '; any man could arrest night-walkers and persons going armed by day or night carrying ' Dagges, or Pistolls '. If the watchman refused to take his turn, or absented himself before sunrise, he rendered himself liable to be presented at Quarter Sessions by the constable, who was himself amenable to the same authority if he failed to keep watch and ward. A custom had arisen, however, of allowing money payments in lieu of service. This convenience may have sprung from the inexpediency of appointing women to act as guardians of the King's peace; for obligation lay upon the house rather than upon its occupants. We therefore find householders, men and women alike, presented both for refusing to watch and to pay for substitutes sent in their places, and occasionally for sending children in their stead.[1]

Day-watchmen or wardmen, as they were called, could be embodied by Justices, constables, or by direction of the State, when necessity arose for a more complete scrutiny of those upon the road; a necessity that, doubtless, with changed and changing social conditions recurred with increasing frequency. Moreover it is to be presumed that, after 1627,[2] ward-men were called upon for duty every Sunday, to prevent infringement of what puritan sentiment of the seventeenth century believed to be a particularly infamous crime : profanation of the Lord's day by travelling thereon without reasonable cause, and by the carrying of burdens. These offences rendered the culprits liable, by an ordinance of 1644, respectively

[1] *Hertford County Records*, vol. i, pp. 368–9, 389; *Somerset Record Society*, no. 28, p. 342. See also the records of Rye in Holloway's *History and Antiquities of Rye.*

[2] 3 Car. I, c. 2 (1627).

to fines of ten and five shillings, raised in 1677, when the regulation again made its appearance on the statute book,[1] to the sum of twenty shillings, for every ' Drover Horsecourser Waggoner Butcher, Higler their or any of their Servants ' who came ' into his or their Inne of Lodgeing upon the Lords day '. Other travellers could go their way with freedom on the first day of the week by obtaining warrants signed by a Justice, a practice already usual as we learn from the ever-helpful Pepys. The English Sunday, slowly developed from the banning of Sunday amusements in the first year of James I, had become a well-recognized and generally accepted feature of social life.

There was one class of travellers who were required by law to obtain warrants or licences, as they were indifferently called, for travel on any and every day of the week : Roman Catholic Recusants. Indeed, they might well have been included in constables' manuals within the category of ' suspicious persons ', so fearful were all classes of designs by them subversive of the existing order. Unlike their more pliable brethren, the ' Church Papists ', they would neither acknowledge the spiritual supremacy of the King, nor receive the communion of the Church of England. They were, therefore, forbidden by Statute to go beyond a distance of five miles from their places of domicile unless they procured licences to be granted by the Privy Council or by two (later four) Justices of the Peace, together with the assent of the Bishop of their diocese and the Lord Lieutenant or deputy Lord Lieutenant of the county wherein the applicant dwelt, with a statement, given under oath, specifying the reason of the journey and the length of the intended absence.[2] Penalties for infringement were severe.

---

[1] 29 Car. II, c. 7 (1677).
[2] ' An Act against Popish Recusants ', 35 Eliz. c. 2 (1592–3); ' An Acte for the better discovering and repressing of Popish Recusants ', 3 Jac. I, c. 4 (1605–6).

Yet the laxity in administering the laws was such
that in practice they enjoyed a large measure of liberty,
procuring licences with ease, and making short
journeys, it may be, without dispensation,[1] until plot
or rumours of plots brought alarm to the public mind
and reinforced the strict execution of the law by order,
ordinance, or proclamation.   After that the traveller
with a tender conscience procured a licence with
difficulty and may be with some delay, for he could not
go beyond his five-mile limit to obtain the required
signatures.   The Watch cultivated an unwonted and
unwelcome degree of interest in his concerns.   If he
went to town some Justice unfriendly to his person
or his religion would in all likelihood tender him the
oath, and, upon his refusal to swear, seize his horse—
if he had the misfortune to live during the reign of
William III [2]—as well as commit him for Quarter
Sessions.   London was forbidden him ; [3] the countryside probably unfriendly.   If he was wise he kept
quiet until the storm passed.

Even this measure of liberty was in principle denied
the priesthood, which was entirely proscribed.   Nevertheless the Roman Catholic clergy moved about the
country ; in disguise it is true, but for the most part
unmolested, visiting the homes of the faithful and
performing their office, until the onset of trouble made
them seek the priest's hole in some mansion of the
rich, or an obscure garret in a mean alley of the town.

Lest it be thought that the religious minority were
alone held in tutelage and a false idea given of their

[1] Possibly also when they made long journeys. As Catholics were
accustomed to go on pilgrimage to St. Winifred's Well and other holy
places, it is reasonable to suppose that, either they ventured to travel
without permission of the authorities, or, when preferring requests for
licences, made false declarations of the intended purposes of their journeys.

[2] 'An Act for better securing the government by disarming papists',
1 Gul. & Mar. c. 15 (1689).

[3] See Proclamations and Ordinances issued during the Commonwealth,
the Popish Plot, and the Jacobite periods ; also 1 Gul. & Mar. c. 9 (1689).

position, it is necessary to add that, such was the fatherly attitude displayed by rulers towards ruled, that the poor were forbidden to leave their homes without a licence from authority—further evidence of this will appear in Chapter VIII—and, during the patriarchal reigns of James I and Charles I, even the great ones of the earth were liable to find their liberty of movement seriously curtailed. Four times between 1603 and 1632 proclamations were issued bidding the nobility and gentry to leave London and live on their estates, so that they might perform the duties required of them as magistrates and landlords. Little good resulted, at least from the two edicts of 1622. Seven thousand families and fourteen hundred coaches were said to have removed in compliance with the orders, yet provisions were no cheaper in London and all the dearer in the country districts whither they went. Moreover so ingrained had the ' new habit ', as it was called, become, that the deportees returned as soon as they dared. Thus, neither in town nor country did the poor benefit by the change. Nevertheless there were some who complied with the Royal Ordinances, as is evident from extant petitions to the King's Secretary of State, following the Proclamation of 1632, for permission to visit London. In December 1632 Lord Chaworth made humble suit to Sir John Coke, Principal Secretary to the King, to move His Majesty to grant him leave to bring his wife with him to London for the sake of her health, presuming that the King would not deny him the comfort, or his wife the means of health, as in obedience to proclamation, they were leaving their son at one of their houses with ' a competent family ' for house-keeping in the country. To show that this was no idle excuse he reminded the Secretary of the trouble he had had some time previously to obtain a pass to the ' Aspa '—Spa—which had done her more good

than all previous experiments—including apparently
His Majesty's touch, when, opinion being that her
disease was the King's Evil, she had sought the cure
of his hand. Two years later Lord Poulett besought
Sir John to procure a licence for his sons to travel
beyond seas for three or four years, and also for
permission for himself to come to London to take
order for their credit abroad, as without a permit he
dared not venture to repair to London. At the other
end of the scale were the ' great multitude of base and
loose people ' who were bidden in 1600 to leave
London on pain of death.

To return to the more immediate subject of this
chapter it is probable that in the long humdrum years
of peace—long in the actual passage of time, brief
in the annals of history—the tax placed upon householders liable for duty was not onerous, nor were
the hindrances caused to peaceable travellers either
frequent or severe. The Watch sleepily walked their
rounds, or dozed away long hours at their stations ;
and, if the constable were complacent or similarly
engaged at home, slipped into the more congenial
atmosphere of the local alehouse.[1] A meeting with
a couple of unsteady roisterers ending in a crack
across an addled pate from a well-aimed watch-bill ;
in London and its suburbs a more severe, and not
always victorious, struggle with young bloods out for
a lark—' muns ', ' hectors ', ' scourers ' were some of
the names they were known by—such were the most
usual and perilous breaks to the night's monotony.
The traveller, if he were respectable and law abiding,
journeyed without let or hindrance except for a per-
functory question at the town's end. Had he a long
journey to go, necessitating an early rising, he could
by a bribe or friendly interest obtain the opening of
the town gates long before sunrise. The worst likely

[1] See Appendix II.

to befall him would be arrest by an over-suspicious watchman and a night spent in tramping the rounds, or if he were well dressed, well spoken, and peremptory of speech, dozed away at the inn or the constable's home fire. Next morning he would obtain his release at the hands of the city fathers or of the local Justice, if not before.

Such a misadventure befell Thomas Ellwood, the Quaker son of an Oxfordshire squire, as he was returning one day in 1661 from visiting Isaac Pennington (the future father-in-law of William Penn), at Chalfont St. Peter's in Buckinghamshire. He was at the time in disgrace with his father on account of his religious belief, and had been lent, by his kind host, a horse to carry him on his way. Relinquishing the horse at Beaconsfield and dismissing the groom who had accompanied him, he proceeded homeward on foot.

'Before I had walked to the Middle of the Town,' he writes, 'I was stopt and taken up by the Watch. I asked the Watchman What Authority he had to stop me, travelling peaceably on the High-way? He told me he would shew me his Authority; and in order thereunto, had me into an House hard-by, where dwelt a *Scrivener* whose Name was *Pepys*. To him he gave the Order which he had received from the Constables, which directed him to take up all Rogues, Vagabonds and sturdy Beggars. I asked him, For which of these he stopped me; but he could not answer me.

'I thereupon informed him what a *Rogue* in Law is, viz. *One, who for some notorious Offence was burnt on the Shoulder*; and I told them, they might search me if they pleased, and see if I was so branded. A *Vagabond*, I told them was *One that had no Dwelling-house, nor certain Place of abode*; but I had, and was going to it; and I told them where it was. And for a *Beggar* I bid them bring any one that could say, I had *begged* or *asked Relief.*

'This stopt the Fellow's Mouth, yet he would not let me go; But, being both weak-headed and strong-willed, he left me there with the *Scrivener*, and went out to seek the Constable, and having found him, brought him thither. He was a young Man, by Trade a *Tanner*, somewhat better mannered than his Ward man, but not of much better Judgment.

' He took me with him to his House. And having settled me there, went out to take Advice, as I supposed, what to do with me ; leaving no Body in the House to guard me, but his Wife, who had a young Child in her Arms.

' She enquired of me, upon what Account I was taken up ; and seeming to have some Pity for me, endeavoured to perswade me not to stay, but to go my way ; offering to shew me a Back-way from their House, which would bring me into the Road again beyond the Town, so that none of the Town should see me, or know what was become of me. But I told her I could not do so.

' Then having sate a while in a muze, she asked me, *If there was not a Place of Scripture which said,* Peter *was at a Tanner's House ?* I told her there was such a Scripture, and directed her where to find it.

' After some Time she laid her Child to sleep in the Cradle, and stept out on a sudden ; but came not in again in a pretty while.

' I was uneasy that I was left alone in the House, fearing lest, if any Thing should be missing, I might be suspected to have taken it ; yet I durst not go out to stand in the street, lest it should be thought I intended to slip away.

' But besides that, I soon found Work to imploy myself in ; for the Child quickly waking, fell to crying, and I was fain to rock the Cradle in my own Defence, that I might not be annoyed with a Noise, to me not more unpleasant than unusual.

' At length the Woman came in again, and finding me nursing the Child, gave me many Thanks, and seemed well pleased with my Company.

' When Night came on, the Constable himself came in again, and told me, *Some of the Chief of the Town were met together, to consider what was fit to do with me ; and that I must go with him to them.* I went, and he brought me to a little nasty Hut, which they called a Town-house (adjoining to their Market-house) in which dwelt a poor old Woman whom they called *Mother Grime*, where also the Watch used by Turns, to come in and warm themselves in the Night.

' When I came in among them, they looked (some of them) somewhat sourly on me, and ask'd me some impertinent Questions ; to which I gave them suitable answers.

' Then they consulted one with another, how they should dispose of me that Night, till they could have me before some Justice of the Peace, to be examined. Some proposed *That I should be had to some Inn, or publick House, and a Guard set on me there.* He that started this was probably an Inn-keeper, and consulted his own interest. Others objected against this, *That it would bring a Charge on the Town.* To avoid which, they were for having the Watch take Charge of me, and keep me walking about the Streets with them till Morning. Most voices seemed to go this Way; till a third wished them to consider, *Whether they could answer the doing of that, and the Law would bear them out in it?* And this put them to a Stand. I heard all their Debates, but let them alone, and kept my Mind to the Lord.

' While they thus bandied the Matter to and fro, one of the Company asked the rest, *If any of them knew who this young Man was, and whither he was going?* Whereupon the Constable (to whom I had given both my Name, and the Name of the Town where I dwelt) told them my Name was *Ellwood,* and that I lived at a Town called *Crowell* in *Oxfordshire.*

' Old mother *Grime,* sitting by and hearing this, clap'd her Hand on her Knee, and cry'd out, *I know Mr.* Ellwood of Crowell *very well. For when I was a Maid I lived with his Grandfather there, when he was a young Man.* And thereupon she gave them such an Account of my Father, as made them look more regardfully on me; and so Mother *Grime's* Testimony turned the Scale, and took me off from walking the Rounds with the Watch that Night.

' The Constable hereupon bid them take no further Care, I should lie at his House that Night, and accordingly took me home with him, where I had as good Accommodation as the House did afford. Before I went to Bed, he told me, *that there was to be a Visitation, or Spiritual Court* (as he called it) *holden next Day* at Amersham, *about four Miles from* Beaconsfield, and that *I was to be carried thither.*

' In the Morning . . . the other Constable came, and I was called down.

' This was a budge Fellow, and talked high. He was a Shoemaker by Trade, and his Name was *Clark.* He threat'ned me with the *Spiritual Court.* But when he saw I did not regard it, he stopt, and left the Matter to his Partner, who pretended more kindness for me, and therefore went about to perswade *Clark,* to let me go out at the Back-door, to slip away.

'The Plot, I suppose, was so laid, that *Clark* should seem averse, but at length yield, which he did; but would have me take it for a Favour. But I was so far from taking it so, that I would not take it at all; but told them plainly, that as I came in at the Fore-door, so I would go out at the Fore-door. When therefore they saw they could not bow me to their Will, they brought me out at the Fore-door into the Street, and wished me a good journey. Yet before I went, calling for the Woman of the House I paid her for my Supper and Lodging, for I had now got a little Money in my pocket again.'

A year earlier Ellwood had had a like experience with a Sunday Watch at Maidenhead while travelling to a Quaker meeting. Had it not been for his smart appearance—he had borrowed a riding coat and a horse from his good friend Pennington—he would probably have had to spend the day in the stocks, for he had no money to pay for his release, as his captor at first demanded.

When the times were out of joint, when the state was in jeopardy from war, conspiracies, or disease, vigilance would be redoubled, urged thereto by imperative orders and proclamations, demonstrating not only in the written word the urgency of the need, but also, to us, by inference, the normal slackness that had to be overcome. Guards would be doubled, mounted men embodied, posts, rails, and gates set up and guard-houses erected. Lesser evils such as the death of the sovereign, a plethora of highway robberies, 'prentice riots, even a plague of Irish beggars or of Quakers—both pests to the official order—would increase supervision in the localities affected. The traveller would be stopped not once but many times in the course, may be, of a short journey and subjected to keen examination from suspicious watchmen. In March 1668 Pepys and a party of friends had much ado to get home 'round by the Wall', after a supper party at the Blue Balls, hard by the Duke of York's theatre, owing to 'prentice troubles. ' . . . we met so many stops by the Watches', he writes, ' that it cost us much time and some trouble, and more money, to every Watch, to them to drink ; . . . and we had like to have met with a stop for all night at the Constable's watch, at Moore-gate, by a pragmatical Constable ; but we came well home about two in the morning.' Eighteen months or so earlier—in August 1666, the great plague year of many English counties—he and his wife, their maid, Mercer, and their two friends, Mr. and Miss Batelier, coming home in two coaches at ten o'clock at night from a supper party at Bow, were examined at Aldgate as to whether they were husbands and wives ; a piece of gratuitous curiosity, with no bearing it would seem, upon any restriction of entry into plague-free London from infected areas

Annoying as these interruptions were to legitimate travellers, they often did not effect the arrest of the very people for whose apprehension they had been instituted—and no wonder if bribery governed results. The gunpowder conspirators upon the arrest of Guy Fawkes, leaving London by one and twos, had no difficulty in escaping,[1] and, joining up with their fellows awaiting results on Dunsmoor Heath, fleeing to the North. One body of fugitives, throwing away their cloaks, covered eighty-eight miles in seven hours, Rookwood riding one horse thirty miles in two hours. Probably the Watch dared not attempt to hinder such large and swift moving bodies of horse-men—one party was forty strong—and most certainly that of Warwick made no resistance when at midnight they broke open a horse-dealer's stable to obtain fresh mounts. But what man could not do, the weather did. Owing to almost continuous rains the tributary streams of the Severn were in flood, the roads next to

[1] It is true the Government were unaware of their names until the 7th November.

impassable, and their progress was but twenty-five miles in sixteen hours, including a short stay at Hewell Grange, where, though now no more than a handful strong, they dared to enter in search of arms and powder. By the time the little band reached the confines of Shropshire the sheriff and his men were hot on their track and their fate was sealed.

Again Charles, after the disastrous battle of Worcester, with a price set upon his head, was able under various disguises to range the West and South, while awaiting an opportunity of escape to France.

If the Watch might on occasion be too venal or too easygoing to give rein to apprehension, the unofficial part of the community, especially in remote districts, was ever ready to take the alarm, whether it was an idle and preposterous rumour, or a credible and probably well-founded report that winged its way by hedgerow, alehouse, and cottage door. It was nothing exceptional, therefore, when the gunpowder conspirators were rifling Hewell Grange, that the Worcestershire folk should have gathered around, fearful of they knew not what ; though news of a rising had doubtless sped from outraged Warwick. Standing at the entrance gates as the rebels passed out, they cried ' For God, the King and the Country ', the answer coming ' For God and the Country and not for the King ', a significant answer that must have dismayed loyal hearts. Seven years later rumour was again abroad ; the Papists were up, the Earl of Huntingdon was slain in his own house. Thereupon Coventry and Warwick, it is said, shut their gates and mustered their soldiers, while at Banbury and thereabouts ' the people made barricadoes and all other manner of provisions, as if they looked presently [at once] to be assaulted '. All these alarms had, apparently, no more solid foundation than that a rumour having reached the timorous King of a Catholic plot against his life, an order had gone forth to disarm papists and imprison suspects, and that, by a coincidence, the Earl of Huntingdon had sent a force to disband some gipsies in Leicestershire. Likewise, in March 1675, Oxford was for eight or nine days in a 'strange consternation', Lilly, the astrologer, having predicted that on a certain day one part of the town would be burnt, and the other swallowed up by an earthquake. In consequence those 'greezy townsmen that had any love for their carcases or money' fled the town ; the country people forswore the market, and Watches were set up in every street to prevent ' the mischiefe fortold'. This led to unexpected trouble, for a gowns-man, 'executeing his office of walkeing that night', clapped all the townsmen he could find into the Castle, which caused ' a great deal of bussel ' and the accusation that the University desired the burning of the town. ' I scarce thinke ', writes our informant, Prideaux, ' a prophecy from God Almighty would have been able to have don quarter as much, or that the town of Ninive did halfe as much fear the destruction foretold by Jonas as our coxcombs this by Lilly.'

Sometimes a trivial, but unusual, incident raised suspicions in the mind of some well-meaning country-man and brought the traveller the unwelcome attention of officialdom. Thus it was when Charles and Buckingham stole away to Spain, in the hope of gaining the Infanta ; none privy to it but the King and a few trusted counsellors. Leaving the Marquis's estate of Newhall in Essex, disguised with beards, and under the assumed names of Thomas and John Smith, with no attendant but Sir Richard Graham, Buckingham's Master of the Horse, they crossed the Thames at Gravesend, and for lack of silver gave the ferryman a piece or two of twenty shillings. This was an unfortunate show of generosity, for it put the man into a ' melting tendernesse '. Believing that they were

lords going oversea to fight a duel, a matter he liked
not between such free-handed gentlemen, he straightway went and told the town officers what had befallen
him, and what he suspected. Customary though it
was to settle a quarrel by means of cold steel, it
countered the Royal will. A show of energy was
therefore deemed advisable. A messenger was at
once sent post to Rochester to have the trio stayed.
It was found they had already passed. Indeed, they
were in some perplexity. Coming to the brow of the
hill beyond that city, they spied the French ambassador
on the road before them, with the King's coach and
others attending him ; a circumstance that made
them balk the beaten road and ' teach post hackneys
to leap hedges '—they had no wish for the French to
gain intelligence of their project, and so, perhaps,
stay their course.

At Canterbury the mayor himself came to seize
them, as they were taking fresh horses. First he alleged
that he had a warrant from the Council to stop them ;
next, finding them unshaken, that the order came from
Sir Lewis Lewkner, Master of the Ceremonies at
court ; and lastly, neither of these serving his turn,
that the advice came from Sir Henry Manwaring,
Lieutenant of Dover Castle. At all this ' confused
fiction ', we are told, ' the Marquess had no leisure
to laugh, but thought best to dismark his beard, and
so told him that he was going covertly with such light
company to take a secret view (being Admirall) of
the forwardness of his Majestie's fleet, which was then
in preparation on the Narrow Seas.' This healed
matters, and they were no more troubled about their
identity, except by the baggage post-boy, who had
been at court, and got a glimmering notion of who they
were ; ' but ', as the narrator, Sir Henry Wooton,
says, ' his mouth was easily shut '. They reached
Dover without further adventure, though, as a result

A POSTBOY

A WATCHMAN

of these hindrances and bad post-horses, not at the hour they anticipated. Thence they set sail on their imprudent journey, with what conspicuous lack of success and of dignity is known to history.

Quickest to scent danger were the peoples of the seaboard districts; their distrust arising from contact with foes more relentless than the sea, more capricious in their onslaught than the most sudden of tempests— piracy and war. Pirates swooped down on peaceful subjects of the peace-loving James to rob and spoil, or gather slaves for Barbary, beating, wounding, and torturing those who fell into their power. French and Dutch sailed up creek and harbour to reconnoitre or make attack on ill-defended forts, stampeding inland the panic-stricken coast-dwellers.

As a consequence hard-set mariners, forced ashore by stress of weather, were regarded as potential enemies and treated as such until they proved the contrary. To disarm suspicion, in the cases about to be cited, was all the harder because the strangers seeking refuge were on pleasure bent, a motive doubt- less beyond the understanding of those who wrung a hard living from the sea.

John Taylor, the Water-poet, made several excur- sions by sea with a couple of his fellow-watermen as crew in a Thames wherry-boat which was little suited to the buffeting even of summer storms. His first misadventure was at Cromer, where he sought refuge one Sunday night in July 1622. Scarcely had he and his two companions leapt ashore and dragged their boat above high-water mark, than some women and children who saw them land became possessed with fear, and ran up and down crying that enemies were come to take the town. Some cried thieves and some cried pirates. The clamour brought the con- stables, then forty men armed with rusty bills. The intruders were taken prisoners, a guard was set upon their boat, and the town was patrolled. Rumour spread; people arrived from three or four miles distant to know what was afoot, and gathered at the alehouse where the trio had sought cover and were being put to keen examination by four constables. Taylor showed them his books and his letters of introduction to persons at Hull and one to the Archbishop of York ; he swore to all these matters, but to no purpose. He had come, it would seem, in a strange manner and suspicious circumstance, to the house of a Papist. While he was suffering at the hands of officialdom his purse was suffering from the thirst of the gaping onlookers, who called for drink and left him to pay the reckoning—four shillings—a trick they were fond of playing upon such helpless victims of their curiosity. The wherry too was suffering. Turned topsy-turvy, bruised and split, with a board torn out in search for arms—a rusty sword was all they carried—she was in a leaky condition when they did ultimately recover her. The examination came to an end and the night passed. Taylor hoped to obtain permission to leave, but he found that one of the rusty-billed militiamen had gone inland some twenty miles to inform the local Justices of the night's alarm. However, the complexion of affairs altered when these two gentlemen, Sir Austin Palgrave and Mr. Robert Kempe, arrived. Taylor's statements were believed, and, the oath of allegiance having been put to all three, they were released. Presents were showered upon them, money, wine, and sugar. Sir Austin gave them a cordial invitation to his home, which Taylor excused himself and his party from accepting. The Cromer men launched their wherry for them, and bore them on their backs to it, but as Taylor laments, they had lost a fair day.

On the second occasion, a year later, in a trip by sea and river to Salisbury, they had successfully put into the old cinque port town of Hastings, and were out to sea again when a renewal of the tempest drove them to seek shelter at Goring—beyond the modern Worthing. No sooner had they found lodging at that rustic hamlet than the constable arrived to learn Taylor's trade, dwelling-place, name, and business, with ' a troope of questions more '—whether he were a pirate, or a lord escaping the kingdom, questions to which Taylor answered him ' according to his plenteous want of wit '. Six miles he wanted to take Taylor and his friends to the nearest Justice, then, reconsidering the matter, stole their oars, and so departed. When, therefore, they rose early next morning to leave unbeknown to the constable—and also to avoid a more numerous host of torturers—they found that they were unable to start. Happily a ploughman found the missing implements a quarter of a mile away, so that they could again battle with more accustomed elements, leaving the unfortunate constable in we know not what trepidation, for fear of pirates and the superior officer to whom he would have to render account.

If in the presence of the Justices—or of pirates— the constable felt himself a lowly creature, in general he wore an air of authority, and was, according to Bishop Earle, more feared than were the magistrates.

' A Constable,' writes Earle, ' Is a vice-roy in the street, and no man stands more upon't that he is the King's Officer. His Jurisdiction extends to the next stocks, where he has Commission for the heeles only, and sets the rest of the body at liberty. He is a scar-crow to that Ale-house where he drinkes not his morning's draught, and apprehends a Drunkard for not standing in the King's name. Beggers feare him more than the Justice, and as much as the Whipstocke, whom hee delivers over to his subordinate Magistrates, the Bride-wel-man, and the Beadle. Hee is a great stickler in the tumults of double Jugges, and ventures his head by his Place,[1] which is broke many times to keep whole the peace. He is never so much in his majestie as in his night-watch, where hee sits in his Chayre of State, a Shop-stall, and inviron'd with a guard of Halberts, examines all passengers. Hee is a very carefull man in his Office, but if hee stay up after Mid-night, you shall take him napping.'

[1] This means ' risks his head by reason of his place '.

CARRIAGE BY LAND AND WATER

Horses

ANOTHER means of keeping the travelling public under observation was that exercised through the monopoly or preference of supplying post horses to travellers, which was assumed by the Crown in various proclamations. Had this resulted in the setting up of posting-houses on all main roads, a very effective instrument of control would have been placed in the hands of government. But such was not the result. The system, until 1635, was limited to the four great roads of the kingdom, and was, moreover, of such an intermittent and shifting character, owing to the exigencies of public affairs and the movements of the Court whence the service issued, that, for many years, no considerable advantage can have been derived from it either by the public, by the postmasters whose salary was increased by the receipts from horse-hire, or by the guardians of law and order.

Initiated, or rather first definitely established, during the previous century for the more speedy dispatch of messengers and other official personages riding on the Sovereign's behalf or by his permission, the service, such as it was, had proved a convenience alike to travellers and to horse-owners, who were liable to have their horses impressed without notice for the use of those riding on commission. So consistently had the ' Through Post ', as it was called, been taken advantage of by unofficial riders on various pretexts that in a proclamation of 1583–4 the public use was admitted, and a fixed charge of twopence a mile instituted for those riding without special commission. The privilege was not without restrictions. No man should ride post except in the company of a guide who was to blow his horn ' so oft as he meeteth companie ' when passing through towns, or at least thrice a mile, and who was to carry, on demand, the traveller's ' male or other cariage ', not exceeding fourteen pounds in weight. He was also to see his employer into the house of the next standing post, or to signify the same to him, if the person was a ' man of sort, that for his pleasure will make choice of his lodging '.[1] Fourpence or a ' guide's groat ' was the charge for this service. No horse was to be ridden more than one stage without the consent of the owner, the stage being approximately a distance of ten computed miles, but very often considerably more.[2] The postmaster, for his part, was to keep four horses and two horns in constant readiness for the Through Post, and to enter the names of all making use of the service in a book and report monthly thereon. His obligation to keep horses did not, of course, abolish his right to cause the impressment of horses, when necessity arose, for the dispatch of those riding by commission.

In 1603, as a result of ' over great libertie of Riders in poste ', further orders were promulgated for the ease of the postmasters, and the more rigorous control of ' such as pretend publique service by speciall

[1] Book of Proclamations, 14 January 1583-4. Thirty-two years earlier the posts on the Dover road had been instructed to have a horn hanging at their doors or painted signs to show that they were post-houses. The custom had either lapsed or was not general. See *The Post Office, An Historical Summary*.

[2] This was specially common in the more remote districts. In 1600 an extension was laid from Bristol to Milford, the stages ranging from ten to twenty-four computed miles. See *Acts of the Privy Council*, N.S. 31, p. 20. In 1660, when Derby was first connected, at Towcester, with the London–Holyhead post, the distances between the stages (as given in a bill of 1666) varied between ten and seventeen measured miles. *Three Centuries of Derbyshire Annals*, vcl. ii, pp. 289-90.

commission. . . . ' The postmasters were empowered to make their own terms and arrangements for horsing non-official travellers, and to raise the fee charged to those riding on public affairs to twopence half-penny a mile. No man was to take horse without first paying the hire, nor load it with more than thirty pounds weight, nor ride it more than seven miles an hour in the summer and six in the winter. Any person disobeying the regulations to the hurt of horse or owner was, upon complaint to a magistrate, to be stayed until he had given satisfaction or security to repay the damage.

Six years later the charge was fixed at threepence a mile. But the lower fee was still and for long after customary in certain places, this being occasioned by the varying lengths of the computed miles in different parts of the country. It would appear, moreover, from a proclamation of about the year 1637, that non-official travellers were still at the mercy of the postmasters who could charge them whatever they choose. The expense of this method of travelling was further increased by the gratuities that the post-officials expected ; at least from those of official rank. This appears from the accounts of the secretary to the Venetian Ambassador who travelled by post to Edinburgh in 1617. He bestowed fourpence at ' the stables ' of each stage, and gave a like sum to the ' post women ', besides sixpence to each postillion as he calls the guide. Fortunately the guide could serve more than one traveller, for on the homeward journey he drove the extra horses before him.

The ' extraordinary charge ',[1] as a writer of the early part of the century calls it, was, however, compensated

[1] The value of money during the course of the century markedly depreciated owing very largely to the influx of silver from the New World. Estimates place the seventeenth-century purchasing power as four, five, or even six times greater than that obtaining in the years before the Great War.

for in the high speed that could be attained by those who choose to ignore the regulations ; as much as ten miles an hour was sometimes accomplished.

The fact that the posts were run at a loss—£3,400 was the deficit alike in 1609 and in 1635 [1]—militated against any expansion of the system. The increasing pecuniary difficulties of the Crown under the first two Stuarts led to inefficiency ; and this to lack of demand on the part of the travelling public. The postmasters' wages remained unpaid for years together. Many fell into debt,[2] some endured arrest and imprisonment. They ceased to keep horses and the letters were carried on foot. Abuses flourished. Horses were impressed without cause and their keep charged to their owners. Bribes were extorted from innkeepers and others owning horses on the understanding that they should not be called upon to supply the service. Stables were broken into during the night without the knowledge of the constables—who should have been present—horses seized and their owners threatened and beaten. Farmers going to market were bereft of their means of getting there. It is even on record that a chief constable, riding to serve a warrant on a defaulting postmaster, was compelled to relinquish his horse for the dispatch of the packet. It is therefore not surprising to learn that the posts to Scotland and Ireland, during the first ten years of Charles I's rule, existed in little more than name.

In 1635 a reorganization took place. The four chief posts were re-established, and services were

---

[1] Proof, indeed, that little was done towards extending the service.

[2] In the *Cal. State Papers Dom.* are to be found a number of petitions which had been sent to the Council by the postmasters praying for redress. Some alleged that they had been obliged to sell their cattle and other goods to maintain the service ; others excused neglect of duty by want of pay ; one complained of the charges to which he had been put by the setting up of a new stage ; another, an old fellow of ninety, that his wages had not been paid for thirteen years, a sum of over four hundred and seventy pounds being due to him. See also *History of the Post Office*, by Herbert Joyce.

promised to Oxford, Bristol, Colchester, and Norwich. Private letters, hitherto carried on sufferance in the official bags—it was called the 'Post for the Packets' —were accepted for transmission to places having standing posts. Competition, though not forbidden, was restricted to known carriers and private messengers. Two years later a letter office was opened in London. In 1644 the advent of a new postmaster was followed by the announcement that there would henceforth be a weekly conveyance of letters from London to all parts of the kingdom. Whatever extension of the posts took place as a result of this, it is certain that many towns long after this date had to be content, and were well content, with the more trustworthy services of the common carriers. Indeed, nearly half a century later, in 1683, we find the Government promising that ' After 14 September next all considerable market towns will be connected with the next post-stage '. Nor was it until the last decade of the century that cross-posts were instituted for the more speedy dispatch of correspondence.

Neither the ordinance of 1654 nor the Act of 1657 made any alteration of a permanent character to the Through Post. The monopoly was re-asserted, and the postmasters were enjoined to keep four good horses at least for the service of travellers. A year later the postmasters on the Chester road, pursuant to orders, published the following advertisement in the *Mercurius Politicus* of the 24th June.

'All gentlemen, merchants, and others, who have occasion to travel between London and Westchester, Manchester, and Warrington, or any other town upon the road, for the accommodation of trade, dispatch of business, and ease of purse, upon every Monday, Wednesday, and Friday morning, betwixt six and ten of the clock at the house of Mr. Christopher Charteris, at the sign of the Harts Horns in West Smithfield, and postmaster there, and at the post-master of Chester, at the post-master of Manchester and at the post-master of Warrington,

Sala Regalis cum Curia Weſtmonaſterij, *vulgo* Weſtmunſter hall

WESTMINSTER HALL.   From an engraving by Hollar

may have a good and able single horse, or more, furnished, at threepence the mile, without charge of a guide; and so likewise at the house of Mr. Thomas Challenor, post-master at Stone in Staffordshire, upon every Tuesday and Thursday, and Saturday mornings to go into London; and so likewise at all the several post-masters upon the road, who will have all such set days so many horses with furniture in readiness to furnish the riders without any stay, to carry them to or from any the places aforesaid in four days, as well to London, as from thence, and to places nearer in less time, according as their occasions shall require, they ingaging at first stage where they take horse, for the safe delivery of the same to the next intermediate stage, and not to ride that horse any further, without consent of the post-master by whom he rides, and so from stage to stage on their journey's end.

'All those who intend to ride this way, are desired to give a little notice beforehand, if conveniently they can, to the several post-masters where they first take horse, whereby they may be furnished with so many horses as the riders shall require with expedition.

'This undertaking began [sic] the 28th June 1658, at all the places above said, and so continues by the several post-masters.' [1]

A proviso in the Post-Office Act of 1660 [2] put a limit to the postmasters' monopoly by permitting travellers to secure horses for themselves if the postmasters could not within half an hour provide them. Even with this concession it was sometimes difficult to procure horses. Jack Verney, when setting out for the east in 1662, was delayed three or four hours at that very important centre, Canterbury, owing to his inability to procure a mount. There were but two in the city, he writes, and those at a very dear rate.

If the traveller had his difficulties the postmaster had his trials. His salary was small, for the Government was well aware that the position was for a variety of reasons coveted by innkeepers; his emoluments were scanty on the less frequented roads; his horses were on occasions lamed, overridden and stolen—horse-stealing was a large and profitable industry. During

[1] *Notes and Queries*, Ser. 1, vol. i, p. 146. [2] 12 Car. II, c. 35 (1660).

the last twelve years of the century, it has been stated,
many postmasters languished in jail through inability
to pay what they owed, and there were few among
them ' who did not trace their misfortunes to the fact
that immediately before and after William's accession
to the throne their horses had been killed or spoiled
through reckless riding or else run away with '.[1]   The
English, indeed, had long been known for their
propensity to hard riding.   This trait, together with
others said to distinguish the nation, is indicated in
a proverb of Italian origin then prevalent : ' England
is the Hell of Horses, the Purgatory of Servants, and
the Paradise of Women '.   As all writers dilate upon
the superior merits of English horses—their gentle
ambling pace, their strength to perform great journeys
—it would seem that English breeds must have had
uncommon racial qualities to endure without deteriora-
tion the hard going on the deplorable national roads ;
or, alternatively, that the vice was not so general as
writers of the period, with their forcible, picturesque
language, would lead one to believe.

For those whose requirements were not met by
the posting system, or whose means would not allow
the ' extraordinary charge ', horses could be hired
by the day or the month.   In the earlier part of the
century a shilling or one and sixpence a day in London
(two shillings for the first day) and a shilling a day in
the country seem to have been the usual charges, the
hirer finding forage and stabling.   Carriers charged
a higher rate; twenty shillings inclusive for a period
of five or six days, this notwithstanding the ' caution
that the passenger must lodge in their Inne, that
they may looke to the feeding of their horse '.   In
return the traveller obtained the advantage of com-
panionship and guidance on his way ; no inconsider-
able benefit, for carriers knew every yard of their

[1] *History of the Post Office*, Herbert Joyce, p. 51.

accustomed route. It was in this manner that young
Coke, son to the Secretary of State, proposed to travel
from Cambridge to London with some fellow com-
moners.

During the second half of the century prices ranged
between six and twelve shillings a week, the hirer
paying on an average one shilling and twopence a day
for horse-meat. In country towns where the single
horse-jobber, or hackney-man as he was called, kept
only a small stable of nags, the difficulty would
occasionally arise of a hirer failing to return a horse
at the time agreed, so losing another would-be hirer
the means of setting out on what might be a long and
urgent journey. Some persons who did not usually
keep horses resorted to a method of supplying their
necessities which was much practised by 'Varsity
undergraduates ; that of buying a horse in preparation
for a journey and selling him again on reaching their
destination. The method had its drawbacks. Sometimes a horse was found upon trial, after purchase, to
be unfit for the journey contemplated. Sometimes the
traveller, arrived at his journey's end, found that he
was unable to sell the beast, and for weeks, perhaps,
while his visit lasted, had to pay for its keep. One
such piece of ill luck befell the well-known Manchester
divine, Henry Newcome, when he paid a lengthy visit
to London. He was fortunate, however, in being
able to put the animal to grass for three months at
Newington, at a total cost of fifteen shillings.

To own a small stable of horses did not exempt the
owner from difficulties, as many a country gentleman
found to his cost when his horses got ill or lamed, or
when the family needs outran the supply. For a great
household such as that of Lord William Howard of
Naworth a large stable of horses was required to provide
for the ceaseless comings and goings of a large family
of sons and daughters, grandsons and granddaughters,

a numerous retinue, and a staff of messengers whom, in the absence of other means of communication, it was necessary to maintain.

The price of horses rose continuously throughout the century. During the first two reigns prices in the North ranged from two pounds to ten, while in the South, in London, twenty pounds was considered, about 1625, a handsome offer for a saddle gelding.[1] It was during the period of the Civil War that the rise became marked. Allowance for a trooper's horse was then, in some cases, as much as ten pounds (1645), or double the amount paid a few years before by Lord William Howard for a riding mare for his son, Thomas. An ordinance of 1656, permitting the export of horses—otherwise prohibited by statute—accentuated the rising tendency of the market. Thus Dr. Denton, who was commissioned a year later by Sir Ralph Verney to buy him a saddle-horse in London, found there was 'scarce anything worth looking uppon under 25*l.*, and those but indifferent neyther'. A little later he writes that he had been asked a hundred pounds for a gelding, ' they pack them so fast into France that now it is but aske and have, even double their value '. After hunting around in Hyde Park and Smithfield he manages to procure a horse for sixteen pounds ten shillings.

In August 1665 Pepys rode, with what pride and pleasure we can imagine, a horse worth forty pounds, the property of Sir George Carteret. Away from the Metropolis prices were lower. In 1674 Winchester College gave fifteen pounds eight shillings and sixpence for a saddle-horse, a moderate price in view of those obtaining in London, but considerable when compared with the six pounds thirteen shillings and fourpence paid for a horse at Swarthmoor in Lancashire for that indefatigable traveller, George Fox, who

[1] See Note A, p. 323.

required, more than any man in England, a sound
and sturdy animal to carry him through his remarkable
nomadic experiences. A Leicestershire Justice, he
tells us, once granted a warrant for his arrest as a
means of seizing his horse.

To those of slender means and those of poor or
indifferent stamina, the pillion-saddle rendered invaluable service. It was no uncommon thing to see
two men riding in this fashion, even those of the
better sort ; but women, naturally, were the most
frequent pillion riders, seated behind husband, father,
son, friend, or servant. Sometimes two women would
ride double, as it was called. A pathetic story is told
how a young married woman, riding behind her future
sister-in-law to Halifax to buy the latter a trousseau
and stopping before the inn door at Sowerby to have
a drink of ale, was thrown by a sudden jerk of the
horse and instantly killed. Indeed pillion riding,
though less arduous exertion than riding single, was
no less dangerous. The accidents recorded of both
classes of riders make a formidable list. Yet some
travellers, having more luck or greater horsemanship,
roamed far and wide without scratch or fall.

There were other drawbacks to travelling on horseback, besides the risk of accidents, a disadvantage not
confined to any one method of progression. There
was exposure to weather ; the riding in mud to the
horse's girths ; the discomforts of driving rain and
snow ; the numbing effect of severe frost ; the hazard
of lying out in a field, if by ill-luck no better shelter
could be reached. Moreover, where hired horses
were employed, there was the distress caused by
unaccustomed saddlery ; a minor annoyance though
a painful one to those journeying afar. But for the
well-seasoned traveller—who was of necessity a good
horseman—there were also advantages. Ground
could be covered at a speed impossible in a coach ;

a hundred miles a day was on occasions accomplished though sixty was more agreeable and thirty or forty more usual in a journey extending over a period of any length.[1] The traveller had entire liberty of action ; and immunity from the inconveniences arising from travelling in a herd. While for all, strong and weak, hardened traveller and novice, there was the cheapness of the old method of travel as compared with the new, whether by the expensively hired private coach or by the more moderately priced stage-coach.

It was probably this consideration which induced Mary Verney, wife of a needy refugee, to make arrangements for her three-weeks-old baby to travel from St. Albans—whither he was being carried by stage-coach—to their Buckinghamshire home, borne upon a pillow before the nurse's husband, upon an easy-going horse, with a footman to run beside. Certainly, that was her reason for riding pillion upon ' a cruell trotting horse ' when, far from strong, she travelled from Claydon to Acton, where a coach awaited to carry her in greater comfort the last seven miles of her journey to London. Others of still humbler means were glad to travel by pack-horse, between the packs, though the pace was slow and not such as to rouse the circulation on a winter's day, and though the wear to clothes in contact with packs must have been severe. Mud, dust, and friction took heavy toll on the garb of all riders, on inner garments and outer ones alike, ' nothing wearing out Llinnen more than riding '. Truly the rider who would be properly equipped had to incur considerable expense. If a gentleman, he required a stout pair of boots—high boots well beeswaxed, and

---

[1] Sir William Dugdale once covered one hundred and three miles in a day. Sir Robert Cary, when he posted from London to Edinburgh with tidings of Queen Elizabeth's death, accomplished the three hundred and eighty-two miles in less than three days, arriving ' beblooded with great falles and bruises '.

perhaps buskins (over-boots) as well in winter [1]—
spurs, saddle, saddle-cloth, bridle, riding suit, a second
suit to wear at the journey's end or by the way, a cloak,
sword, belt, pistol, holster, ' Portmantue ', and a hat-
case. A lady had need of a safeguard—a kind of
over-skirt—a hood, gloves, scarf, perhaps a vizard-
mask to protect the complexion,[2] a side-saddle or
a pillion ' with Strappins ', and a pillion-cloth ; all
of which were apt to be quickly spoilt if not, as
frequently happened to the less secure articles, actually
dropped by the way.[3] It was a serious loss to tradesmen when the gentry took to coach travelling, as will
presently be seen.

In many remote parts of the country the riding
horse was the only means, or only tolerable means, of
getting through the narrow, sunken lanes of rich agricultural land, or over the rough tracks of moor and
mountain. Even Lady William Howard of Naworth,
wife of the celebrated 'Belted Will' and first lady of the
Border country, owned a ' dubble ' gelding in addition

[1] Adam Martindale, writing of a great blow that he had received on the
shin while riding, from the kick of his companion's horse, declared that it
might have cost him his life, as it had done the lives of four of his acquain-
tances, had he not had on a good pair of boots, and also a strong pair of
buskins buckled upon them, such as he then used when riding in winter.
A fine pair of these buskins, or over-boots, is to be seen at the London
Museum. ' Spatterdashes ' was the expressive name given them in the
following century. See Planche, *Cyclopoedia of Costume*, p. 474.

[2] The Misses Fells made purchases of these accoutrements of gallantry
in 1674 and in 1676 ; strange adornment for sober Quaker ladies of country
birth and residence, unless it were to protect the face from wind and rain
when riding. It may also be noted that Mrs. Hater, who travelled by
coach to Portsmouth with her husband and in company with Pepys and
Creed, was masked, so that the connoisseur diarist took her ' at first to be
an old woman '. Afterwards he found that she was a ' very pretty, modest
black woman '.

[3] ' When we had toiled hard to get up to the top of Blackstone hill [or
Edge],' writes Newcome in his *Autobiography*, ' when just on the top my
cloak, that lay between us, was lost, and Mr. Jones rode back almost two
miles to retrieve it. But returning with it the Lord turned all our troubles
into a sense of a great mercy ; for the loss of it would have put a doubt
into us of our journey, laid us under a weary suspense and vexation of mind
all the way.' See Appendix III.

to her coach, which latter was probably used only for visits of state in the neighbourhood, and, occasionally, on short journeys of one and two days' length, to fetch members of that numerous family the last stage of their journey home. On these occasions, it is evident, it laboured under difficulties, for items occur in the Howard of Naworth Household Book such as : ' Hewing a way for the coach beyond Gelt bridg ij^s iiij^d ' ; ' To a manne helpinge one of the coach horsses out of the myre in Brampton parke [one of the Howard estates] xij^d ' ; and ' To Jack the footmane on the hyeway 1st May v^s ', probably for some feat of strength in raising the coach out of a quagmire. Lesser households like that of the Fells of Swarthmoor, in the isolated district of Barrow-in-Furness, kept no wheeled vehicles other than rude, and probably two-wheeled, carts for agricultural use. The wild and mountainous principality of Wales was of course equally unsuited to the new form of traffic. Lord Clarendon (son to the Chancellor) when travelling to Dublin by way of Holyhead after his appointment as Lord Lieutenant of Ireland, had to have his coach taken to pieces and carried over Penmaenmawr. When he ventured to use it in Anglesey, pioneers went in advance to clear a way. Other travellers of less importance had to leave their coaches at Chester. In Devon and Cornwall and in parts of Somersetshire the ways were little or no better suited to the new conditions. It was not until the nineteenth century that the coach and waggon finally triumphed over the riding horse and the pack-saddle.

Coaches

The coach that, during the first half of the seventeenth century jolted over the cobbled streets of great towns or floundered through the mud of country lanes had little resemblance to the comparatively light

Dan. Loggan Delin. et Sculp. cum Privil. S.R.¹

A COACH-AND-FOUR. From Loggan's *Oxonia Illustrata*

and easy running vehicles—a cumbersome relic to twentieth-century eyes—that made such dashing display on the smooth metalled roads of England in the early years of the last century. It was a square, heavy body with domed roof, covered with black leather, studded with broadheaded brass nails, and suspended by great leather straps from upright posts which sprang from the axle-trees. The entrance on either side formed an embrasure, called a boot, for the seating of two passengers ; the only protection for these unfortunate boot riders, or, indeed, for the occupants of the inner part of the coach, being leather flaps or curtains, and, as time passed, an ill-fitting door. Moreover, from the swaying of the coach, the boot had a peculiarly unfortunate effect on some persons ; one youth who experienced its motion declared he was resolved never to ride again in a coach. To be coached was an expression of the time which meant getting used to any violent motion. The coachman had no box-seat such as we know, but sat on a cross-bar or, at best, a cushion, fixed between the two forward standards, his feet resting on the carriage pole. Perhaps it was the result of this insecure seat and a kicking horse that led to the following entry amongst the expenses of the Lady Arabella Stuart's Progress in 1609. ' To the Coachman had [sic] his legg broke—£2 0s. 0d.' Certainly the red cloak and wide sleeves with broad shining lace, said to be the usual livery of the coachman at this time, was not very suitable if contact with muddy roads was of ordinary occurrence. This resplendent individual was aided in his task by one or two postillions where teams of four or six horses were employed.

Such was the vehicle that, in London and the more populous and central parts of the kingdom, grew in numbers and favour. Government might frown upon its accommodation to middle-class use, out-of-work watermen might petition for its suppression, reactionary or interested pamphleteers might inveigh against a conveyance so effeminate and so destructive to trade ; it only multiplied the more. In 1636, it was computed, there were upwards of six thousand coaches in London alone.

The ' Hackney Hell Carts ', as the hired coaches were impolitely termed by their detractors, were the special target of these sharp-shooters. They had made their appearance quite early in the century, but were not allowed to ply for hire in the streets until 1634 when permission was obtained, and a rank formed by the Maypole in the Strand. In a little more than a year the favour was nullified by a proclamation limiting their use to journeys of three miles or more out of London and Westminster. But, notwithstanding the great disturbance they caused to the King and Queen, and notwithstanding the breaking up of pavements and the congestion of traffic imputed to their presence in the narrow streets,[1] the restriction was soon found to be impracticable, and the system of licensing was renewed. Permission was granted to fifty hackney coachmen, with a maximum of twelve horses apiece ; a generous allowance which must have enabled many more than those licensed to gain a living thereby. One authority suggests that the number actually on the streets may have been as high as three hundred. Before the end of the century the official figure had risen to seven hundred.

The private coach, though less reviled than its hireling mate, was not free from censure. It was

---

[1] An order of the Star Chamber, issued as a result of complaints, directed coaches, when returning after the play to pick up passengers at the Blackfriars Theatre, to proceed no further than the west end of St. Paul's Churchyard or the Fleet Conduit, it being ' much more fit and reasonable ' that passengers should go by water or else on foot. Coachmen disobeying orders were to be committed to Newgate or Ludgate. *Hist. of Company of Watermen*, Humpherus, vol. i, p. 224.

said to foster jealousy, pride, and unnatural ambition. Great nobles, such as the Earl of Northumberland and the Duke of Buckingham, vied with one another, it was said, by adding to the numbers in their coach draughts out of ' mastring pride ' ; though one would have thought the condition of the roads excuse enough for the six and eight horses it thus became usual to employ. An honest, blunt-spoken waterman like John Taylor was overcome with ' a Timpany of pride ', when he chanced to ride in the coach of the Lieutenant of the Tower, Sir William Waad. ' In what state ', he writes, ' I would leane over the boote and looke, and pry if I saw any of my acquaintance, and then I would stand up, vailing my Bonnet, kissing my right claw, extending my armes as if I had beene swimming, with God save your Lordship, worship, or How doest thou honest neighbour or good fellow ? ' Truly emotions which ill-beseemed a plain citizen. 'Mastring pride ', compatible with greatness, was presumptuous in those of lesser degree. Nor was ambition more tolerable. ' . . . every Justices wife and the wife of every cittizen must be jolted now ', exclaims another waterman critic of the new-fangled mode. The fraternity, it will be seen, had public morals very much at heart.

The exclusive property at first of the rich and noble, the coach became in due course the necessity of all who, in London and the environs, had any pretensions to social distinction. But it was something more than the plaything of fashion. Cumbersome and jolting and open to the weather, it was, nevertheless, for those unable to stand the rigours of horseback an invention of inestimable benefit. It is true, the benefit might not always be apparent. To a woman or child, sick or in pain, tossing over cobbled streets ; to the mother of an infant crying with convulsive energy over twenty miles or more of rough country road—

one such child, to save its life, had to be left *en route* in the course of a long journey—to the traveller left stranded at the roadside, ten miles from a town, in a coach tipped sideways from the breaking of an axle, or with wheels sunk deep in a quagmire ; to these it might seem but a new form of torture. Yet it entailed neither the exposure nor the physical strain inseparable from the old-style travelling. As to peril, it made little difference which method of transit was adopted, so long as the coachman and postillion were sober and cautious. This, as may be imagined, they were not always in an age when copious drinking and open-handed hospitality prevailed.[1] Although a healthy man might prefer his own gait and his own company on horseback, though a schoolboy or schoolgirl might,

---

[1] The coachmen of Evelyn and of Mr. Henry Howard of Norfolk driving their masters home from Charlton where they had been dining with Sir William Ducie, were so drunk that they both fell from their coach seats on Black-heath, and there they were left, while other servants drove the coaches to London. ' This barbarous custom ', writes Evelyn, ' of making the masters welcome by intoxicating the servants, had now the second time happened to my coachman.' Another master, Timothy Burrell of Cuckfield, Sussex, took a more cynical view of the failing. Again and again in his journal he has made entries of sums, on occasion large sums, that he paid to ' John Coachman ' ' to be spent in ale ', ' to buy him heart's-ease ', and the like. Once he gave John a pound that he might drink all Easter week ; another time he paid the glazier for mending his casement which he had broken at night when drunk. In March 1710 John fell off his coach-box when driving to Glynde, and the saddler had to be paid one pound seven shillings and sixpence, presumably for mending the coach-box, with a further fourteen shillings and eleven pence for ' plasters, ointments, pectorals, purges ', for John's head, eyes, wrist, knee, foot and lung. The fall and the saddler were fatal to him ; he died a few months later. Against nearly every item relating to him, Burrell has made a crude drawing of a tankard or a bottle. Burrell next ventured upon a postillion—we hope he did not encourage him in bibulous tastes. Perhaps the high wages paid to coachmen led to their undoing. John Coachman's wages in 1685 were six pounds a year, whereas the cook received no more than fifty shillings, and the footman thirty shillings. The last named was raised to four pounds a year, when, having been detected in a theft and discharged, he returned after ' a ramble to London . . . almost starved '. *Sussex Arch. Soc.*, vol. iii, 1850. The wages of the Howard of Naworth coachmen ranged from four pounds in 1620 to six pounds thirteen shillings and fourpence in 1640. This was the same salary as the woman housekeeper at Arundel House in London received in 1633.

COACH and SEDAN,

Pleasantly Difputing for Place and Precedent

The *Brewers-Cart* being Moderator.

Spectatum admiſſi, riſum teneatis amici?

LONDON:

1636

Printed by *Robert Raworth*, for *Iohn Crowch*; and are to be fold
Edmund Paxton. dwelling at *Pauls* chayne, neere Doctors-Commons. 16

From a Pamphlet of 1636

and certainly did, chafe at being sent to school in the family coach—the stigma of effeminacy took long to disappear—there were few who did not at some time or other avail themselves of the new convenience.

Certainly the invalid of rank—to digress for a moment—had no need to submit to its joltings, if he were willing to travel at a snail's pace and able to support the additional expense. For such, noble or gentle, there was the horse-litter, a survival from earlier ages, and only to be equalled for ease of movement by the chare or chair, and its foreign supplanter the sedan-chair, which had been introduced from abroad towards the end of the previous century. This popular addition to London street vehicles was fancifully described in 1636 as being ' in a suite of greene, after a strange manner, windowed before and behind with isen-glasse [talc], having two handsome fellowes in greene coats attending him, the one ever . . . before, the . . . other behind. . . . ' Its use was encouraged by the authorities of London, who in 1634 granted a monopoly of letting sedan-chairs to Sir Sanders Duncombe for the express purpose of relieving traffic congestion by initiating competition with the multitude of coaches. Both Sedan and chair occasionally figured on the open road. In the great trek south of 1603 the wife of the French ambassador ' was carried betwixt Edenburgh and London by eight pioners or porters, one foure to relieve the other foure by turnes, carrying her in a chaire with slings '. King James, itinerant even in illness, availed himself as well of a chair as of a litter when in 1619, suffering from ' the stone '—that prevalent seventeenth-century disease—he left Newmarket for Ware and Theobalds. A few years earlier the great Earl of Salisbury set out on what was to be his last journey, making ' many stops and shifts, from his coach to his litter, and to his chair, and all for that ease that lasted no longer than his imagination '. The litter appears to have been in use throughout the century, at first alike for everyday occasions and state ceremonies. Thus Gondomar, Spanish Ambassador to the Spanish-affected James, passed through the London streets amidst the curses and execrations of the soundly Protestant inhabitants, and thus Marie de Medicis entered in pomp her son-in-law's capital in 1638. Later it was used only when ill health or the difficulties of the road precluded the use of the newer methods of progression. It was in a litter that Lady Clarendon surmounted the asperities of Penmaenmawr, and in the same class of gentle-moving conveyance that the Duke of Shrewsbury returned in 1696 from Gloucestershire to London ; a careful piece of stage-managing this, for the Duke was merely feigning illness as a means of evading his personal and public responsibilities as Secretary of State.

The extraordinary popularity of the coach was in course of time justified by improvements in its gait and appearance. The cumbersome body developed the more graceful contour of the later sedan chair. The leather flaps were superseded by glass windows, which though movable up and down, had, it is evident, no protective covering on the inner side of the door. Pepys, on finding that one of his coach windows had been broken within the door, concluded that he had done it himself with his knee, a vexatious accident which cost him forty shillings for a new glass. A greater catastrophe was that which befell the Lady Peterborough. Driving in her ' glass-coach ' she saw a lady whom she would salute, and, thinking the window was open, put her head out through the glass. As the defects of the ' glass-coach '—' the flying open of the doors upon any great shake '—were the subject of conversation which prompted the narration of so queer an accident, this tribute to the clear quality of the glass is the more remarkable. Perhaps the glass had come from the Duke of Buckingham's Glass-works at Vauxhall, which had speedily acquired a high reputation for the quality of the coach-glasses made there.[1]

Experiments were being made to improve the coach in other ways, notably in regard to body suspension and coachman's seat. The newly-formed Royal Society took an active part therein, and during the years 1665, 1666, and 1667 members viewed and tested at Gresham College, St. George's Fields, and elsewhere coaches and chariots—a newer, lighter vehicle—constructed from designs of three of their number, Drs. Croune and Hooke and Colonel Blount. The last named, in his efforts to attain a light, easy-running vehicle, produced scheme after scheme with unflagging zeal and fertile resource. If his projects fell short of success, as probably they did—he retired from the society in the course of 1667—he at least achieved an immortality denied to many greater inventors, for he and his experiments figure in the pages of that keen and interested observer of all things human, Samuel Pepys. A fellow member, Pepys was present at a demonstration ' where the coachman sits astride upon a pole over the horse, but do not touch the horse which is a pretty odde thing ; but it seems it is most easy for the horse and . . . man '. A couple of years later he alludes to a coach-box, no very substantial affair, for he speaks of it as being flung over

[1] According to Aubrey, the first glass coach was brought into England by the Duke of York, shortly after the Restoration. If this statement is correct, the making of coach-glasses in England speedily followed the introduction of the new type of vehicle to this country. George, Duke of Buckingham, applied in June 1663 for a renewal of his patent ' for making crystal looking glasses, coach glasses ', &c. In July of the following year a Proclamation was issued forbidding the importation of various kinds of glasses, including window plates, a regulation that of course led to contraband trade, although the English ' inventors ' had brought the manufacture to perfection, and had undertaken to make glass as cheap as, or cheaper than formerly.

the pole by the kicking of the near horse. David Loggan shows, however, in half a dozen illustrations of different coaches in *Oxonia Illustrata*, that by 1675 the coach-box had a solid-looking platform on which the coachman could rest his feet, although, as far as can be seen, the seat still consisted of a bar or cushion, or possibly a leather strap, fixed between the two forward standards. Pepys describes one coach model designed by Colonel Blount as lying on one long spring ; another, a chariot with springs, highly commended by its inventor, the Colonel, who had driven many miles in it and outdone any coach or horse upon the road, he tested over the cart ruts of Blackheath, and found ' pretty well, but not so easy as he pretends '. Experiments with steel springs had possibly been going on since 1626 when Edward Knapp had been granted a licence for an invention of ' axletrees of iron and springs of steel ' to render coaches stronger, less costly to keep in repair, and lighter ; but although it is said that steel springs were introduced about the year 1670 their use was not general until the middle of the following century.

Somewhat earlier a new type of vehicle had been brought to England by the Chevalier de Grammont, who presented to the King a most magnificent calèche or calash, as it came to be anglicized, which had cost him two thousand louis in Paris. That the ladies should be able to show their charms more freely than was possible in a glass coach was the Chevalier's most excellent intention, but the sequel was unfortunate. No sooner had the Queen displayed herself in the new carriage than both Lady Castlemaine and Miss Stewart, struck by the advantage it bestowed upon the occupant, demanded of Charles the first loan ; a feminine whim which begat a long and fierce contest for supremacy between the old favourite and the new, a brow-beating of the woman-ridden King, and the

A HACKNEY-COACHMAN

final triumph of the new and beautiful star, La Belle Stewart, over her quondam friend and rival.

Coaches could now be had of all sizes. Mr. Henry Howard, brother of the Duke of Norfolk, who kept such regal state at Norwich, had a great coach capable of holding fourteen persons for the convenience of the lady guests attending his New Year's parties. It was said to have cost five hundred pounds ' without the harnesse, which cost six score more '. Other more ordinary coaches were made to carry six or eight persons. The former were described by Sir Ralph Verney in 1652 as being light, ' with one end, and a Bed as are used in France '—perhaps an early variety of the chariot ; the latter had two ends and were considered by him to be ' more apt to breake, and kill horses too '. Chariots to hold two or four persons became fashionable during the post-Restoration period. They cost between twenty and thirty pounds. Sir William Penn, like Pepys an official at the Navy Office, paid in 1667 no less than thirty-two pounds, inclusive of harness, for ' a plain but fashionable chariot '. Fourteen years later Sir William Dugdale, Garter King-at-Arms, was content to give twenty-three pounds thirteen shillings to a coachmaker in St. Martin's Lane for a little chariot, a canvas cover at one guinea, and double harness at four, being extras.[1] Pepys, having agreed to pay fifty-three pounds for a coach, changed his mind, and selected a chariot to hold four, which was already framed but not yet covered with leather. Although he describes it as ' very genteel and sober ', it was sufficiently conspicuous for a solicitous friend to remark that he hoped he ' might not contract envy by it ', a discreet hint that was not acted upon but was later justified when enemies sought to magnify and ridicule the splendour of his equipage by publication of a scurrilous pamphlet.

[1] See Note B, p. 323.

It was a splendour-loving age, and splendour in dress and equipage was deemed the prerogative of high birth. The Duc de Soissons, after an audience with the King in 1660, passed through the streets in a coach ' all red velvet covered with gold lace and drawn by six barbes, and attended by twenty pages, very rich in clothes '. While Ambassador Colbert, eight years later, made his entry into London in a coach of such extraordinary richness that Evelyn, travelled though he was, had never seen the like. King William and Queen Mary's state coach of silver gilt, a present from the States of Holland, in which they passed to the Lord Mayor's feast in 1689, drew forth the praise of more than one writer. Said to have cost sixty thousand pounds, it must have gladdened the hearts of London people who then as now crowded to watch the passing of the great. Their curiosity, however, was often matched by their ill breeding. When the eccentric Duchess of Newcastle took the air in park or suburbs, the rabble afoot, the more select in coaches, would follow and surround her coach. It was her lack of deference to convention, one supposes—her addiction to quaint poses or gestures—that made her a target of popular interest, for her equipage, though rich, was not what would be then called gaudy.[1] On May Day 1667 she appeared in the Park, so Pepys tells us, in ' a large black coach, adorned with silver instead of gold, and so white curtains, and every thing black and white, and herself in her [velvet] cap ', her coachman and footmen being likewise clad in velvet. One would fancy that the coach of his friend Mrs.

---

[1] The Duchess of Newcastle's eccentricity was well known. Sir Charles Littleton, describing in a letter from York, 1665, the progress north of the Duke and Duchess of York, says : ' Hard by . . . mett us on the way my Ld of Newcastle and my Lady, whose behavior was very pleasant, but rather to be seene than told. She was dressd in a vest, and, instead of courtesies, made leggs and bows to the ground with her hand and head.' *Corr. of the Hatton Family 1601-1704*, Camden Soc., N.S. xxii, p. 47.

Lowther—the Pegg Penn of most of the Diary—
displayed on the same festive occasion, was far more
resplendent with its ' richness in gold ', but though
the critical diarist pronounces it to be the finest coach
in the Park, it does not appear to have attracted the
attention of the vulgar herd to any marked extent.

On the May Day of two years later when Pepys
and his wife had the satisfaction of appearing in their
own chariot—discarding the hackney-coaches which,
much to Pepys's chagrin, had had so often to serve
their turn—' the people did mightily look upon ' them
and their coach, with its silver body and gilt standards,
fresh painted for the occasion though the coach was
new ; the horses' manes tied with red ribbons, and the
coachman in a new, green serge livery, with new
green reins in his hands.   It was only when death
visited a house that a sombre appearance was deemed
fitting.   Saddles were then covered with black cloth
or baize, and a black coach was taken into use.   If the
bereaved family did not possess such a one, the
ordinary coach was re-covered in black or a coach
of the requisite hue was borrowed for the period of
mourning

The coach-horses used were of the great or shire-
horse breed and, less frequently, Flemish mares.   The
country gentleman, therefore, could when necessity
arose put his coach-team to agricultural uses, and
conversely, assign to the larger and more powerful
ox draught the task of drawing the coach through
roads unduly founderous.   Indeed, where horses had
been requisitioned during the Civil War, the ox-team
was the natural substitute.   It was in this fashion that
Mrs. Trevelyan travelled from Devonshire to London
to make composition for her husband's estates.

Yorkshire and the Midland counties were the great
breeding centres, and Northampton, Market Har-
borough, and Pankridge (Penkridge) the great marts

for coach-horses, though the last named, the ' greatest
Horse-Fair in the World ' according to Defoe, dealt
more especially with saddle-horses, as did also Malton,
the great Yorkshire exchange.   Prices for harness-horses
ranged from ten to twenty-five pounds and more, according to date of purchase and value of animal.[1] A pair
of grey Friesland geldings for Lord William Howard of
Naworth cost, in the earlier half of the century, rather
over forty pounds, while in 1626 Sir John Coke was
in treaty for five Flemish bay mares at eighteen
pounds apiece, one spare animal being desirable where
four were employed in a draught.   Later, prices rose.
In 1680 the Countess of Sunderland was prepared to
send into Holland one hundred pounds for ' one pair
of the finest, largest grey coach-horses, the most
dappled, the stateliest persons ' that her agent in the
matter could possibly get.   Pepys laid out fifty pounds
at Smithfield for his fine pair of blacks, a result of
considerable research and friendly advice.   This was
probably a necessary precaution, as Smithfield had
an evil reputation for what Pepys describes as ' the
knaveries and tricks of jockeys ' ;   a reputation
commemorated in two contemporary proverbs : ' He
that buys a Horse in Smithfield and does not look upon
him with a pair of spectacles before he buys him, makes
his Horse and himself a pair of sorrowful spectacles
for others to look at ' ;   and ' The Londoners pro-
nounce woe to him that buys a Horse in Smithfield,
that takes a servant in Paul's church, that takes a wife
out of Westminster '—St. Paul's being a regular
meeting-place for the transaction of business and
especially for the engaging of servants.
    The rising prestige of the coach increased the
numbers alike of the parent vehicle and of its offspring,
the chariot and the calash.   In September 1668,
a thousand coaches were said to have assembled in

[1] See Note C, p. 324.

Hyde Park, where, under the command of the Duke
of Monmouth, a muster of the Life Guards was held
in the presence of the King and Duke of York. In
1685 Lord Clarendon, on his departure for Dublin,
was accompanied from London to St. Albans by two
hundred coaches, a mark of friendship and esteem in
which Evelyn took part. Coaches attended funerals,
not only to convey mourners but also as a last tribute
of respect to the dead. At the obsequies of Archbishop
Tillotson (1694) three of the King's coaches partici-
pated, besides many others of the nobility. Numbers
of people honoured the funeral of young Mary
Evelyn ; 'some in person, others sending their
coaches of which there were six or seven with six
horses' notes the bereaved father with mournful
satisfaction.

The coach, in fact, had attained, despite the censures
passed upon it, a position of high honour. Persons
of rank sentenced to death were allowed by special
favour to make their last journey by coach. Thus
Lord William Russell was brought in his own coach
from Newgate to the scaffold erected at the West end
of Lincoln's Inn Fields, 'with a most extraordinary
guard of watchmen and the train'd bands' and
accompanied by Drs. Tillotson and Burnet. Thus
also many a gentleman of the highway made his
pilgrimage to Tyburn Tree in a coach, while his
plebeian companions in distress were carried in a cart
or, still more ignominuously, drawn on a sledge. Upon
those in need of extraneous aid to respectibility the
coach cast a mantle of gentility. Few persons, we may
be sure, suspected the laceman who lived in Durham
Yard and who maintained a coach, of keeping also,
hidden from view, a press for counterfeiting money.

Except for short journeys in and about London by
the 'Hackney Hell carts' previously mentioned, the
expense of coach hire was very high, especially during

the first half of the century, before the advent and during the infancy of the stage-coach services. The charge, early in the century, for a coach and two horses was eight or ten shillings a day ; for a coach-and-three, fifteen shillings, exclusive of horse-meat. But the coachmen, we are told, would not ordinarily go for more than a day's or two days' journey, ' the wayes so farre being sandy and very faire, and continually kept so by labour of hands '. Later the fees were raised to twenty shillings for a coach-and-four, and ten shillings for a coach-and-two ; the respective speeds of thirty and twenty-five miles a day being specified for the summer months within a radius of sixty miles from London. These official allowances did not apparently extend to long-distance journeys ; at least, in practice, the charges came out at very much higher figures.

How great was the cost of hire is best appreciated when comparison is made with the expense of river transport. In 1610 thirty-two shillings was paid out of the Royal Purse for two coaches, one with four horses, to convey some representatives of foreign powers, nervous of a river trip in foul weather, from London to Gravesend, and a like sum for the return of the coaches. A month later a Spanish diplomat leaving these shores, was carried to the same destination by a light river-boat for seven shillings.[1] Sir George (afterwards Viscount) Chaworth, when going on an embassy to Spain in 1621, arranged for ' Two coatches to carye me and my companie wᵗʰ me to Canterburie in two dayes at 20s. a coach for a daie, payeing for theyre comeing back also as for theyr going, 8ˡˡ '. Lord William Howard of Naworth paid in 1628 and 1634 respectively seventeen and eighteen pounds

---

[1] There was also disparity in the cost of transport of goods by land and river. The rates for water carriage were especially low in places on the Thames where the navigation was not liable to interruption. See *History of Agriculture and Prices*, by J. E. Thorold Rogers, vol. v, p. 774.

for coach hire from Enfield and from London to Cumberland and its borders; a rate that would approximate to thirty or thirty-five shillings a day. Yet these were modest charges compared with the twelve pounds exacted from the unfortunate Lady Springett —the future mother-in-law of William Penn—when she hastened from London to Arundel to the bedside of her dying husband. But, while the journeys North were carried out during peaceful summer days, that to Sussex was undertaken by a coach proprietor as a favour, and only after several had refused to entertain the idea. For snow, frost, flood, darkness, and civil war made the venture hazardous—so hazardous, as it proved, that but for the greatest good fortune they would never have reached their journey's end. Moreover, it must be understood, the London coachmen always increased their charges, and were entitled to do so, for journeys into that county 'so full of mud and myre', as the old rhyme has it. Seven pounds was said to be the price, in 1647, for a coach from London to Rye, a trip that by hired nag would have cost a few shillings and no more than eighteen shillings by riding post. The coach, however, was advantageous in one respect. It could save the traveller inn charges, if he were so pleased, by being used for rest at night if the weather were not too rigorous.

Stage-Waggons

Already at the beginning of the century there was in existence a public conveyance for the carriage of passengers paying a fare. This was the long or stage-waggon or caravan, as it was variously called ; in reality, no other than the four-wheeled waggon, hooded with cloth, and used for the transport of merchandise. It was drawn, Signor Busino tells us, ' by seven or eight horses in file, one behind the other, with plumes and bells, and embroidered cloth coverings ', passengers and goods travelling in higgledy-piggledy fashion. These waggons, each of which was capable of holding twenty to thirty persons, traversed the main roads of England. A *Carrier's Cosmography* of 1637 gives the names and terminal places of call of more than two hundred carriers and waggoners, together with a round dozen of foot-posts, clothiers, higglers, and ' demi-carriers '—whatever the last may have been. Fifty years later the number had increased at least by half, to judge by a list published in the first of London's many guide books.[1] If the network was widespread the rate of progress was slow. No more than ten to fifteen miles a day was covered, by reason of the fact that it was usual to carry through the journey, however long, with one team of horses. Convenient for women, children, and sick folk of the poorer classes, it was on occasions used by gentlewomen. In this way Lettuce, daughter of Sir William Dugdale, travelled in 1660 from Coventry to London, probably for reasons of safety. Likewise, a year later, Mrs. Pepys senior, and her daughter, Paulina—who was such a trial and responsibility to her brother—returned home to Brampton, ' Pall crying exceedingly '. Here saving of expense was doubtless the object.

Nevertheless, the stage-waggon was held in great contempt by the vast majority of people, obliged though many of them were to avail themselves of its convenience. Young Edmund Verney, when the family made its customary migration from Buckinghamshire to London, urged that the maids should be allowed to ride up, ' for the very name of a waggon is soe offensive to them '. M. Sorbière, Historiographer Royal of France, ignoring or ignorant of the national prejudice, chose, on reaching England, to make the journey to London by the Dover stage-waggon. It

---

[1] *Angliae Metropolis, or The Present State of London*, by Thomas De Laune, ed. 1690 (1st edition 1681).

was, he tells us, drawn by six horses, one behind the
other, and driven by a waggoner who walked beside
it, clothed in black ' like another *St. George* ', a merry
fellow who fancied he made a fine figure and who
seemed mighty pleased with himself. If the waggoner
was pleased his foreign passenger was of a contrary
humour. Not one of his fellow travellers took the least
trouble to see what became of him at the inns. He
might have been a bale of goods, he declares, for all
the notice they took of him. When he endeavoured
to show civility to the least rustic of his companions
they took it for raillery or an affront. Later, visiting
Oxford, he essayed the superior merits of the stage-
coach. Whether he had come to know the scorn in
which gentlemen who travelled by waggon were held,
or whether it was in the hope of pleasanter company,
does not appear. If the latter it was in vain ; only
the presence of an interpreter, whom he had had the
precaution to take with him, shielded him from
affronts.

Stage-Coaches

At what precise date the stage-coach first appeared
upon the roads of England has never yet come to
light. It may well be that, as a result of the sudden
rise into popularity of the coach during the first
quarter of the century, public vehicles journeyed
between a few important towns as early as the first
years of Charles I, if not earlier. The idea is prompted
by a letter sent in December 1629 by young Coke's
tutor to his father, Sir John, concerning the young
man's desire to travel to London on horseback with
the carrier. Therein he speaks of the tediousness of
the passage by coach ' sitting from 5 in the morning
till almost nine at night, plunging in the cold and dirt
and dark, and that for two whole days with strange
company '. The first definite mention of stage-

coaches relates to the year 1637. *The Carrier's Cosmography* of that date mentions a service of two coaches weekly between St. Albans and the Bell Inn, Aldersgate ; and weekly or bi-weekly services of a ' coach or waggon ' to Hertford and Cambridge. The alternative designation possibly indicates the use of a coach during the summer, and of a waggon during the unfavourable winter season. Doubtless the unsettled state of the kingdom, terminating in Civil War, deterred any growth of the new industry. No further information comes to light until the year 1647, when ' Tide Coaches ', it is stated,[1] were being employed to convey passengers between Rochester and the busy riverside port of Gravesend, the terminus of the Long Ferry from London, which was the usual method of covering the first stage between London and the Kentish coast. It was in the same year that Mary Verney made the arrangements, previously described, for sending her baby by coach to St. Albans, and thence by horseback to Claydon, the stage-coach being without doubt the intended conveyance for the precious burden. Hiring a whole coach was an undertaking that put so great a strain upon her resources that she never resorted to it without questioning expense and alternative means. Taylor, whose trenchant views on coaches have been set forth on a previous page, describes himself and his friends as engaging ' the Southamton coach ' when in 1648 they travelled to visit the imprisoned King at Carisbrooke Castle. The journey from London to the coast occupied three days. Four years later a visitor to Claydon arranged to travel thither by the ' Alsberry coach '.

Further indirect evidence suggests that, by the middle of the following decade, stage-coaches were to be seen on all the great highways radiating from London. From a letter addressed, in February 1655, to Sir

---

[1] *Hist. of Company of Watermen*, Humpherus, vol. i, p. 253.

Ralph Verney, we learn that there were two coaches-
and-six running between London and Southampton,
and that another had been lately set up at Winchester.
During the last month of the same year Marmaduke
Rawdon, a Yorkshire gentleman of fortune, engaged
at Exeter for himself and his friends—five gentlemen
and one servant—a coach-and-six ' wholy to themselves '. They thereby disappointed a Mrs. Fax,
a fellow countrywoman of Rawdon's, who had come
from Plymouth to go to London on urgent business
that would not suffer a week's delay. Being ' a proper
hansome yonge woman '—and a wise one—she waited
until she found the company drinking burnt claret
in the kitchen before their departure, and then made
her request to be accommodated with a seat. As
a consequence she was not only suffered to ride up
with the party free of charge, but was given by Rawdon
the best place at the ' brood end of the coach ', and
further, an invitation to dine and sup with them each
day at their expense ; it was no breach of etiquette,
indeed quite ordinary usage, for the gentlemen to
defray the charges of their lady companions. The
following August 1656, Rawdon found himself the
sole occupant of the two-year-old (or more) York to
London coach. Meeting at an inn *en route* the Newcastle coach, also London bound, containing a gentleman of distinction and three gentlewomen of his
party, the gallant Yorkshireman persuaded two of the
ladies to give him their company in his coach. So dining
and supping all together the party journeyed to London.

In April 1657 an advertisement appeared in the
Mercurius Politicus giving notice of a service to Chester
three days a week, the whole journey to occupy four
days at a cost of thirty-five shillings, with lesser
proportionate charges for towns *en route*. The sub-
joined announcement that fresh horses would be
furnished every day suggests that hitherto the same

horses had been used throughout the one hundred and eighty-four miles of the journey. Two years later the journey was taking five days. Forty-six miles a day had, one supposes, proved an undertaking impossible of accomplishment. A year later a similar advertisement announced services to the North, the North-east, and the West. These included Durham and Newcastle on the first route ; on the second, Preston, Lancaster, and Kendal ; and on the third, Exeter and Plymouth.

The following decades witnessed such an increase in the number of stage-coaches plodding between town and town that comparison may not inaptly be made to the revolution in travel that ensued upon the extension of the railways in the forties and fifties of last century. It is probable that the growth of numbers was accelerated by the action of the unlicensed hackney-coachmen of London, who, to avoid the penalties provided in the Act of 1662,[1] dispersed themselves into every little town within easy reach of London, and setting themselves up as stagers, drove daily to London, where, we are told, they passed the night in carrying fares—we hope with fresh horses. By 1673 almost every town within a radius of twenty or twenty-five miles had a service of one or more coaches, running either daily or thrice weekly to town. The rates for both long- and short-distance journeys ranged between twopence and threepence a mile, a slightly increased charge being not unusual during the winter season. But the long-distance traveller—his seat secured a week, or, in a busy season, a fortnight in advance by payment of ' earnest money ',[2] and the residue paid on taking his seat—had still a considerable item of expenditure, as he travelled along, in the distribution

---

[1] 14 Car. II, c. 2 (1662).

[2] Sometimes even a fortnight was insufficient. Five shillings secured a place in the Norwich coach, 1664 ; ten shillings in the Yarmouth coach, 1689 ; ten shillings in the York coach, 1714 ; and sixteen shillings in the Aylesbury coach, 1662.

of vails. On a journey to York four coachmen successively held the reins, each of whom expected a tip of something like a shilling, besides frequent drinks, which, if we may accept the statement of our informant in these matters—a hostile witness—worked out at three shillings a head each passenger, thus adding seven shillings to a fare of forty or forty-five shillings.

The longer services were for the most part established by carriers and innkeepers, and, less often, by coach- and harness-makers. To the carrier it was, of course, a natural extension of business ; to the innkeeper it was a means of bringing custom to his house. There being many more inns on the main roads than were necessary for the purposes of the stage-coach an innkeeper had, consequently, either to set up as a stager himself or to induce stagers to patronize his inn by granting them special terms for provender. The result appears to have been fierce rivalry between innkeepers on some of the more popular routes, and a speeding up of time-tables between London and certain of the more important towns such as Oxford and Bath. But, as always happens where a trade boom rests on no solid foundation of great economic demand, this competition later subsided.   When De Laune issued the 1690 edition of his guide to London, barely a score of towns had duplicate services, and no more than five—Oxford, Bath, Guildford, Windsor, and Newbury—had any number exceeding this. Nor was the pace of these new-running vehicles any great advance upon previous rates, ' flying coaches ' though they were. How changed is our point of view ! Fifty miles they covered, sometimes more and sometimes less,[1] in a day of twelve or thirteen

---

[1] The ' Flying machines ' of the middle of the following century accomplished no more, if as much. Indeed, during the earlier years of that century, there appears to have been absolute retrogression in the matter of speed.

hours. The stage-coach which accomplished the greatest distance appears to have been the London–Northampton coach which presumably was accustomed to travel sixty-five miles in a day on one stage of its journey ; at least it achieved the feat in 1674 and in 1682 when Sir William Dugdale travelled by it. Five, six, and seven o'clock in the morning were the normal hours of departure. As a consequence it was no unusual thing for passengers to stay the night at the inn whence the coach would start the next day. Such early rising, however, was not the breach of custom it would be to-day ; seventeenth-century England was always early astir. In May 1669 Mrs. Pepys rose on two successive mornings at 2 and 3 a.m. to gather May dew, to the annoyance, it must be owned, of her husband.

Anthony Wood, the antiquary, who, with six or seven others, took part in the inaugural journey of the One Day Flying Coach between Oxford and London, 1669, tells us that they entered the coach—an old-fashioned one with a boot on each side—at the tavern door against All Souls College precisely at six in the morning, and arrived at the Saracen's Head on Snow Hill at seven at night. The fare was twelve shillings in 1669, reduced to ten shillings in 1672. That it was a successful venture is proved by the setting up of a rival service in the two ensuing seasons by two different firms of carriers.[1] That they failed may be ascribed to the fact that they were challenging the monopoly of the licensed University carrier, and flouting the authority of the Vice-Chancellor, who made answer by forbidding

---

[1] Vol. ii, p. 221, of *The Life and Times of Anthony Wood*. Wood adds ' This coach was silenced by the Vice-chancellor's order stuck up in every corner in Oxon, Apr. 15, 1671, because it was set up without his leave.' The editor of Wood's *Life* believes that the coach, though officially discountenanced, continued to run both this season and the next.

WHEREAS the Appointment, Ordering, and Government of all Carriers of what kind soever, Trading to or with the University and Citty of *Oxford*, does of Right belong and appertain to the Chancellor, Masters, and Scholars of the said University, by their Charters, Priviledges, and Customes : the said Carriers to be Ordered and Governed by such Rules as shall be limited and prescribed by the Chancellor of the said University, or his deputy for the time being. AND whereas *Thomas Moore* and *Robert Stonehill* Licensed Carriers of the said University, have undertaken to provide sufficient Coaches and Horses for the Conveiance of Passengers between the said University and the Citty of *London*, which shall in one day Commodiously perform the whole Journey during the Summer half year, (that is to say) from the Twenty sixth day of *April*, being the Munday next before *Easter Terme*, to *Michaelmas* ensuing; for the better regulating of the said Carriers, and Securing the Conveinence of all Passengers who shall happen to go with them, It is Ordered by the *Vice-Chancellor* of the University aforesaid, as followeth.

1. That the Carriers aforesaid shall not demand above Twelve shillings for the conveiance of each Passenger.

2. That they, the said Carriers, shall carry without expectation of farther reward, the necessaries of each Passenger, their severall fardles not being incommodious in their Bulk, and not exceeding six pound in weight.

3. That they, the said Carriers, shall not upon pretence of expectation of Passengers, or any other suggestion, delay the time of their setting out; But before six of the clock in the Morning, be ready over against *Alsouls Colledge* in *Oxford*, and the signe of the Greyhound in *Holborne* in *London*; and Immediatly upon the striking of the Clock of St *Maries* in *Oxford*, and St *Andrews Holborn London* begin their Journey.

4. That the said Carriers shall both at *Oxford* & *London* keep a Book for the Entry of Names of the Passengers, and the receipt of the twelve shillings which shall be laid down upon the entry of their names, and shall be responsible for the fraud or negligence which shall happen either by themselves or Servants in the aforesaid particulars.

5. That the said Carriers shall constantly keep their weekely stages, that is to say, every Munday, Wednesday, and Friday depart from *Oxford*, and Tuesday, Thursday and Saturday returne homeward from *London*.

6. That the said Carriers shall not take upon them to dispose of places in their coach, but shall permit all persons to be seated according to their priority, in taking of their seats, & their respective condition.

7. That the aforesaid Orders and Rules shall not be interpreted to limit or concern those coaches, which shall as formerly perform their Journey in part of two days.

Ap: 5. 1669.   *JOHN FELL Vicechancellor.*

OXFORD
One day
Stage-Coach.

THese are to give Notice to all Persons
that have occasion to go to *Oxford* by
Coach; Let them repair to the
Greyhound in *Holborn*, where they may be
furnished with a good Coach and able Horses, which sets forth every Monday,
Wednesday, and Friday for *Oxford*, performing the Stage in one day; and sets forth
from the *Mitre* in *Oxford* for *London*, every Tuesday, Thursday, and Saturday;
performed if God permit, By

> Widow STONEHILL.
> JOHN FOSSET.

The Stage begins Monday next, being the 17th instant
April, and sets forth precisely at Six in the Morning.

*This coach was silenced by ye vicechanc: order
struck up on every corner in Oxon Apr: 15. 1671
because it was set up without his leave.*

Advertisement Bill of the Pirate Stage-coach set
up between Oxford and London

To London Every Day.

THefe are to give notice that every day in the Week there will be a Coach fet out (at fix a Clock in the Morning) from *Thomas Moor's* houfe over againft *All-Souls Colledge* in *Oxford* which fhall commodioufly perform the whole Journey to *London* in one day, and from the *Saracens-Head* on *Snow-hill* in *London* to *Oxford* again the next day, and fo conftantly for this Summer half-year, *If God permit.*

The Stage begins on Munday next being the 15. of *May*. 1671.

Advertisement Bill of the Licensed Stage-coach

WHereas *Edward Bartlet* hath without Licence from *Me*, prefumed to fet up a Flying Coach to travaile from hence to *London*: Thefe are to require all Scholars and Members of this *Univerfity* not to make ufe of the faid Flying Coach fo fet up by *Edward Bartlet.*

> *P. MEWS Vice-Can,*

Vice-Chancellor's Veto upon the Pirate Stage-coach

members and scholars of the University to travel by the rival coaches.

During the winter half of the year the flying coach was discontinued and the two-day coach, with its average of rather more than thirty miles a day, sufficed the needs of those whom business took abroad—travelling for pleasure was a summer relaxation only. This disproves the assertion, which has been made by more than one modern writer, that stage-coaches were laid up during the winter ' like ships during Arctic frosts '.[1]   It is possible of course that specific ill-paying routes were altogether abandoned during the winter months ; but it is certain that the more usual services were continuous, though of necessity a slowing down of pace occurred.   The writers in question have been misled, we believe, by Thoresby's reference to the York coach being decorated with flowers and ribbons when for the first time it ' passed the road in May ' ;   the custom, delayed on this occasion four days, was connected with the usual and popular May-Day revels.

That the public coaches were usually of obsolete design—as Wood's reference to a boot makes clear—suggests that they were discarded private coaches. Glass windows, it is said, were not common in them until 1680, twenty years after the first appearance of a glass-coach in England.   Some of these vehicles, however, must have been either specially built for or adapted to the particular requirements of public travel, for we read of coach-waggons and waggon-coaches, both alike, probably, stage-coaches with open waggons or baskets attached to the back for the accommodation of lower-class fares and of luggage. In June 1665 we find Mrs. Pepys senior, having put off leaving the sickly town until she had lost her place in the coach, ' fain to ride in the waggon part '.

[1] Smiles, *Lives of the Engineers*, vol. i, p. 169.

Where there was no receptacle for luggage, passengers had to send their trunks by carrier, or, where this was possible, by coasting vessel. With private coaches the luggage was probably strapped on to a platform at the back, hence the following advertisement, one of many, which appeared in the *London Gazette* in 1682.

'Lost on Saturday the 30th of September, between eight and nine a Clock at Night, from behind a Coach, between Aldermanbury and the Turning into Love-Lane, a Hair-Trunk, with the following things in it, a sad coloured Venetian Petticoat, with a Campain Lace at the bottom; a Cherry coloured Sattin Petticoat, Laced to the top with Silver Lace; a purple and white Silk Petticoat; a pair of hair coloured Sattin Stays, Embroidered with Gold and Silver; a Venetian Mantua, hair-coloured and white, faced with black Shag; and some Linnen, marked with an S. Whoever gives notice of the said Trunk or parcel, to Mr. William Bridges Linnen-Draper, at the White Bear in Cornhill, or to Mr. Watson, Merchant in Love Lane, shall have 40*s.* Reward.'

The trunk [1] with its tempting contents had probably been stolen; certainly the 'Portmantle full of Women's Cloaths', lost from behind a coach at the 'White-Horse-Inn at Baldwick' and advertised for a few months earlier, must have been taken by one of the thieving fraternity, who doubtless lingered in the neighbourhood of inn-yards for that very purpose. The platform was alternatively used in private coaches for the accommodation of pages or footmen. 'There are pages in Trunks [hose] that ride behind coches,' writes Mrs. Isham to Sir Ralph Verney about 1652, 'but not many, I know none of your acquaintance that has one but Sir Arthur Haslerigg, and yet I never saw him behind a coch. He is in cloath trunks billited or garded with velvet, silver sword, and silver buckles on his shoes, and silk stockings.' Sir John Reresby relates in his *Memoirs* how his wife and daughter going

---

[1] See Note D, p. 324.

to dine in 1682 with the Earl of Ailesbury ' the perch broke, and two footmen behind it fell under the coach, and were in danger of being killed; but by God's mercy sustained no great harm '. Loggan in *Oxonia Illustrata* and *Cantabrigia Illustrata* gives several representations of coaches with footmen standing behind, which shows that the custom was by this time not unusual. But to return to the history of public vehicles.

Just as the advent and multiplication of the coach and hackney-coach had aroused in the early years of the century a storm of indignation in the breasts of Taylor and his like, so the increase in the number of stage-coaches marshalled the forces of reaction and self-interest in the defence of old custom. In 1673 a certain John Cresset made himself the spokesman of these prejudiced inn-keepers, saddlers, shoemakers, watermen, and their supporting die-hards, and in a well-written pamphlet (to which we have already had recourse) set forth the iniquities of the stage-coaches for the enlightenment of those whom he hoped to enlist in his campaign [1] for the limitation by Parliamentary enactment of their activities to slow, weekly services to shire-towns. Total suppression, he evidently felt, was beyond the power either of his party or of Government to obtain, though not beyond the deserts of the offenders. The dire lot of those whose ' lazy habit of Body ' made them patronize the stage-coach roused him to an eloquence so vivid and so obviously fraught with unhappy memories, that, though it takes the exceptional for the ordinary, it must be quoted at length.

' What advantage is it to Man's health ', he cries, ' to be called out of their Beds into these Coaches an hour before day

---

[1] And not only for their enlightenment. So generous is he of details that, smile as we may at his wrath, we can but feel grateful to him for his pamphlet, which, though it did not effect the end he had in view, was not written in vain.

in the morning, to be hurried in them from place to place, till
one hour, two, or three within night; insomuch that, after
sitting all day in the summer-time stifled with heat, and choaked
with the dust; or the Wintertime, starving and freezing with
cold, or choaked with filthy Fogs, they are often brought into
their Inns by Torch-light, when it is too late to sit up to get
a Supper; and next morning they are forced into the coach so
early, that they can get no breakfast? What addition is this to
mens Health or Business, to ride all day with strangers, oftentimes sick, ancient, diseased Persons, or young Children crying;
to whose humours they are obliged to be subject, ... and many
times ... cripled by the crowd of the Boxes and Bundles? Is
it for a Man's Health to travel with tired Jades, to be laid fast
in the foul Wayes, and forced to wade up to the knees in mire;
afterwards sit in the cold, till Teams of Horses can be sent to
pull the Coach out? Is it for their health to travel in rotten
Coaches, and to have their Tackle, or Pearch, or axletree
broken, and then to wait three or four hours (sometimes half
a day) to have them mended again, and then to travel all night
to make good their Stage? Is it for a Mans pleasure, or
advantagious to their healths and Business, to travel with
a mixt Company that he knows not how to converse with;
to be affronted by the rudeness of a surly, dogged, cursing, ill-
natured Coachman; necessitated to Lodge or Bait at the worst
Inns on the Road, where there is no accommodation fit for
Gentlemen; and this merely because the Owners of the Inns,
and the Coachmen, are agreed together to cheat the Guests?
... Is it for advantage of a Man's Business, that though he have
a Concern of great weight or moment to transact upon the
Road as he goes along, yet if it lie but a stones cast out of the
Coach-way, the Coachman will not drive thither, nor stay
for him at any place,[1] except the Baiting or Lodging-places
where he calls, where they change Horses; and there stay no

---

[1] Travelling to schedule, whatever Cresset may say, was not strictly
observed. The Very Rev. Rowland Davies records stopping, in a stage-
coach journey from Yarmouth to London, at the house of Sir William
Cooke near Bungay to take up that gentleman, and, incidentally, to partake
each of a glass of sherry. Two days later, on leaving Bishop's Stortford,
they were persuaded by the coachman to go by way of Epping Forest, an
unfortunate proposition, for the coach stuck fast in a slough, and they were
forced to walk in the dirt and rain two miles to Epping, each getting wet to
the knees. Thoresby, the antiquary, on one occasion appears to have stopped
the York coach to look for fossils, and another time was hurried out of bed
between two and three in the morning, the coach being 'hasted' by
Captain Crome on the Queen's business, i. e. Queen Anne's.

longer than he pleases neither. To be forced, whatever
accident of sickness or illness happens, to ride these Coachmens
Stages, though never so late in the night, or else to be left in
the middle of a Journey in a strange place? . . . Yet this hath
been many Persons of good Qualitie's case ; though they have
offered to pay the whole Coach-hire, and all the Passengers
charges, to have put into an Inn (late at night on this side the
set Stage) ; yet have they been denyed, forced to ride, though
in peril of their lives, till midnight : And it is not hard to
instance in many that have lost their lives by such usage.'

A gloomy picture, indeed ; enough, one would have
thought, to ensure the speedy demise of the stage-
coach through lack of patronage, without the need of
extraneous assistance.   Yet Cresset is forced to
acknowledge that the ' passage to *London* being so
easie, Gentlemen come to *London* oftner than they
need, and their ladies either with them . . . or quickly
follow them '—to the demoralization apparently of
the ladies who learnt in the metropolis to appreciate
the pleasures of balls and parties, and the concomitant
of fashionable clothes, so that ' nothing afterwards in
the Countrey will serve them. . . . But they must have
all from *London*, whatever it costs '.

The eloquence of Cresset was in vain.   The farmers
were cool.   The innkeepers would not contribute
funds for the campaign ' till the work be effected '.
The gentry were irritated at the aspersions cast upon
them ; and, so double-edged is the weapon of special
pleading in the hands of the over-ingenious, the City
found that the stage-coach services were all to the
advantage of its trade.

Thus stage-coaches grew in favour and, hall-mark
of success, were deemed by the Exchequer in 1694
sufficiently prosperous to contribute to the national
revenue,[1] as the hackney-coaches had already done

---

[1] By 5 & 6 Gul. & Mar. c. 22 (1694) stage-coaches were licensed at a yearly
charge of eight pounds each.   One of several devices for obtaining money
to carry on war, it does not appear to have been more than a temporary
measure.

for the space of thirty years or more. Thus, too, the country ladies continued to bedizen their persons and tarnish their simple natures by contact with the fashionable world of London, while their husbands, heedless alike of the injury to trade and to horse-breeding, recking not of the wars that would come and find them or their children incapable of mounted service in the field, suffered themselves to be drawn about the country in their Indian gowns, silk stockings, and beaver hats—like those sluggard Kings of Ancient Gaul who were carried about their domains reclining on couches set on wheels. Happily, it seems, for the results of Blenheim and Ramillies, they had still on occasion to mount horse to reach the towns whence they could take coach.

To pass from satire to fact. One constant traveller, Sir William Dugdale, was accustomed to use the stage-coach services to the Midlands for no more than one or two stages from London—to St. Albans, Woburn, or Dunstable—where, his servant and horse await-ing, he would mount and ride the remainder of the hundred odd miles to his home in Warwickshire ; or, if he contemplated paying a visit on the way, as not infrequently happened—seventeenth-century travellers saved themselves, when possible, unnecessary journeys —there would be the family coach of his prospective host ready to carry him the last stage of his journey. Changes of conveyance—an irritating disturbance to the spoilt twentieth-century traveller—were of too ordinary occurrence to call forth irate comment in the pages of diarist or letter-writer. Pepys in his busy season of travel, the plague year of 1665, when the King had removed to Hampton Court, the Exchequer to Nonesuch, his wife to Woolwich, with his office in London and later at Greenwich, with the Dockyard at Chatham, and himself moving from point to point— transferred with complete indifference from horseback to coach, and from coach to barge or wherry, unless, indeed, the day happened to be stormy and the water rough.   In August 1663 John Evelyn made one of a party to Scott's Hall, near Ashford in Kent.   First they went by barge to Gravesend, thence rode post to Rochester, and, finally, stepping into a coach-and-six, presumably brought from London for the purpose, completed the journey of thirty or thirty-five miles. A week later they posted back to Gravesend, and sending the coach to London, travelled homeward by barge.

River Travel

As has already been shown, the Thames was, for passengers no less than merchandise, a well-recognized highway of traffic, and one greatly favoured by the authorities, owing to the relief thereby given to street congestion and the saving of wear and tear of the London cobble stones.

Five classes of craft were used in passenger traffic, barges, tilt-boats, wherries, tide boats, and light-horsemen. The public or ' common barges ', as they were designated, made the journey every tide, if wind and weather permitted, between London and Gravesend—the ' Long Ferry ' previously mentioned—and between London and Windsor, with a steersman and four rowers ' in fair tides and five in foul weather ', furnished with sufficient masts, sails, and sail-yards, and . . . a good and sufficient hawser and anchor, to serve in time of distress '. These were the authorized craft, with prescriptive rights, and were licensed to charge twopence each passenger or four shillings the boat load, carrying, it would seem, twenty-four passengers. But their ' preheminence ', to use an expressive seventeenth-century word, was contested by the unofficial vessels and more especially by the tilt-boats, who enticed aboard such richer passengers

A STAGE-WAGGON. From Loggan's *Cantabrigia Illustrata*

A ROWING-BOAT. From the Bagford Ballads

as were unwilling to wait the tedious filling of the common barge ; a policy so successful in the long run that, towards the middle of the century, the common barges were constrained to retire in favour of their rivals. These boats, which derived their name from the tilt or canopy [1] spread over the stern sheets, were manned by five rowers and a steersman ; were licensed to carry twenty and thirty passengers respectively at charges of ten and fifteen shillings the boat load, and were, according to the regulations of 1595, ' not to be overmasted or sailed, whereby the passengers shall be in danger of drowning '. With official recognition the tilt-boats found themselves in the position of having to defend the privilege they had hitherto flouted, against the encroachments of the wherries,[2] light-horsemen and tide boats, smaller craft carrying respectively five, seven, and twelve passengers at prices ranging from six shillings and eightpence to eight shillings the passage.

The competition for public favour between the different classes of watermen was a mere family bickering in comparison with their fierce efforts to resist the ever-increasing popularity of the much-hated hackney-coach. Not only did John Taylor place his mordant pen at the service of his fellow craftsmen, and in three separate pamphlets set forth the grievances of the watermen and the iniquities of their rivals ; but petition after petition was presented to Parliament describing the hardships they and their families endured—forty thousand persons were said to get

---

[1] ' I will pass ', says Davenant, ' the importunate noise of your Water-men (who snatch at fares as if . . . they never had row'd any other passengers but Bear-wards) and now step into one of your pescod-boats ; whose Tilts are not so sumptuous as the roofes of *Gundaloes*, nor, when you are within, are you at the ease of Chaise a bras.' Sir William Davenant, *Declamations at Rutland House.*

[2] The wherries had seats aft ' with sundry convenient cushions ', and very long oars, the oarsmen being ' very dexterous at steering clear of each other '. *Venetian State Papers*, 1617–19, p. 102.

their living by the trade between Windsor and Gravesend—and praying for the suppression of the obnoxious
carriages, or later for their more rigorous limitation.
From 1614, when a bill was introduced in the House of
Commons against ' outrageous coaches ', to 1675
when application was made for leave to bring in a bill
for their restraint, they waged a furious but losing
battle, never gaining more than a temporary advantage.

The benefit of water travel—the speed greater than
that of post-horses, freedom from the delays and annoyances of street congestion, the easy motion and relief
from the ' rude English coaches and the ruder paved
streets '—was outweighed by the manifold inconveniences, the inclemency of travel on the water during
winter weather, the serious accidents due to storms
and unskilled handling, the restriction of movement
to the line of the river, and, lastly, we suspect, the
unpleasantness arising from the quarrelsome, arrogant,
grasping behaviour of the watermen themselves.
Even their champion, Taylor, has to confess that there
are many rude, uncivil fellows in their company as
well as good honest men.

A critic less tender to their failings says : ' when he
[the waterman] is upon the water, he is fare-company :
when he comes ashore he mutinies, and contrary to
all other trades, is most surly to gentlemen, when they
tender payment : the playhouses [1] only keep him
sober ; and as it doth many other gallants, make him
an after-noones man. London-bridge is the most
terrible eye-sore to him that can be. And to conclude,
nothing but a *great presse* [i. e. for sailors] makes him

---

[1] The removal of most of the playhouses from Bankside to Middlesex
was another source of grievance. Taylor states, in 1613, that the players
have all, except the King's men, left their usual residency on the Bankside
and play in Middlesex far remote from the Thames. See ' The True Cause
of the Watermens Suit concerning Players, and the reasons that their
playing on London side is their extreame hindrances with a Relation how
farre that suit was proceeded in, and the occasions that it was not effected.'
Spenser Soc., Facsimile of Folio Ed., 1630.

flye from the river ; nor anything but a great *frost*, can teach him any good manners '. Another writer speaks of gentlemen being baited by ' whole kennels of yelping watermen ' at Westminster-bridge [landing stage], who are ready to tear them to pieces to have two pence rowed out of your purse. Taylor, however, demonstrates that, as usual, there was another point of view, ignored by the public.

' Moreover,' he writes, ' too many there are that passe the bounds of liberality, and spend most prodigally . . . on a thousand vanities . . . but upon a Water-man, that hath rowed till his heart ake, and sweats till hee hath not a dry thread about him, the gentlemens bounty is asleepe, and hee will pay him by the Statute [i. e. according to regulations unaltered since the reign of Queen Mary], or if hee give him two pence more, he hath done a huge worke beyond the merit of Suttons Hospitall [the Charter House].

' I my selfe have often met with a Roaring boy . . . that hath had nothing about him but a Sattin outside to cover his knavery, and that none, of his owne neither, . . . Yet this Gallant must be shipp'd in a paire of Oares at least : but his gay slop [breeches or trunk hose] hath no sooner kist the cushions, but with a volley of new coynd oathes . . . he hath never left Roaring, row, row, row, a pox on you row, . . . and when his scurvinesse is landed where he pleases, hee hath told me I must waite on him, and he will returne to mee presently [at once] and I shall carry him backe againe, and be paid all together : then have I attended five or six hours (like John-a-Noakes) for nothing, for my cheating sharke having neither monny nor honesty, hath never come at mee, but tooke some other pair of Stayres, and in the same fashion coozened another Water-man for his Boat-hire.'

In whatever degree their lack of courtesy—a proverbial theme with seventeenth-century writers—contributed to their undoing, the fact remained that their trade was slowly but surely passing from them. Cresset, whose consideration for the watermen was second only to his hatred for their rivals, declared that many had scarcely a fare a week ; a state of affairs as disastrous to their pockets as it was humbling to their pride, especially to those who, though wearing the badge of some noble lord, gained their daily bread from those whom they affected to despise.[1]   Nevertheless we are entitled to doubt whether their condition was so desperate as the statements of their spokesmen would have us to believe.   Possibly the numbers practising the craft dwindled with slackening of demand.   But, whatever the cause, difficulty was on occasion experienced in procuring their services at the very period of which Cresset writes.   On a windy, rainy Sunday in April 1662, Pepys could find neither boat nor coach to carry him to Whitehall Chapel, where a famous Oxford divine was due to preach. Certainly there was statutory prohibition of Sunday travel,[2] but doubtless watermen, like most other people, disregarded the injunction ; at least four enactments [3] were made by Government and City during the course of the century to suppress their Sunday activities.   Six months later our diarist offered

---

[1] The arrogance of these watermen, attached to the nobility, is shown in a story told by Clarendon.   A waterman having a dispute with a citizen about his fare showed his badge, a swan, the crest of the Earl he served, whereupon the other bade him ' be gone *with his goose* ' ; an unfortunate remark for which he was summoned, fined, and imprisoned until he had paid considerable damages ' *for the opprobrious dishonouring the earl's crest, by calling the swan a goose. Life of Edward, Earl of Clarendon*, vol. i, p. 81, ed. 1827.   How loose was the connexion sometimes between patron and waterman is exhibited in Pepys' statement : ' I did this night give the waterman who uses to carry me 10s. at his request, for the painting of his new boat, on which shall be my arms.' *Diary*, 24 March 1666–7.

[2] 3 Car. I, c. 2 (1627) and 29 Car. II, c. 7 (1677).

[3] *1626, 1641, 1693, 1698.*   What success attended these efforts on the two first occasions does not appear.   In 1693 the rulers of the Company found it so difficult to carry out the directions of the recently promulgated Order-in-Council that the Lord Mayor had to come to their aid, and issue forth a precept to the Aldermen of the riverside wards to appoint constables to attend every Lord's day from eight to eight at the various stairs. The result must have been negligible, for a few months later similar orders were issued.   In 1698 the eight rulers of the Company were ordered by the Court of the Lord Mayor to take it in turn to go out themselves on the Lord's day and suppress the plying of boats within the City's jurisdiction. See Humpherus, *Hist. of the Company of Watermen*, vol. i, *passim.*

eight shillings for a boat to carry him to Whitehall,
without avail, it being the day of the new Queen's
first coming to London. In July of the plague year,
1665, finding no oars to carry him he was 'fain to
call a skuller that had a gentleman already in it', and,
'as he proved a man of love to musique', they sang
together the way down to Deptford with great pleasure.[1]
Had the plight of the watermen been as grievous
as it was painted they would, surely, have braved not
only Government but storm or sickness to gain
a living. Sometimes the lack of watermen was due to
'the press', a method of enforced recruiting for the
navy so little to the taste of the fraternity that, though
their champions made much of their value, past and
potential, to the service, they fled from the river—as
Overbury has related—on rumour of the pressgang.
On the following occasion rumour was silent, or hearts
were uncommonly brave. 'About 12 last night',
7th July 1696, writes Luttrell, 'a presse master and
4 men endeavouring to take some men out of the
western barge passing by Lambeth, the presse master
and one of his men were killed, and thrown into the
Thames, and the other 3 much bruised.'

The vagaries of the English climate were probably
a more serious handicap to the watermen than their
ill manners. In the cold and frost of a winter's day,

[1] To so music-loving a people as the seventeenth-century English singing
on the highway or the river was a natural and agreeable pastime. Pepys,
who had a rare taste for music and some skill in composition (he composed
a setting for 'Beauty, Retire'), frequently enlivened his journeys with
song, on one occasion accompanied by his boy. Another time, while waiting
in a coach outside the Royal Exchange for his wife, he taught her maid,
Mercer, to sing 'the whole Larke's Song perfectly, so excellent an eare she
hath'. Thus the more worldly. Presbyterians and others of low-church
views gave voice rather to psalms. Thoresby, during a four-mile walk to
Kensington, sang to himself part of the 139th psalm, the way being 'most
pleasant' and at that time 'pretty solitary'. All were not so modest. The
father of Abraham de la Pryme, going to Doncaster fair, overtook 'a company of godly Presbyterians who were singing salms as they rid', a proceeding which de la Pryme characterized as 'a great peece of affectedness'
done 'more out of vain glory and pride than piety'.

in the pitch darkness of a winter's night, in the showers and storms liable to occur at any season of the year, the traveller naturally preferred the interior of a coach, or, if necessity gave him no choice, the use of his own legs. An example of this is supplied by Pepys. On the 23rd January 1665–6 there was a ' most furious storme all night and morning '. The next day Lord Brouncker and he went to Deptford, ' the weather being a little fairer '. It was not so for long, as they found when they started on the return journey.

'. . . my lord and I, the wind being again very furious, so as we durst not go by water, walked to London quite round the bridge, no boat being able to stirre; and Lord! what a dirty walk we had, and so strong the wind, that in the fields we many times could not carry our bodies against it, but were driven backwards. . . . It was dangerous to walk the streets, the bricks and tiles falling from the houses, that the whole streets were covered with them; and whole chimneys, nay whole houses, in two or three places, blowed down. But, above all, the pales of London Bridge, on both sides, were blown away, so that we were fain to stoop very low for fear of blowing off of the bridge. We could see no boats in the Thames afloat, but what were broke loose, and carried through the bridge, it being ebbing water. And the greatest sight of all was, among other parcels of ships driven here and there in clusters together; one was quite overset, and lay with her masts all along in the water, and keel above water.'

To prevent accidents, arrangements had been made, in 1595, for the masters of the Watermen's Company to examine all candidates for admission, before permitting them to ply for hire ; a provision which was further strengthened in the first year of James I by an Act [1] regulating the apprenticeship of watermen by reason ' that divers and sundrie people passinge by Water upon the River of Thames, betweene Windsore and Gravesend, have byn put in greate hazarde and danger . . . and many tymes have perished and bin

[1] 1 Jac. I, c. 16 (1603–4).

drowned . . . through the unskilfulnese and want of knowledge or experience in the Wherrymen and Watermen '. However beneficial the result serious accidents continued to occur—and were probably bound to occur—attended at times by great loss of life.[1] '. . . on Sunday last', writes Chamberlain, in October 1622, 'two or three boats were lost in the Thames, both above and beneath the bridge, in one of which ten persons were drowned, some Dutch and some English, who, having been at a marriage at Kingston, and packed thirteen in a wherry, the tempest rising towards eight o'clock at the night, were cast away 'twixt Westminster and the Strand. Only three were saved by strange accidents.' In February 1697–8 even greater mortality ensued from the oversetting of the tilt-boat of the Long Ferry, when, of sixty passengers, not more than seven were saved. A few years earlier a pleasure barge going up river to Twickenham overturned, and drowned four young ladies and a blackamore ; the watermen, ungallant fellows, allowed themselves to be saved. So alarmed was a certain Captain Kay on seeing, one windy day, several boats sink before his eyes that he ordered his watermen to put him ashore at the next stairs.

London Bridge with its nineteen close-set piers was both an added danger, and a serious hindrance to traffic. The water as it passed through the narrow channels—the widest of the arches was thirty-six feet—developed the speed and turbulence of cataracts, rendering it necessary to ship oars and 'shoot the bridge', an undertaking which, requiring the greatest skill on the part of the watermen, was only practicable,

---

[1] In 1619 licence was given to David Ramsey, page of the bedchamber, and to Thomas Wildgoose, to make engines invented by them for ploughing and raising water, and 'to make boats for the carryage of burthens and passengers run upon the water as swift in calms and more saff in stormes then boats full sayled in great wyndes'. Syllabus of Rymer's *Foedera*, p. 843.

or reasonably safe, at certain phases of the tide. A
' shootman ', stationed on the bridge signalled the
easiest passage to take, while below bridge-shooters—
watermen especially skilled in bridge shooting—were
ready for a consideration to guide boats through the
rapids. There were four principal channels or
' navigable locks ', as they were called, of which one
was dangerous owing to the presence of a rock—hence
called the Rock Lock. This, visible at low water, was
more probably encrusted masonry which had fallen
there in 1437 and been suffered to remain. The central
passage was spanned by a drawbridge which was of
considerable benefit to sailing vessels until, towards
the end of the seventeenth century, the mechanism
getting out of order it ceased to be movable.

Prudent travellers, when weather or tide was
unfavourable to the passage, landed above bridge,
usually at Old Swan Stairs, and walked to some wharf
below Billingsgate before re-embarking. Imprudent
travellers, risking the danger, frequently fell victims,
hence the proverb ' London Bridge was made for wise
men to go over and fools to go under '. In Norden's
map of London Bridge, 1624, a boat is shown overset,
and the passengers struggling in the water. Pepys
had the temerity, on occasion, to shoot the bridge in
the dark ; once at least against the tide, when the
men had to grope their way with the pole, which
' troubled ' him before he got through. Another
time he had difficulty in passing up stream. He ' was
fain to stand upon one of the pieres about the bridge,
before the men could drag their boat through the lock,
and which they could not do till another was called
to help them '—doubtless one of the aforementioned
bridge-shooters. Our other celebrated diarist, Evelyn,
was nearly drowned as he shot the bridge at three-
quarter's ebb, by the wherry, in which he was travelling,

Prospect of WINDSOR CASTLE, from the North.

From an engraving by Hollar

colliding with another which was at anchor. It is no wonder that the Master and Surveyor General of His Majesty's Mines devised an engine for raising boats over the bridge.

How keenly severe weather was felt on the water is shown by an entry in Luttrell's diary, under date 13th February 1691–2—a time of great frost and deep snow. 'Seaventeen persons lately pressed and carrying downe the river, 11 of them were found dead in the boat the next morning, by the severity of the weather.' It is true that those travelling the road fared little or no better. On the water, however, the frost if sufficiently prolonged and severe brought compensations. The Thames would freeze and become a solid mass of ice, to the immense satisfaction of the frolic-loving citizens who, congregating to see the sight, would find all the attractions of a fair displayed for them in an unusual situation. Such fairs were held in 1607, 1608, and 1620 ; but all previous meteorological and sportive records were eclipsed in 1683–4, when the river remained frozen from the 6th January to the 9th February, and high carnival was held on the hard-frozen surface. Tilt-boats decorated with flags and streamers were run on sledges, some drawn by horses, and others by out-of-work watermen. Other craft were mounted on wheels, and one called the ' drum boat ' was distinguished by a drummer at the prow. People walked about freely, even venturing below bridge ; propelled themselves on skates—a cavalier importation from Holland—and enjoyed the novel sensation of coach-riding on the ice, more than fifty coaches plying between the Bridge and Westminster. There were streets of shops to tempt the citizens' pockets ; eating-houses to warm the inner man ; a printing-press ' where the people and ladies took a fancy to have their names printed '—

P

gentlemen of birth, one is evidently given to understand, were superior to this attraction. There were horse-races, coach-races, bull-baitings, interludes, and puppet plays to beguile the passing hour, and, more beneficial to the circulation of the onlookers, a fox-hunt, in which the King took part. The roasting of an ox, which, together with the printing-press and the eating-houses, became a traditional feature of all ice-fairs, took place near Whitehall.

River pageants were a notable feature of the Stuart epoch and gave yet another opportunity to the London populace to indulge its holiday spirit. When Charles I and his bride passed from Gravesend to London in the royal barge, with many barges of honour and more than a thousand boats, 'infinite numbers' watched their progress from houses, stairs, and gardens on the banks, and from wherries, ships, lighters, and western barges on the river ; one boat overturned, casting one hundred people in the water, happily without fatality. Notwithstanding the vehement showers, the King and Queen stood publicly, with the barge windows open, out of which the Queen put her hand and ' shaked it . . . all the people shouting amain '. The shake and the shout would have had different purport a few years later. A very dissimilar progress was that of Lord Strafford when, as a prisoner of State, he was conveyed by barge to the Tower accompanied in boats by a large party of his opponents. Two years later a yet more remarkable and unexpected river progress came to pass. On the 11th of January of that year, 1642, the committee of the House of Commons, with Lord Kimbolton and the five members whose arrest Charles had been unable to effect, took water at the Three Cranes. Attended by forty long boats manned by watermen—a thousand had offered their services—armed with small pieces of ordnance, they were carried to Westminster where they were

received by the City Trained Bands and conducted to
Westminster Hall, the while the river was guarded by
one hundred lighters and many small boats, carrying
pieces of ordnance and dressed up with waist-clothes
and streamers as ready for a fight. On the 23rd August
1662 'the most magnificent triumphs that ever
floated upon the Thames' passed from Hampton
Court to Whitehall with another bridal Queen,
Catherine of Braganza. 'His majestie and the Queene',
we read, ' came in antiq shaped barge, covered with
a state or canopy of cloth of gold, made in form of
a cupola, supported with high corinthian pillars,
wreathed with flowers, festoons and garlands', in the
sight of upwards of a thousand barges and boats.

There was scope for much ingenuity in the fashion-
ing of royal barges. The vessel in which King
James I went from Greenwich to Gravesend to greet
his royal brother of Denmark is described as being
built in the fashion of a tower or little castle, enclosed
with glass windows and casements, 'faire carved and
guilt', being wrought with much art, the roof made
with battlements, pinnacles, pyramids, and fine
imagery. It was towed by another barge with thirty
oars. That there were lesser royal barges of more
ordinary appearance is certain, not only for the comings
and goings of royalty itself, but also for the conveyance
of distinguished visitors, and of others of birth or
influence who were making the passage between
London and Gravesend. On one occasion a royal
barge was lent to a party of Quakers—*mirabile dictu*—
who were going down river with George Fox, to wish
him God speed on his setting out for Barbadoes.
These lesser royal barges probably resembled the
vessels in which the nobility and gentry took their
ease ; ' a Sort of Pleasure Boat, at one End of which
is a little Room handsomely painted and cover'd,
with a Table in the Middle and Benches round it ;

and at the other End, Seats for 8, 10, 12, 20, 30, or 40 Rowers.   There are ', our informant adds, ' very few Persons of Great Quality but have their *Barges*, tho' they do not frequently make Use of them.'

The annual water procession, on the morrow of St. Simon and St. Jude (29 October), when the newly-elected Lord Mayor went from London to West-minster to receive the royal approval, was a custom of long standing.   From time to time the river progress was discontinued because of plague, fire, civil strife, or other cause ; and from 1639 to 1655 on account of puritan sentiment.   The Lord Mayor, his predecessor, the aldermen, common councillors, and members of the City Companies in ' gown, fur, hood and scarf ' marched to the waterside, usually to the Three Cranes, where they stepped into gilded barges, the rest of the company either taking boat at one or other of the neighbouring stairs or proceeding on foot to Paul's wharf, Baynard's Castle, or Dorset stairs to await the return of the procession.   As the Lord Mayor passed up stream ordnance would be discharged ' in token of love ', and boats bearing emblematical triumphs or fashioned to resemble strange craft or exotic islands would greet the Lord Mayor and join the procession for the rest of its journey, as well by land as by water. To disguise as much as possible the ludicrous appearance of water triumphs swimming through the streets and lanes of the City, the custom arose, as the pageantry became more and more elaborate, to cover the wheels and lower portions with painted cloths to represent water with fishes swimming in it, two windows being placed in front of each triumph to enable the two men within to direct the vehicle along the crowded thoroughfares.   Sometimes bad weather marred the proceedings.   In 1612 the wind on the water was so great that several of the City Companies' barges being ' in great danger and pain ' had to be

THE FROST FAIR OF 1683–4. From a contemporary print

run aground, while others turned back, so that ' my Lord Mayor, with much ado, came almost alone to Westminster '.

Excursions to Richmond, Hampton Court, and Windsor were popular in the summer season with all classes of London folk, and nearer home, there was pretty rural Chelsea Reach, to which Queen Mary often went in her barge, to be ' diverted there with a consort of musick '. Nor were the lower Reaches neglected, if we may judge from the day's trip undertaken by Mrs. Evelyn and a party of friends from Deptford to the sea and back—which suggests that the charm and benefit of sea air were not, as is commonly assumed, so complete a matter for discovery by eighteenth-century pleasure-seekers.

Although the citizens availed themselves of the Thames for business and pleasure, the river's most important function was the delivery of supplies to the city : hay, straw, and grain from Henley, beans from Hull, oats from Lynn and Boston, coals from Newcastle, building stone from Bullingdon near Oxford. A heavy task it was to keep monstrous-grown London supplied. Owing to the deplorable nature of the roads, and the consequent heavy expense of land carriage, her citizens relied to a very great extent on river transport for the entry of commodities. Yet the Thames as a highway had many shortcomings. The lower reaches from Staines downwards appear to have been in a fair state, thanks to the care of the Corporation of London, whose jurisdiction extended thus far. But the upper river, and more especially the reaches above Burcott, regulated only by inefficient single locks and weirs, usually erected in conjunction with cornmills, with every miller turning the water to his own use—there were said to be twenty-three locks, sixteen mills, and seventeen weirs between Maidenhead and Oxford in 1580—with here shoals, rocks,

ledges, and submerged trees to hinder barges, there
a rushing torrent or perhaps a mere trickling stream,
with pot-holes, with piles and stakes for the convenience
of fishermen and riparian owners—the upper river
must have been most difficult to navigate. Had it
not been that the increasing size of barges was demonstrating the inconvenience of natural waterways—as
wheel traffic was disclosing the insufficiency of roads—
it is possible that no efforts would have been made at
improvements, favoured though river transport was
for commodities in bulk—Taylor tells us that a barge
with eight men could carry more merchandise than
forty five-horsed waggons could do. Whatever was
the cause, legislative action was taken in 1605–6,[1]
and, action having apparently been confined to words,
again in 1623–4.[2] As a result the first double-gated
locks, or turnpikes as they were called, were made on
the Thames, and the bed of the river was cleaned and
made navigable for barges of large burthen between
Burcott and Oxford. Nevertheless, half a century
and more later, barges sometimes lay aground for three
or four weeks in dry seasons, and the reaches between
Burcott and Oxford became, in the words of Anthony
Wood, 'not portable'. Other rivers, where navigable,
supplied important centres of population and distributed local products. Here, likewise, the operation
was hindered by lack of proper conservancy. It was
not until towards the end of the seventeenth century
that, with a few exceptions, measures were taken to
improve these highways of traffic.

Apart from that on the Thames, passenger traffic
on rivers does not seem to have been by any means
common. Mrs. Celia Fiennes who, in the course of the
last decade of the century, visited nearly every county
in England, took occasion to remark at Bristol on the
'little boates wch are Call'd Wherryes such as we use

---

[1] 3 Jac. I, c. 20. Repealed 1623–4.   [2] 21 Jac. I, c. 32.

on the Thames, so they use them here to Convey persons from place to place '. Evidently an unusual feature, or the keen eye and faithful pen of Mrs. Fiennes would have noted it elsewhere ; unless indeed, it had been very common, and then no comment would have been needed.

Bristol seems to have delighted in copying the customs of the metropolis. In 1658 the Mayor and aldermen ordered to be built at the City's charge ' a handsome barge be rowed with eight or ten oars, after the manner of those barges used by the lord mayor and aldermen of London, and other companies there ', twenty pounds being paid to the water-bailiff two and a half years later towards the cost.

The Cross-Channel Passages

To pass from river to sea. For the carriage of mails and the convenience of passengers, official and un-official, packet-boats plied between England and its neighbouring shores. They were small vessels of about sixty tons burthen, had a single deck, and cabins in the high-built stern. From Dover to Calais, Dover to Nieuport, Harwich to Helvoetsluis, Holyhead to Dublin, Port-Patrick to Donaghadee, and from Fal-mouth to Corunna the services ran, at intervals varying from thrice weekly for the shorter passages to fort-nightly between England and Spain. In time of war services to enemy territory were discontinued.

During the second half of the century certainly, if not before, five shillings was the charge fixed for passages in the Dover–Calais and the Harwich–Holland packets. In regard to the latter vessels, M. Jorevin, a French visitor to these shores, advised intending travellers to make agreement in advance with the Master as, though the common price is a crown, ' these seamen are so dishonest, that if you have not made an agreement before departure, they

will make you pay five or six '. Furthermore, he recom-
mended that, as the passage money provided no more
than accommodation, the traveller should provide
himself in advance with provisions, and on board
make a bargain with the sailors for the loan of something to rest on during the night. Neglect to do so
led to daily disturbance and even to blows. Whether
incidents of such a nature occurred on the Dover
packet does not appear ; in any case the passenger
must have felt like a plucked pigeon by the time he
reached port. In addition to the five shillings passage
money, a further five shillings, and probably more,
was exacted at Dover by the horde of officials who
battened upon him ; these included the Transcriber
of his pass, the Clerk of the Passage (who exacted,
as custom-dues, fourpence for each trunk and twopence
for each portmanteau), the Water-Bailiff, the Master of
the Ferry (who transferred him from shore to ship),
and the Searcher who searched for contraband or
refrained from so doing according as he received only
his modest due or a gratuity in addition—largesse
wisely spent, for there were, we are told, as many
filchers as searchers. Only in regard to the engaging
of the Master's cabin, at a charge of five shillings, was
the traveller at liberty to decline. At Calais the Master
of the Ferry appropriated no more than threepence
each passenger for transferring them ashore. But as
the ' brawling sharking fellows ', his deputies, would
not release their human freight until they had received
sixpence apiece, the plucking of the pigeons was not
suffered to be interrupted while feathers remained.

Although numerous statutes and proclamations forbade the export of gold and silver ' either as coins,
jewels, Bullion, Plate or vessels ' [1] travellers were
allowed to carry small sums of money out of the kingdom. Fynes Moryson, writing in the early part of the

---

[1] Proclamation, 1607.

BANK OF THE THAMES AND LONDON.   From an engraving by Hollar

century, gave twenty pounds as the limit. This was scarcely a generous allowance to those who contemplated a lengthy sojourn abroad. The restriction must have put the conscientious traveller in a quandary. Indeed, apart from contraband, it was a nice question whether it were better to travel with gold and silver and risk the attention of highwaymen (if not searchers), or to have letters of credit and perhaps lose on the exchange. This question perturbed Mary Verney when she was making preparations to cross to France. To the searchers likewise fell the task of detecting persons who were deemed dangerous to the State ; an arrangment that must have proved advantageous to suspects, for Evelyn, writing of Dover under date 12 August 1650, tells us ' money to the searchers and officers was as authentic as the hand and seal of Bradshaw himself, where I had not so much as my trunk opened '. Elsewhere, we are told, that there were as many filchers as searchers. Father Francis Slingsby must have been either unfortunate or particularly severe in his moral code. Returning to England from Rome, where he had been received into its Church and consecrated priest, he had all his books and papers taken from him by the searchers ' for a welcome in these parts '. He was glad, however, to ' swallow up that misfortune and say not a word, lest that by seeking to recover them ' he might have betrayed himself. For the Lords of the Privy Council knew that he had turned Catholic, and he was therefore ' fain to keep close '.

The packet-boats had no monopoly of passenger traffic. The traveller could, if he wished, make the crossing by merchantman, or, if he procured a pass, by Government vessel. It was in one of the King's ships, *The Ninth Whelpe*, that Sir William Brereton crossed from Waterford to Minehead ; an expensive journey, for it cost him one pound and ten shillings

in vails, including ten shillings for the use of the
Master Gunner's cabin—the Captain's cabin had been
engaged by another passenger. Payment would seem,
however, to have varied according to rank, for his
untitled companion gave only ten shillings, to be
distributed among the crew. On another occasion he
crossed, from Gravesend to Holland, in a fifty-ton
pink with sixty-seven passengers, including two
women and four children, and under decks as large
a consignment of goods as could be stowed. It must
have been a relief to spend six hours at Queenborough
eating lobsters while waiting for a favourable tide,
but not a very good preparation for a voyage.
Indeed, the unpleasant conditions on board ship must
have affected many travellers who, under other circumstances, would have been good travellers. ' To
avoid the ill smelles of the ship,' says Fynes Moryson,
the traveller ' may in Summer Carry red Roses, or
the dried leaves thereof, Lemmons, Oranges, and like
things of good odour, and in Winter hee may carry
the route or leaves of Angelica, Cloves, Rosemary,
and the foresaid Lemmons, Oranges and Rose Leaves '.
He also gives good advice how to avoid sea-sickness.
When the Venetian Ambassador, who had engaged
a ship for the crossing to England at a cost of twenty-
two crowns, arrived on board the vessel with his
staff, he discovered that she was already ' crowded
with passengers of every description, musicians,
women, merchants, bearded Jews, tatterdemalions
and gentlemen crowded together '. Luckily berths
had been engaged for the distinguished strangers,
though they were not very commodious, that assigned
to his Excellency being ' so low and narrow that it
could not even contain four persons '. Their provisions for the voyage consisted of ' good beer, yet
better Rhenish, excellent French claret with capital
Mayence ham and a flask of Spanish aromatico '.

Evidently the chaplain, Busino, who describes the
journey, was not affected by the conditions aboard.

M. Jorevin, on making the adventure to England,
chose a Dieppe merchantman bound for London, on
account of the Master's familiarity with the English
tongue. Had he based his choice upon a knowledge
of seamanship it would have been more to the point,
for the voyage proved not only unpleasant but
hazardous. First, the galliot which carried him from
shore to ship filled with water. Secondly, when he
was embarked and under way, the wind rose to such
a height that sails had to be shortened during the
night, which prevented the passengers from sleeping.
Thirdly, the master lost his way in the dark. And,
lastly, arrived off the Downs, they found the wind
against them, and had to put into Margate harbour.
There, the wind still proving contrary, the passengers
were landed, minus luggage, and had to make their
own way to London.

According to a contemporary guide-book, the short
sea-crossing between France and England occupied
three hours, but four or five were more usual. Sometimes ships were becalmed, as on the occasion when
Congreve took to an open rowing boat in mid-Channel,
to enable him to reach Calais the same evening, having
started at four o'clock in the morning. This was
accomplished after five hours of hard rowing by the
French oarsmen who, we conjecture, had set out in
the hope of gaining a fare and a reward suitable to
their exertions. The packet-boat did not arrive until
the following morning. Ports became crowded
whenever storm or contrary winds prevailed. In
February 1617–18 three hundred sail were said to
have taken shelter in the Downs on account of rough
weather, ' more than ever were heard of to lie there so
long '. Sometimes ships were delayed by unfavourable
winds for two or three weeks. King William, on his

way to Holland, offered, like Canute, an example of
the limitation of kingly power by actually returning
all the way from Margate to Kensington when he
found that adverse weather conditions were likely to
prevail for some time to come.   The unfortunate
King of Bohemia (who had no kingly power to be thus
limited) was kept windbound at Flushing for five
weeks, and only reached England after the ship in
which he was a passenger had been twice unsuccessfully launched.

On occasions, the traveller had not only to await
passable weather conditions, but found, when at sea,
that the crossing was likely to occupy as many days
as usually it took hours to effect.   Such was the case
when M. le Maréchal de Bassompierre, the old companion in arms of Henry IV, was returning from an
unpleasant mission to England, his train swollen with
seventy French priests, banished from Court and kingdom.   Arrived at Dover, the party awaited a favourable
crossing for four days.   They then set sail, only to
find themselves the plaything of a storm which carried
them first towards Dieppe and then back again to
the Downs.   There they were forced to set foot to
earth and return to Dover.   Finally, after a fortnight's
stay in port (at the cost of fourteen thousand crowns
to the brave and generous Marshal) the retinue and
equipage were embarked.   But it was not until five
days later, after throwing overboard two coaches,
containing forty thousand crowns' worth of wearing
apparel, brought as gifts for the French Court, and
losing twenty-nine horses by death from thirst, that
the unhappy party accomplished the twenty-one miles
to Calais.

This was a calamitous journey indeed ; but others
of almost equal severity if not of equal misfortune can
be named.   Marie de Medicis, when coming to
England in 1638, was seven days at sea and three days

outside Harwich, whither her ship had been driven
by a storm, before it was possible for her and her ladies
to disembark, and meet the critical gaze of those who
had hurried thither from Dover to receive her.
Although the Queen herself was ' insensible to the
fatigues of the sea ', her ladies were ' a little in disorder '
having been ' more attentive to the alleviating their
uneasinesses, than the preserving their beauty '.

Her daughter, Queen Henrietta Maria, had a yet
more trying experience four years later, when she set
out from Scheveling to rejoin her warring spouse.
Her ship, the *Princess Royal*, accompanied by eleven
transports, filled with ammunition and stores for the
royal forces, was convoyed by the Dutch Admiral,
Van Tromp, who later gained distinction fighting the
English Commonwealth.   No sooner had they got
under way than a tremendous north-east wind arose,
tossing the ship in such fashion that the ladies of her
suite, expecting death hourly, wept and screamed,
until the daughter of Henry the Great bade them
comfort themselves, for Queens of England were
never drowned.   And comforted they were, until
going below, the tempest rising, they were tied into
small beds and suffered the horrors of sea-sickness.
Soon pandemonium reigned.   The officers crowded
into the Queen's cabin ; the ladies who were already
there, believing that death would engulf them at
any moment, insisted on confessing themselves to the
Capuchin fathers of the Queen's suite, who, being as
ill as any of those present, were not able to give due
attention to their task.   As a result the penitents
shouted out their sins aloud, regardless of others, and
only intent on obtaining instant absolution, a
spectacle that amused the Queen, who, free from fear,
was apparently equally free from sea-sickness.   She
supposed, so she related years after to her old governess,
Mme. de Motteville, that the extremity of their fears

took away the shame of confessing their misdeeds in public. Whenever the storm abated, and eating and drinking were going forward, ridiculous attempts were made to serve her in state, the attendants tumbling over one another with screams and confusion— another laughter-raising episode. No alarm could stifle her mirth. Yet it was a fortnight of pitching and tossing ere they touched land ; and not then the craved-for land of England, but the wild Scheveling coast of Holland whence they had set sail with twelve stout ships, and to which they now returned but ten strong, two having succumbed to the fury of the sea. When again the undaunted Henrietta set out, a quick and prosperous voyage brought her to Bridlington Bay, and to all the hazards and disasters of the long-drawn Civil War.

Entering port, in an age when charts, or sea platts as they were called, were crude and ships not easy to manœuvre, was, as may be well imagined, likewise fraught with danger and difficulty. Of this John Chamberlain, the lively correspondent of Sir Dudley Carleton, had experience. After three of four baffled attempts to cross from Flushing, and a long wait at that port—others less patient or more reckless went to the greater and varied hazards of a land journey to Calais—he embarked in an English pink, carrying threescore passengers and three pilots, one of Dover, one of Sandwich, and one of foreign origin. Thence they set sail, in company with four more pinks, for England. A sore tempest arising, they were two nights and two days at sea, and then were driven up as high as Yarmouth. There,

'. . . offering to enter into the haven, the tides being spent, we struck upon the bar, where, if we had stuck, we had been all lost. But it pleased God we got over, and with full sails, beat upon the head or piles so as, if the ship had not been new and strong, she had been split or beaten in pieces. In this fear and confusion, some endeavoured to leap upon the piles when she came close (for she struck upon them four times), some few made shift to scramble up, but four of our company, leapt short, whereof three were drowned and in our sight, and one beaten against the piles all to pieces. We got them all taken up and buried. In the mean time, some boats came from the shore, but would not approach us without orders given to take in but three or four at once. The seas went very high, and it was dangerous landing; so that, till I had seen the success of four boats, one after the other, I would not stir; and, as it pleased God, I had the best passage, most of the rest being washed over head and ears, or overtumbled in the landing.'

It is no wonder that skippers arranged their sailings so as to make a landing during the hours of daylight.

With the perils of the deep were associated the man-made perils of capture and pillage, by free-lance pirates in the earlier years of the century, later by enemy men-of-war and their irregular forces known as privateers. In 1635–6, with the nation at peace with all the world, we find the Master of His Majesty's packet-boats writing to complain that his company had been robbed of all they had by Captains Russet and Tasset of Calais, ' who ordinarily lie close to the shore near St. Margaret's, and there watch for all that come out of Dover road, to take or leave at their pleasure. The packet now for Dunkirk they dare not carry, nor will go any more to sea without good provision of men and ammunition.' The very persons of travellers were not safe. Some weeks earlier Captain Roussel of Calais (perhaps friend Russet in another guise) had taken five muskets and all the passengers' money from the Dunkirk packet, while his brother pirate, Tasset, had dared to take possession of the Baron Rochecour from a shallop of Calais.

Some twenty years earlier the Lord-Deputy of Ireland, Lord Chichester of Belfast, had to wait more than a month at Chester, or West Chester to give it its full and old-time designation, ' not daring to adventure the

passage without a convoy from his majesty to secure
him against the pirates, which are said to lie in wait
for him in those seas, to ease him of the burthen of such
provision money as he carried over with him, amounting to a good round sum of some sixteen or seventeen
thousand pounds'. Ultimately, six or eight ships
were sent to conduct him over 'and to scour those
seas in a little their return'.

In time of war not even convoys were safe from
molestation. In July 1649, when Prince Rupert and
his men were harrying the seas, Evelyn going to
France embarked in the packet-boat which, having
been pillaged on several occasions, was now for the first
time guarded by a pinnace of eight guns. Nevertheless, they were chased for some hours by a Royalist
privateer, who, however, dared not attack their ship,
and who was finally chased by them and their companion, until he got under the protection of the castle
at Calais, and they were forced to desist. It would
doubtless have gratified the master of the packet—
if not the loyalist Evelyn—had he known it, that some
of these cavaliers had themselves suffered some
months before at the hands of pirates. A French
man-of-war, carrying Clarendon and others of the
Prince's adherents to the Royal Fleet, was pursued and
attacked by six or seven Ostenders—freebooters,
though they had the King of Spain's commission—the
passengers robbed of all they possessed, money,
jewels, clothes, valises, trunks ; the servants of the
very shirts off their backs ; and all taken as prisoners
to their captors' home port. Thence they were indeed
suffered to depart, but without any real satisfaction
for their losses, the whole population, as Clarendon
believed, including the magistrates, or 'lords of the
admiralty', being in league with the marauders.
Assuredly the occupation was lucrative and well
organized, with ramifications all over the continental

THE FLIGHT OF QUEEN MARY BEATRICE, 1688

From a contemporary print

Northern seaboard ; intelligence of likely booty being sent from port to port irrespective of frontier.

The cross-Channel traffic again suffered heavily during the Dutch and Spanish wars of the following decade. So hazardous did the crossing become that Sir Ralph Verney, writing in 1656 to his young son, due home from Holland, advised him to bring nothing more ' then the cloathes uppon your Back, & those the Worst you have, for tis reported the passengers (by reason of our Warre with Spaine) are often pillaged. . . .' Some said that the Parliament ships were freest from capture, but this does not appear to have been the universal opinion. Luce Sheppard, on whom rested the responsibility of conveying the Verney children and their cousins to France, had heard it said that the ' schallopes ' were freest from robbers and ' doe pase much this summer time ', but, she adds, she ' durst not venture the gentillwemen in a schallope', which was open to all weather and most in danger of being cast away. However, though the seas were ' very full of pirats ', they successfully crossed in their ' sheepe ', free from all danger.

To a man of adventurous and roaming spirit like Fynes Moryson the sudden discovery, upon lifting of a fog, of a couple of Dunkirk privateers, the hurried flight, the rapid changes of course to outwit the swift chasing pirates, the firing of the guns to summon help from others of the fog-scattered convoy, the preparation for fight, if fight they must—to him and his like such a voyage presented a not unpleasing excitement. But to a woman like Luce Sheppard, with the care of young children ; to Mrs. Evelyn and Lady Browne, her mother, who, though three days at sea before they reached Rye, with ' seventeen bales of furniture and other rich plunder ', passed unscathed through the Dutch fleet, being taken for ' fishers ', the passage can have held nothing but heavy anxiety.

Indeed, to many a woman the risk of seeing her iron-bound and yellow hair-trunks, her cabinets and linen cases, and all the bundles of treasures dear to her heart, pillaged by the enemy must have weighed more heavily than the possibility of death.

Treacherous though the Channel might be, it was to many an avenue of escape to be sought at risk of life and limb, from worse dangers threatening at home. But it was no easy task to leave England, especially in time of danger, real or fancied, to the State. None could enter or leave the country without a licence to be obtained from duly constituted authority, and then only by subscribing, on demand, to the Oath of Allegiance. Moreover, during times of stress, there were few that were not liable to be taken by the Watch or by other port officials for examination before Governor, Commissioners, or Mayor. Luckily for those ill-disposed towards the ruling powers, Mr. Mayor —and we suppose his colleagues too—was not always inclined to have his privacy invaded, especially during night hours when he was abed.

To make unauthorized comings and goings yet more difficult, an order went forth in 1615 that all merchantmen other than those known, and therefore above reproach, were required to use only the ports of Dover, Rye, and Sandwich, an order that was surely flouted with impunity all the way from the North Foreland to the Isle of Wight, the stretch of coast that, we take it, it was meant to cover. More effectual, probably, was the order of 1650, which required that vessels bound for Holland should take on board no more passengers after they had passed Gravesend; when searches were to be made of all passengers, those with passes not exempted, ' the present conjuncture requiring more than ordinary diligence '. Nor were private landing-stairs, or bridges as they were called, allowed at Gravesend at this time, ' but only the common bridge that so there may be better watch kept, and account taken of all persons and things that shall there go on board or ashore '.   At times shipping was altogether stopped, whether it were merely to enable the Princess Elizabeth to cross in state to Holland by pressing mariners to man the fleet, or whether it were peril to the State that dictated such a measure.

Where there is a will there is a way.   The hard-pressed Recusant, the delinquent Royalist, or the scheming Jacobite would counterfeit a pass, or procure one in a false name,[1] and thus armed trust to the venality of his compatriots and to their habitual slackness, to secure safe passage overseas.   In desperate need he would make for a quiet stretch of coast—and there were many in those days—where merchantmen were not unwilling, for a substantial bribe, to smuggle live cargo to an alien shore.   Pursued, the fugitive might find himself even in mid-Channel baulked of escape, and led back prisoner whence he had come.   It was a strange coincidence that brought about the capture of Sir John Fenwick, the well-known Jacobite conspirator, upon the discovery of the plot to assassi-

[1] Evelyn, writing under date 12 August 1650, describes how, arriving at Canterbury on his way to France, he was ' surprised by the soldiers, and having only an antiquated pass, with some fortunate dexterity I got clear of them, though not without extraordinary hazard, having before counterfeited one with success, it being so difficult to procure one of the Rebels without entering into oaths, which I never would do '.   As he had a few weeks previously obtained a pass from Bradshawe, President of the Council, enabling him to transport himself, two servants and other necessaries to any port in France, the reason of his embarrassment is not apparent ; unless, indeed, the oath of allegiance had been required of him and by him refused.   Sir Ralph Verney, M.P., refusing to take the Covenant and deeming it advisable to seek refuge in France, obtained the following pass under an assumed name, and was thus enabled to reach the coast in safety.
    ' To all Captaines and others whom it concerns.
London.   These are to require you to permitt and suffer Mr. Ralph Smith and his wyfe and his man and mayde to passe by water to Lee in Essex and to returne.   So they carry nothinge of Danger.
                    November the 30th 1643.
                            By Warrant of the L[d] Maier.
                                Jo: Beadnege.'

nate King William. Striking out for Romney Marsh
with a friend—both were well armed and mounted—
he was passing near Rochester when he recognized,
and was recognized by, a messenger (detective) who
was conveying two prisoners to London. Threatening
the man, he escaped. But the messenger raising the
hue and cry, he was followed to New Romney where he
and his bedfellow, a Jacobite solicitor, were arrested
on the eve of their sailing for France. Thence he was
brought back to London where prison and death
awaited him.

More to be pitied was the attempt of the charming
and hapless Lady Arabella Stuart to escape from the
realm of her harsh and unfeeling cousin, James. She
had fallen in love with and secretly married William
Seymour, heir to the Suffolk-Tudor line. This union,
when he heard of it, alarmed the King, who was as
timorous as he was obstinate ; for not only was
Arabella closely allied to the throne of Scotland, but
Seymour was the undoubted claimant to the throne
of England, according to the disregarded will of
Henry VIII. The errant couple were accordingly
placed in restraint, Seymour in the Tower, Arabella
in the care of Sir Thomas Parry at Lambeth. But the
King did not even then feel secure on his throne.
He transferred his cousin to the keeping of the Bishop
of Durham, and arrangements were made for her to
proceed to his episcopal seat. She refused to go and
was ultimately removed in a litter by force, in a state
bordering on collapse. At Barnet, whither she had
been carried in two removes, she was allowed a month's
respite. The rest we will describe in the words of
Mr. John More.

' On *Monday* last in the Afternoone my Lady *Arabella* lying
at Mr. *Coniers* House near *Highgate* [a mistake for Barnet],
having induced her Keepers, and Attendants into Securitie by
the fayre Shew of Conformitye and Willingness to goe on her

L'HEVREVX DES EMBARQEMENT DE LA REYNE AV PORT DE
HARWICH

MARIE DE MEDICI AT HARWICH

From a contemporary print

journey towards *Durham* (which the next Day she must have don,) and in the mean tyme *disguising her selfe by drawing a pair of great French-fashioned Hose over her Petticotes, putting on a Man's Doublet, a man-lyke Perruque with long Locks over her Hair, a blacke Hat, black Cloake, russet Bootes with red Tops, and a Rapier by her Syde,* walked forth between three and four of the Clock with Mr. *Markham* [an attendant]. After they had gon a foot a Myle and halfe to a sorry Inne, where *Crompton* [servant] attended with their horses she grew very sicke and fainte, so as the Ostler that held the Styrrop, said *that Gentleman would hardly hold out to* London. Yet being set on a good Gelding *astryde* in an unwonted Fashion, the stirring of the Horse brought Blood enough into her Face, and so she rid on towards *Blackwall*; where arryving about six a Clock, finding there in a Readiness two Men, a Gentlewoman and a Chambermaid, with one Boate full of Mr. *Seimour's* and her Trunks, and another Boate for their Persons, they hasted from thence towards *Woolwich*. Being come so farre they bade the Watermen row on to *Gravesend*, There the Watermen were desirous to land, but for a double Fraight were contented to go on to *Lee* : Yet being almost tyred by the way, they were faine to lye still at *Tilbury* Whilst the Oares went a land to refreshe themselves. Then they proceeded to *Lee*, and by that tyme the Day appeared, and they discovered a Shippe at Anchor a Myle beyond them, which was the *French Barque* that wayted for them. Here the *Lady* would have lyen at Anchor expecting Mr. *Seimour*, but through the Importunitye of her Followers they forthwith hoisted Saile to Sea-warde. In the meane while Mr. *Seimour* with *a Perruque and Beard of blacke Hair* and in a tauny Cloth Suit, walked alone *without Suspition* from his Lodging out at the great West Doore of the *Tower, following a Cart that had brought him Billets*. From thence he walked along by the *Tower Warfe* by the *Warders* of the fourth Gate, and so to the *Iron Gate*, where *Rodney* [a friend] was ready with Oares for to receive him. When they came to *Lee* and fowned that the *French* Ship was gon, the Billows rising high, they hyred a *Fisherman* for twenty Shillings to set them aboard a certain Ship that they saw under Saile. That ship they found not to be it they looked for, so they made forwards to the next under Saile, which was a shippe of *Newcastle*. This with much ado they hyred for 40*l.* to carry them to *Calais* . . .

'Now the Kyng and the Lords being much disturbed with

this *unexpected Accident,* my Lord Treasurer sent Orders to a *Pinnace* that lay at the *Downes* to put presently [at once] to Sea,[1] first to *Calais* Roade, and then to scoure up the Coaste towards Dunkerke. This *Pinnace* spying the aforesaid French Barke which lay lingering for Mr. *Seimour* [really they were almost becalmed], made to her, which thereupon offered to fly towards *Calais,* and endured thirteen Shot of the Pinnace before she would stryke. In this Barke is the *Lady* taken with her Followers, and brought back towards the *Tower*: *Not so sorrye for her owne Restraynt, as she should be glad yf* Mr. Seimour *might escape, whose Welfare she protesteth to affect much more than her owne.'*

Seymour did indeed escape, and lived to re-enter into the good graces of James. Not so poor Arabella. For four long years her loving, rebellious, high-wrought spirit withered in the Tower, and then it was all-merciful death which released her from the grasp of her implacable kinsman.

---

[1] In truth, not one but many vessels were sent in pursuit by the thoroughly alarmed King and his advisers. A lighthorseman with twenty musketeers was sent out as low as the Nore to search all ships, barques, and other vessels. Houses were searched at Leigh. A ship was ordered to stand out for Calais, another dispatched to the Lords at Greenwich to send away in haste ' with galleys open '. While these were preparing, an oyster boat with six men in her and with shot was sent out, as were some light fishing-craft. It was one of these, *The Adventurer,* which had the ' honour ' of capturing the runaway Princess in mid-Channel, and of bringing her back to England. See the *Life and Letters of Lady Arabella Stuart,* by Elizabeth Cooper, vol. ii.

V

INNS, ALEHOUSES, AND OTHER LODGING

' THE ancient and principall True use of Innes and Victuallinge Houses was for the Receipte, Relief and Lodginge of wayfaring people travellinge from place to place.' Such was the pronouncement of an Act of the reign of James I,[1] and such the doctrine of the authorities in their dealing with houses of entertainment.

The individual known in more recent years as the ' bona fide traveller ' was permitted to obtain drink at hours forbidden to local residents. He was also entitled to receive lodging—innkeepers and alehouse-keepers being required to ' keep one or more spare Beds for lodging of strangers '—and, if refused without good cause such as lack of room, could, through the medium of the constable, force admittance, though ' how the officer shall compell him is not yet set down '—to quote the words of a constable's manual. Failing this he could indict the innkeeper or alehouse-keeper so refusing. Tavern-keepers, on the contrary, were forbidden to harbour travellers, as appears from a presentment in 1599–1600 of a tavern-keeper of Hitchin, who was charged with ' exposing bread and beer as well for men as horses ', and using ' lodging for packmen, whereas in truth the same house was never hitherto used as an inn '.[2] Further, innkeepers and alehouse-keepers were not allowed to receive guests for whom they would not answer ; a paradoxical situation, unless, as we suppose, the action of the constables in forcing admittance relieved them of

---

[1] 1 Jac. I, c. 9 (1603–4).   [2] *Herts County Records*, vol. i, p. 30.

responsibility thereunto. As the execution of the laws in seventeenth-century England never equalled their stringency of wording, it is reasonable to suppose that the host of the wayside inn or the village alehouse never hesitated to flout the law when it suited his purpose to do so, though he might lose his recognizance and his livelihood thereby. Accordingly we find more than one indictment, and more than one chronicler, relating the difficulties experienced in finding house-room. Nicholas Brooks, fishmonger, having left his house in Southwark on Friday, 30th December 1664, and lodged first at the ' Flower de Luce ' in St. Albans and the two following nights at the ' Redd Lyon ' at Luton, found on reaching Wheathampstead about four o'clock of the Monday afternoon that neither Thomas Wethered nor Roger Austin, host of the Bull, would receive him. Had he not given a quarter of a pound of ' tobackee ' and two flagons of beer to John Skale to guide him to the ' Tinn Pott ', where he found good entertainment for himself and his two horses, he might have had to spend a night of dis-comfort and anxiety without doors. No more than ten days or a fortnight before he had been robbed by nine horsemen between Watford and Edgware, and, ' usuall traveler ' though he was, can have felt in no valiant mood. George Fox, the Quaker, who we must admit was an uncomfortable guest for any innkeeper, with his strange, unconventional ways, and his frequent collisions with the authorities, had, on at least two occasions, to seek shelter beneath a hedge-row. Even the jovial Taylor and sober Mrs. Fiennes were sometimes hard put to it, especially in the more remote districts, to find a night's lodging.

The cause, we believe, was twofold. First, accommo-dation was meagre in all but the great inns. Secondly, the consumption of liquor by the local inhabitants—the beer, ales, wines, and strange mixed drinks so

¶ **Certaine wholesome Obseruations and**

Rules fo Jnne-keepers, and also for their Guests, meet to be fixed vpon the
wall of euery Chamber in the house ; but meant more specially for the good of
Mʳ. *Henry Hunter* and his wife, of *Smithfield*, his louing brother and
sister, and of the Guests which vse their house.

---

1. E Reade of Inkeepers that they were of ancient time, as in *Ios.* 2. *Iudg.* 1 9. verse. 2 1.22.
2. Our Sauiour in the Gospel commends the vse of Innes. *Luke* 1 0. ver. 3 4. and brought to an Inne.
3. Yea Christ himselfe by his owne presence did sanctifie the vse of Innes by eating his passeouer there. *Mat.* 26.18.
4. In *Acts* 2 8. there is expresse mention of an Inne with approbation and liking. They came to meet vs at the market of *Appius*, and at the three Tauerns.
5 Common experience sheweth all men what vse there is of Innes for ease of Trauailers, that their bodies which are the members of Christ, and Temples of the holy ghost appointed to a glorious resurrection, may be refreshed after wearisome labour.
6 It must not be accounted a small matter to affoord house roome, lodging, rest and food to the comforts of Gods children.

Rules for Innekeepers.

1. THough your house (as an Inne) bee open for all men to come vnto, yet account honest men your best guests : euer hold their company better then their roomes.
2 Amongst honest men, 'et such as be religious withal, be most welcome. The feet of the Saints are blessed, and often leaue b'essings behind them ,as we read of *Ioseph. Gen.* 3 9. 4. 5.
3. Of religious and godly men let faithfull Ministers haue heartiest intertainement. The feet of such as bring glad tidings of peace and good things, oh how beautifull are they. *Rom.* 1 0. Such as receiue a Prophet in the name of a Prophet shal haue a Prophets reward. *Mat.* 1 0. Be not so glad of your gain, as that you may pleasure such.
4 Because your guests be Gods children, and their bodies the members of Christ, let their vsage for meat, lodging, diet, and sleepe bee such as becomes such ; worthy personages , as bee heires with God, euen fellow heires. with Christ. *Rom.* 8.
5. In seruing and louing your guests, remember you do serue and loue God, who takes all as done to himselfe, which for his sake is done to his. *Mat.* 2 5. 3 4. 3 3. 3 6.
6. Content your selues with an honest gaine, so vsing your guests as they may haue an appetite to returne to you when they are gone from you.
7 Make choice of good seruants , such as know God and make conscience of their waies: for these are likeliest to be true, faithfull, diligent, and cheerefull in their seruice; also such will best please your best guests, and will not iustly offend your worst Moreouer, God will cause your busines to prosper best in the hands of such.
8. Giue your seruants no euill example in word or deed, beare not with their lying, deceit, swearing, prophaning of the Sabbath, or wantonnes. Cause them to keepe the Lords day holy, going to the Church by turnes : examine them how they profit by Sermons, loue such seruants best, as most loue Gods word.

Rules for Guests.

1. VSe an Inne not as your owne house, but as an Inne; not to dwell in but to rest for such time as ye haue iust and needfull occasion and then to returne to your owne families.
2. Remember ye are in the world as in an Inne to tarry for a short space; and then to be gone hence.
3. At night when ye come to your Inne thanke God for your Preseruation : next morning pray for a good Iourney.
4. Eat and drinke for necessity and strength, and not for lust.
5. At table let your talke be powdered with the salt of heauenly wisedome, as your meat is seasoned wich material and earthly salt.
6. Aboue all abhorre all oathes, cursing and blasphemy, for God will not hold him guiltlesse which taketh his name in vaine.

FINIS.   T.W.

An early broadside

beloved of seventeenth-century palates—must have far outweighed in value the profits to be derived from an occasional traveller, who, in the case of a disorderly house, might do positive injury to business by inform- ing against it.[1]   So great a part did the ' inordinate hauntinge and tiplinge in Innes, Alehouses and other Victuallinge Houses ' play in the daily life of both rich and poor that the mischief was proof against alike the sporadic efforts of Parliament to reduce it and the more constant and effective pressure of Justices in Quarter Sessions with their powers of suppressing alehouses.[2]

To dwell at length upon the drinking habits of the nation, or upon the devices of the authorities for regulating the several categories of hostelries, would fill many and somewhat tedious pages.   We will pass, therefore, to a general description of the better-class English inn, seeing it, as far as we can, with the eyes of the seventeenth-century traveller ; though the first place must be accorded to a writer of slightly anterior date, or we should lose a picture as detailed and perspicacious as a little Dutch masterpiece.

' Those townes that we call thorowfaires have great and sumptuous innes builded in them,' writes Harrison, ' for the receiving of such travellers and strangers as passe to and fro. The manner of harbouring wherein, is not like that of some other countries, in which the host or goodman of the house dooth chalenge a lordlie authoritie over his ghests, but cleane otherwise, sith everie man may use his inne as his owne house in England, and have for his monie how great or how little varietie of vittels, and what other service himselfe shall thinke

[1] ' In old times the ale-house windows were generally open, so that the company within might enjoy the fresh air, and see all that was going on in the street ; but as the scenes within were not always fit to be seen by the " profanum vulgus " that passed by, a trellis was put up in the open window. This trellis, or lattice, was generally painted red.' The term lattice frequently became equivalent to an alehouse. *Hist. of Signboards*, 1866, J. Larwood and J. C. Hotten, as given in a note to the *Bagford Ballads*, vol. i, p. 402.
[2] See Note E, pp. 324–5.

expedient to call for. Our innes are also verie well furnished with naperie : bedding and tapisterie especiallie with naperie : for beside the linnen used at the tables, which is commonlie washed dailie, is such and so much as belongeth unto the estate and calling of the ghest. Ech commer is sure to lie in cleane sheets, wherein no man hath beene lodged since they came from the landresse, . . . If the traveller have an horsse, his bed dooth cost him nothing, but if he go on foot he is sure to paie a penie for the same : but whether he be horsseman or footman if his chamber be once appointed he may carie the kaie with him, as of his owne house so long as he lodgeth there. If he loose oughts whilest he abideth in the inne, the host is bound by a generall custome to restore the damage, so that there is no greater securitie anie where for travellers than in the gretest ins of England. Their horsses in like sort are walked, dressed, and ·looked unto by certeine hostelers or hired servants, appointed at the charges of the goodman of the house, who in hope of extraordinarie reward will deale verie diligentlie after outward appearance in this their function and calling. Herein neverthelesse are manie of them blameworthie in that they doo . . . deceive the beast oftentimes of his allowance by sundrie meanes,'—an unhappy fact attested by several other writers.

Next he refers to other and yet more dishonest practices of innkeepers and their servants, a blot upon the fair fame of English inns, with which we shall deal more conveniently later. Adverting again to the great inns he says :

' . . . it is a world to see how ech owner of them contendeth with other for goodnesse of interteinement of their ghests, as about finesse & change of linnen, furniture of bedding, beautie of roomes, service at the table, costlinesse of plate, strength of drinke, varietie of wines, or well using of horsses. Finallie there is not so much omitted among them as the gorgeousnes of their verie signes [1] at their doores, wherein some

---

[1] The ' noblest sighne post in England ' was said to be that at Scole in Suffolk, the house of which had been built in 1655 for James Beck, a merchant of Norwich. Extending across the road it was carved with ' a great many stories, as of Charon and Cerberus, of Actaeon and Diana, and many others ', while the sign itself, the White Hart, hung down in a ' stately wreath '. See the *Journal of the Very Rev. Rowland Davies*, Camden Soc. 68, and Sir Thomas Browne's Works, vol. i.

doo consume thirtie or fortie pounds, a meere vanitie in mine
opinion, but so vaine will they needs be, and that not onelie
to give some outward token of the inne keepers welth, but also
to procure good ghests to the frequenting of their houses in
hope there to be well used.'

It is little wonder that Fynes Moryson, the traveller,
writing some forty years later, exclaims ' the World
affoords not such Innes as England hath,[1] either for
good and cheape entertainement after the Guests owne
pleasure, or for humble attendance on passengers,
yea in very poore Villages, where if Curculio of
Plautus should see the thatched houses, he would fall
into a fainting of his spirits, but if he should smell the
variety of meates, his starveling looke would be much
cheared '. He too makes comment upon the crooked
ways of the ostler, and then passes indoors.

' Another servant gives the passenger his private chamber,
and kindles his fier, the third puls of his bootes, and makes
them cleane. Then the Host or Hostesse visit him, and if he
will eate with the Host, or at a common Table with others, his
meale will cost him six pence [later eightpence and twelvepence were common charges], or in some places foure pence
(yet this course is lesse honourable, and not used by Gentlemen) : but if he will eate in his chamber, he commands what
meate he will according to his appetite, and as much as thinkes
fit for him and his company, yea, the kitchen is open to him,[2]
to command the meat to be dressed as he best likes ; and when
he sits at Table, the Host or Hostesse will accompany him, or
if they have many Guests, will at least visit him, taking it
curtesie to be bid to sit downe : while he eates, if he have
company especially, he shall be offred musicke, which he may
freely take or refuse, and if he be solitary, the Musitians will
give himm the good day with musicke in the morning. It is
the custome and no way disgracefull to set up part of supper
for his breakfast : in the evening or in the morning after

---

[1] M. Jorevin, as a patriotic Frenchman, was more restrained in his
appreciation. ' One is as well treated here ', he writes, ' in the taverns and
inns, as in France, and as neatly lodged, the manner of this country being
pretty much like our own.' *Description of England in the 17th century*,
by Jorevin ; Grose's *Antiquarian Repertory*.

[2] See Chap. VIII, ' On the Road ', p. 238.

breakefast, (for the common sort use not to dine, but ride from breakefast to supper time, yet comming early to the Inne for better resting of their Horses) he shall have a reckoning in writing, and if it seeme unreasonable, the Host will satisfie him, either for the due price, or by abating part, especially if the servant deceive him any way, which one of experience will soone find.'

As will be seen from the foregoing, the great inns of the age were very different from the hotels of to-day. If dishonest practices were occasionally resorted to by the servants, the guest was treated with hearty, old-fashioned hospitality. The host—so long as he remained sober—was the host, in no less degree than the private gentleman who welcomed his friends for love of their company. He would so entertain his guests at supper with ' merry tales, and true Jests ', as to make their weariness clean forgotten ; his daughter, perhaps, would play on the virginals, though it might be but indifferent well ; he would take it both as a duty and a pleasure to act as guide to those who wished to visit the sights of his city, and, at least on one occasion, did give ' a perfect account ' of the town's history from its infancy upwards. His wife—if, indeed, the lady was not, as frequently happened, sole proprietor [1]—would greet them on arrival, may be, with a cup of sack and a dish of hot salmon, saying, if of the Northern speech, *may God thank thee*. One of this kindly tribe of women treated a quartette of weary travellers ' as if she had been a Mother rather then an Hostesse '. In truth, the English inn was mirror of the English manners of

[1] There was a tendency to regard alehouse licences as suitable provision for invalids and widows who might otherwise require assistance from the rates. Thus we find Tho. Grunwin of Wheathamstead petitioning the Hertfordshire Bench that, as he was sickly and not able to work and maintain his family, and as they were ' civill honest persons, and situated by the roadside at a fitting place for the relief of passengers, and formerly an alehouse ', the Justices might grant him a licence ' to draw and utter beere '. *Herts. County Records*, vol. i, p. 246.

THE REINDEER INN, BANBURY

the day : a homely atmosphere in which the host felt
at ease with his guests, whether they were lords or
lackeys, and where the traveller in his conversation
showed no strain of supercilious or class-conscious
reserve.

As in the sphere of intercourse generally, there was,
of course, a reverse to this pleasing picture. Hosts
were to be met with who were surly and overbearing.
Hostesses there were who ' could only Dress fine and
Entertain the soldiers '. It was of this type of ' Handsome Hostess ' that Bishop Earle wrote ' She is the
Loadstone that attracts men of Iron, Gallants and
Roarers [or Roaring boys as they were sometimes
called] . . . Her lipps are your wel-come, and your
entertainement her company, which is put into the
reckoning too, and is the dearest parcell in it '. The
favours of a sprightly hostess were not the only items
which were on occasion put into the reckoning. The
traveller might find himself paying for the honour of
being lodged at the inn of an alderman, or of a gentleman of ancient lineage : a circumstance which might
be turned to good account. Thus at the ' George '
at Lancaster the host was well acquainted with the
affairs of the shire, as his brother ' Mr. Covile was both
a Justice of the Peace, and a chiefe Gaoler ', and could
thereby procure his guests ' some commaund of the
Castle '.

High charges were sometimes tempered with
generosity, if we may believe M. Misson, a recorder
of English customs who was not always accurate in
his statements. At Christmas, he tells us, the custom
prevailed of not fully charging for the viands eaten on
that and the two following days. At Leeds, on market
day at the sign of the ' Bush ', writes Mrs. Fiennes,
' any body that will goe and Call for one tanchard of
ale and a pinte of wine and pay for these only shall be
set to a table to Eate wth 2 or 3 dishes of good meate

and a dish of sweetmeates after '. She regretted that she had arrived a day too late to benefit by the custom ; ' however ', she adds, ' I did only pay for 3 tankards of ale and wt I Eate, and my servants was gratis '. The custom had once been general in Yorkshire but was dying out, despite the cheapness and plenty in the North—and the high price of ale—compared to the prices ruling in the South.

In the reign of Charles I prices in the northern half of the kingdom were said to be a third of those current in the South. In that of William III, ' a five Shilling Ordinary [1] in many places of *England* ', it was declared, ' would hardly produce what Sixpence or to be sure Twelvepence would here '—Yorkshire. Lady Elmes (a Verney by birth) and a party of friends, who fled in 1665 from the plague-stricken capital to Knaresborough, paid no more than ten shillings a week each ' in pention ' for themselves and seven shillings a week for each servant, ' with lodgens in '. It must be owned the accommodation left much to be desired, but of this more anon.

According to Harrison there were no worse inns to be found than those in London, and probably few dearer. Evidence of this is difficult to obtain, as diarists and others never gratify the reader's curiosity by giving the particulars needed for a just estimation of cost. A visit to London of eight weeks less than one day paid by Pildrem, steward to Lord Howard of Naworth, cost three pounds eighteen shillings and sixpence, or a trifle over nine shillings and sixpence a week. Nineteen years later Lady Verney found herself ' att very great charge ' when, coming from France in the hope of obtaining removal of sequestration from the Claydon estate, she tarried in London. Twelve shillings a week she paid for a chamber for herself and another for her maid ' twoe

[1] See Note F, pp. 325–6.

pare of staires high, fires, candles, washing, breakfast
and diet besides '. There appears to have been little
or no rise of prices for accommodation in London
after the Restoration. M. Sorbière, in 1663, found
that fair lodgings could be obtained in the neighbourhood of the New Exchange and Whitehall for a crown
a week. Cresset, in reckoning the average cost of
a visit to London from York, Chester, or Exeter,
allowed a like sum or six shillings a week for house-
room. The inn charges at Newmarket were very
extortionate where as much as a guinea a night was
exacted—doubtless when the Court was in residence.[1]
The busy riverside port of Gravesend also gained
notoriety by the rapacity of its innkeepers. Some
foreign diplomats were charged ten shillings per head
for each meal in the year 1617, at a time when the
value of money was still relatively high.

The crowding of inns for race meetings, fairs, and
other events was as great then as now, having regard
to the size of the population and the number of
dwelling-houses. Moreover, guests tolerated accommodation that neither the most hard-pressed nor the
most inconsiderate of hotel-keepers of to-day would
dare offer to clients. The Very Rev. Rowland Davies,
who, as Chaplain to an Orange Regiment under orders
for Ireland, was proceeding thither in the company of
his own brother and of the Earl of Orrery in the spring
of 1690—the fateful year of the Battle of the Boyne—
found, on arrival at Chester, the inns so full that
' had not the earl got a billet from his colonel at the
Golden Lion, we must have stayed in the street '.
There they obtained very ill stable accommodation
for their horses and ' a dog-hole of a lodging ten times
worse ' for themselves. He and his brother lay in

---

[1] ' I intend ', writes Sir Charles Littleton in 1682, ' to goe to Cambridg,
and the next day to Newmarket, and come away the same night, because
I despaire of lodging.' See *Hatton Corr.*, Camden Soc., N.S. xxiii, p. 15.

a bed not five feet long nor four broad, placed under
a pair of stairs in such a position that they could not
both at once get near it ; one being forced to stay in
the Earl's room while the other went to bed. Lady
Elmes, though relieved of the dangers and unpleasant
sights and sounds of London in plague time, was none
too happily situated at Knaresborough. ' . . . the
horrid sulfer watter ', which was ' as bad as is posable
to be imajined ', she found pleasant ' to all the doings
we have within doores, the house and all that is in
it being horidly nasty and crowded up with all sorte
of company, which we Eate with in a roome as the
spiders are redy to drope into my mouthe, and sure
hathe nethor been well cleaned nor ared this doseven
yerese, it makes me much moare sicke then the nasty
water. Did you but see me,' she continues to her
brother, Sir Ralph, ' you wolde laughe hartily att me
but I say little of it to whot I thinke. Then to mend
all this, the[y] goe to supper att halfe an ower after
six, soe I save a bitt and supp bye myselfe 2 owers
after them, which is the plesantest thinge I doe
heare '. She was as unfortunate in her habitat
at Astrop Wells, a watering-place in Northamptonshire frequented by seventeenth-century health-
seekers. ' . . . instead of the sweet woodbines and
jesamine att Claydon,' her old home, she writes, ' I
have the stincke of sower whay & cheese, which is
so strong in my chamber I know not whot to doe . . .
not a coale of fyer can I get to burne one smale bitt
of perfewme, fast I must the night, heare not being
athor [either] master or maide att home, candle there
is not a bit, soe I have sent to borrow one '. Thoresby,
the antiquary, had to share a bedroom with two and
three other persons on several occasions. This caused
him some chagrin on account of want of privacy for
saying his prayers. Happily, the seventeenth-century
traveller was neither squeamish about want of cleanli-

INTERIORS OF INNS. From the Roxburghe Ballads

ness, nor, as a rule, a stickler for privacy.[1]   The accommodation offered to guests in private houses was no whit better.   When Pepys and his wife visited Sir George Carteret at the Royal Lodge in Windsor Park, they were given a passage-room where they 'slept not very well because of noise'.   At Lady Wright's seat, Dagenham Park, Essex, the diarist, on one occasion, slept with the Chaplain, and on another with Mr. Brisband, a 'good scholar and sober man' who entertained him with an account of Rome, 'which', writes Pepys, 'is the most delightful talk a man can have of any traveller'.

It was not only races, fairs, the propinquity of war, or dread of contagion that brought business to a locality.   An election or the Assizes would throng with a motley crowd the town where such an event was in progress, for both were regarded by the society of the neighbourhood, gentle and simple alike, as occasions for convivial intercourse.   Sir Thomas Browne, writing of the polling-day at Norwich of May 1679, hazarded the opinion that there were five or six thousand horses in the town, besides a great number of coach-horses.   There was, he adds, a strange consumption of beer, bread, and cakes.   Abundance of people slept in the market-place, 'and laye like

---

[1] How lacking were our ancestors not only in the amenities we at present enjoy, but in the measures of cleanliness that we deem necessary in the interests of public health, the following extract from the *Autobiography* of Sir Simmonds D'Ewes makes clear. 'In our passage to London', he writes of his childhood's days, 'we lay at Blandford, at the sign of the Red Lion, where shortly after we had alighted, I desiring to walk into the gardens, took with me one of my grandfather's clerks, named Thomas Tibbs. We first passed through the stable-yard, where I seeing divers fowls picking upon the dungill, like a true child, ran presently towards them to have catched them ; but the place where they stood, being a shiny puddle and only covered over with some dry litter, not long before thrown out, I sunk into it suddenly above my knees, and was very seasonably rescued and pulled forth by the said clerk that came with me, who thereby slipped in deeper himself. Being come into the house we were assured from all hands, that if I had passed on but one foot further I had been swallowed up in a deep pit, digged there on purpose to receive the stable-dung. . . .'

flocks of sheeps in and about the crosse '. The chance traveller who arrived in the midst of such proceedings —Mrs. Fiennes had a gift for striking towns in Assize week or at polling time—found himself at best provided with the worst lodging at the highest rates, and with small prospect of sleep. Had his nag any go left in it, he did well to escape the tumult and ride five or ten miles farther, though no more than ale-house accommodation offered itself there.

The hostelries of a market town were never places of quietude, for the giving of food and shelter to the wayfarer was but a part of their multiple calling. Should the country gentlemen wish to frame a petition for presentation to King or Commons, choose a Parliament man, or partake of a feast, it was to the inn they resorted. Was a meeting of the Justices convened, it was at the ' Mitre ', the ' Crown ', or the ' George ' they assembled. There, the young and convivial gathered to play shovel-board and less reputable games of chance ; the quack to vend his nostrums, and the pedlar to chaffer his wares, showing now a wonderful spit worked ' without Jacks, Lines, Weights, Strings, or Pullies ', and now ' a new invented bridle with screws '. There, too, the bone-setter came weekly on market days to set limbs broken in riding accidents or by other misadventure ; and the showman to display for a fee of sixpence each his seven-and-a-half-foot giant, his monster woman, or his ' groaning elme '. It was the head-quarters of the Recruiter who came to decoy the young and innocent into taking the King's shilling, and the haunt of spies sent by Government to learn the disposition of the country or the intricacies of a plot. To the inn-yard drove his lordship and his lordship's family in three or four coaches with a train of twenty or thirty retainers. Thither were brought prisoners on their way to assize town or distant gaol : delinquent Lords

in their own coaches with a stout guard of soldiery,
and, may be, with the Tower gaoler, gentleman-porter,
and warders in attendance ; Quakers, Jesuits, Popish
Recusants, Regicides, Jacobites, a-horseback, in public
coach [1] or waggon, some treated with the consideration
due to their position or with respect for their opinions,
others shackled and in ragged garments, or like the
mere common malefactor—who might also be brought
thither—with their feet tied below the horse's belly.
In fact, the inn was a public house in a more true and
comprehensive sense than that which holds to-day.
Folks came and went at will, to stare at a famous—or
infamous—prisoner or listen to the examination of
a suspect. They would crowd the inn-yard to hear
Fox or one of his disciples speak ; magistrates,
soldiers, townsfolks—believers and scoffers—asked
or unasked, would invade his room, smoking and
drinking, sometimes at Fox's expense—when, as like
as not, high words would be raised. Indeed, given
the drunken habits of the day and the lack of self-
control evinced on all sides, the inn can have been no
place for the traveller craving peace and quiet. Did
a troop of soldiers come to billet at an inn, the ears of
visitors would be assailed by the din of their coarse
oaths and coarser talk. On occasions they would be
deprived of their very beds for the greater comfort
of the officers—such at least was the case during the

---

[1] Edward Parker, whose uncomfortable ride in the boot of a coach has
already been noted, travelled some part of the way on that occasion with
Colonel Hutchinson, the Regicide, who had been taken, as he tells us, 'in
this last Plott', and was being carried to London. *Archaeologia*, No. 20,
p. 443. From Mrs. Hutchinson's *Memoir* it would seem that, for at least
part of the way, the Colonel travelled either in his own coach or in one
privately hired. His experiences at the ' Talbot ' in Newark, whither he
had been taken from his home at Owthorpe before proceeding to London,
had been in no wise pleasant. He had been put into ' a most vile room ',
deemed unfit for the Duke of Buckingham's footmen, and had received such
insolent treatment from Tomson, the host—who had already shown his
enmity by leading a party to Owthorpe to search for arms—that he had
' snatched up a candle and laid him [Tomson] over the chaps with it '. This
outburst brought him temporary relief by removal to another inn.

Civil Wars. Even the Justices, when they came to town for Quarter Sessions, could not ensure good order at their hostelry. At Wells in 1633–4 there were brought before the outraged magistracy five delinquents, Thos. Merefeild, Thos. Gappy, Richard Loake, William Wilson, and William Bull. They were charged that they

'did sitt upp all or the greatest parte of the night, Disorderly Drinkinge, quarrellinge and hoopinge, to the greate Disturbance to some of the Justices of the peace and others then Lodginge in the same Inn, and that some of the said Justices beinge soe Disturbed were enforced to rise out of their bedds, Doubtinge least there might have bynn some murder Comitted amongest them, and came unto the said parties requiringe them to leave of their Disorders, and to betake themselves to their bedds, who were by the said Companie affronted with very contemptious and uncivill speeches.'

What became of the disorderly five does not appear, but two, at least, attempted to exonerate themselves by giving information of the 'uncivill speeches' of their companions ; and the Court, 'in regarde of the example and frequent number of offences in this kinde thought fitt to comend the Consideracoñ thereof unto his ma^{ts} Attorney Generall' for him to take some course against the delinquents. And this was at a time before the hand of authority was enfeebled by Civil War.

More serious in its result was the brawl at Matlock's, or Maddox's, posting inn at Doncaster in January 1681. The Earl of Eglinton, three Justices of the Peace, and some others being there one night drinking and gaming at cards :

'. . . about 3 a clock that wild Lord having lost, and they reckoning their losings, Matlock sd my Lord I hope you remember 3li I won of you at such a cock-fight, the Lord denyed, he affirmed, it came to provoking language, at last Earl Eglinton drew his rapier, made a passe at Matlock, run him thro the thigh, not content with that he runs him quite through the belly, none of the company offering to hinder only Justice Blithman at last stept to him, pluckt his sword from him, but the man dyed by ten a clock that day, and the Ld is sent prisoner to York . . . he gave 100*li* to have yrons kept off.'

That the quiet and respectable traveller was often glad to avail himself of private lodgings must now be apparent. The Rev. Henry Newcome congratulated himself when he arrived at Scarborough with his wife and friends and found that the innkeeper, Mr. Saunders (to whom he carried a letter of recommendation !) was obliged, owing to lack of accommodation, to place them at the house of a merchant. They had ' two neat rooms ', a landlady who was ' mighty respective ' to them, and an ordinary by themselves at eightpence a meal, which saved them fourpence a day and freed them from ' mixed company '. On their visit to Scarborough the following year they were still more fortunate. Riding towards their destination they overtook and entered into conversation with a Mrs. Dickinson who had been staying in London since Christmas, and that very day was going home with a little lad before her. Just before reaching the town she invited them to take up their quarters at her house, merely for ' company sake '. They did not accept, for they had been civilly used by Mr. Saunders the year before. Moreover, Mrs. Newcome feared infection, it being July of London's great plague year, and the lady newly come thence. The inn, however, proved to be crowded to its utmost capacity. So, upon Mr. Saunders agreeing to stable their horses, and the Doctor having assuaged Mrs. New-come's fear, they ' reassumed ' Mrs. Dickinson's offer and went to her house, where they had two excellent rooms and lived by themselves for a third part of what it would have cost them at the inn.

To give shelter to benighted strangers was a prime law of hospitality. In Scotland, where inns were few and far between, it was customary for travellers to go from one nobleman's house to another, little pleasing though these were to Southern refinement ; at least so says Mrs. Fiennes. Venturing across the Border she was so appalled at the lodging offered her by the wayside, and so fearful that she would not get a bed to lie in between Eskdale and Edinburgh, that she promptly retraced her steps homewards. On one or two occasions when faced with the prospect of poor alehouse accommodation or none at all, she found shelter with kindly farmer or Quaker folk. At ' Nether Sugar ' (Lower Shuckburgh ?) near Warwick, ' a sad village ' where she could find no lodging, Sir Charles ' Shuggberys ' (Shuckburgh ?) seeing their distress, ' being just night and the horses weary wth the heavy way ', took compassion on her and her party and treated them handsomely, giving them a good supper, served on plate, and very good wine and beds. He had learnt of their distress from his wife, who had happened to meet them on the road while they were looking for accommodation and of whom they had made inquiries.

John Taylor, the Water-Poet, was full of wrath when he was denied hospitality by servants at a house in South Wales, though he had no other introduction than that of a servant who had guided him thence from the house where he had slept the previous night. Nor would he have had any prospect of a night's lodging, had he not chanced to be overtaken by a fellow-traveller who offered him entertainment. Certainly the wide heath beneath and the wider firmament above, which had so nearly been his night's lodging, seem to twentieth-century thinking a fair resting-place on an August night, far better than some of the habitations in which, during the course of his adven-

turous travels, he sought refuge ; such as the weaver's
cottage at Hastings which had

> No meat, no drinke, no lodging (but the floor),
> No stoole to sit, no Locke unto the doore,
> No straw to make us litter in the night,
> Nor any candlesticke to hold the light ;

or the alehouse at ' Neatherstoy ' (Nether Stowey,
Somersetshire) whose reception and entertainment of
Taylor shall be presently narrated. Even the empty
fisherman's cottage at Dungeness with its cable and
ropes for bedding seems cheerless in comparison to
a heather couch beneath the stars.

Mrs. Fiennes who, considering her station in life
and her sex, was as bold and enterprising as the
Water-Poet, had on one or two occasions to endure
conditions which were almost as bad. At Hart-
whistle in Northumberland, though there was an inn,
they had no hay for fodder and would get her none,
and when her servant went to procure some, they
became angry and refused her lodging. She was
therefore ' forced to take up in a poor Cottage wch was
open to the Thatch and no partitions but hurdles
plaistered. Indeed ', she continues, ' the Loft as they
Called it wch was over the other roomes was shelter'd
but wth a hurdle . . . the Landlady brought me out
her best sheetes wch serv'd to secure my own sheetes
from her dirty blanckets, and Indeed I had her fine
sheets to spread over the top of the Clothes : but noe
sleepe Could I get, they burning turff and their
Chimneys are sort of fflews or open tunnills that the
smoake does annoy the roomes ', The houses thereabouts, she adds, are but little better than those of
Scotland (of which she had had a dismal experience)
and but little better kept.

Alehouse accommodation was in many places almost
as primitive and unsavoury as the homes of the poor.
Their discomforts and inconveniences were usually

taken in good part by travellers, and were regarded
more as occasions for jest than for censure. Pepys
and his little party, stranded at an alehouse on Salisbury
Plain, ' made merry ' when, rising in the morning,
they found that their beds were lousy. Nor had he
any qualms or compunction in turning a poor pedlar
out of bed, so that he and his wife and their two girls,
Betty Turner and Deb. Willet, could have a night's
rest, the two girls sharing a truckle bed in the Pepys'
room. Moreover, the host was ' a sober, understanding
man ' who could talk to his sociable guest ' about this
country's matters, as wool, corne, and other things ',
and make merry at supper with Bristol gossip about the
manning of a new ship ' with none but men whose
wives do master them '.

Fortunately for the Pepys' household they did not
have to take up their quarters at what had been the
' Rose and Crown ' at Nether Stowey, to which Taylor
' extreme weary ' came one summer's day of 1649—
the year of Regicide. There he found the hostess
out of town, mine host sufficiently drunk, the walls
and ceilings adorned with ' rare Spiders Tapestry ',
and the smoke so palpable that he could scarce see
anything else. Mine host ' swing'd off ' half a pot
to him, bidding him be merry, and asked if he would
like any powdered beef and carrots for supper. Taylor
answered, with all his heart ; then, being weary of
the house, went and sat three hours in the street
where the host often visited him. At last seven o'clock
struck, and Taylor returned indoors to see if supper
was ready, his ' hungry selfe halfe starv'd with expectation '. He found the fire out, no beef boiled, mine
host fast asleep, and the maid attending to the hogs.
Awakening the master, he asked him where the beef
was, but got no other answer than that he desired him
to be content with eggs fried with parsley. Taylor
then asked to be shown to his room, which he found

'sutable to the rest of the house'. There he stayed until nine o'clock expecting supper, when the host came and told him that there were no eggs to be had. So, purchasing a piece of bread and butter, he went to bed. But it was only to receive torments from 'an Ethiopian Army of Fleas'. The exact account of the appearance of his enemies and his methods of execution are best left to the publications in which his experiences have appeared. At last weariness and watching began to enforce sleep upon him, so that in spite of the fleas' 'teeth' he began 'to winke'. Then three children began to cry, and for an hour's space he was kept awake—and occupied. The children being hushed asleep, the game began among the dogs, and the dogs had no sooner done bawling than day-break appeared, and the hogs began to cry for their breakfast. He therefore arose, and, 'almost sleeping', continued his travels.

The standard of comfort—discomfort perhaps would be the better word—at the 'Rose and Crown' was certainly not equal to that of Walton's 'honest ale-house' with its 'cleanly room, lavender in the windows, and twenty ballads stuck about the wall', its two beds with white linen sheets smelling of lavender, and its handsome, civil hostess.

There were many alehouses and inns which, apart from motives of comfort, it was advisable for the honest traveller to avoid. Allusion has already been made to the way in which the ostler would 'deceive the beast oftentimes of his allowance'. But this petty form of theft did not always satisfy his cupidity. He sometimes entered into league with those gentle-men of the highway who plied their nefarious trade in his district. Moreover the chamberlain (the modern 'boots' or chambermaid), and in some cases the host himself, acted as most useful intelligence officers to the fraternity.

'Certes', exclaims Harrison, 'I beleeve not that chapman or traveller in England is robbed by the waie without the knowledge of some of them : for when he commeth into the inne, & alighteth from his horsse, the hostler forthwith is verie busie to take down his budget or capcase in the yard from his sadle bow, which he peiseth slilie in his hand to feele the weight thereof : or if he misse of this pitch, when the ghest hath taken up his chamber, the chamberleine that looketh to the making of the beds, will be sure to remoue it from the place where the owner hath set it, as if it were to set it more convenientlie some where else, whereby he getteth an inkling whether it be monie or other short wares, & therof giveth warning to such od ghests as hant [haunt] the house and are of his confederacie, to the utter undoing of manie an honest yeoman as he journeth by the waie. The tapster in like sort for his part dooth mark his behaviour, and what plentie of monie he draweth when he paieth the shot, to the like end : so that it shall be an hard matter to escape all their subtile practises. Some thinke it a gay matter', he adds, ' to commit their budgets at their comming to the goodman of the house : but thereby they oft bewraie themselves. For albeit monie be safe for the time that it is in his hands (for you shall not heare that a man is robbed in his inne) yet after their departure the host can make no warrantise of the same, sith his protection extendeth no further than the gate of his owne house : and there cannot be a surer token unto such as prie and watch for those booties, than to see anie ghest deliver his capcase in such maner.'

Clavel, a repentant highwayman, in his *Recantation of an ill ledde Life*, tells us that not only were chamberlains tempted to forswear the paths of virtue by large bribes, but were often placed by their thievish employers in situations for the express purpose of obtaining information. Innkeepers themselves were as much tempted as their servants to turn accomplice, for, as Clavel explains, the highwayman ' spends full thrice as much in wine & beare ' as peaceable and sober guests. This was especially liable to happen with the smaller houses of entertainment. Some acquired unsavoury reputations, such as the ' Unicorn ' at Bruton and Dollinge's house at Shepton Mallet, both in

Somersetshire. The latter according to the constable, who reported five highway robberies in the neighbourhood in the space of eight days, was a place of weekly resort of ' many lewd and suspicious persons ', some of whom were taken and executed, presumably for their share in the robberies. Some houses appear to have been designed for the express purpose of defying law and order. The ' Lepords Head ' at Ware had a ' privye place ' for hiding stolen goods and suspicious (suspected) persons. The landlady boasted, if our informant speaks truly, that, at the press, she had hidden five men from the constables, and that she could convey men ' from chamber to chamber into the back-side '. ' There is not ', declares the informer— who had been in league with the lady—' such a house for the purpose within a hundred miles.'

Harrison's assertion that travellers at inns were immune from theft clearly overstates the case. In the first place the most upright of hosts could not guarantee the respectability of his guests. As an instance we may cite the misfortune of Anne Harrison, the Chester carrier, who tarrying the week-end at the ' White Lyon ' Inn, ' London Cony ' (Colney) in Hertfordshire, in compliance with the law forbidding Sunday travel, had a pack broken open and several things stolen. Suspicion fell upon Thomas Bradley, who, having accompanied her for some miles on the road thither, and likewise spent the week end at the ' White Lyon ', had risen at four o'clock on the Monday morning and departed, without paying for his diet and lodging ; a suspicious circumstance that was certainly enough to cause his condemnation, though he protested that he had not been guilty of the theft, and had only left without payment because he had no money to discharge the debt. Secondly, there were innkeepers whose cupidity had no limit. In 1659–60 Hugh Davy, a servant, while staying at the ' White Hart ' at North

Curry in Somersetshire, was led to drink to such excess that he stayed two nights instead of one, as he should have done. He then found that his money, amounting to about fifty shillings, had been taken out of his purse. On complaining to the landlord, Robert Saxton, he was advised by that artful gentleman to tell his master that he had been robbed in the forest of 'Ratch' (Neroche) ; 'but', the statement continues, 'he believes that either Robert or John Saxton do know of the taking away of his money'. Alexander Johnson in his *Lives of the Highwaymen* describes how some highwaymen and the landlord of a solitary inn conspired to rob a benighted traveller who came thither for lodging. First one of the highwaymen pretended to be an old acquaintance with the stranger. Then they all insisted on him supping with them, and when question of payment arose, they tossed for it in such a fashion that their intended victim had to pay— the goodly sum of three pounds. The traveller had by this time begun to suspect the quality of the house, and, on going to bed, barricaded his door with all the movable furniture of the room. His precaution was in vain. The thieves, entering by a secret door carried off his money and his clothes and left him bound, only to return a few minutes later in the company of the landlord and bewail his misfortune, saying that *They would find out the Rogues, if they went to a Conjuror.* Although the victim felt convinced that they were his despoilers, he thought it prudent, for fear of his life, to pretend to believe them. The next morning he was under the necessity of borrowing some old clothes of the landlord and returning home, having no money to prosecute his journey any further. Johnson's tales are not all credible, but this may well have happened in some remote and dishonest house.

Equally without substantiation but equally credible is the story, told in *The English Rogue*, of another

dishonest host ; but one who practised a more gentle
method of thievery.   The household consisted of
landlord, landlady, son, daughter, chamberlain, tapster,
hostler, cook-maid, scullion, and two or three boys,
' all alike, knavish enough '.

' My Landlord ', says the supposed narrator of the history,
Mistress Dorothy, ' . . . although he commonly had the best
Custom of any house in the town, yet he would practice wayes
to gain, and bring in more ; among other wayes, he used this
for one. He would take his Horse in an Afternoon, and ride
out some ten or twelve miles, and so return home again ; but
he seldome came home, but he brought Guests with him,
which he would take up by the way, thus.
' If he saw a parcel of Travellers, who he thought to be
good fellowes, and fit for his purpose he would then enquire
which way, and how far they travelled ; to this they commonly
answered, directly ; and if they were for our Town, then he
would joyn with them ; and soon after, his second question
would be, to know if they were acquainted at the Town, and
at what Inn they would take up their Quarters ; If they were
strangèrs, and by that means indifferent of the place where
they should lodge ; then he told them, that the best Inn in the
Town was his House, but not naming it to be his, or that he
had any Interest in it, but only that he knew there was a good
Hostess, who had a handsome Daughter that would use them
well ; and he seldom missed with this Bait to win them to
agree to go thither with him, and accordingly to bring them
home with him. But if they would not agree upon the place,
and he saw there was no good to be done, then he would pretend
some excuse to stay behind them, and would wait for such
company as would at all points be for his turn ; and with them
would he enter the House as a Stranger : indeed he would
call the Chamberlain, Hostler, and Tapster, by their Names ;
but they, who knew their Duties, would in no case shew any
Duty to him. Then would he, as being acquainted in the
House, tell his Fellow Travellers what provisions there was
for Supper, and would be sure to draw them up to the highest
Bill of Fare he could. If the Hostess, or her Daughters company were desired, he would be the forwardest to call them, and
only treat and converse with them, as of some small acquaintance ; after supper, he would endeavour to draw on the

Company to drink high, and use all possible means to enflame the reckoning; and when he saw they were well heated with wine, and the fury of their expences was over, he would pretend, out of good Husbandry, to call for a Reckoning before they went to bed, that they might not be mis-reckoned, or staid from the pursuit of their Journey in the Morning : to this they would commonly agree, and the Sum total of the reckoning being cast up, he would be the first man that would, without scruple, or inquiry into the particulars, lay down his share, and by his examples, the rest would follow ; if any did question the dearness of the Victuals or the quantity of the drink, he would by one means or other take them off, protesting that the Hostess was too honest to mis-reckon them, and that he had kept a just account himself, and was well satisfied ; or else he should be as cautious from parting from his money as any of them ; and then they, not distrusting him further, would by his example pay the shot. Thus would he many times, by his Crown or six shillings share, mis-reckon on them sixteen or twenty shillings ; especially if they came to high drinking : and then the reckoning being paid, they went to bed, he retiring with his wife, and he would lye abed in the morning, and let them march off alone ; but if they, in the Morning, did fall to drinking again, taking a hair of the Old Dog, then would he up, and at them again, make one at that sport, and many times put them out of capacity to Travel that day, and so keep them there to his profit, and their expences ; he shifting his Liquor, and in the end, shifting himself out of their Companies, when he had seen his Conveniency, leaveing them to pay roundly for their folly. If they enquired after him, my Hostess would pretend he was a Chance Guest, as they were, only, she had seen him the last year, or such like ; and thus he would force a Trade, and enjoy his pleasure and profit, by joyning them together ; and this course did he frequently use when Guests came not in of their own accord ; so that our house was seldome empty.'

Sometimes the dishonest innkeepers, rapacious for still larger profits, or hankering after excitement, took to the road. The famous ' Captain ' James Whitney is said to have been persuaded by one of his highwaymen guests to leave the small inn which he owned at Cheshunt, and prey upon those whom he had hitherto served. Bracy, captain of a gang which operated in the Midlands, combined both trades. Betrayed by one of his own servants, he was entrapped in his own house, while visiting his wife who lay there dying. He met his doom, as, attempting to escape, he endeavoured to make his horse clear the fence which bounded his premises at the back.

VI

HIGHWAYMEN

'THEEVES in England are more common then in any other place, so farre as I have observed or heard,' says Fynes Morison, the traveller; 'but', he continues, 'having taken purses by the high way, they seldome or never kill those they rob.'

Of their reluctance to do murder we shall speak later. Of their numbers, the cause may be sought in the rapid expansion of trade and commerce in the sixteenth and seventeenth centuries, coincident in the former period with a vast increase in the vagrant population, a result of social and economic changes. The evil legacy of vagrancy was, indeed, so great that, although the laws initiated under Elizabeth may and probably did reduce, to some extent, the numbers of workless nomads, it was beyond the organized resources of the State to do more than mitigate the pest. To this aspect of seventeenth-century life we shall revert in a later chapter.

The methods employed for the suppression of highway robberies were little, if at all more effective. Reliance was placed, as was necessary where no police force existed, on a sense of civic duty which was, in the main, beyond the scope of the seventeenth-century intellect. The chief burden lay on the hundred within whose limits the robbery had been committed, the inhabitants being bound, on the raising of hue and cry by him who had been robbed, to bring the thief to justice, or on failure to do so, to reimburse the victim to the extent of half his loss. The limiting of responsibility to half-losses had been effected by

Ego, non sum Ego.

GENEROSI ÆTATIS Suæ 25. VERA ET VIUA EFFIGIES IOHANIS CLAUEL

That I may neither beare anothers blame
Through wronge suspicions nor yet act Yᵉ same
At any time hereafter, but prove true
Loe to be knowne yow haue my face at viewe
Rich Meighen Excud: in Cœmiter: Stⁱ Dunstan: An: 1628

JOHN CLAVEL THE HIGHWAYMAN

a statute of Elizabeth,[1] as a result, so it was stated, of the more frequent putting into execution of the law, the consequent inability of the hundreds to meet their liabilities, and the negligence of parties robbed in prosecuting their aggressors while they had remedy at law to recover damages without indictment. It had further been enacted, to stimulate the pursuit and capture of highwaymen, that other hundreds called upon to follow the hue and cry were to be equally liable for half the loss sustained, if it were shown that they had neglected pursuit.[2]

It is no wonder that the highwayman, mounted on a swift horse, and knowing the lie of the country, with an ill-directed, ill-disciplined, and perhaps half-hearted rabble to pursue him, should frequently escape the hands of justice. Moreover, the traveller with a tender regard for the gentlemen of the road, and, probably a due appreciation of their power, often refrained from raising hue and cry, having no liking for putting the noose round the neck of a fellow-creature ; highway robbery, like other felonies, was a hanging matter. ' . . . if doctor [Denton] dos intend to dou anything with the country [i.e. sue the county],' writes Lady Hobart, ' he shold have conseled the men though he knew them, for they will surely hang them.'

If England was indeed more subject to highway law than other countries, at least marauding, during the first half of the century, was not on a scale to force further legislative action. Towards the end of the year 1623 and again in 1625 highway robberies were indeed sufficiently numerous near London to cause concern to the authorities charged with the keeping of law and order. On the first occasion Secretary

---

[1] 27 Eliz. c. 13 (1584–5). By the Statute of Winchester, 13 Edw. I (1285) the duty of full restitution had been imposed upon defaulting hundreds.

[2] Under Charles I Devonshire Quarter Sessions sent persons to prison for refusing to go with the hue and cry.

Conway wrote, on the instructions of the King, to the Lord President of the Council desiring that body to consider the best means of repressing the evil, and reviving the laws, suggesting that strict watches should be kept in and about London, that vagrants should be restrained and punished, and that the Lord Mayor, Aldermen, and Recorder should be consulted. Two years later the Lords of the Council wrote to the local authorities for London, Middlesex, and Surrey directing them to search all suspected hostelries, to stay all horses of doubtful ownership, and to bind over all suspicious characters—measures that do not seem to imply any great menace to authority. It was rather the lawlessness engendered by Civil War, and the lack of employment consequent on its cessation, that first brought to the fraternity an access of numbers sufficient to disturb the equanimity of Government. In May 1647 the Sheriff of Oxfordshire certified ' That many troopers, Irish and others, who had been in Arms against the Parliament, robbed all passengers, and that he had raised the Posse Comitatus, and apprehended about one hundred of them '. If any improvement followed it was but temporary. In September 1649 General Fairfax issued a proclamation to Army Commanders urging them to apprehend all robbers, and promising high rewards for those captured. Within a week twenty of Captain Hind's band committed forty robberies near Barnet in the space of two hours. Possibly it was this outrage which moved Parliament, a few weeks later, to offer a reward of ten pounds to any one who caused the apprehension of a burglar, highwayman, or other robber, to be paid on conviction. Further, proclamation was made that all papists, delinquents, and suspicious persons were to be disarmed ; that the laws against vagrants were to be enforced ; and that informers who had been convicted of any of these offences might be reprieved.

Within the next three months twenty-eight male-factors, principally robbers, including Captain Rey-nolds of the late King's Cornish forces, were hanged together at Tyburn. Under various guises the reward held good for the next six years.

It may well be doubted, however, whether there was any real diminution of the evil, while discontent, flaming at times into armed resistance, overspread the land. In 1655 Cromwell, as well to check the pre-valent lawlessness as to destroy political opposition, tried the experiment of dividing England into twelve military districts, under the rule of Major-generals, with a militia force of over six thousand men at their command. But the régime was short-lived. In two years the new engine of Government was broken. Yet some good may have resulted therefrom. When three years later the monarchy was restored, stable Government assured, and the disbanded soldiery replaced in civilian occupations, the country became tolerably free, for some time, of the highway incubus.

In December 1668 a proclamation was issued for the apprehension of twenty-four highwaymen, belong-ing to one gang, whose names and aliases were specified. Direction was given at the same time to those who let horses near London, to deliver lists of the same to the Justices ; and those who lent horses to highwaymen were threatened with severe punish-ment. This was followed eleven months later by the offer of a double reward, that is twenty pounds, for the apprehension of four of the gang, who were still at large. In 1677 the Government, in an endeavour to enforce due observance of Sunday rest and to raise revenue, took away from the traveller his claim to reparation if his loss occurred on that day, and appro-priated the fine incurred by the errant hundred to its own uses. That this right had been for many years denied the traveller appears certain from the remarks

concerning Sunday travel made by Clavel, the highwayman, of which an account will be given later.
From this time forth proclamations offering the
customary reward of ten pounds appeared at recurring
intervals ; palliatives, doubtless, that diminished
activity for a season. The very fact that recourse was
had to this form of publicity demonstrates that security
was more than usually disturbed, for proclamations
were only issued on extreme provocation, as we learn
from an incident recorded in the Memoirs of Sir John
Reresby. When Sir John approached Charles II, and
asked him to issue a proclamation offering a reward
of twenty pounds for the apprehension of the redoubt-
able Nevison, who had broken gaol and was threatening
death to several Justices, the impecunious monarch
answered that a proclamation would cost him one
hundred pounds, but that he would order twenty
pounds to be paid by the sheriff of the county in which
Nevison was captured to him that took him, and that
the offer would be published in the *Gazette* ; which, as
Reresby remarks, was the same thing.

With the coming of the Revolution and the advent
to power of a monarch whose title was challenged by
a large section of the people, the evil developed like
a virulent epidemic. A study of Narcissus Luttrell's
day-book (*A Brief Historical Relation of State Affairs*)
unfolds the course of the disorder, and reveals a state
of lawlessness creditable neither to the Government
which permitted it nor to the nation which submitted
to it.

During the year 1690, the second of the new reign,
as many robberies were recorded as in the previous
eight years. By October the roads were infested with
robbers. A proclamation was issued the last day of
the month reciting the many murders, robberies, &c.,
which had occurred, the connivance of innkeepers and
others, and the negligence of the Watch. By February

of the following year the statement was made that,
during the winter, there had never been known, 'in
the memory of any man living', so many robberies
as had taken place in London and the adjacent parts,
of hats, periwigs, cloaks, and swords ; an indication
that the footpad, as well as his more dashing compeer,
was at work. For the rest of the year entries concerned
captures rather than exploits of highwaymen. In
1692 operations began in earnest, more than twenty-
four robberies occurring between May and November,
the booty including five hundred guineas from the
Earl of Marlborough, fifteen thousand pounds from
seven Western coaches (by twelve highwaymen), and
a like sum from the Manchester carrier. During the
year the fraternity lost twenty-seven highwayman and
suspects captured. In November so prevalent were
robberies that parties of horse were ordered to quarter
in towns situated on the great highways. In December
lawlessness reached such a height that Whitney, the
greatest highwayman of his day, was emboldened to
offer terms ; first, that he would keep the roads clear
for the sum of eight thousand pounds a year ; secondly
—in conference with two peers of the realm—that
he would bring thirty stout men and horses to the King's
service, on assurance of pardon. The offer was refused;
the King would grant no more pardons. Thereafter,
despite fewer travellers, robberies increased in alarming
fashion—there was 'noe travelling the roads' towards
the close of the year—and, though Whitney was
captured, and duly suffered the penalty for his crimes,
the contest waxed fiercer.

During 1693 thirty-nine robberies or attempted
robberies were recorded. In February a list of forty
highwaymen and their haunts, and in April a list of
double that number, including the names of several
women, were given to the Lord Chief Justice. The
number taken during the year amounted to forty-five

or forty-six highwaymen and suspects and twenty-four horses. The following summary of the entries in Luttrell's diary gives some idea of the character and extent of the depredations for this one year. Of course some of the instances set down may be mere gossip of doubtful veracity. On the other hand, it should be borne in mind that stray references, set down in a work such as this, record no more than a small percentage of the whole number of murders, assaults, and robberies which had been perpetrated. For instance no mention is made by Luttrell of the robbing by three men in vizard masks of Pepys, his nephew, his nephew's wife and other ladies as they were driving to Chelsea in the Pepysian coach on Michaelmas Day of this year, when Pepys was deprived of some three pounds in money, a silver ruler, a gold and silver purse, and a magnifying glass, although one of the ladies was enabled to save a bag of money thanks to the gallant Pepys who had conjured the men to be civil to the ladies and not affright them ; no wonder that the average highwayman was ruthless.

JANUARY.

Three coaches robbed of £200 on the Epsom road.
Five waggons on St. Albans road robbed.
Robbery of maltsters near Devizes.
Unsuccessful attack on a goldsmith near Acton, one highway man killed, one wounded.
Ten highwaymen rob and maltreat countrymen near Barnet.
Three highwaymen unsuccessfully attack three coaches on Gad's Hill.
Robberies between Highgate and Barnet.

FEBRUARY.

Two gentlemen set on by footpads in St. George's Fields, Southwark, robbed, stripped, and bound ; one said to have died of cold.

MARCH.

Postboy robbed and wounded between Penzance and Marazion.

APRIL.

'Mr. Penn of Bucks' robbed.

Gentlemen and servant attacked by four highwaymen near Devizes; one highwayman killed, two wounded.

A goldsmith and his companion set on near Stratford, Essex, by eight highwaymen; goldsmith killed while trying to escape; the other submitted himself to be robbed.

JUNE.

Worcester coach and two Oxford coaches robbed near Stokenchurch; two horses killed.

Unsuccessful attack on two gentlemen near Reading; one highwayman captured, two wounded.

Butcher robbed near Bagshot; three highwaymen taken as result.

JULY.

Robberies on Tunbridge road by six highwaymen.

Great robberies in Epping Forest; many horses killed.

SEPTEMBER.

Unsuccessful attack on Harwich postboy; one highwayman killed.

Six coaches and some waggons robbed on Finchley Common.

Gentleman robbed going to Greenwich.

Harwich Mail robbed for important letters.

OCTOBER.

Oxford coaches robbed by six highwaymen.

NOVEMBER.

Ship's Purser robbed on Hounslow Heath of six thousand pounds' worth of diamonds which he was bringing from Plymouth to London merchants. Hundred sued.

DECEMBER.

Nine persons robbed and killed by five highwaymen, and two pilots robbed between Gravesend and Rochester.

Robberies near Beaconsfield. Pursuit by Hue and Cry; the Captain (Reynolds) shot and taken.

A King's Messenger robbed returning from Kensington to London.

As a result of this last-mentioned attack the King ordered a nightly patrol.

The following years, 1694–5–6, showed a considerable decline in highwaymen's activities ; the slow but effective result, one concludes, of the increased reward of forty pounds offered by proclamation, September 1692, for information leading to the capture of a highwayman ; and also, probably, of the impressing of persons who could not account for their way of living (February 1695). Whatever the cause, travellers enjoyed comparative freedom from molestation—for these few years.

With the signing of the Peace of Ryswick in 1697, fresh hordes of lawless, devil-may-care men were let loose upon the peaceful countryside ; and there ensued a recrudescence of activity, not to be compared to the proceedings of a few years before, if we may judge by Luttrell's records, but none the less disturbing to the authorities who had to wage war on men who had been fighting the country's battles. Already, in October 1697, the Hertfordshire roads were so highly dangerous for persons to travel with any quantity or sum of money that the Chief Constable of Hertford gave order to the petty constables of the parish of St. Andrew's (and doubtless to others under his command), to provide six able-bodied men ' well armed with muscots, carbines or gunes ' for the protection of the hundred. Six months later the Lord Chief Justice sent out an expedition to break up a large gang of highwaymen, burglars, and cattle-stealers who were plundering the countryside from the shelter of Waltham Forest. Though the bandits were scattered for a while, it took another expedition, this time composed of dragoons, to suppress their forays on the Cambridge and Newmarket roads. The following year, day and night patrols of horse and foot-guards were placed upon the roads leading from London, the favourite haunt of the highwaymen. Guard-houses were erected in Hyde Park, to hinder the marauders from

Capt. Hind Robbing Col. Harrison in Maidenhead-Thicket.

using it as an eyrie whence to pounce upon likely prey travelling the ill-famed road to Kensington. As the further course of this epidemic lies beyond our sphere we will pass to a consideration of the public attitude that allowed such a state of lawlessness to endure.

To the myopic vision of the seventeenth century little or no moral obloquy attached to him who plied the trade of highwayman. As the ' Cashiered Soldier ' succinctly put it :

> To beg is base, as base as pick a purse ;
> To cheat, more base of all theft—that is worse.
> Nor beg nor cheat will I—I scorn the same,
> I'll purse it, I—the highway is my hope,
> His heart's not great that fears a little rope.

It was indeed this ' little rope ', dangling like the sword of Damocles above him, that brought to the highwayman not a little of the pity that might so well have been bestowed on some other of the unfortunates, generated by the harsh penal laws of the century. As sober John Verney expressed it : ' 'Tis great pity such men should be hanged.' Had not the public imagination quickened upon the romantic figure of the highwayman and his dashing exploits, it is certain that his misfortunes would not have called forth its sympathy. Yet how few must there have been of that traditional gallant breed celebrated in verse and prose, and how many the rough savage brutes whose crimes deface the pages of Quarter Sessions Records and other unvarnished documents ! But so it was ; human sympathy was aroused and kindly emotions stimulated by the almost certain fate which overtook those who lived upon their fellows. Thus, whenever a well-known and respected gentleman of the highway was to make his pilgrimage to Tyburn, the route thither would be thronged as for a royal procession. The hero of the hour, bravely clad, a nosegay at his breast, passed with good-humoured sallies and as

much dignity as gyves and a common cart or sledge
would allow, to the ill-omened tree where, with a laugh
and a jest, amid general regret and the tears of tender-
hearted women, he would make a speech of wit or
bombastic repentance, and so take leave of the world
he had flouted.[1]   On one occasion, so great were the
crowds upon the wall of St. Sepulchre's Churchyard
on the route of the procession, that it gave way, killing
one person and wounding several others.

Yet, unless the highwayman was singularly unfortunate, he had more than one chance of returning
to an honest way of life.   If he had influential friends
his chance of a reprieve once or twice was doubly
certain—though, to be sure, when robberies were
exceptionally frequent, it was difficult for any to escape
the gallows.   That it was possible to ply the trade
through a generation of proclamations the long career
of Rumbold testifies.   Even authority was tender to
the highwayman on occasions ; for its own purpose.
In 1626 Secretary Coke offered to the Lords of the
Council one Duckett, a condemned felon, and member
of a band who ' robbed up and down, eight or nine in
a company, with pistols, like Robin Hood and his
men ', deeming him suitable to be sent overseas for the
King of Denmark's army.   Whether Duckett was sent
does not appear, but the Lord Chief Justice sent a
strongly worded letter to the Lord Privy Seal warning
him of the evil effects of granting reprieves.   Such
recognition of the danger of condoning vice was
unusual.   Sir Ralph Verney, as upright a man as any in
the kingdom (he refused to subscribe to the Solemn
League and Covenant, and his estate was in consequence
sequestered), used the whole weight of his influence to
extricate his two highwaymen cousins from the consequences of their actions.   He gave them money
(to one he allowed twenty shillings a week after his

[1] See Note G, p. 326.

coming out of jail), he lent his wig as disguise, to assist in an escape (highwaymen were very devils at escaping), he obtained reprieves and pardons for them. Nor was he singular in his efforts to stay the course of justice. In like fashion his relative, Lady Hobart, used her powers of persuasion, when need arose, in the legal circles in which she moved. Nor did these good people show the slightest compunction in admitting their erring kinsmen to their homes. To Claydon came Dick Hals—in a cart with the cook-maid, it is true—and upon the invitation of Lady Hobart. Some time later, during a lapse into honest ways, he figured as an invited guest at the wedding of her granddaughter. Charles II, whose royal dignity indeed sat lightly upon him, gave audience to William Nevison, highwayman and hero of the hour after his famous ride to York [1] (falsely attributed by a later generation to Dick Turpin) ; granted him a pardon, and, with his characteristic knack of finding the happy word, dubbed him ' Swift Nicks ', a name by which he was ever after known, even to the extent of its figuring as an alias in Royal Proclamations for his apprehension.

To the Verneys it was a huge joke when Sir Ralph's

[1] His famous ride to York was the outcome of his being recognized by one whom he robbed at Gad's Hill at four o'clock in the morning. Knowing that nothing could save him, if once within the arm of the law, but the proving of an alibi, he immediately fled upon his blood bay to the North. Crossing the Thames at Tilbury, he passed through Chelmsford, where he baited his horse and gave him some balls, Braintree, Fenny Stanton and Huntingdon, where he again halted, and so down the North Road to York, two hundred and fifty miles from his starting-point. Arrived a little before eight p.m., he went straight to the bowling-green, and there engaged the Lord Mayor in talk. Thus, when arrested a short time afterwards, he was successful in disposing of one of the counts against him, the robbery at Gad's Hill, and was thereby enabled to obtain his acquittal. Proud of his achievement he could not for long keep a silent tongue, and soon the world was privileged to acclaim the hero and his deed. See Harper's *Half Hours with the Highwaymen*, vol. ii, an agreeable history of the lives, known and traditional, of the highwaymen of the seventeenth and eighteenth centuries. Smith (vol. 2, p. 5) gives the place of robbery as Barnet, the hour as five o'clock, and the arrival at York as six o'clock.

uncle, Dr. Denton, and his wife were robbed on the highway. One of his aunts vowed that the thief was Sir Ralph's younger brother, Harry, who was not ill-pleased with the imputation, though Lady Hobart was persuaded he would have liked the money better than the jest. The joke was carried still farther when another relative, invited to stay with Sir Ralph at Claydon, entreated his prospective host to shut his brother up ' for fear he meet with us as the Dr. was mett with '.

The Verneys were not singular in numbering highwaymen among their kinsfolk. The profession was well suited to gentlemen down on their luck who could shoot straight and ride like the wind. Younger sons who had lost all at cards or at horse-racing found this an easy method of supplying their wants, and many an empty purse was replenished on Newmarket Heath. So too did Cavaliers, and later, Jacobites, dispossessed of their livelihood. Indeed, it became fashionable in highwaymen circles to impute political motives to their deeds. An ostentatious display of loyalist sentiment elevated the profession to a higher plane. In June 1691 Walker, of the ' Golden Farmer '[1] gang, who was apprehended and carried before the Lord Chief Justice, declared that he did not own him for judge, King James being his lawful sovereign. In November of the following year ' 15 butchers going to Tame Market to buy cattle, were robbed by 9 highwaymen, who carried them over a hedge and made them drink King James' health in a bottle of brandy '—pleasant highwaymen these—' and bid them sue the country '. It by no means followed, however, that these demonstrative gentlemen had suffered, or were willing to suffer, for legitimist principles.

[1] The ' Golden Farmer ' was William Davis, who, as was afterwards discovered, combined the trade of honest farmer with that of highwayman.

Many, and among these some of the most skilful
exponents of the highwayman's art, had no right to
crest and coat of arms ; for the profession was re-
cruited from the shiftless, the naturally dishonest, and
the adventurous of all classes—clergymen, university
graduates, scholars, merchants, tradesmen, soldiers,
farmers, yeomen, labourers, and servants. In January
1691/2 ' Parson' Richard Smith, a lecturer for Chelsea,
was accused of robbing on the highway and of having
in his possession a gold watch which he had stolen on
Finchley Common ; charges which he denied. It
was said that he had already been condemned in the
country ; and furthermore, that he had persuaded
one of the witnesses against him to break open Chelsea
College (Hospital) and steal the plate. Both universities supplied recruits. Cambridge was the Alma
Mater of two well-known members of the fraternity,
Augustine King and William Cady, son of an eminent
Norfolk surgeon ; and though Oxford does not supply
any names to the roll of highway graduates, it had the
distinction of being a very nursery of crime, if, as it is
said, scholars were responsible for the robbery of the
Oxford coach in December 1692. As to the soldiery,
it was not only those who were disbanded and without
employment who caused trouble to the authorities.
The Dragoons, who were sent out to suppress robberies,
and the Guards, who did not at this epoch live in
barracks, included in their ranks men who added to
their pay by exertions on their own account. Among
others who took to the highway, mention may be made
of a barrister, a prizefighter, a waterman, butchers,
bricklayers, &c. Strangest of all, perhaps, is the
story of the butler and the footman, servants to a
gentleman at Eltham, who with truly marvellous
audacity took the opportunity, whenever their master
was away, to sally forth to Blackheath in search of
purses, until one day they were recognized by one of

their master's guests and promptly denounced for
what they were. Knighthood itself was not free from
the stigma of the gallows, if stigma it was. Twice was
Sir George Sandys indicted for robbery on the highway, once at Kensington and once at Wapping.
Acquitted on the first charge, he was, on the second
occasion, convicted and hanged, his lady and son being
at the same time committed to prison as accomplices.

Although the highwayman and his exploits might
be fit object for jest or admiration at home and in the
tavern, his potential activities on the road bred wari-
ness, not to say extreme caution, in the traveller, and
gave rise, in seasons of exceptional violence, to a sense
of disquietude and apprehension. To travel well-
armed was an ordinary precaution. Weapons gave
the traveller heart to set out on his journey, though
when the test came the sword might never be un-
sheathed and the pistol never cocked. Persons of
distinction were not infrequently granted escorts.
The Grand Duke Cosmo of Tuscany, who visited
England in 1668-9, was guarded between Dorchester
and Blandford by a troop of militia, to prevent any
untoward accident while he was crossing the Downs.
Some years later Sir John Reresby, Sheriff of York,
took the precaution of travelling from York to London
well guarded, for fear of some of his ' back friends and
highwaymen, having caused one of the chief of them
to be taken not long before '.

Humbler folk, who depended for their safety on
their own exertions, were glad to seek the company of
their fellow travellers. The Rev. Adam Martindale
delayed his return to the North, when on visit to London
in 1649 for ordination, ' for company to come safely
downe with, for there was great robbery by the way,
especially neare Dunstable '. Unhappily for him,
on his second day's journey, eight miles out from
St. Albans, his horse fell sick and was scarce able to

go a foot's pace, so that the company left him in the most dangerous part of the road. ' I was a little suspicious ', he wrote, ' of every one I saw follow me. . . . With much adoe, sometimes riding softly and sometimes going on foote, I got to Brick-hill about noone, where my horse being well cherished, became heartie, and carried me freely to Daintree [Daventry] that even.' The company deserved a drubbing from the highwaymen for leaving him in the lurch.

Such was the atmosphere of suspicion engendered by the activities of the highwaymen that to suspect or be suspected of predatory designs by fellow travellers was no rare occurrence. A great man (his name does not appear) overtaking Fox and his companions in Wales, and suspecting them to be highwaymen, would have had them taken up at the next town had not Fox been ' moved of the Lord ' to speak to him. So thoroughly impressed was the great man by Fox's earnestness and transparent honesty that he invited the party to enjoy his hospitality, and was ultimately won to the doctrine Fox expounded. Mrs. Celia Fiennes had similar fears, probably with better reason, when riding from Sandy Lane to Whitchurch :

' 2 fellows all on a suddain from the wood fell into the Road, they Look'd truss'd up wth great Coates and as it were bundles about them wch I believe was pistolls, but they dogg'd me one before the other behind and would often Look back to Each other, and frequently justle my horse out of the way to get between one of my servants horses and mine, and when they first Came up to us did disown their knowledge of the way and would often stay a little behind and talke together, then Come up againe, but the providence of God so order'd it as there was men at work in the fields hay making, and it being market day at WhitChurch, as I drew near to it in 3 or 4 mile was Continually met wth some of the market people, so they at Last Called Each other off and soe Left us and turned back ; but as they Rode with us 3 or 4 mile at Last they described the places we should Come by, . . . wch shew'd them noe strangers to the Road as they at first pretended.'

Sir George Wheler had a still more alarming experience when travelling from Oxford to London. Moreover, he carried a jewel of great price for his lady love, besides a gold watch, twenty guineas, and some silver, and was sensible of the great risk he ran, for his journey was known to several of his friends, and to his jeweller, Mr. Pargiter, ' who was called a Jew '.

' To conceal the Time of my Return ', he writes, ' I knew was scarce possible among so much acquaintance ; all that I could was to conceal the way I designed to Returne which I did, ffor I went downe the town as to goe by Beconsfield Road, but as soon as I was out of East Gate turned Nor'wards, and went to Sir Ralf Varney his house in Buckinghamshire, where I was kindly entertained all night. . . . The next day. . . . Staying after Diner too long, night overtook me before I could reach Alsbury. Within a mile or two of this town I came into a deep and narrow Lane, covered over with trees in the hedges, so close that I could see neither way before me, nor skie above me, nor anything about me. Having Pistols before me, I drew one and held it in my hand, So that I could Span it in a moment for ffear of a surprise. I was not, I suppose, above half way down this Lane but on a suddain two or three men cald out Stand ! Stand ! ! Stand ! ! ! ffearing them to be Robbers I Blustered also &c., til we came to a Parly, and I demanding what they would have, they told me they were the watch sent to Stop all Passengers, ffor that there had been Robberies committed that Day upon Uxbridge Common ; That every body had been Robbed that past that way from nine or ten in the morning til one or two in the afternoon, which was the time I should have bene there from Beconsfield had I gone that Road. So I desired these men to conduct me to the towne and shew me the best Inne and I would Reward them.'

How thankful travellers were when they safely passed noted robbing-places such as Maidenhead Thicket, Gad's Hill, Shooter's Hill, Finchley Common, Hounslow Heath, Watford Gap, Sherwood Forest, and Stone Gate or Stangate Hole on the North Road near Grantham, many devout phrases and ejaculations in diaries and autobiographies testify. Generally travellers took the prudent course of letting themselves

I. Nicholls delin.   I. Acton Sculp.

Iohn Cottington *alias Mul-Sack, Robbing* γ^e Oxford Waggon
Wherein he found four Thousand Pounds in Money.

be despoiled of their belongings, often without protest, as was indeed wise. Quakers, naturally, submitted without cavil, and were no doubt excellent game for the huntsmen of the road. Once however the Christian precept of turning the other cheek was of material as well as spiritual value, if we may believe the story given by Maria Webb in *The Fells of Swarthmoor Hall and their Friends*. Leonard Fell, having been deprived by a highwayman of his money and his horse, warned his assailant against the evil course he was pursuing. Upon the other threatening him, he declared that he would not give his life either for his money or his horse, but that he was willing to do so for his, the robber's, soul ; an answer which so touched the miscreant's heart that he instantly restored both money and horse. If Fell gained an adherent, the sect lost one when Jacob Halsey, a Quaker, it is said, turned highwayman and robbed travellers in the ' language of the Lambs ' though not in the dress ; probably because the plain Quaker garb was not a good disguise.

Sometimes, when the crucial moment arrived, coach passengers would endeavour—with what success may be imagined—to pursue the two opposite lines of conduct. Captain Alderman Briggs, Burgess for Norwich, was for resistance when the Norwich coach, in which he was travelling, was stopped between Barton Mills and Thetford. But his sword being taken from him, his man (prudently) disappearing, and none of the passengers joining with him—they had little to lose, ' passengers usually travelling with litle money '—he was constrained to see the coach robbed and the coachman despoiled of fifteen pounds which he carried for the purchase of a new horse.

Where resistance was put up and shooting started, it was usually the attacked, and not the attacker, who paid for his temerity ; but not always. It might be a bodyguard of servants accompanying my Lord's or my Lady's coach who, unusually full of fight, would make the attackers retire with scars of battle upon them. This happened when Hind and Allen attacked Cromwell, while he was travelling in his coach between Huntingdon and London, attended by seven servants. Hard riding enabled Hind to escape, but Allen was captured and suffered death for his audacity. Or, it might be, that the battle would be won by no more than a gentleman and his man fighting against odds. Upon the victors of such gallant and successful exploits the sentimental public showered impartially the same measure of applause that, had the issue ended differently, might well have been bestowed upon their opponents. Thoresby mentions on several occasions having passed safely, somewhere in the locality of Grantham, ' the great common, where Sir Ralph Wharton slew the highwayman ' ; evidently a deed long remembered by travellers, conscious of the hazards of the road. Richard Dawson (a connexion of the Verneys, and head of the Vauxhall glass-works) and his servant Kit were justly famous in their day for their practical and courageous endeavours to suppress robberies in their neighbourhood. Meeting cunning with cunning, they would drive out to Kennington Common—a favourite lair of the high-waymen—disguised, sometimes as old ladies, and, when attacked, would rush out at opposite doors, take their assailants in the rear, handcuff them, put them inside the coach, and then drive off in triumph. It is related that, though they had many fearful struggles, they were always victorious.

If we may judge from the accounts given us by Luttrell, Johnson, and Smith, the great ones of the earth were frequent sufferers at the hands of the fraternity. The Duchesses of Albemarle and Ports-mouth, the Duke of Monmouth, the Earls of Dorset, Marlborough, Oxford, Plymouth, and Rivers, Peter

Bradshaw and Harrison, the Regicides, the Archbishop of Canterbury, Nell Gwynn, and Judge
Jeffreys, were all called upon to stand and deliver—
how the highwayman must have enjoyed fleecing the
savage lawyer ! In June 1698 there appears to have
been quite an assemblage of rank and fashion on
Hounslow Heath when ' 3 highway men rob'd
between 30 and 40 persons one after another . . .
among whom were the duke of Northumberland,
lord Ossulton, sir William Clark, &c., and attempted
the duke of St. Albans, but he was too well attended ;
they took from them considerable summs in gold and
silver, watches, &c., but were extreamly civil to the
duke of Northumberland, and returned all they took
from him ' ; what was the reason for this unusual
generosity does not appear.

Clavel,[1] in his *Recantation of an ill ledde Life*, shows
the traveller, in rhymed verse, how he is to comport
himself to avoid being robbed. As it gives some
insight into the practices of highwaymen and into the
habits of travellers, a brief paraphrase seems pertinent
to our subject.

First, you must keep secret your intention of setting
out on a journey, and forgo asking your neighbours,
kinsmen, and friends to breakfast or sup with you
preparatory to your start ; though they drink healths
to your good return they may be plotting to have you
robbed. Thus has he known a father betray his own
son, a brother his brother, a friend ' Most deare in

---

[1] John Clavel, b. 1603, was a gentleman and heir-presumptive to his
uncle, Sir William Clavel, a Devonshire squire. In 1626 he was taken up
for being concerned in various robberies and brought before the King's
Bench, where he pleaded that he had never struck or wounded any man,
had never taken anything from their bodies, never cut girths or saddles, or
done any corporal violence. Condemned, he was reprieved and set free,
principally, it is said, through the instrumentality of Queen Henrietta
Maria. The *Recantation* was written while he was in prison, and
subsequently published, running through three editions.

outward shew ' his friend. Ten times more dangerous
is it for you to make choice of a stranger as travelling
companion. He may be a highwayman in disguise,
and by making you suspicious of other company on
the road, will draw you away to where his confederates
lie in wait to attack. Surprised, he will draw his
sword, and they will ' hacke, and hew against each
others Till threatned to be *shot*, you give the word, and
bid him yeeld '. When you raise hue and cry he will
lead you the wrong way, or, if you chance to meet and
suspect one of his company he will say you are mistaken, for he viewed his assailant well when, in the
scuffle, his vizard (mask) fell off.

Associate with none, unless, indeed, you find
persons rather willing to lose than have your company.
To ride on the sabbath is ill-advised. Not only is it
the day for rest and prayer, but being so, none ride
on that day but those that have great affairs to do and
means to effect them. The roads are therefore quiet
and the highwaymen active. Moreover, if you are
thus robbed, the judge in conscience will deny you
compensation.

To detect whether your fellow-travellers are highwaymen or no, take occasion to stop short, and see if,
unwilling to let you go free, they do not slack pace.
If, however, they continue on their way, still have a
care when again you overtake them. Beware of the
traveller who muffles his cloak over his face ; of him
who asks inquisitive questions ; and of those who
whisper between themselves.

Perhaps you ride with a friend, and are presently
joined by another rider, a ' seeming honest man '.
You are two to one, and therefore have no suspicions.
Not so your honest fellow-traveller, who, when two
miles further three other of his companions join you,
' shakes, Trembles and quivers ', and cries ' friends
we are way-laid '. By such trickery he finds out

whether your purse is richly lined and worth robbing. Then, instead of being three against three as you imagined, you are two against four.

Perhaps you are marked as a prize worth taking. There will ride up to you cheek by jowl a countryman dressed in a russet doublet, leather breeches, steeple hat with greasy brim, and rolls of hay twisted round his legs above his hob-nailed shoes. Carrying a goad and mounted on a wad of straw, he will begin to chat with you, and you, amused with his silly answers and country speech, will be taken unawares, when, whistling Robin Hood or some country catch, he seizes you the while his companions, who rode at a distance behind, come up to fleece you.

Ride rather by night than day with any sum you are afraid to lose. Then you will be free of highwaymen at least (of padders he is uncertain), for they know themselves at a disadvantage in the dark, and believe that none ride at night with aught worth stealing.

As highwaymen are wont to keep station on the great highways, picking and choosing their victims, travel, therefore, along the by-roads.

To bustle up close when riding by any dangerous place only works more surely your own overthrow, for the thieves, sallying out, will compass you about. It is best, therefore, to keep a butt's length apart at least. Scattered troops are never set upon for fear of some escaping and raising the alarm.

Always go to the relief of those beset. If despite these injunctions you suddenly discover you are in thieves' company, don't show alarm. Draw your sword as soon as they. If they find you resolute they will be overawed and afraid to kill you, for they know that by taking your life they endanger their own, and will find no safe hiding-place.

You yield, our mentor comments severely, too patiently, and are content not only to be robbed but to let your aggressors go free, for, if they are not captured, you still have all restored and what care you ? Moreover, you often double and misname the sum of your loss, knowing that the hundred will come to composition with you. When you come to tell the story of your loss, though you ' were rob'd fairely, and but two to two '—thus the seventeenth-century mentality—you say that there were four, five, or six assailants, and that you fought about an hour, and, having cut and slashed your harmless clothes yourself you say it was done in the fight, though you gave without resistance.

If you are surprised, and have no other course open but to yield, give fair words, and then you will have better treatment.

Do not put your hand over where your money lies, as is frequently done ; the thieves are thus told where it is hid ; nor believe them when they tell you that you shall have all restored if you wait with them in hiding until they seize the person for whom they wait. You not only become an accessory to their crime, but are duped as well, for having accomplished their task they will leave you destitute with the rest.

Remember that, after an encounter, highwaymen always ride across country to some town where they abide the night. They know that ' None use to travell thus athwart to tell ' the history of their loss, and to describe their assailants. Next day, they are gone ere the lazy hue and cry comes to make inquiry. Then will ' some poore silly fellow ', placed in authority ' Through some wretched wilfulnesse ', arrest those that never meant harm, yet being apprehended often lose their lives. Scour, therefore, to left and right of you, and, if at night you miss your quarry, ' a carefull spy Next day shall surely see them riding by '. If, however, the thieves light on a great sum, then they will ride straight to their rendezvous in the city,

which is a sure shelter for thieves.[1] Should their
operations have taken place to the East of London,
Westminster, Holborn, or the Strand will be their
goal ; if to the North, then Southwark, Lambeth, or
Bankside. When any one has lost his purse to thieves,
there a Watch is placed at the country's cost. Thereupon travellers, thinking it impossible, being thus
guarded, that they should lose their money, grow
careless, and the thief can ' doe his list, and freely
passe, The watchmen nere the wiser ; for they stand
Setled at one place ', and know nothing of what is
passing beyond their station. Or, if they do happen
to be present at an encounter, being ' poore, silly, old,
decrepped men that are Fitting for nought else ', they
stand ' Amaz'd affrighted ', not daring to make a
sound, until the robbing done and the birds flown,
they set to crying ' Thieves, Thieves '.

As appears from the foregoing the life of the highwayman was one of trickery and violence—and, on
occasion, of malice. A gentleman of the road like
Captain Hind or Claude du Vall, who raised his hat
as he made his request, and who, on receiving his due,
returned a few shillings to the late owner to carry him
on his way, was a rarity. Yet neither of these highwaymen could lay claim to gentle blood. Likewise few
travellers, we fancy, understood the amenities of the
highway as did Sir Richard B——, who with the
utmost *sang-froid* and generosity offered his despoiler,
Captain Whitney (Captain was, mostly, a courtesy
title in the profession), a breakfast with a fowl or two,
an invitation which was accepted by Whitney to the
extent of drinking the knight's health from the
contents of a passing beer-waggon. In fact the road

[1] Luttrell makes frequent mention of highwaymen being taken in London.
Under date 28 September 1695, he writes, ' Some highwaymen were taken
in Drury Lane with a considerable summ of money about them, being pursued
out of Dorsetshire, where they robb'd the receiver general of that country.'

was a rough school, and gentle breeding was soon
forgotten in the lust for booty and the pressure of
self-preservation. Thus on the 30th July 1669 a gang
of eleven highway robbers, all gentlemen according
to the True Bill brought in at the Middlesex Quarter
Sessions, attacked on the highway near Hillingdon
and maltreated Ursula Hobson ; assaulted, beat, and
wounded Sir Robert Vyner, Knight (the rich goldsmith and banker), and assaulted Bridget Hyde 'an
infant of sixteen years ', daughter and heiress of the
late Sir Thomas Hyde (and step-daughter of Vyner),
robbing her of three silk hoods worth thirty shillings,
a scarf, and a lace handkerchief each of the same
value, and an amber necklace worth twenty shillings.
One of these gentlemen was acquitted, three were
found guilty and sentenced to be hanged, while of
the remaining seven no notes disclose the fate.[1]

If gentlemen could possess themselves of the
finery of one who was little more than a child, it can
readily be understood that the traveller on horseback
was as likely to lose his riding-cloak, coat, gloves,
handkerchief, and hatband as his money and valuables,
or, if he rode well mounted, his horse, saddle, and
bridle. No fish was too small for the net of the
highwayman, and no person beneath his notice except
the indigent. Maltsters, graziers, farmers coming
home with well-lined purses, postboys with valuable
packets and useful Government dispatches,[2] carriers
with their waggons loaded with goods in transport—
Nevison made them compound for safety by regular

---

[1] See Middlesex Session Rolls, vol. iv, pp. 88-9. It is possible that the
assault upon the young lady was a form of revenge. See Chap. VII, pp. 186-7.

[2] Postboys were attacked as well for the intelligence to be gained and
turned to profit, from the letters and dispatches of Government officials,
as for the values to be found in letters and packets. In 1654 the mail was
stopped and robbed within a mile of St. George's, Southwark, by a band of
mounted men, who, having opened all letters and found no money, broke
open the packets, scattering the contents. They all made their escape.
Mercurius Politicus, 25 March 1654, as given in Inderwick's *Interregnum*.

tribute paid at certain inns—itinerant merchants, men and women, who toured the country with stocks of cloth or silk, ribbons and lace, glass or cutlery, some with stout riding nags and heavy-laden packhorses ; none were rejected by the fishermen of the roadside.

Sheepskins were the lure that made William Taylor, one February day of 1615, attack Simon Steele, merchant, of Dumfries, in that wild border-county of Cumberland ; pull him off his horse, draw his sword, and assault him, and take both skins and horse, offering at the same time their return for the sum of twenty-nine shillings, ' whereof ', we read, ' though he [Steele] complayned to a Justice, yet could he get noe redresse '. If he could not get redress, this much satisfaction would be his. If ever the thief were caught his end was sure and speedy ; for in the North the scales of justice were tilted yet more heavily against the accused than in the more peaceful and law-abiding south where thieves formed a smaller proportion of the population and mountain fastnesses were unknown.[1] And even there it was found necessary that the rules of procedure in the courts should be framed to secure the conviction of the guilty rather than the safety of the innocently accused. Taylor, probably, was no more than a footpad; a mean and lowly profession despised by the aristocrats of the highway but none the less dangerous to the peaceful traveller, as Evelyn found to his cost. It is thus, under date 11th June 1652, that he writes of his experience.

' The weather being hot, and having sent my man on before, I rode negligently under favour of the shade, till within three

---

[1] ' The [North] country ', says Roger North in his *Life of Baron Guildford*, ' is yet very sharp upon thieves ; and a violent suspicion there is next to conviction. When his lordship held the assizes at Newcastle, there was one Mungo Noble (supposed to be a great thief) brought to trial before his lordship, upon four several indictments ; and his lordship was so much a South country Judge as not to think any of them well proved ' and so released the man ' much to the regret of divers gentlemen who thought he deserved ;to be hanged.' Vol. i, p. 179, ed. 1890.

miles of Bromley, at a place called the Procession Oak, two
cut-throats started out, and striking with long staves at the
horse, and taking hold of the reins, threw me down, took my
sword, and hauled me into a deep thicket, some quarter of a
mile from the highway, where they might securely rob me, as
they soon did. What they got of money, was not considerable,
but they took two rings, the one an emerald with diamonds,
the other an onyx, and a pair of buckles set with rubies and
diamonds, which were of value, and after all bound my hands
behind me, and my feet, having pulled off my boots ; they
then set me up against an oak, with most bloody threats to
cut my throat if I offered to cry out, or make any noise ; for
they should be within hearing, I not being the person they
looked for. I told them that if they had not basely surprised
me they should not have had so easy a prize, and that it would
teach me never to ride near a hedge, since, had I been in the
mid-way, they durst not have adventured on me ; at which
they cocked their pistols, and told me they had long guns too,
and were fourteen companions. I begged for my onyx, and
told them it being engraved with my arms would betray them ;
but nothing prevailed. My horse's bridle they slipped, and
searched the saddle, which they pulled off, but let the horse
graze, and then turning again bridled him and tied him to a
tree, yet so as he might graze, and thus left me bound. My
horse was perhaps not taken, because he was marked and
cropped on both ears, and well known on that road. Left in
this manner, grievously was I tormented with flies, ants,
and the sun, nor was my anxiety little how I should loose
in that solitary place, where I could neither hear nor see any
creature but my poor horse and a few sheep straggling in
the copse.

'After near two hours attempting, I got my hands to turn
palm to palm, having been tied back to back, and then it was
long before I could slip the cord over my wrists to my thumb,
which at last I did, and then soon unbound my feet, and
saddling my horse, and roaming a while about, I at last per-
ceived dust to rise, and soon after heard the rattling of a cart,
towards which I made, and by the help of two countrymen,
I got back in to the highway. I rode to Colonel Blount's, a
great justiciary of the times, who sent out hue and cry
immediately. The next morning, sore as my wrists and arms
were, I went to London, and got 500 tickets printed and
dispersed by an officer of Goldsmiths' Hall, and within two

days had tidings of all I had lost, except my sword, which had a silver hilt, and some trifles. The rogues had pawned one of my rings for a trifle to a goldsmith's servant, before the tickets came to the shop, by which means they escaped ; the other ring was bought by a victualler, who brought it to a goldsmith, but he having seen the ticket, seized the man. I afterwards discharged him on his protestations of innocence. Thus did God deliver me from these villains, and not only so, but restored what they took, as twice before he had graciously done, both at sea and land.'

That travellers' horses were welcome booty to the highwaymen may be ascribed to the fact that they had need of a constant supply of good, sound, and if possible swift, mounts. To take them from those of their victims who rode fine—and unmarked—animals was one way of satisfying their necessities. But there were others. Stray horses were to be found on the road, left there by careless riders ; others were plucked under the eyes of the ostler from the inn-yard. It is besides probable that there was a big surreptitious trade in the capture and sale of horses to needy highwaymen and others. As a consequence advertisements in the *London Gazette* for the return of lost horses were of no unusual occurrence. The following, though it has no obvious connexion with highwaymen, has a characteristic seventeenth-century flavour that must needs find place here ; moreover what should a seaman, if seaman he were, want with a horse, unless to sell it to the fraternity, or turn highwayman himself ?

' Rode away with from the Bull Inn in Darford in Kent, on Sunday last was three weeks, the 20th of January, a Brown punch Horse, about 13 hands high, with a small Star in his Forehead, a little Gauled near the Off shoulder, a little bob Tail, a brown hairy Saddle, the Stirrup Leathers, Bridle and Cruppers are all marked with the Letters R.G. burnt in with a marking Iron. The rider of him pretends to be a Seaman, with a pair of Red Striped Breeches, a pair of sad coloured Dutch Stockings with white Stitches all along the middle behind, and the Clocks all work'd with White, he hath a pair of thin Pumps, hath a large head of Hair, curls well, Visage pale, and full of Pockholes. If any can give notice of them to Mr. Robert Glover at the Bull in Darford aforesaid or to Mr. Lucas at the Spurr Inn in Southwark, if all [sic] for the Horse have a Guinea reward, or if both Horse and Man, three Guinea's reward.'

The highwayman who for lack of horseflesh had to turn padder felt himself a sorry creature. Yet a quick-witted padder, with his different method of working, had no need to envy his more lordly colleague, and could on occasion get the better of a gentleman of the road, as De La Pryme shows in a vivid and unaffected little roadside episode.

'. . . a great lusty man-servant' of Mr. Parrel of Wroot (in the Isle of Axeholme, Yorks.) got 'a maggot into his head' to turn padder, so he acquainted his master with his resolution, explaining that it would be a much easier and more profitable way of living. His master dissented, but all to no purpose. 'And so, next morning, away he went, with a good clubb in his hand; and being got in the London Road, somewhere about Newark or Grantham, there overtook him on the road, a genteel man on horseback. John letts him come up to him, and taking his advantage, he catches hold of his bridle, and bidds him stand and deliver. Upon which he of horseback, being a highwayman himself, he began to laugh that a thief should pretend to rob a thief! " But ", says he, " harken, thou padder, I'm one of thy trade; but surely, thou'rt either a fool or one that was never at the trade before." " No, Sir ", says John, " I never was at this trade in my life before." " I thought so ", says the highwayman; " therefore, take my advice, and mind what I say to you. When you have a mind to robb a man, never take hold of his bridle and bid him stand, but, the first thing you do, knock him down, and, if he talk to you, hit him another stroke, and say, ' Sirrah! you rogue, do you prate? and then ', says the highwayman, ' you have him at your will '," etc. Thus they walk'd on for about a mile, the highwayman teaching the other his art; and as they were going a by way to a certain town, they comes to a badd lane. Says the padder to the other on horseback, " Sir, I am better acquainted with this country than perhaps you are, this lane

is very badd, and you'll indanger [of] lying fast, therefore you
may go through this yate [gate], and along the field side, and
so miss all the ill way." So he took his advice, and going that
way the padder went the other way, and coming to the place
where the highwayman should ride through a ʻgapp into the
lane again, this rogue, this padder, stands under the hedge, and
as soon as ever he sees the highwayman near him, he lends him
such a knock over the head that he brought him down immediately. Upon which he began to say, "Sirrah, you rogue, is
this your gratitude for the good advice that I gave you?"
"Ah! you villain, do you prate?' And with that gave him
another knock. And so, having him wholy at his mercy, he
takes almost fifty pounds from him and gets upon his horse, and
away he rides home to his master at Wroot, by another way,
as fast as he could go, and being got home he goes to his master
and tells him, saying—"Tash! master, I find this a very
hard trade that I have been about, as you sayd it would prove,
and I am resolved to go no more, but be contented with what
I have gott. I have got a good horse here, and fifty pounds in
my pocket, from a highwayman, and I have consider'd that
I cannot be prosecuted for it, therefore I'll live at ease," etc.'

The master must have been surprised at the unwonted wit of his servant (who had no character for
such) and the folly of the highwayman. Perhaps he
too was a novice, or, more likely still, no highwayman
at all. Such tricks were sometimes employed by peaceful travellers to avoid spoliation at the hands of the
fraternity.

On occasions footpads and highwaymen acted in
combination. More usually the two branches of the
profession went their separate ways ; the footpads
to haunt the confines of London, and beyond—
St. George's Fields, Westminster, Knightsbridge,
Chelsea, Hampstead ; the highwayman, singly, in
pairs, or in bands of varying sizes, to range further
afield. The outer suburbs and the nearer stretches
of the great highways were the hunting-grounds for
those who based their operations on London. Sometimes a half-dozen, dozen, or even a score or more

gathering together, they would attack and rob all who travelled the highway, killing travellers' horses to hinder pursuit. This was not infrequently a prelude to more advantageous business, the seizure of rich booty known to be on the road. It might be two or three hundred pounds, under the charge of the Oxford carrier, Bartlett, or, more tempting and more difficult of capture, five or ten thousand pounds of tax money, coming up in the Worcester or the Manchester waggon, under guard of armed men and possibly of mounted horse.[1] If this should happen, the despoiled travellers would be herded into a field and there guarded until, the capture effected, they would be dismissed, to find their way as best they could to the nearest town.

There were times when the depredations of the highwaymen roused, even in the lethargic veins of the country folk, a desire to rid themselves of the parasites. So it was that, in 1617, when the ruined gamesters and others who recouped themselves on Newmarket Heath proved a more serious menace than usual to the peace of the countryside, the countrymen assembled at the point where the Devil's Dyke intersects the main road, disposing themselves so as to shut off from flight a party of five highwaymen who had been engaged in robbing a coach of considerable booty. But their strategy failed. The highwaymen, knowing that in any event their offence was a hanging matter, charged right through the party, firing and

---

[1] In December 1691, the Worcester waggon containing four thousand pounds of the King's money, was stopped in broad daylight near Gerrard's Cross, four miles from Uxbridge, by sixteen highwaymen. Four persons were in charge of the waggon, and being within a mile of their inn, fancied themselves secure and walked on, leaving two men on foot to guard it. Having laid their blunderbusses in the waggon, these two were pursuing the even tenor of their way, when the waggon was attacked and plundered of two thousand five hundred pounds, which was all the thieves could manage to carry away. See Sydney's *Social Life in England from the Restoration to the Revolution*, pp. 288-9.

wounding four of their number, and so got clear away.

More successful were the efforts of the people of Middlesex to rid themselves of Jackson (alias Dixie) and his four confederates, Williams (alias Matchet), White (alias Fowler), Parkhurst, and Slader. On the 16th March 1673–4 three of the number had robbed the Windsor coach in broad daylight in sight of about a dozen gentlemen, well armed and mounted, who pursued them five or six miles before they lost sight of them. This roused the country, as will appear later. Two days later the entire gang robbed two coaches in Bedfont Lane near Staines. Supposing themselves to be discovered by a gentleman's servant in a green livery who was a-hunting, and who, upon sight of them, made hastily across the fields towards Acton, they bent their course to Harrow-on-the-Hill. Though they supposed themselves to be pursued they saw no one till they reached that town. There they found forty or fifty men ready to receive them with guns, pitchforks, and other weapons. Turning they made their way down the hill only to find a great number of horse and foot waiting for them at the bottom. Nevertheless they made the countrymen— according to their confession—run into the houses for shelter, while they rode on to Kilburn, Hendon, and Hampstead Heath, hotly engaged all the way, so that, though it was no more than ten or eleven o'clock in the morning when they left Harrow, it was six o'clock in the evening ere they reached Hampstead. Daylight was fading. Powder and shot had long been exhausted. Some had lost their swords, and most were sorely wounded. Two hundred men were assembled to stay their course, and there, in the deep hollow road at North End, the five dauntless highwaymen fought for an hour, until, one of their number mortally wounded, and the rest exhausted, they were over-

powered. Thence they were conveyed to Newgate,
and thence a few weeks later to the Sessions' House
for trial. All four were found guilty on one or more
of the fourteen indictments and all were hanged,
Jackson being gibbetted on the scene of his last stand,
opposite what is now the estate called ' Wildwoods ',
between two elms which for long remained standing
and were known as the Gibbet-elms.

VII

TRIALS AND TRIBULATIONS

Such was the lawlessness of the age that highway robbery was only one of several dangers that menaced the security of the road. No traveller was safe while the assassin, the drunken reveller, and the irresponsible rough were allowed to wreak their wills with none to hinder them except the sleepy Watch. Even the confines of the town and of the court were not safe to life and limb. In 1611 Lord Herbert of Cherbury, passing through Scotland Yard with two lackeys in attendance was attacked by Sir John Ayres and his servants, in full view of twenty or thirty of the knight's friends and passers-by ; these did practically nothing to stop the affray until, the attackers becoming worsted by the courageous peer, the partisans of Sir John drew him away to Whitehall stairs and the river. Security was no greater during the second half of the century. In 1670 Lord Ormonde was attacked and kidnapped by Colonel Blood and five accomplices, as he was driving in his coach up St. James's Street. He would have been carried to Tyburn and there hanged, as it is said, by the dauntless adventurer—the same who subsequently made the attempt on the Tower Regalia— had he not by vigorous resistance and the help of his footman managed to escape. The same year Sir John Coventry, who had alluded in open Parliament to the King's pleasures, was waylaid at night in the Haymarket at the instigation, it is said, of the King, taken from his coach, and his nose slit to the bone; an indignity upon a Member so strongly resented by the House that a Bill was brought in and passed, making the offence of mutilation a felony punishable by death, without benefit of clergy. So little was thought of the drawing of blood—especially where the motive could be imputed to politics or religion—that George Fox, the Quaker, and two companions were unsuccessfully ambushed while riding in Radnorshire by a Justice's Clerk and his friends, for no other reason, Fox alleges, than their Quaker faith, which made them obnoxious to the authorities to whom was entrusted the maintenance of peace. Nor was this the end of the adventure. No sooner had he and his friends escaped from the ambushers than they came upon a drunken man afoot, with a naked rapier in his hand, and shortly after met two women and two men, one of whom had just rescued one of the women from the armed brute, and had had his thumb cut off in the struggle. Fox on finding the miscreant's horse, presented it to the victim to enable him to ride to the nearest Justice of the Peace to raise hue and cry.

Men of so-called honour who could stoop to assault or assassination for personal and political ends had no scruples, as can be readily understood, in abducting fair and rich heiresses, if it pleased their fancy or their interest so to do ; though, judging from the references in Pepys, Luttrell, and the Verney *Memoirs*, the undertaking was never or rarely fraught with success to the abductor. Miss Bridget Hyde, the victim of the eleven gentlemen highwaymen, was the object of many unsuccessful attacks upon her person. Heiress to an estate worth more than three thousand pounds a year and stepdaughter, as has already appeared, to the rich banker-goldsmith, Sir Robert Vyner, she went through a form of marriage when only twelve years of age with her cousin, Mr. Emerton, who having then failed to keep her in his possession tried again and again to retrieve his mistake. One most daring seizure has found record in the Verney Papers.

Cornet Wroth, who was doubtless acting on Emerton's behalf, while taking an after-dinner coach airing with Sir Robert and his stepdaughter near their country house in Middlesex one day in July 1678, drew a pistol on his host and, having six or eight troopers to assist him, carried off the young lady in another coach. A wheel of the vehicle breaking he laid her across his horse, and so rode to Putney Ferry where another coach lay waiting. Pursuit, however, gained on them and the girl was recovered, speechless from fright, as well she might be, ' but the gallant Cornet escaped '. The King, it was said, was so angry that he declared that if Wroth was condemned he would ' not meddle ' in the matter to save him. The marriage was finally declared null, but not before Miss Hyde had announced her union with Lord Dumblane (subsequently second Duke of Leeds), and had bestowed upon the first aspirant to her hand and fortune the sum of twenty thousand pounds.

To persons of humbler rank, especially to the weak or aged, the danger lay in unpremeditated attack by drunken rowdies and by those lusting for blood. Evidence of this is to be found in Quarter Sessions Papers. The following extracts from the Somerset-shire Records relate to those years of unrest and uncertainty, 1658–9.

' Information of John Westover of Wedmore that as he was returning home from Brent fair last Michaelmas day he met in a dark place of the way certain men (named), one of whom tore half his cloak off his back and struck him so that he fell off his horse. One of the men named said that he saw men fighting and Westover struck with a pike staff or raven's bill.'

' Complaint of Robert Tyte the elder of Stalbridge gent., that on the night of 1st September he met certain persons (named) of Charlton Horethorne in a narrow lane, one of whom struck him on the head with a piked staff saying they had a warrant for him, but it was not shown. He demands the good behaviour against them.'

' Information of Maud wife of Thomas Collar of Woolavington given to Edward Sealy 2. Aug. 1659. As she was returning home by herself from Bridgwater market on or about 7th July, Adrian Towes of Marke overtook her and calling her ugly toad demanded her name ; he then knocked her down and demanded her purse, to which, hiding her purse she replied that she had bestowed all her money in the market. He then said " I think you are a Quaker," and she denied it, he compelled her to kneel down on her bare knees and swear by the Lord's Blood that she was not, which, to save her life, she did. Another woman then came up and rebuked the said Towes whereupon he struck her down ' athwart ' her saddle into one of her panniers.'

Though it does not appear that the imbibing of strong liquors was responsible for any of the above-mentioned assaults, the prevalent vice was undoubtedly the cause of much of the unreasoning violence displayed. Fiendish in its apparent aimlessness was the attack by ' some rude drunken fellows ' on an old man, Will Taylor, and his son, Jeremiah, as they were coming home from Leeds one February night of 1680–1. With a great staff they struck the old man from his horse into a ditch and, not content with that, as soon as his son helped him to his feet, belaboured him again, striking out his eye so that he lay, our informant adds, at Holbeck ' in hazzard '. These doubtless were raw Yorkshire lads who knew no other law than that of their own instincts. But what of the under-sheriff of Norfolk, Mr. Verdon, who, with a party of friends, returning home ' pretty merry ' from Newmarket, where they had presented an address to the King, took occasion to murder a man, it is said, without any provocation !

A drunken man is as dangerous to himself as to others. Therefore, it is not surprising that we read again and again of drunken travellers being found by the roadside with broken limbs, and of others lying drowned in ditch, pond, or river. Though it was not unusual, after a drinking bout at a gentleman's house, for a servant to be sent home with an unsteady guest, even this did not always save the well-liquored from disaster. One gentleman-of-the-law of Halifax ' having been drinking himself very drunk at Mr. Fox-crofts ', and being sent homeward with a man and lanthorn to guide him, set spurs to his horse, not knowing what he did, and ran straight into the river Calder, and was there drowned ; a melancholy and sensational end not unappreciated by the Halifax folk, hundreds of whom ' walkt on Lords day by the waterside to spy if they could find him '.

There was danger, too, in the quick, uncontrolled temper of men of all classes—a defect so general as to suggest that it resulted from hard drinking—and in the sword which lay close to the ready hand of noble and gentle. Even those of plebeian origin and training, if they did but serve the quality in the capacity of lackey or coachman, must needs settle their reckon-ings and support their dignity by a display of cold steel.[1] A quarrel between a hackney-coachman and a fare was enough to draw blood ; and a block of traffic in a London street more than enough to cause death to one or other of the participants. ' Last night ', writes Luttrell in 1694, ' the Earl of Warwick wounded a hackney coachman in 3 several places, and thereon was secured ' ; ' . . . by coach to White Hall ' writes Pepys, ' the coachman on Ludgate Hill 'lighted, and beat a fellow with a sword.' And again, ' To West-minster Hall, and in King Street there being a great stop of coaches, there was a falling out between a drayman and my Lord Chesterfield's coachman, and one of his footmen killed '. Fox, walking up Ludgate Hill while the traffic was blocked with coaches coming from the Lord Mayor's feast, saw a man with a naked rapier jump out of Secretary Thurloe's coach, and run

[1] A Proclamation dated 29 September 1660, forbids footmen and lackeys to wear swords in London and Westminster. *Cal. State Papers Dom.*, 1660–1.

up to a carman who was standing near by, who promptly 'uppe with his slinge & knockt out his braines'. Fox bade the onlookers put the injured man back into the coach, but Mr. Secretary refused to receive him, letting him die, as he did shortly afterwards, in the road. Sometimes the assailant escaped the retaliatory blows only to fall victim to the anger of an infuriated mob. Young Mr. Gerard, aged about 17, taking his mother to see New Bedlam— mad-houses were welcome sights of the town—was insulted by the drunken porter and his wife. Drawing his sword, he ran the man through the groin. Thereupon the rabble, coming up, fell upon the lordling, nearly pulled him in pieces, thrust him into prison, and then broke the windows to come at him again. He was rescued by the Lord Mayor and given shelter for the night in that gentleman's house. Already, a year previously, ' being in drinke ' he had killed a footboy in St. James's Park by striking him under the ear.[1] Retribution commonly falls alike upon guilty and innocent. The Countess of Bath driving past New Bedlam and being taken for the young nobleman's mother—a Frenchwoman and therefore all the more obnoxious—had her coach broken to bits by the crowd and her footman knocked down.

Fox in a curious Quaker story supplies us with another instance of the quick temper and imperious

---

[1] ' Last night the Ld Cornwallis and Mr Gerrard, the Ld Gerrards son, being in drinke, abused the sentinells in St James Parke, and, after, Mr Gerrards meeting Capt With's footboy, upon what provocation is not yet known, strucke him soe that the boy fell down dead. The sentinells cryed out murder; whereupon they both fled, but were pursued into Sr Stephen Fox his house. My Ld Cornwallis appeares and declares that he wase going up the staires when the boy wase killed; but heareing murder cryed he returned to Mr Gerrards and his servants, who said that their master only hit the boy a box on the eare of whch he dyed. Mr Gerrard absconds himself, and ther appeares noe bruise on the boy but just under his eare.' *Hatton Corr.*, Camden Soc., vol. xxii, p. 126, 18 May 1676. This young gentleman was Charles Gerard, eldest son of the first Earl of Maccles-field by Mdlle de Civelle. See *Dict. Nat. Biog.*

ways of the ruling classes. Cheshire, not London, was the scene. Sir Geoffrey Shakerley, a Justice of the Peace, riding along a road with his man servant came upon a young man, a Quaker, who was standing with some laden horses beside a mill. The road being narrow the young man could not get the horses quickly out of the way, whereupon the magistrate raised his cane to beat the young man, but found himself quickly disarmed, and the cane laid upon the road. Then he took out his pistols, but was relieved of them in the same expeditious manner, and so with his rapier. The servant asked for the return of the weapons, and to this the Quaker agreed on the promise that his master should do no mischief with them. Next Shakerley sent his man to fetch the constable and a Bible, so that he could tender the oath of allegiance and supremacy to the oath-abhorring Quaker. All the while he sat his horse opposite to the young man and the laden horses. The servant returned saying that he could find no constable, and that the people were so poor he could get no Bible. Master and man then set off to find a constable, while the young man, having bided their return some time without avail, passed on over a common with his horses. Shakerley, having failed to put his plan into execution, and spying his victim, followed him to the town, where he found a constable and a clergyman and then and there made ready to write out a ' mittimus ' to send the Friend to gaol for disarming him. The others, however, dissuaded him, giving as a reason for lenity that the young man was in his old clothes, and that his father was a very honest man, though, in truth, he was ' the veryest drunkarde in the tounde [town] & used to beate his son '; so that he had ' beene used to disar...e his father of his weapons . . . which made him soe expert in that worke '. Such a noise, however, did the affair make in the county, and so fearful were the young

man's friends of vindictive action on the part of the
Justice, that they persuaded him to remove from the
vicinity.

To the peaceable seventeenth-century traveller at
ordinary seasons, it is probable that potential dangers
from robbery and assault were less disquieting than
the inconveniences and petty annoyances incidental
to travel ; such as the inclemency of the weather, the
difficulty of obtaining post-horses, the ill-will of host
or ostler, the propinquity of disagreeable coach
travellers, or the vagaries of a riding companion unduly
suspicious of all others upon the road—one who would
choose this or that road, or bait long before nightfall,
in the belief that he was being shadowed by persons
intent to rob him.

In time of war the hazards and inconveniences of
travel were increased. Soldiers were lawless : authorities were distrustful. As a consequence the traveller
who was of a nervous or apprehensive nature could
have had little or no peace of mind while upon the
road, although he might often reach his journey's
end without incident. If of the old faith the licence
to travel would be procured with the utmost difficulty.[1]
If of sound religious or political views, he might still
have to obtain a pass. Nor did this free him from
official interference. Watches would in all likelihood
be suspicious, and guards inquisitorial. His pass
might not be honoured ; his horse or horses might
be seized ; his progress barred ; and he himself laid
hold of by hectoring soldiery. Lady Verney, when
she left London for Claydon in 1647, could scarce
get ' a nagg ', and had to go round by way of Berk-
hampstead to avoid the soldiers. Even so, she found
them at Uxbridge fighting at four o'clock in the
morning.

Happier by far were those young and adventurous

[1] See Note H, p. 326.

SOLDIERS. From the Roxburghe Ballads

'FLEEING FROM THE PLAGUE'. From a contemporary print

spirits to whom a chance-met fight presented welcome relaxation from the daily round. Of such was Colonel Hutchinson's coachman who, borrowing a horse from his master, one day of 1659, for the purpose of being let blood at Nottingham, found, on arriving at his destination, that the cavaliers had risen against the fast decaying Commonwealth. Taking a case of pistols, and thinking ' more of shedding than losing blood ', he followed in pursuit of the warring factions, and finding the insurgents in rout, killed one (according to his own account), and returned home with a cravat and other spoils of war, although he had previously engaged to go on the cavalier side. Of such also was Sir John Reresby. Hearing, one day in 1661, that Venner's followers were making a stand in Caen Wood, near Hampstead, he took one of his coach-horses (in default of better mount), and setting his man upon the other, scoured the wood by moonshine until just on midnight when they found their quarry, who received them with musket and shot and then decamped. Probably there were none who enjoyed the alarums and excursions of war so thoroughly as the scholars at Thame Rectory, of whom Anthony Wood was one. Soldiers were quartered in the house, and beguiled the boys with talk in hours of preparation. Skirmishes, not one but several, took place at their very door. Best of all, the day that Borstall was to be surrendered to Parliament, the boys were given ' free libertie ', of which many availed themselves, to walk the four miles to that stronghold, where with hundreds of others they watched the proceedings from outside the works.

But our business lies with the difficulties and dangers experienced by the peaceful traveller. More strictly relevant, therefore, is the history of the war-time journey undertaken by Mrs. Wandesford, widow of the Lord Deputy of Ireland, in company with her three young children, to one of whom, a daughter, we are indebted for its graphic record. Leaving Chester (where they had been besieged) in 1643 for their home in Yorkshire, they travelled with a pass issued by Colonel Shuttleworth of the Parliamentary forces. They had in their train several servants and tenants, and no more than two trunks filled with linen, the rest of their possessions having been lost in Ireland, whence they had been forced to flee. They reached Warrington in safety, ' though with much difficulty, by reason of the interchange of the king's armies and the parliament's '. There they heard ' alarums ' of attacks by the King's forces from Chester, but as these proved only a ruse to awaken the diligence of the home forces, they were able to pass without hindrance next day to Wigan. This town, ' zealous for theire king and church ', had been plundered the previous spring by the Parliamentary forces. They found it ' sorely demolished, and all the windowes broaken ', and the people, at their first coming, scared lest they had been of the enemy. But hearing that Mrs. Wandesford was niece to a famous bygone divine of their town, they flocked to see her, ' using all the civilities and kindnesses imaginable to her '. Continuing their journey next day, they came to a place on the borders of Lancashire called Downham. There they were stopped with harsh language and abuse by a Parliamentary corporal and his men who refused to honour their pass. Swearing and threatening that the travellers should be ' striped ', they took them to a ' pittiful house ' where they were forced to lie all night, the while their captors continued to threaten them as kinsfolk of the hated Lord Strafford. They allowed one of the servants, however, to go with an escort to Colonel Shuttleworth, ten miles off, who, upon sight of his own pass, declared his displeasure at their treatment and sent his own nephew to convey the party to the

limits of his command.   Thereafter they passed unmolested to Snape, near Bedale, where they stayed
for a season with Mrs. Wandesford's eldest daughter,
as her own jointure house was unsuitable for residence
owing to frequent hostilities in the district in which
it was situated.   Later they set out for York, only to
find, when they had gone half way, that the city was
about to be besieged and, therefore, impossible to enter.
  Thus far the peaceful non-combatant intent upon
his or her own peaceful errands; a happy and fortunate
being compared to many who travelled the road in
the long drawn years of strife.   Such were yeomen-
farmers bereft of all by plundering soldiery, their
goods and stock sent in one direction, themselves
driven off in another to the accompaniment of snapping
firelocks ; yokels, torn from the plough and driven
to battle by well-primed muskets in the rear ; London
militiamen, homesick for the counter in Cheapside;
the wounded packed into waggons and jolted for
hours at a stretch from one town to another ; the
fugitive passing by stealth—hiding in barns or under
hedges while the clatter of hoofs or the tramp of
many feet told of danger—until the wide sea and an
alien shore brought liberty, or discovery, prison and,
it may be, death.   So the King for six fateful weeks
after Worcester fight won his way through manifold
dangers.   And so, too, Captain Hind, cavalier and
erstwhile highwayman, after that same disaster, leapt
the city wall and hid beneath hedgerows and bushes
until, the search for fugitives abating, he made his
way afoot to London where, under an assumed name,
he lived securely for five weeks.   He was then denounced to the Speaker, secured, arraigned at Reading
on an old charge of manslaughter, and, the indictment
failing, hanged for treason at Worcester.
  Other fugitives there were whose sole offence lay
in their religious and political opinions.   Such a one

was Dr. Peter Heylyn, chaplain to Charles I, Prebendary of Westminster Abbey, and Rector of Alresford in Hampshire.   Incurring the animosity of the Puritan party, he left Westminster for his country home.   Upon war breaking out, and hearing that Waller with a troop of horse was being sent to take him prisoner, he fled to Royalist Oxford.   His living having been sequestered, his goods and chattels seized and dispersed, he and his wife lived for a time upon the proceeds of the sale of the coach and horses which had brought them to that town.   When this money had been spent, not having any means of procuring any more, he sent his wife to London and himself ' went out of *Oxford* a. d. 1645, walking as a poor Traveller through the Countrey, and disguis'd both in his Name and Habit ; . . . in the likeness usually of an honest Country-man, or else of a poor decayed Gentleman, as indeed he was '.   So wandering ' like a Jew, with a Groat in his purse, and somtimes without it ', he passed from place to place like the patriarchs of old, finding hearty entertainment amongst friends of the royal party.   Once he was betrayed by a ' zealous She-*Puritan* ', wife of a true-hearted Cavalier.   But having warning from the husband's two sisters (the husband was away from home) that intelligence had been sent to the Parliamentary soldiers of his presence there, he went out at a back door and down a pair of garden-stairs, and tramped all night to more trusty shelter.   Wearying of this kind of life and obtaining supplies of money, he settled with his wife and eldest daughter at Winchester ' in the House of a right honest man, one Mr. *Lizard*, with whom they Tabled a good while '.   Winchester was then a strong garrison for the King.   As he was near Alresford—his old home—' he would go somtimes in disguise to visit his old Neighbors, who he knew were true and faithful to him '.   Those halcyon days quickly vanished.

Winchester was delivered up to his enemies. Every
house was full of soldiers, quartered upon the inhabitants. Fortunately for Dr. Heylyn, he was staying
in a house which had been formerly occupied by
Papists and had a secret chamber entered from
behind ' an old Beds head ' by a door so neatly made
like the other wainscot of the chamber that it was
impossible for strangers to find it. There he could
hear thè mirth and raillery of the soldiers in the adjoining chamber, and their gaming at cards and dice.
Taking his opportunity to leave such dangerous
quarters he put on his travelling robes, with a long
staff in his hand, and, it being market day, walked
out of the town with the country crowd. He had not
gone many miles when, ' some stragling Soldiers
lighting on him, and catching hold of his hand, felt
a Ring under his Glove, which through hast of his
escape, he forgot to pull off ; which no sooner discover'd, but they roughly swore he was some Runaway
Cavalier : the Ring being hard to get off, the poor
Doctor willingly helped them ; in which time came
gallopping by some of the Parliaments Scouts, who
said to their Fellow-soldiers, " *Look to your selves,
the Cavaliers are coming* " ; at which words being
affrighted, they took that little money that was in his
Pocket, and so rid away without further search, and
he good man jog'd on to the next Friends House with
some pieces of Gold that he had hid in his high shooes,
which if the Rogues had not been so hastily frighted
away would have been undoubtedly found, and might
have cost him his life by further suspicions of him '.
But, although the doctor's pilgrimage of suffering was
to continue for two more years, his season of peril was
over ; he was not again molested. In 1648 he was
permitted to live at his brother's home, Minster Lovel.
Later he made composition for his temporal estate
and removed to Lacie Court, near Abingdon, where he

entertained friends and strangers of the King's Cause, many of whom were homeless and fugitive as once upon a time he had been. At the Restoration he recovered his Prebendal stall at Westminster.

The plague, which in six great epidemics—and many minor ones—harried seventeenth-century England from end to end, was as disturbing as the broils of war to free movement. Markets were closed, fairs prohibited, and highways diverted. Towns which were free of the dread disease forbade intercourse with those infected,[1] and strict Watches were kept to prevent the ingress of travellers suspected of coming thence. Camps were set up outside the town for the reception of suspects, and in some cases for the isolation of those who had had the temerity to harbour others more cunning or lucky, who had slipped through the cordon. None were allowed to receive guests without notifying the fact to the constables. In some instances prohibition went so far as to order the departure of ' all Strangers and Tradesmen . . . not settled accordynge to the lawe ' in the town. Carriers and stage-coaches were forbidden to journey to the infected localities. In fine, every effort was made by healthy communities to ban intercourse with the plague-stricken.

It was easier, however, to isolate the unhappy cities than to exclude their pestiferous inhabitants, whose only thought was to flee the fate which probably awaited them in their own homes. To take London as an example. As soon as a heavy rise in the Bills of Mortality suggested an impending epidemic, the better classes left ; the landowners to their country estates, others to make their homes with relatives more happily situated, or to await the passing of the visitation in distant and health-giving spas. The ' Hurry of the

[1] See Note I, p. 327.

People was such for some Weeks ', says Defoe in his
Journal of the Plague Year, 1665, ' that there was no
getting at the Lord-Mayor's Door without exceeding
Difficulty ;   there was such pressing and crouding
there to get passes and Certificates of Health, for such
as travelled abroad ; for, without these, there was no
being admitted to pass thro' the Towns upon the Road,
or to lodge in any Inn . . .'   Later, when panic set in,
the poorer sort, without let or leave, spread themselves
throughout the neighbouring counties, finding what
shelter they could in barns, out-houses and self-made
huts, unheeding the vexation and alarm they caused
their involuntary hosts and neighbours.   Hospitality,
charity, common humanity, fled before the terror of
the plague :

' . . . away they trudge thick and threefold ; ' says Taylor of
' The Wonderful Yeare ' of 1603, ' some riding, some on foote,
some without bootes, some in their slippers, by water, by land,
in shoales swom they *West-ward* : . . . Hacknies, water-men and
wagons were not so terribly imployed many a yeare ; so that
within a short time, there was not a good horse in *Smithfield,*
nor a coach to be set eye on : . . . the sight of a [Londoner's]
flat-cap was more dreadfull to a Lob [country bumpkin] then
the discharging of a caliver : a treble-ruffe . . . had power to
cast a whole houshold into a cold sweat . . . to *Bristow* [went]
. . . an honest knowne citizen.. . . with other company, travelling
thither . . . and setting up his rest not to heare the sound of
Bow-bell till next *Christmas,* was not withstanding in the hye
way singled out from his company, and set upon by the
Plague. . . . The rest, at that word, shifted for themselves, and
went on, hee (amazed to see his friends flye . . .) yeelded ;
and being but about fortie miles from *London* . . . he calld
for help at the same inne, where not long before he and all his
fellowe pilgrimes obtained for their money (mary yet with
more prayers then a beggar makes in three termes) to stand
and drinke some thirtie foote from the doore . . . presently [at
once] the doores had their wooden ribs crusht in pieces, by
being beaten together : the casements were shut more close
than an usurers greasie velvet powch : the drawing windowes
were hangd, drawne and quartred : not a crevis but was stopt,

not a mouse-hole left open ; . . . mine hoste and hostesse ranne over one another into the back-side, the maydes into the orchard, quivering and quaking, and ready to hang themselves on the innocent plumb-trees. . . . As for the tapster, he fled into the cellar, rapping out five or six plaine countrey oathes, that hee would drowne himselfe in a most villainous stand of ale, if the sick *Londoner* stoode at the doore any longer. But stand there he must, for to go away (well) he cannot, but continues knocking and calling in a faint voice . . . : he might knocke till his hands akte, and call till his heart akte, for they were in a worse pickle within, then hee was without, hee being in a good way to go heaven, they being so frighted that they scarce knew whereabout heaven stoode, onely they all cryed out, *Lord, have mercie upon us* . . . the poore man standing thus at deaths doore, and looking every minute when he should be let in, behold, another *Londoner*, that had likewise bene in the *Frigide zone* of the country, and was returning . . . to the heaven of his owne home, makes a stand at this sight, to play the physition . . . he leads him into a field, a bundle of strawe (which with much adoe he bought for money) serving instead of a pillow. But the destinies hearing the diseased partie complaine and take on, because he lay on a field-bedde, when before he would have been glad of a matresse, for very spight cut the threads of his life . . . the church nor church-yard would let none of their lands : maister Vicar was struck dumbe, and could not give the dead a good word, neither Clarke nor Sexton could be hired to execute their office ; no, they themselves would first be executed : so that hee that never handled shovell before, got his implements about him, . . . and so layde him in the . . . earth : . . . and learning, by his last words, his name and habitation, this sad traveller arrives at *London,* delivering to the amazed widdow and children, instead of a father and a husband, onely the out-side of him, his apparell. But . . . the bringer of these heavy tydings . . . the very next day after his comming home, departed out of this world, to receive his reward in the spirituall court of heaven.

' . . . I could draw forth a catalogue ', remarks Taylor, who well remembered the epidemic, ' of many poore wretches, that in fields, in ditches, in common cages, and under stalls (being either thrust by cruell maisters out of doors, or wanting all worldly succour but the common benefit of earth and aire) have most miserably perished.'

In 1636 many country inns and alehouses ' un-chang'd their signes ' because they would harbour neither whole nor sick. The gentry, on the other hand, shunned as unsafe all places of public resort. Lady Elmes, whose purse-strings were not easily unloosed, made plaint in the summer of 1665, when leaving Knaresborough for the Midlands, that to lie at gentlemen's houses, as she must do, would cost her she knew not what.

Defoe, in his *Journal of the Plague Year*,[1] 1665, gives a graphic description of the flight from London of a party of men and women ; their wanderings around the eastern purlieus of the city ; the stratagems they used to circumvent the Watches placed upon the roads, to stop the passage through towns and villages of such as them ; the hostility of the inhabitants ; the means they took to obtain food ; and, finally, their long sojourn in Epping Forest, first in a tent, then in huts, and later in a disused house. There were, it is true, some exceptions to this general attitude of hostility. In the epidemic of 1625 Hendon and Tottenham distinguished themselves by relieving the sick and burying the dead, a display of humanity not to the liking of the Lords of the Privy Council, who ordered the Middlesex Justices to see that the in-habitants of those places removed the ' multitudes of inmates ' and newcomers, and received no more such undesirable visitors. The King's Palace at Theobalds was not far away, and must needs be protected from contagion. In July 1665 the Grand Inquest of Hertfordshire made presentment ' that severall persons doe dayly come downe from the cytie of London in great numbers with their families and goods to inhabitt in several places in our countie, to

---

[1] Although this *Journal* was composed many years after 1665, at which time Defoe was a small child, and is consequently a fictitious narrative, it follows closely in essentials the accounts of earlier writers. See *A History of Epidemics in Britain*, by Charles Creighton, vol. i, pp. 649–51, ed. 1891.

the great danger of infecting of the same, and also
that severall persons in this countie bring downe greate
quantities of raggs to the great annoyance and danger
to infect the same '. Annoyance, indeed ; for infection, it was thought, could be communicated without
direct contact.

Apart from runaways few cared to leave home.
Those whom business took to London in the late
summer of 1665 found the shops shut and the streets
deserted, except for pest-coaches, coffins, and beggars
—many with the tokens of plague upon them—who
implored alms of the passing traveller. So early as
the 22nd July Pepys writes : ' I by coach home
[coaches were later avoided for fear of infection], not
meeting with but two coaches and but two carts from
White hall to my own house [near the Tower], that
I could observe, and the streets mighty thin of people '.
In the following September, when the disease in
London was at its height, young Taswell went very
reluctantly, on his father's command, from Greenwich
to London to deliver some letters on his behalf—the
post thence was probably stopped. Only on being
provided by his sire with angelica and aromatic herbs
(used as preventives), some eatables in a bag, and
some Spanish wine, so that he need eat no London
food, did he venture into the city. There the usual
distressed objects met his sight, some beckoning to
him, some carrying away their dead upon biers—the
regulation that burials should be made by night only
was disregarded during the first three weeks of
September when the plague was at its height. Delivering his letters to a Mrs. Harrison, nurse of the Taswell
family and sole survivor of her own family which
had comprised seven children, he was greeted with a
loving embrace, an unwelcome attention which happily
had no injurious result. Thence he returned straight
home.

Though the plague-stricken were strictly forbidden by law to leave their homes—persons so offending were deemed, 1 Jac. I, c. 31, felons if they had sores, otherwise rogues—it was impossible to keep the distraught or terrified victims from wandering, or to prevent the destitute from begging. In Hampshire in July 1666—the epidemic of 1665 did not attain its greatest virulence in the provinces until the succeeding summer—they broke out (of the pest-house probably), visited the better sort who, they doubtless thought, were escaping more lightly than they, and opened the gaol, so that the Royal White Train Bands had to be mustered to suppress them. Nevertheless, as Cary Gardiner (a Verney by birth) observes, 'wee are afrad of all wee meet, they ramble a bout . . .'

The more extraordinary dangers and difficulties which beset the path of the traveller have now been dealt with ; and the commoner risks and more trivial disturbances claim our attention.

The roads, such was their state even under the most favourable climatic conditions, accounted for much discomfort and many accidents. Riding falls were common—how common only those who have conned the diaries and autobiographies of the time can judge. This was usually the effect of the horse putting his foot into a hole, disguised, often enough, by mud or a thin crust of hard soil. Slipping on or breaking through an ice-coated road was a common mishap in winter. Thoresby frequently led his horse on such occasions. The stones too, which so plentifully bestrewed the roads, gave their share of trouble, laming horses and wearing thin their shoes, so that in rough country like the Cumberland Fell district, new shoes had to be put on every two or three days. Moreover good smiths were hard to come by in remote parts. Nor was it only neglect that made the roads dangerous. If the countryman failed to appreciate the benefit to himself and his fellows of well-kept roads, he did appreciate the sand and gravel that could in many parts be quarried from their surfaces, suffer though he might at Quarter Sessions for his contravention of the law. Travellers had to beware of the resulting pitfalls, and, furthermore, in some parts of the country, of coal and lead shafts, notably in Lancashire, Yorkshire, Somerset, and Flint. For no consideration was paid by miners either to rights of passage on the King's highway or to the dangers resulting from unprotected pit-heads.

In the blind, hollow lanes, very general in some parts of the country, the discomforts of the perpetually sodden ways were enhanced by the difficulty, if not impossibility, of passing or being passed by others upon the road ; it might be the sheriffs of the county and their retinue, official and unofficial, proceeding in state to the county border to receive His Majesty's Judges. Adam Martindale's daughter, riding before her employer's coach, was actually run into owing to the drunken coachman's furious driving, happily without injury. On the broader roads the rider's difficulty was to keep to the track, owing alike to the pack-horse drivers, panniers, whifflers, and market women who, stoutly contending for the way, compelled the rider in one mile's travel to cross twenty times to one side, and owing also to the tracks themselves being frequently so ill-defined that they were lost in moor or meadow. Twice within a few miles between Faringdon and Malmesbury did M. Jorevin lose his way, and wander in woods and meadows until he found persons to direct him back to the road. His first rescuer told him that he would have great difficulty in getting again into the right road ; but this may have been with an eye to the shilling he subsequently received for guiding him there. Even the stone-paved causeway was sometimes a source of trouble. Loosely set stones made horses trip, precipitating their owners into mire or bordering dyke, and occasioned the wedging of coach wheels. Thus when Mrs. Fiennes was travelling by coach along the pack-horse road to Bath she had to call the help of several men to extricate an imprisoned wheel.

Indeed coaches were in such a rudimentary stage of their evolution that they were as little fitted to traverse the roads as the roads were to carry them. Accidents, as a result, were in the order of things. Perches would collapse, wheels come off, bolts and axle-trees break. This last was a common mishap. The Bedford coach in which the Rev. Henry Newcome was travelling broke two axle-trees in one day ; the private coach of a Norfolk gentleman broke two in a furlong, making it necessary for him to send the offending parts in a dung-cart to be mended at Bishop's Stortford. Overturning, owing to the rough surface of the roads, was as common as it was dangerous. In some cases it led to the killing of the occupants. Pope, whose coach was overturned into a ditch— through the running away of the horses—was almost suffocated before he managed to break the glass windows, and then he was in danger of drowning, for the coach sinking deeper, the water gained, and he was only rescued just in time. Even the King, Charles II, suffered the misfortune which so frequently befell his subjects, being overset when travelling in the dark near Holborn with the Dukes of York and Monmouth and Prince Rupert, happily without injury except to his royal dignity. How it occurred Pepys, our informant, did not know, ' but . . . the torches did not, they say, light the coach as they should do '— leaving the holes and ruts therefore unseen by the royal coachman.

The weathercock nature of the English climate is seldom appreciated by those who live within its in-

fluence. To this rule the seventeenth-century traveller
was no exception. Although he chose by preference for
his expeditions the long, warm days of summer, he had
a hearty dislike of the heat and dust which frequently
attended journeys in that season. The one he shunned,
if he could, in the middle hours of the day ; the other
he bewailed, as well he might, for the pulverized state
of the roads must have been splendid quarry for the
wind. Evelyn actually curtailed a tour he was making
in North-east England on this account. In winter the
traveller was in far worse plight. The wind cut his
face, and half-froze him within. The roads were at
best pitfalls for the unwary, and at worst deep in snow,
or lost in flood-water ; for rivers and streams, checked
by no proper system of land drainage or river conservancy, oftentimes spread over contiguous, and
sometimes wide areas—some roads were commonly
under water during the winter season.[1] In that event,
if his business were urgent, he might have to take
a circuitous route. Nor was this always possible ;
so widespread and devastating were on occasion the
floods.[2] Summer showers, indeed, might well delay
him ; or, worse still, the sudden onset of a storm and
fast rising waters might cut off his retreat, so that like
the cattle in the field he would have to swim to land.
But then the ' washes ', though they rose quickly,

[1] Such was the highway ' called the Ryse ' between Glastonbury and
Meare in Somersetshire, and adjacent to the river Brue. Liability for its
repair being unknown, the Bench desired two of the local Justices in 1629–30
to examine the inhabitants of both parishes and to make some order for
the repair of the road and the setting up of posts ' by the river's side to
distinguish the river from the highway upon high waters '. *Somerset
Record Soc.*, No. 24, p. 114.

[2] Served with a subpoena to give evidence at Lancaster while living in
Cheshire, Adam Martindale was faced with three bad choices ; to venture,
though he was sick, riding in the rain before the waters of the Mersey rose—
the Mersey was apt to flood ; to risk death by drowning when the waters
were out ; or to forfeit one hundred pounds, a serious loss for a poor,
non-juring clergyman. He chose the first alternative, and, by riding no
more than twelve miles a day, arrived safely at his destination, though he
felt desperately ill on arrival.

fell again in a few hours, leaving the roads practicable
though unpleasant enough, with ruts full of water.

Of all weather abominations severe snowstorms
were the worst, here with the drifts piling up man-high
and more, and there treacherously powdering the iced
surface of the road. During the Great Frost of 1683–4,
travellers on Salisbury Plain, exposed to the full
severity of the weather, were frozen to death in the great
snows then prevailing.   Some years later (1708)
Thoresby, the antiquary, travelled the North Road to
London in weather as distressing if not as severe ;
an experience he portrays with such vivid concern
that, as exemplifying seventeenth-century travel, a
brief account of it will not be inappropriate here.

Leaving Doncaster on the 27th December with
a companion, Alderman Milner, he found the ways
better than he had expected, though the waters had
been out in the neighbourhood of Doncaster. They
reached Barnby Moor that night. Next day they
found ' some of the ways very bad, especially about the
Eel-pie-house near Tuxford, where the ice breaking
in, it was both troublesome and dangerous '. They
ferried over the Trent, also several meadows, then rode
' for above a mile together, very deep to the saddle
skirts frequently, and dangerous, especially upon a long
causeway, which the guide was forced to plumb every
step '; had they slipped they would have been plunged
into water of a considerable depth. Sleeping at
Grantham, they found, next morning, that much snow
had fallen. This retarded their journey, obliging them
to attend upon the Lincoln coach, so that they reached
no further than Stamford, each having had a fall.
Next day ' by reason of the prodigious quantity of
snow and drifting of it ' there was no passing either
for horsemen or coaches, though the coach drivers
knew every step of the way—four or five of these
vehicles had already been overturned. No guide

would venture forth, nor did the farmers around dare attend market. One sojourner at the inn where Thoresby was staying, a clergyman, was only thirteen miles from home, but he was as securely tied as he who lived twenty times as far away. Indeed, a stout heart, infinite patience, and a well-lined purse were necessary to those who went a-journeying in winter. When Thoresby and thirteen fellow-travellers—one a parliament man who was due at Westminster for the Session—at last set out, four days later, their guide turned back at the mile's end, not daring to adventure further for fear of his life. At Royston the people came running out of their houses to stare with amazement at the venturesome party ; and at Enfield, Thoresby having the mischance to break through the ice, his horse plunged almost belly deep into quagmire, so that the water ran in at his pockets, staining his papers, as well as into his boot-tops. No wonder that travellers had special riding suits of thick cloth, and jack-boots with double fronts of the stoutest leather.

The uncertainty of the English climate sometimes caught the traveller unprepared. Pepys, after waiting long one August day for unexpected rain to cease, borrowed a coat of a fellow-wayfarer for sixpence, and then pitied the poor man because he was without protection! At Biggleswade, in July 1661, the weather proved so cold that he was glad to buy a pair of woollen stockings to put over his thread ones. Another time he bought a pair of old shoes for four shillings from the landlord of the inn at Puckeridge where he had stayed the night, but on that occasion the purchase was not made as a result of bad weather but of the swelling of his feet so that he could not get on his boots. A youthful friend of the sons of Sir Thomas Browne who went with them for a tour into Derbyshire was armed against the weather with no more than an open-sleeved doublet. This circumstance caused

much sport to his two companions when, between
Tuckesford and Chesterfield, the rain came down so
heavily that his sleeves spouted water, which made
them liken him to a whale. He was in a ' lamentable
pickle ' and pretty well soused by the time they reached
their inn, after seven hours travelling at two miles
an hour, and in no condition, we may be sure, to
continue further that day. The Brownes, however,
having crawled upstairs to a fire, and well dried
themselves without and liquored themselves within,
were intent upon continuing. Stormy though the
weather was, they wished to take advantage of the
guidance of some Derbyshire ' blades ' who were
bound like themselves for Bakewell. So on they went.
If he of the open-sleeved doublet had any malice in
him it must have done him good to see what their
precipitancy led them into. The way and the weather
were no whit better. The rain came down in floods
from the hill-tops, washing down mud and forming
a bog in every valley ; a trial made doubly hard for
these sons of Norfolk by the craggy ascents and ' almost
perpendicular descents ' which they were forced to
ride down at breakneck speed, if they were to keep in
sight their conductors, who, mounted upon horses
well used to the country, careered always ahead. At
length ' a friendly bough that had sprouted out beyond
his fellows ' gave the leader such a brush of the jacket
that it swept him off his horse which, not caring for
his master's company, ran away. This gave the
strangers opportunity to overtake their guides, and
propose more sober riding. It was all in vain however.
No sooner had they started again than they ' thundred
away ' at such a pace that the strangers were soon
outpaced. When at last the leader halted, at the top
of one of the highest hills thereabouts, they found that
he of the open sleeves was missing. Young Edward
Browne thereupon rode back on their tracks ' hooping

and hallowing' until, afraid that he too might be stranded, he rejoined the mountaineers who told him that there could be no staying with the thick mists of closing day drawing in upon them. They therefore precipitated themselves valleywards into the drenching rain, where all their ' tackling faild and hee that fared best was wet to the skin '. To add to their misery they were upon such an uneven rocky track, full of great holes and with rapid currents, that their hasty leader plunged into a dirty hole and fell over his horse's head, his face, by good luck, smiting a soft muddy place which gave him a mouthful of dirt. Thereafter they rode at more leisurely pace. So up hill and down dale and across swollen streams they arrived at Bakewell, a little after dark. At this place they found good entertainment for themselves, but none for their horses ; there was neither litter nor oats and they were forced ' to lay abroad this wet night, poor jades, in a cold rotten medow which made their hides as tender as you might rub the hair of them as easily as the bristles from a scalded pig '. Having dried their clothes—contrary to Derbyshire custom and precept ' when all is wet to the skin hold out yet ' —they got into the best bed in the house, ' somewhat softer than a rock ', and, wearied with travel, ' snorted out the night '. Next morning saw them sight-seeing ; and then, a serenade of the bagpipe and breakfast over, a happy meeting with the lost one took place, who, as they purposed to ride to two of those ' Wonders of the Peak ' so gratifying and full of awe to the seventeenth-century mind, ' the Devil's Arse ' and ' Eldon Hole ', very prudently bought ' honest Jarvis ' the host's cinnamon coat for eight shillings. The rest of the tour was of a more agreeable nature, and does not, therefore, come within the design of this chapter.

Many qualities then as now went to the making of a good traveller ; patience, prudence, an unruffled

temper, a fair share of wisdom, and quick perception
to shun the many pitfalls that bestrewed his path.
Of these qualities none were so necessary, when it
came to fording rivers and streams, as prudence and
a keen eye. So quickly did the waters rise in the swift-
flowing streams of the North, that even those well
versed in the local lore of depths and currents could
not always get across in safety. It was thus Mrs. Thornton's brother, George Wandesford, perished on the
31st March 1651. Having bidden his footman,
James Brodericke, ' an Irishman, and an excellent
runner ', meet him at Richmond, Yorkshire, at two
o'clock that day—footmen were foot-men in those
days, and frequently Irishmen—he set out alone from
his mother's house at Hipswell towards the River
Swale. Meeting a wedding party

' he asked the people whether the Swaile might be riden.
They said that there had bin a flood, but it was fallen, for some
one had crost the water that morning. Soe he, biding the
people joy in theire marriage, went very slowly towards the
river ; and, as we heard aftterwards by two men which saw
him on [from] the other side, he went down as cairfully and
slowly as foot could fall. Nor was the second flood come so
high till he was in the midest of the river ; but when it comes
from the Dales it falles with a mighty, mountaineous force
sudainly, as I can myselfe testifie, whoe . . . was very nigh
perishing in that water, once or twice . . . two men . . . per-
ceaving a gentleman goeing downe to the water . . . seeing
afarre of that the flood came sudainly, and mightely downe,
made haste to the Swale, and see[ing] only his horrse getting
out of the river, where he had bin tumbled in all over head,
and by swiming had gott out and shaked himselfe. They gott
hold of his bridle . . . perceaved it to be his horse, made a
great search for my brother but could not find the bodie ;
with great sorrow and lamentation they ran to Easby and
Richmond, raising all the townes. . . . Great and infinitt was
the search by thousands of people from that time [Monday,
31st] till Wednesday following,' when his body was discovered,
' it beeing fallen into a poole neare Catterick Bridge, above a
mile from the place he was drowned.'

Many travellers were saved from disaster by the superior sagacity of their horses. The Rev. Oliver Heywood was crossing the River Calder when he found it so deep that he turned back ; then thinking that he must be in the right way went in again to his horse's belly, whereupon the animal refused to go farther. Searching again he found an ' ebbe and safe ford ', and crossed over without mishap. He heard later that he had been on the edge of a dangerous whirlpool and had he gone farther he must have been ' irrevocably swallowed . . . up '. Pope as a young man had a like experience. He was crossing the Thames at night in a coach when the horses refused to go a step farther, though the coachman urged them on. Other travellers then came up, and they learnt that, not only were they nowhere near a ford, but were on the brink of a hole twice as deep as the coach.

In truth, crossing a river at night was almost as dangerous as crossing it when in flood, and he did well who awaited the coming of day at an inn or alehouse on the hither side, or who took his course to the nearest bridge. Not that bridges were altogether secure, as we have already demonstrated. Prudent Mrs. Fiennes, finding that the bridge over the Lynn, between Ely and Huntingdon, was surrounded by water, took the precaution of ferrying over. The carriers, more used to the risk and preferring to save the expense—twopence each horse—kept to the submerged road, full of holes and quicksands as it was. Nevertheless Mrs. Fiennes, though she had perforce to make use of ferries—especially during her tour in Devon and Cornwall—had no love for them. The wet and cold of the passage never failed to give her a chill— miserable fore-knowledge that must have made the journey from Plymouth to Hoile all the more trying, for, besides switchback lanes deep in clay, with sloughs and holes full of water, there were three ferry-crossings to be effected ; the first, Cribly [Cremyll ?] Ferry, being ' a very hazardous passage by reason of 3 tydes meeting ', and though but a mile long, taking at least an hour with seven or eight rowers.   In a September storm of 1693 the Plymouth-Saltash Ferry-boat, higher up, was cast away, three men and three horses being drowned.

The passage of the Humber from Hull to Barton was, in the words of Defoe, ' an ill-favoured, dangerous Passage '.[1]   How unpleasant a crossing it could be Sir John Slingsby knew, when, fearing for the safety of his family after the taking of Newcastle by the Scots, 1640, he took his wife, his wife's sister, a Lady Vavasour, and his own children from Scriven in York-shire to his brother's house in Lincolnshire.   Upon leaving Hull they found not only a cross wind, which increased the difficulty and danger of sailing, but such a number of ships in the harbour that it was a hard task to clear them.   They actually fell foul of one vessel, breaking a piece of the forepart of their boat. This put his wife, his sister-in-law, and Lady Vavasour into such a fright that they never ceased weeping and praying until they came ashore at Barton ;   a concert in which his son Thomas, ' affrighted wth the waters ' joined with such vigour, that it seemed ' as if he would have bust himself '.   A groat each man, and a shilling each horse was the charge for the passage half a century later.

We learn from Pepys the hindrances encountered in crossing the Thames below bridge.   Sometimes the

---

[1] Defoe, writing in the following century, describes his passage 'in an open Boat, in which we had about fifteen Horses, and ten or twelve Cows, mingled with about seventeen or eighteen Passengers, call'd Christians : we were about four Hours ', he continues, ' toss'd about on the *Humber*, before we could get into the Harbour at *Hull* ; whether I was sea-sick or not, is not worth Notice, but that we were all sick of the Passage, any one may suppose, and particularly I was so uneasy at it, that I chose to go round by *York*, rather than return to *Barton*, at least for that time.' *Tour*, vol. ii, p. 142, ed. 1724.

ferrymen were not to be found when wanted—this
occasioned a merry frolic in the Isle of Dogs, the
Carterets, and Pepys, though ' oars ' had at last
arrived, taking a fancy to sleep all night in the coach,
with the glasses drawn up, wine and victuals being
brought them at daybreak. Sometimes at ebb tide
the horse-boat could not be got off—an annoying
obstacle for Sir George and Lady Carteret and Pepys
speeding to young Carteret's wedding with the Lady
Jem. Montague at Dagenham, for they only arrived in
time to meet the bridal party returning from the church.
At Gravesend, on one occasion, the wind and tide
being contrary and the boat loaded with young
Carterets, two saddle-horses, and the invaluable Pepys,
watermen had to be engaged to tow them across ;
a business that was preceded by unpleasant and fierce
haggling, the watermen asking twenty shillings for
the crossing and Pepys refusing to pay, using at the
same time his official position by swearing ' to send
one of them to sea '—' and will do it ' he adds—
whereupon, happily, other rowers undertook to do the
job for half the sum. Young Carteret and Pepys once
spent an hour at Greenwich Ferry crossing the water
' to and again ' to get the coach and horses over. The
carriage of vehicles by ferry was also a risky business.
The York stage-coach being ferried over the Trent
near Newark, November 1694, overset the boat, so
that the three passengers therein were drowned. The
mingling of passengers and horses was not infrequently
a cause of trouble. Both Sir John Reresby and the
Rev. Henry Newcome record being knocked over by
horses as they were stepping out of ferry-boats ; the
baronet, who was ever unfortunate, as he himself
records, had thereby his shoulder put out of joint,
which necessitated the summoning of a bone-setter.

The accident which befell Sir Charles Littleton
as he was passing the ferry at Richmond, Yorkshire,

on the 1st January 1679–80, was not only dangerous but strange. Writing to Lord Hatton to wish him a good New Year he says :

'I had like to have made an ill end of the old one, for yesterday as I was passing the ferry at Richm^d [Richmond, Surrey], my hors leapt over board wth mee on his back into the river, and presently [at once] turnd on one side and mee on his back, my feet hanging in both stirrups. But what wth the flounsing of the hors and my own endeavors I soone was free ; but then was so intangled wth a p^r of greate French bootes and many cloathes, I was not able to turn myself as I lay on my back ; but yet kept myself above water, till Thom Brok leapt out of the boate and pulld me up, being then not out of my depth. And so I gott well ashore, and my hors swam a greate way down the river, till at length he found the way too to the shore, and neither of us, I hope the wors. For my own part, I neither then nor since have found the least cold by it.'

That there was much to exacerbate the temper of the seventeenth-century traveller is apparent ; but no explanation can excuse the ill manners and reckless temper that were often displayed as well at the ferry side as in coach or inn. Fox and his companions at the Mumbles near Swansea, having been refused passage to Cornwall by one shipmaster, had actually got their horses into the boat of a more complaisant owner, when some gentry came up and threatened to pistol the master if he allowed the Quakers passage, a threat that effectually lost them passage across the Bristol Channel, and resulted in their proceeding inland to make the long round by road. An even more discreditable scene occurred at Selby, Yorkshire, of which the unfortunate, and hasty-tempered Sir John Reresby was the central figure.

'. . . a quarrel happening between my company and some others about first going into the boat, I was struck over the head with a cudgel, which provoked me to wound one or two with my sword. This gave so great an alarm to the country people there met together upon the occasion of the market, that I was encompassed and two gentlemen with me and our servants, and after a long defence pulled off my horse, and had certainly been knocked on the head, had I not been rescued by my Moor, who got hold of the man's arm that had me down, as he was going to give the blow. Being got up again, I defended myself till I got into the house of an honest man, that gave me protection till the rabble was appeased.'

The crossing of estuaries was as difficult and uncertain as it was dangerous, on account of the vagaries of tide and sand.   Although Lord Clarendon in his progress as Vice-Roy Elect through North Wales to Holyhead, reached Conway in time to make the river-crossing there, he had, owing to the failure of the ebb tides and the high winds prevailing in the broader part of the Menai Straits, to take the long and circuitous route over rocky Penmaenmawr, and thence across the water by the narrow Bangor passage. Indeed, Lord Bulkeley's coach and servants sent from Anglesea to Penmaenmawr for Lord and Lady Clarendon's use narrowly missed being cast away.   John Bramston (subsequently knighted), his father, the Lord Chief Justice, and two friends, were in like peril when, on their way to Ireland in the year 1631, they made the same crossing.   Wallie, son to the host of the Red Lion at Chester, had told them that the speediest cross-channel passage was from Holyhead, but that they must ride, for the coach could not go thither—as Lord Clarendon subsequently discovered and as has been described in a previous chapter.

' . . . soe away we went next day,' writes Sir John.   ' One Mr. Fountain and Sir Thomas Cary went alonge with us, and passinge over the mountains Pen Men Maure, in the narrow passage wee met a gentleman, of whom Mr. Fountain and Sir Thomas inquired how the tyde was, whoe told them we might pass well if wee made hast, soe they putt on, wee followinge, not knowinge what had passed.   Soe soone as they were downe the mountaine they fell to gallopinge.   Neither my Father nor my selfe understood at first the meaninge ; but,

findinge the water grow deeper, for it came in rills, wee suspected the sea might be comeinge in, as it was, and soe I desired
my father to gallop too.   The sands, save only in those rills,
were carpet wayes.   At last wee came to the place where they
were (I meane Sir Thomas and Mr. Fountain), expectinge the
ferrie boat, which was at Beaumaris, and the ferrimen drinkinge.
Wee all made as loud a call as we could.   We did see some
fisherboats, and being in great perplexitie and feare, we all
rode on brest up the streame, purposeinge to trie if our horses
(the worst comeing to the worst) would carrie us over.   I askt
my father if he could swim ; he sayd when he was younge he
could.   Sayd I : Wee will keepe up the tyde, and with the
help of our horses, and by swimminge, we may either gett over,
or else some of the boates may take us in.   At last the ferrie-
men sett out, and came to us, tellinge us we were in noe dainger-
but by such tyme as we and our horses were on board, a ship
might have rode between us and the shoare behind us, and all
was covered with water where wee stood long before we gott
to Beaumaris.'

Mrs. Fiennes, crossing the Dee from Flint to
Neston, and fearing the shifting sands and deep holes,
took the precaution of engaging two guides.   It was
at least a mile (probably a mile and a half by modern
estimation) before she came to mid-channel, ' wh^{ch} was
pretty deep and with such a current or tyde wch was
falling out to sea, together wth the wind [that] the
horses feete could scarcely stand against it, but it was
but narrow . . . and so soone over '.   The sands were
deep enough, she says, to swallow up a coach or
waggon.   These, doubtless, were the quicksands which,
in March 1687, broke the stage-coach as it travelled
from Neston to Chester ;   an accident that would
have left the children of Sir Charles Porter stranded
but for the timely assistance of Bishop Cartwright's
coach.

Difficult and dangerous as was the crossing of
estuaries, it is nevertheless a fact that travellers often
preferred the smooth sands, treacherous though they
were, to craggy ascents and descents inland—striking

testimony to the primitive state of the roads. Charles
Cotton—the poet and continuator of *The Compleat
Angler*—availed himself of the sands of Dee when
travelling with a guide from Chester to Flint, but only
by dint of hard spurring did he and his companion
arrive dry shod. Still more dangerous was the crossing
of Morecambe Bay from Ulverston to Hest Bank—
the direct and usual route of the people of Furness to
their market town of Lancaster. ' A dreary distance
of about fourteen miles,' it was practicable for no more
than a few hours each day, when low water left the bay
to a great extent uncovered. Though the least
treacherous route was brogged out with tree stumps,
the ever-shifting streams of the Leven, Kent, and Keer
made the employment of guides, with cart and horse,
necessary for strangers, if not for the well-accustomed
Furness and Lancaster folks. Many travellers, in
particular the inexperienced and over-merry, lost their
lives in attempting to make the passage. The parochial
records of Cartmel-in-Furness are crowded, it is said,
with instances of death by drowning on the sands. In
one instance that has come to our notice, that of
Miles Hubbersty, the Quaker, it would appear that
treachery of man and not of nature was the cause of
death. He was, according to Fox, ' destroyed by
a wilful, wicked man, being the carter, who clapd
his hook in his cloak & drew him from the freinds
near 100 yards, so that he was strangled and drowned '.
Could this deed of homicide have been perpetrated
by the guide whose task it was to save imperilled lives ?
Perhaps, for the lives of Quakers were not accounted
so sacred as those of other men.

It will be apparent to the reader that guides were
often necessary adjuncts to travel in localities with
which the traveller was unfamiliar. For those riding
post, professional guides were of course to be obtained
at the post-houses. Other travellers were glad to

engage the services of stout countrymen, obliging innkeepers and ostlers, and, sometimes, chance-met carters and carriers. The last-named, by long and constant familiarity with every quagmire, rill, precipice, or other danger-point upon their routes, made splendid guides. The Rev. James Brome when travelling in Derbyshire with the young sons of Mr. Van-Ackar met ' a plain but sensible Peasant, going homeward with his Cart loaded with Stones ; the poor Man ', he continues, ' readily complied with our Proposals [to act as guide], whereupon taking a Horse out of his own Team, and leaving the rest to graze thereabouts, till his return, our Pilot began to steer forwards ', and carried them safely to their destination, discoursing the while, in answer to their questions, upon the character of the country and the people, and upon the unknown extent of the moors over which they were passing. More usually countryfolk, except those who were used to act as guides, could rarely direct the inquiring stranger farther than two or three miles from their homes. In Derbyshire the people seldom left the confines of their dales. Primitive folk were these, to whom shoes were an encumbrance to be worn by the better sort only, for Sunday show. The young Brownes, going from Buxton towards Chester, had a guide who, ' for the credit of the businese went a little way with his shoes on ', but it was not long before Edward saw him throw them behind a hedge. When questioned he explained that the hardness of the way forced him to it.

It was difficult in bad winter weather and at harvest-time to get any one to undertake the none too pleasant business. Taylor, during the harvesting season in Wales—a country where guides were always necessary owing alike to the difficulty of the region and the scant familiarity of the people with English—was forced to pay two and three shillings each day for guides, and had besides to bear their charges for meat, drink, and lodging. They ' had rather ', he says, ' reap hard all the day for six pence then to go ten or twelve miles easily on foot for two shillings '. As he describes himself as ' ascending and descending almost impassable mountains, and Break-neck stony ways ', the miles having in length what they lacked in breadth, the preference shown by the labourers for the accustomed work in the fields was without doubt judicious.

When a guide had been procured, it was not safe to reckon that his knowledge and skill would be equal to the task of finding his way across open country, not to speak of mist-laden moors or the intricacies of forest tracks. Thus, to the chapter of woes endured by John Chamberlain on his way home from Holland— the long wait at Flushing, the hazardous voyage, and the still more hazardous landing at Yarmouth—yet one other distress was added.

' I will only tell you,' he writes to Sir Dudley Carleton, ' that, tarrying that night at Yarmouth, we went the next day to Norwich, and so toward London, and the first night our guide lost his way on Newmarket Heath ; so that we wandered up and down in rain and blustering weather, and extreme dark, till after eleven o'clock, whereas we might have been at our lodging anon after seven.'

Pepys was often apprehensive of being lost. On one or two occasions his guide failed him, but he was never thereby delayed for more than an hour or two. Once, riding with a guide in the dark through Windsor Forest, he found his way by help of the moon, which recompensed him, he said, for all the pain he had taken in ' studying of her motions '. Luckier was Mrs. Fiennes who in the course of her travels through the length and breadth of England never once met with a guide who failed to carry her to her destination ; though one put her into an awkward predicament by losing her bundle of night-clothes. Gentlemen sometimes, as a friendly act, conducted their friends or erstwhile guests across difficult and perhaps dangerous ground. Travellers who were familiar with the country through which they were passing were only too willing to play the guide to strangers whom they chanced to meet or overtake upon the road. That it was hazardous to accept such proffers, however well meant, the following history of Adam Martindale will show.

When chaplain to Lord Delamere, he was sent in 1673 by his employer from Cheshire to Burton-on-Trent there to consult with a certain Dr. Cotton about the health of two of his Lordship's sons. At Uttoxeter, hearing that the waters were very high around Dove Bridge, by which he had to pass, he inquired for a guide. A young fellow-lodger in the house in which he was staying was about to make the same journey and offered to guide him through the waters, a proposal he accepted. Both being well-horsed they passed the danger zone in safety. His surprise was keen, therefore, when, having reached dry land, his companion told him that he had never passed that way before. It was increased, however, when he made his return journey, for he found ' the water being voided out of the lane ', that it was full of quagmires on both sides with only a narrow path of sound ground in the middle. Only by divine providence, he remarked, had their horses been guided ' through that strait way '. If they had been overthrown into the deep water which lay on either hand, it would have been much if they had escaped with their lives.

The Puritan mind was wont, of course, to take the most serious view of whatever befell. It affected him not only with a ready apprehension of trouble, but also with a desire to record the trials that had been put upon his erring soul and the mercies vouchsafed by his All-Merciful God. Hence Nonconformist divines and those of like disposition recorded in their diaries misfortunes that others of lighter humour passed over in silence or greeted with a jest. That the Rev. Henry Newcome felt that ' all the providences ' were directed against him, when he and a party of friends and relations took a ' pleasure trip ' from Wymington to Cambridge, can cause no more surprise than that he should have taken the punishment as directed solely against himself.

' Six horses we were ', he writes, ' and nine persons, and we seemed to design more pleasure than (it may be) was fit for us '—so worked the Puritan mind. ' The weather being good this day, we set out about nine. By that time we had rid a little above two miles, my cousin Hannah fell in a dry ditch and pulled her horse upon her, and cut her brow very sadly. I was much affected with it, and could have been content to have turned again. But we turned into a little town called Newton, to Mr. Trot, the minister's house, and got the wound dressed, and balsam put into it, and the wound bound up, and she was very hearty, and concluded, (after two hours' stay) to go forward ; and just as they were fetching out the horses, Dr. Bletso, a relation of theirs, came by, and so came in and sewed up the wound and put on a plaster ; and this was a providence that a little alleviated our trouble, and encouraged us again, and we set out on our way. We came not to St. Neot's (which was but ten miles) but Mrs. Katherine Robinson, one of our company, was tired and ready to fall off her horse ; then was I forced to take her, and Rose [his daughter] rode single nine miles ; but then it rained, and was so cold on that plain champaign between St. Neot's and Cambridge, that Rose was weary, and we were forced to change again. But Mrs. Katherine could not ride insomuch that we were forced to go a foot's pace, and it was late and rainy. We light at the Crown, where our lodging was bad, and the worst light to me that night, lodging in a pitiful cockloft, where were two beds full besides of men that lived in the Fens. And it was the saddest night of rain that had come of long. The next day it rained all day, insomuch that we could not stir out into the fair [the celebrated Stourbridge Fair] of all day. The Wednesday morning, being September 13th, we went to the fair, which was sadly dirty, and altogether unpleasant to be in. It was a fair remarkable for the great and sudden inundation that drowned all the lower fair, quite up to the Proctor's booth, to the great loss of many. We set out about three, intending for St. Neot's that night, but in our way also was strangely prevented. Mrs. Robinson thrown off her horse at the Bridge, and dragged by the foot in the stirrup. She got up, was dirtied sadly, but yet unhurt, and after half an hour's stay on her, we essayed to march again, and at the town's end met our company coming on foot back again, which amazed me. But we were forced to return to our inn again, for my poor cousin Hannah was fallen into a pond, and so we got to the same lodgings, got her to bed, and were forced to stay at Cambridge this night also.'

However, after all these misadventures they arrived safely at Wymington, ' and it pleased God my cousin Hannah after mended of her eye, and had no hurt by her other fall into the pond '.

Almost as unpleasant, though not quite so full of peril, must have been the Pepysian trip to Brampton and the Fen country in September 1663, yet the Diarist was merry enough between whiles. First Mrs. Pepys, having drunk some cold beer at Bunting-ford, began to be sick. She became so pale that her husband who was alone with her in a ' great chamber ', their friends being out of the way, ' thought she would have died, and so in great horror, and having a great trial of my true love and passion for her, called the maids and mistress of the house, and so with some strong water [brandy] she come to be pretty well again '. Whereupon, his fright over, he called their travelling companions to supper in the great chamber, and became ' very merry in talk '. Next day one of their fellow riders had two falls, ' once in water, and another in dirt ', despite which they continued very merry. From Brampton, Pepys, his uncle and cousins went to pay a business visit to some cousins living at Parson's Drove, a troublesome journey across the fens, where their horses sank to their bellies. He found it a ' heathen place ', and his cousins living

' in a sad, poor thatched cottage like a poor barne ', peeling hemp. Though he found interest in their occupation—he found interest in most things—he was nevertheless ashamed of their company when he supped with them at the miserable inn to which they repaired. Still more unpleasant was the news brought them that one of their horses had been lost out of the stable, a misfortune that was somewhat lightened for the Diarist when he learned that it was not his, but his uncle's mount that was missing. They were suspicious of a London lawyer's clerk who was lodging next door and had him secured. So, ' about twelve at night or more ', our friend Pepys went to bed, ' in a sad, cold, stony chamber ' ; to be awakened soon after to hear the good tidings that the horse had been found—and, we suppose, the unfortunate Londoner released. Next morning Pepys found that he had been cruelly bitten by gnats, a mishap that might have been worse. They went over sad fens to Wisbech and concluded their business, not entirely to their satisfaction. Next day he picked up his wife at Brampton and they proceeded homeward. It proved a pleasant journey until they reached Biggleswade, where they had to employ countrymen to lead them through the long and danger-ous waters which had flooded the country thereabouts. Their troubles were then over, though next day Mrs. Pepys was very discouraged at the prospect of the long journey to London. They rode, however, easily to Hatfield, and there she procured the favour of travelling in an empty coach to London for the sum of two shillings and sixpence.

VIII

ON THE ROAD

ALTHOUGH the great days of pilgrimage were gone when knights and squires, monks and nuns, merchants with forked beards, yeoman ' clade in cote and hode of grene ', and all the other company of ' sondry folk ', rode in fellowship to Canterbury, there was yet great diversity of persons and equipage to give life and colour to the road ; a diversity unknown in these days of rapid movement, levelling men and manners to dull uniformity. Even the pilgrim's staff might still be met with on the road ; but of this more later, when the mighty of the land have had the consideration due to exalted rank.

Chief of all road users was the King, chief not only by right of his position as head of the state, but also by reason of the numbers that formed his train and the disturbance his passing caused to the countryside. The Divine Right of Kings might be questioned, but the ceremonial pertaining to royalty was not one jot abated. Nobles, Courtiers, Ushers, Sewers of the Chamber, Sergeants at Arms, Gentlemen-Waiters, Pages, Trumpeters, Sergeants-Trumpeters, Footmen, Porters, Messengers, Heralds at Arms, Yeoman of the Pad-horse and of the Sword, Grooms of the Pack-saddle and of the Great Horse, Sergeant of the Close Carriage, Harbingers, Sumptermen, Bottlemen, the Waymaker, the Coachmen, the Knight-Marshal, and King's Poet, formed the royal train and made up an assemblage of some hundreds of persons. All these King James I took with him on his progresses, to the distress of the countryfolk who had to lodge and feed

G g

these persons, supply the royal larder, and deliver carts
and teams for conveyance of the royal baggage. Payment was made, it is true, but the rates fell far short of
market prices, and even so, the money was not easily
secured from the royal purveyors, whose duty it was
to supply the royal household, and whose pleasure and
profit it was to fleece the conscribed by the selling of
exemptions and the abating, delaying, and withholding
of payments.[1] In 1615 when the King was proceeding
to Salisbury and the Queen to Bath, the counties
through which they were to pass made petition to be
spared the honour, ' in respect of the hard winter,
and hitherto extreme hot and dry summer, whereby
cattle are exceeding poor, and like to perish every-
where '. The petition was unheeded ; the progresses
went their allotted ways. Indeed, the following
winter James went to Newmarket with ' twenty earls
and barons attending, and such a number of principal
gentlemen ' that it caused wonder how they could all
lodge ' in that poor village '. But he too had his
difficulties. His requirements were large; his revenue,
notwithstanding his privileged position, insufficient
to cover them ; his purveyors, we may suppose, as
ready to cheat their master as to defraud those whom
they forced to cater for his necessities. For his journey
to Scotland in 1617 he had difficulty in raising the
hundred thousand pounds required, though he resorted
to forced loans from London citizens and others of
his richer subjects. On this occasion he took with him
fifty gentlemen pensioners, and twenty-four of the
Chapel Royal, while many things were sent for his
use, including ' all manner of furniture for a chapel '
and more especially ' a pair of organs that cost above
£400 ', and ' pictures of the apostles, Faith, Hope,
and Charity, and such other religious representations ',
all under the charge of Inigo Jones. ' . . . how welcome

[1] See Note J, pp. 327-9.

they will be thither God knows ', adds our informant, John Chamberlain. For the Queen's stay at Bath, though it was but a ten days' visit, a sum of thirty thousand pounds was needed.

The cities that were so honoured had likewise to bear the brunt of heavy charges. The streets had to be repaired and swept, gravelled, and garnished with camomile and other herbs ; [1] all obstructions, such as rails and midden heaps had to be removed. Window-frames, doors, and pumps were newly painted, stone-work whitened, the Royal and City Arms new 'tricked', and boughs from neighbouring woodlands set up at the street doors. Mayor and aldermen had to pur-chase new gowns, and their attendants to be newly decked in ' hats, feathers, stockings, Gartas ' and other apparel, besides receiving wages for their services. Moreover, there were gifts to be bestowed upon the King, Queen, Prince, and Nobles—if not silver-gilt cups and bowls, necessitating perhaps a visit to London, at least pairs of handsomely embroidered gloves—and fees to be given to the horde of lesser officials who attended the royal travellers. All this had to be paid for by city and citizens, not to mention the cost of lodg-ing and dieting their exacting and not always welcome guests. At Cambridge in 1615, during the first of two visits paid to the town that year, over two hundred pounds

[1] For the visit of James II to Oxford in 1687, order was given that the highways along which he was to pass were to be ' thick with gravell that noe horses or coaches could be heard to tread or go '—a desirable measure on noisy cobbles ; but, says Anthony Wood, the ' abundance of raine that fell (the next day after the king came in) turned it all to dirt, and the citizens were forced to hire people to shovel it up and carry it away in carts in North Gate street '. Rails and posts before houses were removed, and ditches filled in, but the King and his retinue preferred ' the common way in the middle of the street '. That the strewing of leaves and herbs was an act of courtesy as well as ceremony is shown by a touching mani-festation of sympathy and homage rendered, in July 1647, to the hapless Charles I and his children. ' The King's Children coming to *Causham* [Caversham] to meet their Father, great Numbers of People flocked thither to see them, and strewed the Ways with green Boughs and Herbs.' White-locke's *Memorials* . . . , ed. 1732.

were spent by the Corporation, and nearly six hundred pounds by the University, for the nine or ten days' festivities. In 1612 the town of Leicester, which had only just recovered from the contagious sickness, wrote to the Earl of Harrington, its influential neighbour, begging his lordship's help for the repair of its town, then much decayed, and pleading to be given assistance from neighbouring towns in the cartage of stone, gravel, and sand for its roads, so that the King might 'without danger perform his Highness's intended progress'. It was unlucky that the town was free of the plague. Had the dread disease still lingered there, the ushers who went in advance to make arrangements for the royal progress would not have given a clean bill of health, and the town would have been saved the burden of a visit.

It was easier for the court to avoid plague-stricken towns than it was to avoid the plague itself. During the royal tour of 1603 the court was ' contynuallie haunted wth the sicknes, by reason of the disorderlie companie' which followed them, forcing them to move from place to place, and infect all places through which they passed. A disorderly company it must have been, thieves being not unknown. One ' plaied the Cut-purse ' from Berwick to Newark in the inaugural progress to England, 1603, before he was caught and executed ; and his execution (without trial) raised a grave constitutional question.

Not only were the royal travellers followed by an army of retainers and their hangers-on, but the roads along which they passed were lined with loyal subjects. In the great progress South of 1603, so great were the multitudes that came to rejoice at the sight of the new King that James—who ' hated the bustle of a mixed multitude '—' was faine to publish an inhibition against the inordinate and dayly accesse of people's comming '.

Lords, gentlemen, city brethren, country-folk, suitors
—noble and ignoble—pressed one another to catch
sight of his royal person, ' the better sort ... to observe
and serve ; the other(s) to see and wonder '. At
Stamford ' a company of honest poor suitors ' came on
high stilts to prefer a suit against the Lady Hatton.
At Royston he was met by the High Sheriff, Sir Edward
Denny, clad in a rich suit of dun colour, attended by
a ' goodly companie of proper men, being in number
seven score ', dressed in ' blew coates with sleeves
parted in the middest, buttoned behinde in jerkin
fashion ', with white doublets, hats, and feathers, all
mounted on horses with red saddles, who awaited his
coming with ' a gallant horse ' richly caparisoned as
gift for the royal traveller ; while towards Standon
the Bishop of London met him with ' a seemely
company of Gentlemen in tawny coates and chaines
of gold '.   But it was the good folk of London and
Middlesex who made greatest demonstrations of joy ;
as dwellers in or near the heart of the kingdom they
had doubtless felt more keenly than upland peoples,
the general sense of uneasiness and insecurity which
prevailed during the final, long-drawn months of
Elizabeth's reign. The multitudes of people, as he
neared London, were such ' in highwayes, fieldes,
medowes, closes, and on trees, that they covered the
beautie of the fieldes '. Fighting for place, injuring
and hurting one another, they shouted and cried and
cast up their hats—' of which many never returned
into the owners' hands ' until ' he passed by them over
the fields, and came in at the back side of the Charter-
house '. A few years later the same loyal folk came in
such numbers afoot, or horseback, and in coaches to
salute the King and Queen of Denmark, as they came
from Blackwall through the London suburbs, that
there was hardly way left for the royal company to
pass onward to Theobalds, where lay strewn upon the

highways green oaken leaves bearing the words
' Welcome, Welcome ', writ in letters of gold. When
the return journey was made to the Danish fleet,
anchored in the Thames off Gravesend, the neighbouring Rochester was invaded by a host of sightseers so
' that thousands could get no lodginges or meate for
their money '. Again, when in 1638 that unfortunate
Queen, Marie de Medicis, came to seek refuge with
her more ill-fated son-in-law, Charles I, the reception
accorded her was such, if we may believe her chronicler
M. de la Serre, as would have befitted an Elizabeth or
a Catherine the Great. At Harwich, where she landed,
and all along the road to London crowds of persons
of all ages gathered ; nor did a start at daybreak deter
them from assembling. At Chelmsford the neighbouring peasantry, men and women, mustered 'without
any other order or command than . . . their own zeal '.
Some led by a violin and others by a bagpipe they
' received the Queen, dancing to the sounds of these
instruments, enlivened by a thousand acclamations
of joy '.

An improvised entertainment was a favourite
method of attracting the attention of royal travellers.
Queen Anne (of Denmark), returning from Bath and
Bristol and receiving due notice, made a stand at the
Wansdyke, where the Vicar of Bishop's Canning,
dressed as an old bard, and his scholars in ' shepherds'
weeds ', received her with a four-part song, com-
mencing :

> Shine, o thou sacred shepards' Star,
> On silly shepherd swaines,

to the great liking and content of the Queen.

To organize such a wayside serenade for the King,
her husband, would have been scarcely possible.
James loved hunting no less than scholarship. It is
said that he often followed deer (presumably when not
on progress) for the space of eight whole days, relays

of horses being posted in various places to enable him
to keep up the chase.[1]   His progresses consequently,
if primarily intended for intercourse between monarch
and subjects, were made the occasion of much hunting
and hawking.   Sometimes, on his summer tours, he
went no farther than the Midland counties, visiting
first one country mansion and then another.   Travelling
no more than six to twenty miles a day, he spent his
days in hunting and hawking, and his nights in feasting,
dancing, and the witnessing of masques.   Even the
long journey to Scotland was enlivened with his
favourite sport—a cause of disappointment, without
doubt, to many gathered upon the highway to watch
his passing, and most certainly of perturbation to the
Mayor and Commonalty of his good city of Lincoln,
for, assembled at the appointed place of meeting
outside the town, they found that ' by reason his
Majesty hunted along the heath ' he came not by the
highway to the rendezvous.   They met him eventually
near Queen Eleanor's Cross, and, next day, had the joy
of accompanying him when, descending from his
coach, he mounted ' his horse caprisoned of state '
and made his state entry into the city.

The entry of persons of Royal birth into corporate
cities—and sometimes of others of note—was always
a matter of ceremony, whether it were the monarch
himself or foreign princeling.   First a watchman was
stationed in a tower to give notice of the guest's advent,
or a messenger was sent to watch the exalted personage's
movements and report his approach.   This having

---

[1] Busino, Chaplain to the Venetian Embassy, our informant on this
matter, gives a curious description of James on horseback. ' . . . in riding
he cares for nothing, never holding the reins in his hands, but relying
entirely on the address, agility, and dexterity of his grooms, who run on
either side of him, keeping pace with his horse : it is indeed true that he
now and then gets some awkward falls, but this is attributed to the hot
temper of the hackneys here, rather than to any other cause.' ' Diaries and
Despatches of the Venetian Embassy at the Court of King James I ',
Rawdon Brown, *Quarterly Review*, July 1857.

been done the church bells summoned the citizens
and others to the Guildhall or other place of assemblage
whence they sallied forth for some distance on horseback and in coaches, accompanied on occasions of
state by the Lord-Lieutenant of the county, the High
Sheriff, and the militia, to attend the distinguished
traveller on the last stage of his journey to the city
gates, where mayor and aldermen awaited his arrival.
In March 1680–1, when Charles II and his Queen
arrived at the East Gate of Oxford for that short and
stormy session known as the third Whig Parliament,
they found awaiting them eighteen constables of the
city and suburbs with painted and gilt staves, four
sergeants at mace, two on horseback, and two on foot
with their silver staves erected, the mace-bearer, the
Town Clerk with a chain of silver-gilt about his neck,
the Mayor in a scarlet gown with a livery on one side,
and the Recorder in a black gown on horseback upon
the other, the Aldermen, Bailiffs, and ex-Bailiffs all in
scarlet and fur, each with a livery servant by his side to
lead his horse, and the rest of the House and Common
Council, about sixty, in black gowns faced with fur.
When the King's coach stopped the Mayor and
Recorder knelt down by the coach-side upon a mat,
the latter making a speech in English, the former
offering the ' gestamen ' of his authority (that is to
say, the mace).   Rich gloves were then presented to
the couple and the procession made its way into Oxford.
First came the city brethren and their retainers, then
the King's coach, followed by the Life Guards—post-
restoration Royalty seldom travelled without attendant
Guards—the coaches of the Royal retinue, the
Lord Lieutenant with his horses of State led before
him, the High Sheriff, and the gentlemen of the
county and their liveries, the county troops ' buff-
coated and well horsed ' bringing up the rear.   As
the King passed to his lodgings in Christ Church, there

King Charles the 2⁴ in Disguise riding before M.ᵗ Lane by which he made his Escape: the Lord Wilmot at a distance. Clarendon Vol. 3. Pag 440.

were 'such shoutings, acclamations and ringing of
bells, made by loyall hearts and smart lads of the
layetie of Oxon '—so writes the Royalist Wood—
' that the aire was so much peirced that the clouds
seemed to divide.   The generall cry was " Long live
King Charles ", and many drawing up to the very
coach window cryed " Let the King live, and the
devill hang up all roundheads " ; at which his
majestie smiled and seemed well pleased '.   So great
was the press that the coach was scarce able to pass,
and the rain was driven backwards ' by the verie
strength of voices and hummings '—humming seems
to have been a usual expression of approbation at this
time—and, lest we might think this phenomenon
incredible, Wood adds for our convincement, that he
' did partly observe it ' from a stationer's shop.   The
King, it seemed, had prohibited any public reception.
Nevertheless the University authorities went in a body
to his lodgings to make him speeches of welcome ;
contrary to practice they had not ridden out to the first
milestone to give greetings.   Very different was the
Royal departure a few days later.   Having by a strata-
gem dissolved the obnoxious Parliament, Charles,
after a hurried breakfast, departed by a back staircase,
and stepping into a private coach, unattended by guards
or footmen, set out for Windsor, the Queen and retinue
following at four o'clock the next morning.   Panic
ensued among the alarmed Whigs, who, having entered
Oxford in such triumphal fashion, with bows and
ribbons and large retinues of armed horsemen—a little
matter Wood does not deign to mention—now left it
as though flying for their lives, so that the price of
horses doubled, and the roads outward were thick
with men a-horseback and in coaches hurrying to
their homes.
     Even at less critical seasons the loyal among the
town and gown contrived to make a good showing with

pageantry, speech-making, and acclamations. Sometimes there was an unrehearsed effect, as in 1687 when
James II, visiting the town, arrived at the milestone
where the heads of the University were assembled.
The usual Latin oration having been delivered, and
the Bedells' staves offered to the King, the Superior
Bedell of law, Christopher Wase, 'being a meer
scholar, and troubled with shaking hands, could not
get on horsback, but was helped up, and when he was,
he could not hold his staff upright, but cross ways,
because he would hold the bridle, which caused
laughter in some and anger in others '—who doubtless
felt the indignity put upon the University more than
the humour of the incident.

King William, too, had a popular reception when
in 1695 he made a progress to Lincoln and Nottingham. More considerate than some of his Stuart
predecessors, ' he was accompanied with not above
twenty nobles from London and his guard, besides
the gentlemen that he had picked up in the country
as he came along '. Moreover, he brought with him
all his own provisions—purveyance had been abolished
—though at Lincoln he made little use of them,
' eating nothing there but a porringer of milk '. At
prayers at the Minster, the day after his arrival, the
people so thronged about him, ' that he could scarce
get any wind ', until he made a sign for them to stand
off. Indeed, his coming made a ' vast noise in the
country, and prodigious number of men went from all
parts to see him ; even from York, and Carlisle, and
Newcastle itself . . . there was so many that people of
all sorts were forst to ly in stables and barns, and every
thing was so exceeding dear that it is incredible. The
parriters ' (apparitors, messengers of the Ecclesiastical
Courts), continues our informant, Abraham de la
Pryme, ' were sent out, all ten miles round about
Lincoln, to bid the clergy come in to kiss the king's

hand, and all the constables had order to acquaint
towns and gentlemen with the king's comeing to
Lincoln '. Thus was it in times before a daily press.

The reception of official personages was fraught
with almost as much ceremony as that of Royalty
itself. When Sir John Reresby first entered York
as Governor of the city, he was met upon the road by
the High Sheriff, citizens, and gentlemen of York,
to the number of four hundred, together with one
company of foot ; the cannon of Clifford's Tower
being fired as he arrived within the city precincts.
Lord Clarendon, in his progress North as Lord-
Lieutenant designate of Ireland, was met two miles
outside Chester by a gathering of the county gentry.
Through the suburbs he passed between the town
militia, who wore red coats lined with black, while in
the city itself ' My Lord Ferrers's regiment ' lined the
route. Just within the city gates the Mayor and
Aldermen stood upon a scaffold, in their ' formalities ',
whence the Recorder greeted him with a speech of
welcome. It was, said the recipient of these honours,
impossible to make a greater show, though the King
had been there himself.

Much ceremony encompassed the visits of foreign
princes to these shores, even though they came
incognito, as did the Grand Duke Cosmo of Tuscany.
This young man was given something like a royal
progress when, in 1669, he landed at Plymouth and
proceeded to London. Guns boomed when his frigate
entered the Sound ; guns greeted him as he stepped
ashore. A ceremonial reception by the civic and
military authorities ensued, followed by a procession
through the town between a double line of soldiers
under arms, with colours flying, to the sounds of trumpets and drums, and ' the festive shouts and acclamations of a very numerous population '—the town
numbered, according to the chronicler of these events,

some twelve to fifteen thousand inhabitants. They filled not only the streets, the windows, and the roof-tops, but the shrouds and riggings of the ships in the dock. At every village through which the royal traveller passed, the cheerful sounds of the church bells greeted his ears. At every town which he visited the Mayor and Aldermen in ' their habits of ceremony ' their mace-bearers before them, came to pay their respects. At Basingstoke—a wretched timber-built town—they tracked him to the parish church, whither he had gone sightseeing, and offered a public reception which he declined. So, too, the principal county gentlemen would journey a mile or two to bring him into town, while others would flock to his inn or private lodging to bid him welcome to their county. At Salisbury the ladies of the neighbourhood, likewise anxious to behold the distinguished visitor, would have assembled at the inn to watch him sup, had not the gallant heir of the Medicis frustrated their design by paying them a visit at the house where they had gathered to await the royal supper-hour. Two miles outside Basingstoke he was met by a troop of fifty-four men of the Royal Regiment of the Earl of Oxford, who had come thither by command of the King to attend upon him. He accepted a small escort for his baggage, and dismissed the rest after a brief roadside inspection. Contrary to his orders the whole troop appeared next morning, and, refusing to be dismissed, accompanied him to Egham. This, doubtless, was a precaution taken to convey him safely over the robber-infested Bagshot Heath—an escort of Train Bands had, as we have already seen, been similarly employed across Dorchester Downs. As he drew nearer to London he met coaches, one after another, laden with nobles and gentlemen who had come to greet him, either on their own behalf, or on that of the King or the Duke of York. Thus his train grew until, at

Brentford, he desired them all, with the exception of his personal retinue and a few of the greatest nobles, to go on before him, in order to preserve his incognito. Thence he took coach with a few compatriots, followed by the deputy Master of the Ceremonies, his adjutant with the luggage, and a coachful of nobles. Through a ' truly delicious ' country, studded with villas and country houses, he passed to London—passing at such a speed that Pepys, who was one among the throng of persons who drove, walked and rode towards Brentford to meet him, could see little of him beyond the impression that he seemed ' a very jolly and good comely man '.

Allowance must be made for the loyal zeal of court chroniclers and others. There were many we know who grumbled not a little at the inconvenience caused to themselves and to the country by these royal journeys. Yet so strange and indefinable is the glamour of royalty, these malcontents were no doubt as forward as the most loyalist of their neighbours to line the highways and gaze upon the countenance of monarch or prince. It is probable that in one class of persons, those on travel bent, not the most infectious enthusiasm could overcome the displeasure and irritation that the royal movements generated ; at least if, as we surmise, the experience of Thomas Ellwood and Guli Springett was not altogether exceptional. Guli Springett—later to become the wife of William Penn, Quaker and founder of Pennsylvania —was the owner of an estate in Sussex, and at this season of her life, 1669, no more than twenty-two years of age. Thither she was sent by her mother, in charge of Ellwood, her old school-fellow and a valued friend of the family, to stay with her uncle Springett and conduct business with her tenants. They set out from Chalfont St. Peter's, the home of Guli's mother, tarried the first night in London, and next morning took the

Tonbridge road.   At Sevenoaks, where they put in
to bait, they had much ado to get either provisions or
room for themselves and their horses.   The house
was full of guests, and those not of the better sort, for
the Duke of York was on the road that day on his way
to the Wells, and divers of his guards and the meaner
sort of his retinue had nearly filled all the inns of the
town.   Leaving John Gigger, Guli's servant, to take
care of the horses, Ellwood procured a little room for
her, and, having seen her into it, went to the kitchen
' and with much ado by praying hard and paying dear '
got a small joint of meat from the spit to stay their
appetites, which ' were all pretty sharp set '.   They
left the inn as quickly as they could and rode on, for
the roysterers who swarmed there had looked very
sourly upon them, as though they grudged them both
the horses they rode and the clothes they wore.
Coming to a ' Spot of fine smooth sandy Way ' upon
which the horses trod softly, they did not hear a knot
of roysterers following them until Ellwood, who was
abreast of Guli and talking to her, heard a little noise,
turned, and saw a horseman coming up on the farther
side of her horse, having his left arm stretched out
ready to take her about the waist and lift her backwards on to his own horse.

' I had but just Time ', he writes, ' to thrust forth my
Stick, between him and her, and bid him stand off ; and at
the same Time reigning my Horse, to let hers go before me,
thrust in between her and him, and being better mounted than
he, my Horse run him off.   But . . . he slipt by me, and got
up to her on the near Side. . . . To prevent which, I thrust in
upon him again, and in our jostling, we drove her Horse quite
out of the Way, and almost into the next Hedge.
' While we were thus contending I heard a Noise of loud
Laughter behind us, and turning my Head that Way, I saw
three or four Horse-men more, who could scarce sit their
Horses for laughing, to see the Sport their Companion made
with us.   From thence I saw it was a Plot laid, and that this

rude Fellow was not to be dallied with ; wherefore I bestirr'd myself the more to keep him off, admonishing him to take Warning in Time, and give over his Abusiveness, lest he repented too late. He had in his Hand a short thick Truncheon, which he held up at me ; on which laying hold with a strong Gripe, I suddenly wrenched it out of his Hand, and threw it as far a Distance behind me as I could.

'While he rode back to fetch his Truncheon, I called up honest *John Gigger,* who was indeed a right honest Man, and of a Temper so thoroughly peaceable, that he had not hitherto put in at all. But now I rouzed him, and bid him ride so close up to his Mistress's Horse on the further Side, that no Horse might thrust in between, and I would endeavour to guard the near Side. But he, good Man, not thinking it perhaps, decent enough for him to ride so near his Mistress, left room enough for another to ride between. And indeed so soon as our Brute had recovered his Truncheon, he came up directly thither, and had thrust in again, had not I, by a nimble Turn, chopt in upon him and kept him at a Bay.

'I then told him, I had hitherto spared him ; but wish'd him not to provoke me further. This I spake with such a Tone as bespake an high resentment of the Abuse put upon us, and withal pressed so close upon him with my Horse, that I suffered him not to come up any more to *Guli.*

'This his Companions, who kept an equal Distance behind us, both heard and saw, and thereupon two of them advancing, came up to us. I then thought I might likely have my Hands full, but Providence turn'd it otherwise. For they, seeing the Contest rise so high, and probably fearing it would rise higher, not knowing where it might stop, came in to part us ; which they did, by taking him away, one of them leading his horse by the Bridle, and the other driving him on with his Whip, and so carried him off.'

One of the roysterers, however, stayed behind. A heavy shower happening to come down, he and our travellers all took shelter beneath the same well-spread oak, whereupon he tried to excuse his colleague's behaviour by saying that he had drunk a little too liberally. The excuse held no weight with **Ellwood** who told him that one vice could not excuse another ; that they all had abetted their friend in his attack ;

that he was not ignorant whose livery they wore, and was well assured that the Duke, when he heard of their action, would call them to account for their outrageous behaviour. Upon this, the frightened retainer begged hard of Ellwood that he would pass by the offence, for it would mean the utter ruin of the young man were the Duke to hear what had occurred. Having said all he could without any sign of Ellwood's relenting, he rode off, followed at a more leisurely pace by the other travellers. At Tonbridge, Ellwood and Gigger kept close on either side of their charge, a precaution which Ellwood thought well justified, for, though it rained hard the streets were thronged with men who looked very earnestly upon them but did not offer them any affront. As a result of this misadventure it was late before they arrived at their destination. When Guli told her uncle of the treatment to which she had been subjected he resented it highly, and would have prosecuted the culprits had not Guli chosen to pass by the offence, having been so well preserved from danger.

Retainers of princes and nobles were prone to arrogance ; for like master like man. Great noblemen, aware of their exalted position in the State, were accustomed to receive marked deference from all inferiors, while their retainers not only claimed privileges for their masters but like consideration for themselves. The high notions sometimes conceived of what was due to noble blood are shown by the following letter written from Tunbridge Wells by John Verney in 1685.

'Yesterday morning Capt. Henry Wharton comeing to the Wells, bade a Coachman drive out of the way for the D[uke] of Norfolk was comeing, but the coachman haveing broke some harness, said the D. of N. must waite if he came, or words to that effect, on which Harry W. knockt him downe, then Dr. Jefferyes (Broth: to the L^d Ch.J.) lookt out of the coach & askt the reason of the action ; the Captaine bade him come out of the coach, & he would serve him soe too ; this hath

CATHARINE OF BRAGANZA AT PORTSMOUTH

CATHARINE OF BRAGANZA AT HAMPTON COURT

angered his Lordshipp, but I presume (for the Duke's sake) tis husht up.'

Habituated though the age was to ostentatious display, the *cortège* of the Marquis of Winchester called forth comment when, in 1687, he travelled South from Scotland with four coaches and a hundred horsemen in his train ; a display of numbers that was accentuated by extravagancies of deportment and manner of living, for the Marquis was acting a part. Not liking the methods of government of James II, but anxious to avoid committing himself to the opposition party, he counterfeited a disordered mind, with such success that some among his friends were deceived by the follies in which he indulged. That the retinue was remarkable for its size for any person not of royal blood is made clear by comparison with that of the Duke of Newcastle, husband of the whimsical Duchess. Though the latter ' travelled indeed like a great prince ', he was accompanied by no more than three coaches and about forty attendants on horseback when he and his family migrated from London to Welbeck. Even so, it was sometimes impossible for the whole party to be lodged at the same inn. Perhaps greater display was made by the nobility in the earlier years of the century than was possible after years of destructive civil war. Giovanni Scaramelli, Venetian secretary in England, writes in a dispatch of 1603 ' the drain on private purses is enormous, to such an extent that even the smaller members of the Council, the lesser Peers and gentlemen, appear in public with forty or fifty pack-horses and some with teams of horses to the number of one, two, or three hundred horse with double sets of livery, one for the valletaille and the other for the gentlemen of the suites '. However it may be, Lord William Howard of Naworth, as great a noble as any in the land, was content to travel with twenty-four men and twelve (? spare) horses when

he journeyed from Thornthwaite to London in April
1620, usually a matter of ten or eleven days. Five
years later he had no more than six in his company ;
yet the expenses of the journey, eighteen pounds ten
shillings and twopence, almost equalled the cost of
the previous journey. It was customary, whenever
Lord and Lady William Howard left Naworth Castle
on a journey, for a crowd of poor people to gather at
the gate to wish them God speed, while others awaited
them at some turn in the road. Nor were their
attentions ever suffered to pass without distribution of
largesse to the needy and deserving.

Nobles passing to the Continent as Ambassadors
Elect travelled in a manner befitting the exalted rank
they were assuming. When Lord Roos set out for
Spain in 1617—' in a good and fair ship of the
king's, called *the Dreadnought*'—he took with him
six footmen ' whose apparelling stood him in £50
a man, eight pages at £80 a-piece ', twelve gentlemen,
to whom was entrusted one hundred pounds each for
their habiliments, and twelve ordinary servants ' who
were likewise very well appointed '. His twelve
sumpter cloths ' stood him in better than £1,500 ' and
' All his other provisions were suitable '. But this
display did not approach the regal splendour with
which the Duke of Buckingham prepared to go to
Paris in 1625 to escort the new Queen, Henrietta
Maria, to England. His train was to consist of six
or seven hundred persons ' at least ', Lords, Knights,
Privy Gentlemen, Grooms of the Chamber, Chief
Yeomen, Yeomen of the second rank, with grooms
attendant upon them, Master Cooks and second Cooks,
Pages, Footmen, ' Labourers-selleters ' (saddlers ?),
Huntsmen, and Stablemen—most with one or more
rich suits apiece—together with ' Three rich velvet
Coaches inside, without gold lace all over ', with eight
horses in each coach and six coachmen richly suited,

eight score musicians, similarly clad, and twenty-two watermen ' suited in sky coloured taffaty all gilded with anchorgs and my lords arms'. That Buckingham did not dazzle the eyes of the French court with this splendour of display was due to the death of the old King, James—which offered the favourite increased opportunities for political activity at home—and, possibly, to the distaste the French already felt for his person. As a consequence, when he did reach Paris, after the royal wedding, his arrival was as unexpected as it was unwelcome—to the French court if not to the neglected Queen of Louis XIII, into whose dull life he brought for a few brief weeks at least the semblance of romance.

Ambassadorial splendour has to be paid for, as one French representative to the court of St. James learnt in a fashion as lowering to his dignity as the sea-sickness that he dreaded.

' The French ambassador went hence on Sunday morning,' writes Chamberlain in January 1620/1, ' having sent away the most part of his train two days before, being himself such a fresh-water sailor that he rather chose to go by coach through all the foul ways, than take the benefit of the river to Gravesend; and endures the sea so ill, that, at his coming, he lay sick at Dover two days before he could recover himself, and was often heard here to say that he would give a thousand crowns that he were well over. He was followed to Rochester by divers shopkeepers of the Exchange for satisfaction of wares delivered to some of his followers, to the value of £400. How they sped I heard not; but perhaps he thought that might be abated, having bestowed £1000 or £1200 among them.'

Judges riding circuit—and ride they did in the earlier part of the century—were followed by a train of law-officials, barristers, and servants. Nor was this all. To the boundary of each county there rode to meet them a cavalcade embracing the chief elements of the countryside ; the High Sheriff, in fine apparel, his tenants and his retainers, the latter in new livery for the occasion, some with javelins and halberds, two trumpeters at their head, followed by a varying but usually large assembly of the county gentlemen who regarded it as a privilege to escort the representatives of the King through their county, and a pleasure to offer, when occasion served, the hospitality of their homes. Their lordships were wont to mitigate the ardours of travel and the routine of duty with a view of the sights [1] and a taste of the good cheer of the countryside. As they drew near the waiting cavalcade the trumpets sounded, the retinue and the gentlemen uncovered, the Sheriff alighted from his horse or his coach, and advancing towards the King's emissaries, who had likewise set foot to ground, bowed and made a complimentary speech. Then mounting again they passed to the assize town—if not to some mansion for the night—where with trumpets sounding and bells pealing, they defiled through the crowded streets to the judges' lodgings. There we should leave their lordships to their learned deliberations, their junketings, and all the brave show of assize week, were it not that the Hon. Roger North, who rode the circuit as a barrister towards the end of the century, gives us a passing glimpse at their ways of travel while demonstrating the sagacity of horses.

' I was very hard as to fatigue in those days, riding for the most part a trotting mare, and ever esteemed my horse the easiest time I passed. It was observable that horses that had gone once or twice came to understand their trade, and to know the trumpets sounded their ease and accommodation, and at the first clangours of them the horses would always brisk up as at good news. I observed also my horse would not, though a year after, forget a by-lane by which he had passed to a gentleman's house, but would make his proffer to go that way.'

In the lawless borders of the North the usual retinue was reinforced. The tenants of the several

HORSES AND VEHICLES

From Loggan's *Oxonia Illustrata*

manors through which the circuit passed were bound
by long custom to guard their lordships through their
precincts ; but ' out of it ', says North, ' they would
not go, no, not an inch to save the souls of them '.
A strangely medieval appearance they must have had
as, seated upon small nags, with short cloaks, great
beards, and long, broad, basket-hilted swords stuck
in wide belts and touching almost to the ground,
they came up one by one to his lordship (Baron
Guilford) and chatted with a familiarity born of
entire ignorance of the punctilio of good breeding.

Another link with the past were the bands of
Catholic pilgrims that wended their ways to one or
other of the Holy Wells, which were the only objects
of veneration left them in post-reformation England,
except for a few chapels and monastic ruins such as
the Priory at Knaresborough and the neighbouring
chapel of St. Robert, which was of great renown among
the faithful, St. Robert, the reputed founder, being
revered as the worker of numerous extraordinary
miracles. On occasion they travelled in large numbers,
though whether split into small parties does not appear.
Such a politic course of action would have alike
eliminated close scrutiny by the Watch and avoided
giving offence to the countryside through which they
passed. A party of about thirty pilgrims, men and
women, came in September 1605 to the Holy Well of
St. Winifred in Flintshire—a favourite resort with
Catholics, where, according to Protestant description
were ' certain stones that look white But streak'd with
pure red which they say is her blood '. The party
included Father Garnett, Superior of the Jesuits in
England, who wished, so we read, ' to shake off the
business about London ', and to do what he could at
friends' houses by the way. For the last part of the way
the ladies of the party walked barefoot—a penance,
indeed, on the rough Welsh roads—and one whole

night was spent in devotional exercises at the Well before the return journey was started. Such was the pilgrimage as it appeared on the road, and such it doubtless appeared, and no more, to some among the party who prayed for the well-being of King, Country, and Holy Church before the Shrine. But sinister influences were at work, shaping for generations the destiny of the Catholic faith in England. Among the travellers was Rookwood. Among the hosts who entertained the party on their leisurely course there and back were John Grant and Robert Winter, all three participants in the maturing Gunpowder Plot, which within three months was to shake England from end to end and involve the Superior of the Jesuits in the political ruin of his party. Twenty-four years later there came to the same Holy Well another band of pilgrims—a fact duly noted by the Privy Council. Over fifteen hundred persons took part in this progress, including one hundred and fifty priests and such eminent persons among the laity as Lord William Howard, the Earl of Shrewsbury, Sir Cuthbert Clifton, Sir John Talbot, and Lady Falkland. To the Protestant section of the population the Well was remarkable for the number of beggars that infested the neighbourhood and the diversity of people frequenting it, ' some . . . cursing, and others at pray'r, Some dressing, some stripping, some out, and some in '. No wonder that the pilgrims of 1605 chose the night time for their devotions.

So many references have been made to the gentry travelling the road that we may well pass, without further description of their methods and their manners, to a short survey of all, gentle and simple, who might have been found travelling the King's highway during the second half of the century.[1]

---

[1] The following incidents and details are taken, with one exception, rom real life. The exception is the coach-journey to London of Sir Francis

To take Oxford as starting-point. South-eastward, towards London, a party of University dons and their servants lumber in coaches and six, Vice-Chancellor, Proctors, Bedells, and the like. They are going to prefer a petition to His Majesty or to Parliament ; to bring a lawsuit against their perpetual adversary, the City of Oxford ; or, possibly, to elect a new Chancellor. If they journey Northward, mounted and habited in stout riding-suits, they go a-visiting their Chancellor in Scotland upon the affairs of their community. Along the same road—that to Banbury and the Midlands—travels Clarencieux King-at-Arms in a coach and four, his clerk and a herald-painter with him. They are making a tour of these parts to new ' trick ' the coat of arms of the county gentry, and register them afresh in the books of visitation. Banbury, it is to be hoped, unlike Oxford, will have no horse-racing occurring in its vicinity, or Clarencieux will have but scanty records to take back with him to London. It may be, however, that he is travelling to the country mansion of his Grace, the late Duke, whose funeral he is to attend in his official capacity. Then, later, we shall see him, in his hood and gown, with his colleagues and a score or more of servants clad in mourning cloaks, riding before the hearse, which is adorned, as are the six horses drawing it, with arm-emblazoned escutcheons, while behind follow more than fifty coaches and a great number of mourners afoot. Very different is the funeral he now passes by, the body laid on horseback upon a board, a few sad-eyed mourners in the rear. A pitiful sight, yet not so pitiful as the little procession that, turning the next bend in the road, comes into view ; a party of soldiers, and in their midst a venerable prisoner, too ill to sit

and his family—this is a free adaptation of the journey of Sir Francis Wronghead described in Sir John Vanbrugh's play *The Provok'd Husband, or a Journey to London,*

a horse, stretched across the animal's back, his jailor astride behind, while a brother in distress, bent and aged with sickness and captivity though he be, stumbles afoot, his legs so heavily shackled that a boy walks beside him to bear up, by a length of cord, the weight of the iron links between. These are priests who are being taken from one prison to another for trial at assizes. It is spite rather than fear that accounts for the plight of him who is afoot.[1]

To infrequent travellers the setting out on a journey, however long anticipated, causes some trepidation. But, once mounted and well upon the highroad on a fine October day—byways find no favour with those who ride by ones and twos—travellers' qualms will disappear. So ride a trio on the North Road ; husband and wife pillion-fashion, the youth, their son, upon a borrowed nag. They are full of good spirits ; young hopeful because he is going to London to be apprenticed to a mercer in the New Exchange, and, with the spectacles of youth, sees fame and fortune before him ; his parents by reason of the gaieties they are minded to enjoy upon this, their first visit to the capital. Their heads full of the wonders of London— the Court, the theatres, the Mulberry Garden—they will be lucky if they meet with no rogue to cozen them out of their money. It 's ten to one they lose that fine, new red pillion cloth before they return to the sheltered homestead in Lincolnshire—and, may be, their sturdy gelding too, for horse-stealers are much about just now. As they ride down the main street

---

[1] It should be explained that a spectacle such as this was more common to the first half of the century than to the second. Indeed, these two incidents belong to the years 1610 and 1642. See Challoner's *Memoirs of Missionary Priests* (ed. 1843), vol. ii, pp. 44 and 203-4. After the Restoration of the Monarchy, 1660, persecution of the Catholics was of a less oppressive character. With the launching of the ' Popish Plot ', 1678, the old feelings of fear and hatred once more had play, and for a few years, prison, ill-usage, and, in some cases, death, were the portion of those who were so unfortunate as to be denounced by Oates and his fellow perjurers.

of Royston they pass a waggon, heavy laden with passengers and goods, rumbling in the opposite direction. In it there rides one who, ten years before, had, like young hopeful, set out joyfully for London. Now dismissed from his position as school usher, his money gone, he and the portionless gentlewoman, his wife, are being jolted homewards in the carrier's waggon, half-starved, and half-clothed in chill October weather. Let us hope that past sins will be forgiven, and a ready welcome greet them as they cross the threshold of the old home. With them goes another in distress, a young woman, daughter of a North-country minister. Six months before some fugitives from the plague had inspired her with a desire to see London life. Breaking from home she had gone thither into service, only to be smitten, first with plague and then with small-pox. Now, bereft of her good looks and her situation, with her lovely brown hair shorn for its worth, she is hastening home with the few shillings she yet possesses—and with the remains of a ' lusty goose-pie ', cased in twig-work, which the carrier with whom she travels brought her from home on his journey up. A mother's greeting awaits her ; otherwise, the goose-pie would never have made the three weeks' journey from Yorkshire to Middlesex.

As young hopeful and his parents leave Royston they come upon a multitude of coaches, riders, and pedestrians, all passing outwards, and in the midst some who trudge with disconsolate looks, though clad in riding-suits. There has been a great race between two footmen, the King's lackey having challenged a fleet-of-foot butcher of the town. Five or six thousand persons have been to see the contest, so it is said, and they are now going homeward, most of them with lighter pockets than they carried there, for the favourite, the royal lackey, has been defeated. Those booted and spurred stragglers are both penniless

and horseless, having wagered away all their possessions. How envious they must feel of the mud-
bespattered rider who bears down upon the throng,
and, who, having threaded his way through their
midst, rides swiftly out of sight to the South. Like
enough he is a royal messenger carrying dispatches.
Perhaps he goes to announce a royal birth or death.
It may be he comes from Yarmouth or King's Lynn,
with the first tidings of a battle at sea. A sorry
spectacle he will make at court, welcome though he
be, ' his face as black as the chimney, and covered with
dirt, pitch, and tar, and powder, and muffled with
dirty clouts, and his right eye stopped with oakum '.[1]
Almost as swiftly rides the physician going to an
urgent case. A country practitioner, he is well used
to the saddle, for he spends much time in going from
patient to patient ; though sometimes a critical and
remunerative case may detain him some days or a week
at a bedside, until he is called elsewhere. His London
colleague may keep a coach for his dignity, if not for
his convenience—hackney coaches and wherries make
convenient substitutes—but he knows that his dignity
would soon be prostrate in Waggon-rut Lane on
a December afternoon. The dissenting minister is
as often on the road. He too favours a sound nag,
as he goes about the country visiting the sick, baptizing
infants, and preaching, as well in adjoining counties
as in his own neighbourhood. A still greater traveller
than he is the Romish priest to whom is entrusted
the spiritual well-being of a wide district. Homeless,
enduring all weathers, afoot or on horseback, he passes
from mansion to mansion, cottage to cottage, sometimes openly, but frequently in secret, sometimes by

[1] It is Pepys who portrays in such fashion the arrival of a messenger
from the Fleet. This news-carrier, ' Mr. Daniel ', brought Pepys, from
Harwich, the first tidings of the engagement known to history as ' The
Four days' Fight ' (1 June 1666), a hard-fought battle which ended in the
defeat of the English and the victory of Van Tromp.

night, at other times by day ; then wet and weary and hungry though he be, he is often fain to lie in barn or coppice until night falls and he can enter without fear of discovery the home that is awaiting his ministrations. There are others too, whose lives are largely on the highway ; process-carriers, public-messengers for the dispatch of business, private errand-goers carrying letters, gifts, and the like.

Leaving our trio of riders to pursue their quiet, and we hope, uneventful way to London, we will go forward and watch other travellers upon this great corridor to London from the North and the Eastern counties.[1] Turning into the highway at Puckeridge, a smart new chariot attended by two liveried horsemen proceeds briskly to the South. In it travels a young Suffolk squire and his new-made bride. They are for London and mean to taste its gaieties though they go ostensibly to buy some of the new walnut furniture to deck the old half-timbered mansion of their fathers ; later, may be, they will replace the old hall with a fine, red-brick structure. Speedily they overtake the slow lumbering coach of their neighbour, Sir Francis, the new-made Parliament man, who is carrying his wife and daughters to London for the session. Despite the utmost efforts of the four coach-geldings, the two cart-horses, Ralph the coachman, and Giles the ploughman, who has turned postillion for the nonce, their progress is of the slowest. And no wonder.

[1] The North road was a usual way out of London for traffic to Newmarket, Bury St. Edmunds, and Norwich. Ogilby in his *Itinerarium Angliae*, 1675, and in his revised pocket edition of 1699—called *The Travellers' Guide*—completely ignores the road through Epping Forest to Bishop's Stortford. No doubt travellers preferred the somewhat longer route by the North road (whence they diverged at Hoddesdon, Ware, Puckeridge, or Royston) for the way through Epping Forest was poor, and likelihood of attack by highwaymen probably greater on that lonely stretch of highway. Nevertheless, as the incident related in Chap. IV, p. 93, note 1, shows, the direct route through the Forest was used, to the distress of the stage-coach travellers who were persuaded by the coachman to follow that route.

Behind, in the basket, lie four ' portmantel '-trunks and a great deal box, with Tom the serving man and the pet monkey to keep guard. On the coach-box beside Ralph sits Doll the cook-maid, who has as little liking for her insecure perch as for the back seat within, which she has just vacated. Inside rides Sir Francis, my Lady, the young squire, and the three young ladies, with Mrs. Bess, my lady's maid, a fat King Charles spaniel, and around and upon them an assortment of boxes and baskets, the latter well stuffed with a cargo of eatables and drink, to stay their hunger on the way ; cold boiled beef, biscuits, cheese, plum cake, beer, sack, brandy, cherry-brandy, Tent-wine, and plague-water to ward off the sickness. They have already spent four hours by the roadside, the fore-wheels having collapsed under the heavy load, and are like enough to have more adventures before they reach Westminster. Neither Giles nor Ralph is in a state to thread with needful circumspection the busy streets of suburbs and city. Already, twenty-five miles or so from London, the road carries two diversely assorted streams of traffic, sluggish at times but never ceasing for long. Here are wains heavily laden with malt for Ware ; the horse-teams, as the coach comes up to them, strain hard to pull aside from the centre of the hard-rutted way. Here a string of pack-horses trot Londonwards to the jingle of the leader's bell, their dorsers filled with herrings, mackerel, whiting, and sprats from Yarmouth. The stream is all to the Southward now, for it is market day in Ware. Now they pass waggons laden with market produce ; atop of one, taking a ride, sits a woman weaver surrounded by her yarn. Now a farmer's wife, seated on horseback, trots by, her panniers full of butter and eggs. Once or twice a litter of pigs or a flock of geese are overtaken being driven to market ; or a pedlar woman with pack strapped on back. She is in company

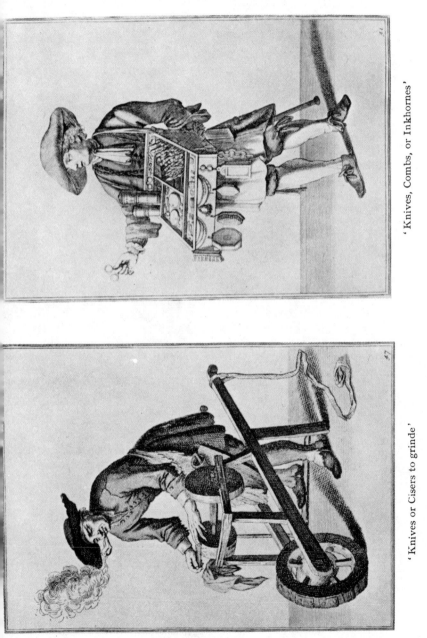

'Knives or Cisers to grinde'   'Knives, Combs, or Inkhornes'

FROM TEMPEST'S CRIES

with a blind man who carries his stock-in-trade, a
bundle of switches, under one arm, his other free to
tap, tap, with his staff. Through Ware the coach jolts
and blunders, between carts and horses, market-goers,
cattle, and other live stock—unaccustomed work has
sobered Giles's and Ralph's morning exhilaration—
until country is reached once more. But the traffic
does not cease. Farmers' wives and farmers' waggons
they now meet and pass. As they turn a sharp bend
in the road they come upon a man with three fierce
fighting bulls. It is probable that these are going to
a church-ale at Stanstead or thereabouts, for they
take a by-road on the left, leaving the road clear for
the sluggish-moving coach.[1] But not for long. A
cloud of dust upon the horizon indicates a herd of
cattle. They are being driven from Cambridge to
pasturage nearer London, before the advent of winter
renders their removal impossible. Fortunately for
Giles and Ralph, they turn aside on to some firm grass
that now appears beside the road, inviting ease to tired
hoofs. Presently the Bury coach passes by, going
Northward, with Bury tradesfolk, like enough, homing
after their half-yearly jaunt to London to lay in fresh
stock-in-trade. A little later and they overtake Southgate's Norwich waggon, Southgate (or Suggit as he is
frequently called) himself walking beside it and talking
to a dusty, travel-stained youth—though his suit be
new fustian bought for the journey—who is footing it
to London to take upon himself a situation, his worldly
possessions tied in a handkerchief, save five precious
shillings worn next his skin.[2]

[1] See Note L, pp. 329–30.
[2] In this fashion William Lilly, the astrologer, first went to London.
Son of a Leicester yeoman, he took leave of his father, then in Leicester
gaol for debt, on 4 April 1620, and ' came along with Bradshaw the carrier,
the same person with whom many of the Duke of Buckingham's kindred
had come up with. . . . It was ', he continues, ' a very stormy week, cold and
uncomfortable : I footed it all along, we could not reach London until
Palm-Sunday, the 9th of April, about half an hour after three in the

So Giles and Ralph and their load travel onward, the coach groaning and creaking, the party inside—again including Doll—growing more and more sleepy. Slower and slower they go, for the horses, unused to two long days of travel, are growing very tired. It is eight o'clock and quite dark before they reach the west end of the town, and both Giles and Ralph are lulled to security, if not to sleep. A few minutes later the coach, now proceeding down Castle Street, veers to the right. There is a grinding noise of wood rubbing wood, and the coach stops, firmly wedged between the posts of Cranbourne Alley. It is impossible at that hour of night either to advance or retreat. The travellers, sleepy-eyed and silent,—they are too weary to grumble—gather as many boxes and baskets as they can carry, for the coach must lie on the edge of the town all night, and tramp the few hundred yards which separate them from their new winter home in Leicester Fields. Giles and Ralph tumble into the coach and there sleep until morning light enables them to manœuvre the coach from its awkward situation ; honest, peaceable sleep disturbed but once, and that to send flying a couple of thieves who open the door intent on divesting the coach of its cushions, curtain, and fringe.

To dismiss with a passing glance the poorer wayfarers of the seventeenth century would be to ignore an important and, in retrospect, if not in fact, a picturesque element of life upon the road ; one, moreover, that in the efforts of government to suppress the nomadic tendencies of the lowest stratum of society, was subject to special restrictions. Owing to many and

afternoon, at which time we entered Smithfield. When I had gratified the carrier and his servants I had seven shillings and six pence left, and no more ; one suit of cloaths upon my back, two shirts, three bands, one pair of shoes, and as many stockings.' Next day his master bought him a cloak, of which he was very proud, and he ate white bread, a delicacy to which he was not accustomed.

diverse causes—the abolition of serfdom, social unrest, disease, rebellion, and civil war—vagrancy had become during the previous century a great and admitted evil ; an evil that was fostered alike by the increase of pasturage at the expense of arable farming, and by the dissolution of the monasteries that had catered for the well-being of the vagrant classes, and upon suppression, had even supplied recruits to their numbers. Act succeeded Act and Proclamation succeeded Proclamation, but still a vast (if somewhat reduced) army of landless, indigent, and, for the most part, work-shy peasants continued to wander the land, picking up a bare subsistence by thieving or begging as temperament or circumstances dictated, and causing, during the earlier half of the seventeenth century, almost continual embarrassment to the authorities concerned with their suppression. Occasionally, as in 1626 when preparations were being made for war, or when pestilence was feared, stern measures would reduce their numbers ; though what became of them— whether they merely took to the waste lands of the less settled parts of the country—does not appear. Once, in 1624, the more able-bodied of the men were impressed for service in the Palatinate, and marched, or rather were driven, to Dover, where they became so riotous that the town was for a week or more menaced with starvation and ruin. As often as vigorous action reduced their numbers, an influx of Scotch or Irish— the latter brought over secretly to West-country ports —would swell the total anew. Again the Government would stir local authorities to action. Marshals would be appointed to stimulate the vigilance of the constables. Watches would be set up at cross roads, and the immigrants returned to their respective countries, the Irish being sent to their ports of arrival, and thence shipped home at the expense of those same ports which had permitted them to land

The classes of vagrant persons deemed, by Act of Parliament, rogues and vagabonds were many ; the penalties to which they were exposed, though little deterrent to the confined vagrant, were both odious and obstructive to the well-disposed and legitimate traveller. It was accordingly necessary for the poor honest traveller to obtain a certificate from the corporation or parish wherein he (or she) dwelt stating that he was of good conduct ; that he had dwelt in his town or parish a certain number of years ; and that it was necessary for the maintenance of his business or his health that he should be allowed to pass and repass through certain towns. The document terminated with the request that churchwardens and others would take into favourable consideration his—the bearer's— case, and further his desires. Thus armed he could pass in safety about his business, seek his health at Bath or Buxton, or go to London to be touched for the King's Evil. Without it he ran the risk of being taken up by the constable and carried before a Justice of the Peace, who might order him to be stocked—that is put in the stocks—or ' stripped naked from the middle upwards, and . . . openly whipped untill his or her body be bloudye ', and afterwards sent with a pass from constable to constable to his place of birth or last residence. If he strayed from the authorized route, he exposed himself to like ignominy.

With a testimonial the disabled soldier and the disabled or shipwrecked mariner went to their last places of legal settlement, allowances being given them by county treasurers for relief in transit. With a testimonial too, granted by a Justice, Constable, or Tything Man and entered in the parish book, the harvester went to work in places distant from his home —that is to say, if he did what the law required of him. Evidence, however, suggests that constables at haytime and harvest suffered wayfarers to pass. un-

molested ; and thereby let pass habitual vagrants. On
more than one occasion the laxity of the constables in
enforcing the law at this season of the year received
unfavourable comment at the hands of higher authority.
Indeed, it is reasonable to suppose that the constables
were little disposed to intercept a wayfarer who went
quietly on his way neither begging nor stealing, nor
in any manner raising the ire of parishioners; unless,
of course, they were roused to action by a renewal
of orders or by some motive of a personal or parochial
character. What with their own business and that of
the parish the constables were busy men, and although
allowances were made to those who lodged passing
vagrants and, on the other hand, a penalty could be
enforced on those who failed to carry out the law,
they had enough to do with thieves, poachers, and the
more obstrusive kinds of vagrants, without concerning
themselves with persons whose sole offence lay in
their failure to have provided themselves with certificates of travel.

That there were exceptions only proves the rule.
Thus we find an Irishman, who described himself as
Nicholas Farles, serving-man, arrested in May 1635
by the Watch at Ottery St. Mary Devon, as he travelled
on foot towards London, without a pass, from Penny-
cum-quick, Cornwall, where he had landed. His case
proved no ordinary one and beyond the jurisdiction
of Sir Peter Prideaux before whom he was taken; for
he carried a little box which, he said, the Countess of
Westmeath had charged him to deliver to the Earl of
Clanricarde in London. This contained ' certificates
under the hand and seal of the Bishop of Meath
testifying orders of Neilan Feranan, a Romish priest
. . . for the enlarging of the said Feranan '. How he
fared does not appear, but, as he confessed that he
was a Roman Catholic, and as further he declared
that he would never take the Oaths of Supremacy and

Allegiance, it is probable that his further course was from constable to constable—if not under the charge of a messenger—and his destination a London prison.

Some vagrants there were who were neither averse to casual employment of an easy roaming nature, nor particular in regard to the sanctity of property. It seems probable that Richard Jackson ' late of Elaston in the county of Stafford, laborer ', belonged to this intermediate class, using his trade of drover ' to lend colour to his vagrancy ', according to the expressive seventeenth-century phrase. His story, as told to Sir Henry Legh, knight, has the merit of disclosing something of the ways of a little-known class of wanderer. On Tuesday the 3rd of June 1634,

' hee was hyred at Congerton [Congleton] in Cheshire by one Mr. Tompson, a Graszer whoe dwelleth at Northampton, to helpe him drive a drove of Cattell towards Derbye and that they lodged that night at Newcastle at the sign of the Starre but knoweth not the Inkeepers name, And that on Wednesdaye they travelled from thence to Stone, & soe to a Bridge supposed to bee Wolsley bridge, neare to the wch bridge hee saith they lodged that night at the sign of the Lyon but knoweth not the name of either his hoste or hostes there And from thence on Thursdaye came to Derbye about foure of the Clocke in the Afternoone, where he was paid for his labour of dryvinge by the sd Mr. Tompson & by him discharged and further saith that uppon Wednesdaye hee lefte Uttoxeter on his right hand to goe to Derbye, and denyeth that he was any of the three dayes spied at the house of Mr. Richard Morton vicar of Spoonedon. And saith uppon Thursdaye hee went to Marton from Derbye whither he came much about sunsett, & layd there all night in a barne belonginge to an Alehouse, the owners name whereof he knoweth not & uppon Fridaye went hee knoweth not whither & lodged that night hee knoweth not where, the like hee saith for Saterdaye, saving that on Saterdaye night hee laye under a hedge, and uppon Sundaye after morninge prayer hee came to Elaston & undertooke to drive Cattell for one Mr. Scattergood towards Belton Fayre, and haveinge driven that afternoone & all that night hee came the next morninge being Mondaye to Belton Fayre And beinge

asked how hee came by an apron, & a stockinge that were found
uppon him, saith that he found them on Munday last in the
Road Waye cominge from Belton Fayre towards Burton,
where he was apprehended as a Vagrant, & beinge sent towards
Derbye, was stayed by Mr. Morton aforesd uppon Supposition
of felony and by him brought before Sir Henrye Legh at
Egginton.'

Notwithstanding the discouragement of vagrancy,
some of the vagrants were upon the road by order of
authority.   These were indigent persons, who, unable
longer to support themselves and their families, were
sent from constable to constable to their places of birth,
or last known domiciles, there to be maintained at the
expense of the parishes that received them.   But so
little liking had the parishes for the charge, and so
difficult was it in some cases to determine the legal
domicile of these impotent folk, that it was no uncommon thing for them to be sent like shuttlecocks back
and forth between village and village, until Quarter
Sessions, in desperation, made some order for their
maintenance.[1]   One woman, Dyonese Indoe, was sent
six times by pass from London to Martock in Somersetshire and back to London.   That she had a mind to
live in Martock ' where she pretended one William
Indoe, her husband, [had] Dwelt ', is evident.   Though
ultimately adjudged to dwell in London, in the parish
of All Saints, Barking, where both she and her husband
had been in the service of a deal merchant—eighteen
days being allowed her for travelling thither—she was
again, two years later, at Martock, where she complained to one of the judges of the Western circuit that
the inhabitants refused to make provision for her.
What became of Dyonese does not transpire, but
Martock was given order to maintain her until good
cause to the contrary could be shown at the assizes.
Rather different, and probably more deserving of

[1] See Note M, pp. 330–31.

sympathy, was the case of Lyonell Wills. Two years
previous to his application to the Justices in Quarter
Sessions at Wells, Somersetshire, he had married
without the consent of the parish of Tintenhull wherein
he dwelt—in such fashion parishes restricted their
liabilities for relief. Having failed through intimidation to obtain houseroom—under-letting was forbidden
by law—he had been forced to travel from place to
place with his wife and children, so that he feared, as
he told the Justices, that he would ' in thend bee taken
as a vagrant '. As the Justices ordered his settlement
at his old home he probably avoided this misfortune.
Not so William Porter, ' a very poor and impotent old
man '. From Eddington, also in Somersetshire, where
twopence weekly was allowed for his support, he was
obliged in order to obtain better relief—' about
a fortnight sithence '—to visit some friends at Shap-
wick. There the constable had taken him up and
had had him ' grievously whipped ' and sent away.
It is satisfactory to know that the Justices thought
fit to relieve Porter and admonish the over-zealous
constable.

Two other unfortunates were Frenchmen, Abraham
Ally Giles Bruaneere and Anthony Southwin—such
their names to English ears—who were taken ' travellinge and begginge without anie Certificate testifyinge
theire quallity or Condition '. They had been set
ashore, as they told the Taunton Bench in July 1651,
by an Ostend man-of-war who had boarded their
bark which was in transit to Swansea, and had
been forced to beg for sustenance. The court in
consideration of their misfortunes refrained from
imposing corporal punishment ; ' yett by force of the
statute in such cases made and provided ' ordered
that they should be sent from parish to parish and from
officer to officer, to the port of Lyme, their place of
landing, thence to be transported to their native town

PILLORY   WHIPPING

From the Bagford Ballads

A VAGRANT

From the Roxburghe Ballads

of Rouen, ' with the first conveniencie ', six days being
allowed them to reach the coast.

Where parishes were unable to make provision for
the destitute through their own poverty and the
numbers dependant upon them, the bench granted
licences to certain of their poor to beg, usually within
the confines of their hundred. Badges were provided
to be worn by those licensed upon the breast and back
of their uppermost garments. Similar licences or
briefs, were granted to collectors for hospitals and gaols
and to persons rendered destitute by the firing and
destruction of their homes—no rare occurrence in
those days of lath and plaster and half timbering.
Whole towns had sometimes to beg aid of the charit-
able. Quite a trade arose to supply the fraudulent
with passes and briefs. In the West, counterfeiting for
the Irish importees became so profitable a business that
it was carried on by many who should have known
better : schoolmasters, Justices' servants, and the like.
Sometimes the impostor was discovered and suffered the
penalty of the law. But ' there is many a slip . . .' One
' very lame man not able to travel more than one mile a
day ', who, with his wife, was arrested in Somersetshire
travelling with a pass purporting to have been signed
by a Wiltshire Justice, managed to escape in the night
and get away, despite the hue and cry sent after him.

Space forbids mention of more than a few of the
trickeries resorted to by the many and various rogues
who flourished at this period, and who figure so largely
in the prose and verse of contemporary publicists and
ballad-writers.

A versatile exponent of the art of begging was ' the
Cunning Northerne Begger ', whose doings are recorded in a ballad of the reign of Charles I. In ragged
garments he takes his seat by the roadside (usually
at the bottom of a hill), until he spies a coach or some
mounted gallants approaching. Then rising upon his

crutch he cries : ' good, your worship, good sir, bestow one poor denier, sir ',[1] obtaining which he spends it at the Pipe and Pot. In various characters he ranges about the country. Sometimes he is a poor maimed soldier, though he has never been abroad except on the road. Anon, he is a sailor in old canvas clothing, with a tale that six Dunkirkers have taken all and left him nothing. Sometimes he crawls upon the ground like a one-legged cripple. At other times he maltreats his flesh so that it seems to fester, and with plaster on it feigns the falling sickness (epilepsy). Then, as if sightless, with a boy beside him, or groping his way, or led by a dog, he goes to the highway, where with cords in his hands he begs of all who come nigh. Turned into a country-fellow, with a child at his back and a ' Doxie ', or pretended wife following, he cries alack, his house and goods are burned. Though he sometimes gets the lash, it is better to beg than to steal and go to the gallows.

An impostor who knew how to work not only upon the sympathies, but also upon the fears of the country folk, was the individual known to the profession as the Abraham Man, and to the world at large as the Bedlamer or, more familiarly, as Tom o' Bedlam. Although he had never been inside Bethlehem Hospital—Bridewell was more likely—he went about feigning madness, with a brass plate on his arm, and, sometimes, with a self-inflicted branding mark, signifying that he had been discharged and was licensed to beg by the governors of that hospital, which was not true ; licences to beg were never issued by these authorities. With his skin black and blue as from beating, he would ' by many Phantastick tricks ' obtain bacon and other victuals from ' silly Country

---

[1] *Denere.* ' Denier : m. *A penny, a deneere* ; *a small copper coyne, valued at the tenth part of an english penny* ; . . . also, the price of a thing.' 'A French-English Dictionary Compil'd by Mr. Randle Cotgrave with another in English and French,' 1650.

people '. But he also deceived many who should have known better, as appears from the Household Account Book of the Fell family (of Swarthmoor Hall in Lancashire), where, under date 15 November 1673, we find ' given to a bedlamer by sist^r Lowe^r & sist^r Susannah 6d. '. Probably there was no intimidation in this instance. Farther North, in the Border Counties, they frightened people in their houses, says Roger North, ' taking what they listed '. One of these rogues was tried before Lord Guilford ' for killing another of his own trade whom he had surprised asleep, and with his great staff knocked on the head ; and then bragged that he had given him " a sark full of sere bones ", that is a shirt full of sore bones. He would not plead to the country because there were ' horsecopers ' amongst them, till the press was ready [peine forte et dure] and then he pleaded and was at last hanged '.

Working separate districts singly or in parties, gangs of thieves and beggars roamed the country during the summer months. A description of these vagabonds who aped the ways of gipsies, given in *The English Rogue*, which first appeared in 1665, will show their methods and manners while travelling the road. The author, ' Meriton Latroon ', claimed to have had actual experience of the life. Clothed in rags pinned and stitched together—so that, as he says, had he been forced to take them off he could never have put them on again—his face stained with green walnuts to give him the appearance of a gipsy, he joined the company of hookers (stealers of clothes by means of a hook), dummerars (who sought charity by feigning to be dumb), swigmen (fraudulent packmen),[1] and the like, who made up this brotherhood of deceit.

' We Muster'd above threescore old and young, and because we were too great a company to March together, we were

---

[1] There were many other specialists in the profession of thieving, each with a descriptive name.

divided into three Squadrons. The first Squadron that led
the Van, was ordered by our Commander [a ruffler who robbed
poor wayfaring men and market women] to stick up small
boughs all the way they went, that we might know what course
they steer'd . . . we had every one his Doxie or Wench, who
carried at her back a *Lullaby-cheat* [infant], & it may be
another in her Arms. When they are weary of carrying them
they take their turnes to put them in a pair of Panniers, like
green Geese going to market, or like Fish in Dossers coming
from *Rye*. Where note, that each division hath a small Horse
or two, or else Asses to ease them of their burdens. Some of us
were clad Antickly with Bells or other toys, merely to allure
the Country people unto us, which most commonly produced
their desired effects. In some places they would flock unto us,
in great quantities, and then was our time to make our Markets.
We pretended an acquaintance with the Stars . . . and so
possessing these poor ignorant people with a belief that we
could tell their fortunes by inspection into either hands or
faces ; whil'st we were seriously looking thereon, one of our
diving Comrades pickt their pockets, or with a short sharp
knife, and a horn on the thumb *nipt* their *bungs* [picked their
pockets] . . .

' Thus we rambled up and down the Countrey : and where
people demean'd themselves not civil to us by Voluntary
contributions, their Geese, Hens, Pigs, or any such mandible
thing we met with, made us satisfaction for their hide-bound
injuries. Our revenge most commonly was very bloody. . . .
The usual sacrifices . . . were innocent Lambs, Sheep, Calves. . . .
We seize the prey, and leave the Tragical part to our *Morts* or
women to act ; the *stage* on which they perform their parts, is
either some large *Heath*, or *Firze-bush-Common*, far from any
House. This being done, and night approaching, we repair
to our Dormitories, or Houses of rest, which are most usually
Out-barns of Farmers and Husbandmen, which we make choice
of in some poor stragling Village, who dare not deny us, for
fear ere the morning they find their Thatcht Houses too hot
to hold them.'

It was, doubtless, one or more of these beggar-
bands that the Devonshire Justices of the reign of
Charles I had in mind, when they ordered the setting
up of a weekly Watch to search and arrest rogues and

vagabonds, ' some whereof pretend to be petty chapmen, others peddlers, other glassmen, tynckers, others palmesters, fortune readers, Egiptians, and the like ', who ' some-time . . . meet by thirty in a company both upon the highwaie and in the night tymes in ale houses and other cottages and obscure places and howsses of evill reporte, soe as his Matie's better subjects are not only much prejudiced but terrified '.

Real gipsies, with their strange speech and strange ways, wandered the country as they had wandered it for a hundred years and more, notwithstanding the repressive measures that for long had been meted out to them in vain efforts to rid the country of their presence. Often they were confused with the beggar-bands just described. Thus the gang of fifty persons who were in 1703 committed to Hertford gaol for 'travelling about telling fortunes and calling themselves Egyptians ' may or may not have been of that strange race of wanderers.

It was not only gangs of twenty ruffians and more who intimidated the countryfolk. Even one sturdy beggar dared ' by threats and menaces ' to extort money and victuals from those who lived in houses remote from neighbours. Such a one was Thomas Roades, a ' poor gentleman ', born at Edgeworth (Edgware), a ballad-singer by profession, who wandered about the country, as he told the magistrates, hunting as well as singing—a damning confession to make to the bench, if by that he meant poaching. Though ' too stout-hearted to beg ', he called and asked, as was his wont, for a cup of beer at the house of John How of Hemel Hempstead and, when the woman of the house came to shut the door upon him, he punched at her with his staff. It is perhaps to his credit that after this he desired to be called not by his father's name, but rather by the many names the country people had given him.

More refined methods of obtaining money from pockets none too well lined were gaming, quackery, fortune telling—of course much practised by the gipsy fraternity—and other ' subtle crafts '. It was by the second and third of these methods that Joseph Haynes, gentleman, James Domingo, and Sarah, ' his pretended wife ', earned their living. Coming into Ware one day in 1676—the woman in man's apparel— and having distributed bills to give notice of their arts, they told fortunes for sixpence apiece, and sold an elixir for the curing of ' almost all deseases '. But Ware, unlike Bishop's Stortford where the trio had made twenty pounds, was evidently a disease-free town, little given to probing into the mysteries of the future, for Haynes got no more than five pounds and three maydenheads '—coins of Elizabeth—together with ' a broken shinne ', while Domingo earned about twenty-six shillings. Sarah, we suppose, being a woman, received nothing but what her companions chose to give her. Many of those who went from town to town vending quack medicines were foreigners. Setting up their stages in churchyards, inns, or on commons, they sold their strangely compounded pills and potions to the wondering yokels, who were ever ready to credit foreigners with miraculous powers of healing. The ' High-Dutch Physitian ', James The-mut, mentioned by Anthony Wood, was doubtless a practitioner of superior attainments—that is to say in the art of effrontery and deception—for his practice extended to the Quality. Coming to the ' Saracen ' in Oxford in 1661, he dispossessed the University physicians of their patients. Within a month of his arrival he ran away 'and cozenned his patients of grat quantity of money that he had taken of them beforehand '.

And the penalty for all this trickery and fraud ? It was severe in law if not in practice. The culprit ' if dangerous to the inferior sort of people ' might be branded and pressed for the navy,[1] or banished the realm—a euphemism for service in the plantations. Should he return without licence, or on second conviction, he could be hanged as a felon without benefit of clergy. For those not deemed incorrigible or dangerous—probably those we should call first offenders—the punishment was whipping and stocking and passing to their last places of residence or, if domiciles were unknown, a year in the House of Correction. But as with highwaymen so with rogues. The severity of the law rendered it largely innocuous. The graver punishments were probably seldom or never imposed. Moreover, notwithstanding the thievery, intimidation, and violence suffered by the peaceful inhabitants of the countryside, and notwithstanding the monetary inducement offered them and their officers for the apprehension of offenders, they tolerated and even encouraged the rogues and vagabonds in their midst.

Vagrants were news-carriers and gossip-mongers in an age when periodicals were both rare and brief and news slow of travelling. As Cotgrave said,

> If one should refuse to talke with every Begger,
> He should refuse to have company sometimes.

There were persons, even of the more substantial kind, who went so far as to harbour them voluntarily in their barns and outhouses. One ' cherisher of wandring beggars ', Mr. Hannibal Baskervyle of Bayworth, Oxfordshire, ' built for them a larg place like a barne to receive them, and hung up a little bell at his backdore for them to ring when they wanted anything '. He had been several times indicted at Abingdon

---

[1] According to the wording of the Act (1 Jac. I, c. 7, 1603-4) they were to ' otherwise be adjudged perpetuallie to the Gallies of this Realme . . .' As the use of galleys had never been extensively adopted in this country, and as, in 1608, the Navy contained but four decayed galleys, it is reasonable to suppose that in effect, incorrigible rogues were pressed for service in the fleet.

Quarter Sessions for the offence of harbouring, says Anthony Wood who found him a ' melancholy and retir'd man '. The Hertfordshire Quarter Sessions Records give a number of instances of gentlemen, yeomen, and others being indicted as ' lodgers of rogues '. One John Bourne was called upon to answer for ' entertaining and harbouring several Egyptians in his house, who go robbing people of their goods '— an unpopular person with his neighbours if the charge were true.

Though the law was modified in practice it was wide in scope. Yet here again, we fancy, clemency—in this case wise clemency—prevailed. Many persons entirely innocent of any intent to defraud came within the definition of rogues and vagabonds. Thus players of interludes, minstrels, harpers, fiddlers, jugglers, bearwards, and the like were subject to arrest and summary punishment if they made performance on the village green, in the great barn, or at the Castle gate ; unless, indeed, they had obtained licence from the King's Master of the Revels or his deputy, a procedure, and doubtless an expense, that were deterrent to poor, ignorant, wayfaring folk.[1] Such manner of living was calculated to be harmful to the morals of the people and, furthermore, a cloak for vagabondage and sedition, as to some extent it must have been. Under the Puritan régime of the middle years of the century even the favour of a licence was withdrawn, and those who continued to flout ' Gods wrath and displeasure . . . to the disturbance of the peace thereof ', did so at the risk of terrestrial as well as divine punishment. Itinerant merchants were likewise under official ban during the early years of the century ; for wayside trading not only gave pretext for vagabondage and sedition—as performances did in the case of players—but ran counter to the interests of the

[1] See Note N, pp. 331–2.

shopkeepers, an important section of the community, owing to the competition the latter thereby suffered. To suppress itinerant trade was impossible. In 1618 Government, recognizing the logic of the situation, or as they expressed it in their proclamation, finding the trade ' useful when well supervised ', opened an office for the licensing of chapmen who procured testimonials from two Justices of the Peace. Such licences, however, did not permit vendors to trade in towns except at fairs or during the hours of market. These hawkers were of invaluable service to country-women precluded by their work in field or garden or at the loom from going to town ; or, may be, hindered by long distance and inclemency of weather, from venturing upon the journey thither. But our business lies not with the homekeeper.

If the way was unpleasant or hazardous for the good-wife, how must it have been for the pedlar with a pack on his back, though it were only filled with ' women's tryflinges ', gloves, pins, combs, laces, pomanders, beads, brooches, thimbles, thread, shears, and such other odds and ends as vanity or wont declared needful to woman's person ! There were others besides the pedlar who made the weary round from cottage to cottage, selling or mending and gossiping the while ; the glassman with his basket of drinking glasses and other vessels, the crateman with his earthen butter-pots at his back, the clothier with rolls of cloth and holland at his saddle-bow, the knife grinder with his little cart and rotary wheel, the tinker who mended or sold kettles, skillets, and lanterns, the hawker of books and ballads—a character suspected, and not unjustly, by authority as a distributor of seditious songs and for-bidden pamphlets—and the travelling carpenter who would mend and make that which was beyond the skill of farmer or goodman. Often enough it was the shrill intonation of a woman's voice that floated

across the hedgerow with ' Buy my drinking glasses ',
' Scotch cloth, d'ye want any Scotch cloth ', or one
or other of the wonted cries that told the housewife
her cupboard could be supplied ; it might be at
no other expense than a few coney-skins given in
exchange.

Some sold wares of their own manufacture, if not
to the cottager and her richer neighbours, to chapmen
or shopkeepers at country or city inns. Others carried
butter and cheese ; poor women these, generally,
harried it may be by the measures taken to prevent
cornering of foodstuffs or profiteering within the area
of purchase. Forestalling, engrossing, and regrating
were the terms by which these offences against the
interests of the community were known. Traders
known as ' badgers ', wholesale dealers in farm and
dairy produce and other ' dead victualls ', with two,
three, four, or six ' horses, mares, or geldings '—the
number allowed was carefully prescribed on the licence
issued to them—bought in the fairs and markets of
one county or district to sell in those adjacent or not
far distant, the itinerary no less than the means of
travel being carefully defined. It was sometimes stipu-
lated upon the licence that the badger should return
with a load different from that which he carried on
the outward journey, such as salt, salt-fish, oats, or
some other commodity which was needed by the district where the licence was issued. In similar fashion
permits were granted for the transfer of cattle and for
the supply of provisions to towns. That even well-
known badgers were sometimes lax in obtaining
permission to trade, the following petition to the
Somersetshire Justices, 1609–10, makes clear.

' We the Constables of Taunton in the Countye of Soṁst
and others of the same Towne doe pray yoᵣ good woᵣˢ to grant
to Durstoun Briddian of Wedmore yoᵣ lawfull licens to bringe
Butter to oᵣ Towne of Taunton, ffor that he is staied by

Brudgwater [Bridgwater] menn, and Cannott com thrugh the same, not Haveinge a licence, and we will rest bound to yoᵗ good Worshipps for the same. Wee know that he or his wife is heare this som time [summer time] twice every Weeke With one or two horselading of Butter.'

Probably the Bridgwater men had some score to pay off against Taunton. If a recognized badger failed to arm himself with the necessary licence, we can well believe that many small traders went their rounds without authorization. One lacked money to pay for the recognizance demanded and, finding himself un-molested, saved that which he earned for more profit-able purposes. Another, for some reason, had for-feited the confidence of the licensing authorities. A third failed to obtain official sanction through excess of numbers applying. A fourth, disliking formalities and more happy-go-lucky than his colleagues, did not bother himself to apply and chanced the consequences. Thus probably they reasoned and acted. But some-times retribution came upon those who had the temerity to ply their trades without permission, as the records of the Middlesex Quarter Sessions for the seventh and eighth decades of the century make evident. Doubt-less the city companies exercised a stimulating influence upon the neighbouring magistracy. The penalties meted out to most of the delinquents, however, were mild compared with those it was permissible to inflict upon them as convicted rogues and vagabonds—further evidence that the law was never rigorously enforced. Of the half-dozen or so cases cited, one was found not guilty—a test case, probably, to obtain a judicial decision as to the rights of the Glass Sellers' Company without the city ; one was pardoned, two were fined—twelvepence in the case of a knife-grinder who confessed ' this grave indictment '—and three were sentenced to be whipped. Of these last, one, a woman, had her punishment deferred, which probably meant remission, while the other two, who had been guilty of ' craftily and deceitfully using the art of buying and selling Scotch cloth and Holland cloth and wares pertaining to the art and faculty of linendrapers ', were sentenced to be stripped naked from the middle upwards, and to be whipped till their bodies should be bloody ' at the whipping-post *prope* Charing Crosse '.

Though penalties were often mild, the instruments by which punishment could be inflicted were not suffered to be hidden from view.

> In *London* and within a mile, I weene,
> There are of Jayles or Prisons full eighteene,
> And sixty Whipping posts and Stocks and Cages,
> Where sin with shame and sorrow hath due wages.

So wrote John Taylor in 1630. The shame and sorrow and even the mere sight of these castigators of the evil-doer were, may be, intended to deter and intimidate the unruly.

There was yet one other class of traveller, innocent of evil intent, against whom, from the middle of the century onwards, the vagrancy laws were put in force—the Quakers. It was in 1647 that George Fox, son of a Leicestershire weaver, started upon his long pilgrimage in the cause of the new-found faith which inspired him. Such was his success that within a few years he had gathered many to his fold, rich and poor alike, but mostly of the middling sort. With the zeal common to revivalists he and his followers spread the truth as they conceived it. They spoke on the race-course and at the fair ; in the market-place as by the wayside ; to the Sheriff and the Justices as to the labouring folk. They argued in church with the parson, interrupting on occasions the service, and all the time heedless of the uproar their remarks or their mere presence might and did create.

In consequence, while they gained converts they

alienated those to whom their belief made no appeal, as well the vulgar herd as those to whom was entrusted the keeping of law and order. From the poor they received stoning and beating ; from the rich stripes and imprisonment. Even the Quaker Mayor of Cambridge scarcely dared to walk the streets of the city he governed, for fear of ill usage from the scholars. At the sister university two women Friends who visited the city in 1654 were dragged through a dirty pool and then held under a pump, for water to be pumped into their mouths ; on the principle, one supposes, of washing out lies. It is said that one of the women was on the same day permanently injured by being thrown over a gravestone. Had the Quakers carried on their propaganda with tact and discretion, it is probable that, while the Commonwealth was in being, they would have been left in freer enjoyment of their religion and of their liberty. Cromwell was not unfavourable to their tenets, and granted Fox more than one interview, endeavouring, it would seem, to induce him to gentler methods of persuasion. As it was, the disturbances caused by him and his disciples forced the Central Government to uphold the actions of the local authorities. It was not long before the law was put in motion against them, and as disturbers of the peace, as blasphemers, heretics, and seducers, as rogues and vagabonds they were sent to jail or whipped and returned to their homes. In 1657 the vagrancy laws were extended, owing to the disturbed state of the country, to include all who wandered without sufficient cause. As a consequence Friends were at seasons and in places subjected to a persecution degrading to their dignity, peculiarly satisfying to their enemies, and, we may add, hindering to their labours. Under the rule of the major-generals in 1656, Watches were set up in the highways of Dorset, Somerset, Devon, and Cornwall to arrest 'suspicious persons '.¹ Of those apprehended many were 'Friends', twenty-one persons belonging to the sect being taken in the highways of Devon during one month and sent to Exeter jail.

'They brought [them]', writes Fox, 'before the Justices & some clothiers & other men they whippt off [worth] abut 100 or 80 [pounds] a yeere which they tooke uppe not abuve 4 or 5 miles from there familys that was goeinge to mills with there cloath. And when freindes was gott amongst the watches Itt woulde bee a fortnight or 3 weekes before they coulde gett out of them againe for noe sooner had one party taken them & carried them before the Justices and they had discharged them but then another woulde take them uppe & carry them before other Justices.'

A great deal of needless cost, as Fox remarks, but a means of spreading the truth among officials.

Again, after the passing of the Quaker Act, 1662, the West became active in the persecution of Friends; though, as will appear, the Justices, as before, were not all agreed upon the course to be pursued. Meetings were broken up by warrant and Friends arrested. The prisoners, when told to present themselves before the Justices—to save the expense of their carriage thither— not unnaturally refused, pointing out at the same time that such procedure was contrary to the dictates of the warrants.

'& then', says Fox, 'they was feign to hire carts & horses & wagons to carry ffreinds in : where they lifted them uppe

¹ In September 1656 Devonshire Quarter Sessions gave orders that as 'now lately divers other persons styled by the name of *Quakers* disaffected to the present Government, do wander up and down the country, and scatter seditious books and papers to the deluding of many weak people ', all constables should cause good watches and wards to be kept for the apprehending of all beggars, rogues, vagabonds, wandering, idle and sus- picious persons 'and that they likewise apprehend all such persons as travel under the notion or name of *Quakers* without a lawful certificate testifying from whence he came and whither he is travelling, or shall have or do scatter, publish, or own any such seditious books or papers as afore- said, or shall interrupt or disturb any minister in the congregation or other- wise '. They were to be brought before some Justice of the Peace to be dealt with according to law. See Quarter Sessions from Q. Elizabeth to Q. Anne, A. H. A. Hamilton, pp. 164–5.

& carryed them in there wagons and carts & when they came
before a Justice hee was moderate & woulde it may bee gett
out of the way, & then they were forct to carry them before
another : so that they was almost 3 weekes carryinge & cartinge
ffreinds uppe & doune from place to place : & then the oficers
came to lay there charges upon the tounde [town] & the
toundspeople woulde not pay it but made them pay it them
selves & that broake the necke of there persecution.'

Then as now money spoke with no uncertain voice.
The two Conventicle Acts, 1664 and 1670, brought
fresh pains and penalties to these seekers after Spiritual
Truth.   Still persecution ebbed and flowed, as the
grasp of authority alternately relaxed and tightened.
With the reign of Papist James, 1684, came gradual
relief, and with the Act of Toleration, 1689, reasonable
security for Friends to enjoy their form of worship
and to go their ways unhindered and unmolested.

The laws against vagrancy, and also the laws
against Sunday travel, affected Friends with peculiar
force owing to the extensive, and in some cases
almost continual travels that many underwent in the
cause of the faith.   There were travelling ministers,
women as well as men, who went from district to
district, putting up at the houses of Friends of the more
substantial kind to hold meetings in parlour or orchard.
One of these propagators of the faith, Roger Haydock,
travelled in Holland and the three kingdoms 32,727
miles by land and sea from the time he first went abroad
in the ministry at the age of twenty-four.   Another,
Samuel Waldenfield, journeyed forty thousand miles
during the last twenty or thirty years of the century,
and then his labours were not ended, for he subsequently covered many a league more in England,
Scotland, Ireland, Holland, and Germany.   There
were those who took upon themselves the task of
visiting their more unfortunate brethren in prison,
offering sometimes their own persons to the jailers
to relieve sick or long-suffering comrades. So Margaret

Sutton travelled from Westmorland to the prison at
Bury St. Edmunds, in the hope of giving respite to
George Whitehead. Likewise Anne Downer, a
preacher of London, walked two hundred miles to
visit Fox when he was incarcerated in Langston jail
—for some time immured in a dungeon called Dooms-
dale, as a result of refusal to pay either for his own keep
or that of his horse. There were others who felt
impelled to publish the truth throughout the length
and breadth of the land. Some of these were religious
maniacs, as William Sympson who ' went three years
Naked and in Sackcloth in the days of Oliver . . .
through Markets . . . and to Cambridge, stark naked
. . . and . . . through London '.

As prisoners too they travelled many miles, not only
in the guise of vagrants passed from constable to
constable, but as prisoners newly arrested or in course
of transfer from one prison to another. Fox was once
' tossed ', as he felicitously expresses it, three times
between Worcester and London—not to speak of
a fourth journey undertaken during temporary release
—his presence at Worcester Sessions and Assizes
alternating with appearance before the Judges of the
King's Bench. Finally the High Court of Justice
quashed the sentence of Premunire which had been
passed upon him at Worcester and after fourteen
months of bondage he was released. The degrees of
restraint imposed upon Fox—and upon other prisoners
for faith—varied according to circumstance or malice.
Arrested at his wife's home, Swarthmoor in Furness,
he was guarded by thirty horse and foot to Lancaster
jail.

' . . . they woulde not lett mee ride of my own horse ', he says,
' but sett me of a lite horse behinde the sadle : & they would
not lett mee speak to freinds : & . . . a great noise they made
& very rude & wicked they were : & they tooke my knife from
mee . . . And soe they beate the poore horse : and made him

kicke : & I slipt off the horse againe : & then they lifted me
uppe behinde the sadle again : & led the horse with a haltar
till they came to the Carter forde [the passage across Morecambe Bay] : & it beinge very deepe they lett mee gett one
[on] of my owne horse : & then they led mee through the
water.'

As Fox passed along singing praises to the triumph-
ing power of the Lord one ' wicked fellow ' kneeled
down in the roadway and, lifting up his hands, blessed
God that he was taken prisoner. Arrived at Lancaster
Fox refused to give bond for his appearance before
the King's Bench. The Sheriff, thereupon, concluded
to send him to London with a party of horse ; then,
on considering what the charges would be for maintenance on the way, he determined to send him up
guarded by the jailer and some bailiffs ; until,
thinking again, he judged that the expense would still
be overmuch. Finally he asked his prisoner to put
in bail to be at London on a certain day of the term.
To this Fox replied that he would not put in bail.
Nevertheless, if he were permitted to travel with one
or two friends, he might ' bee in London such a day
if the Lord did permitt ', and that he would bear all
charges. So, journeying in leisurely fashion for three
weeks and holding meetings the while, he reached
London where in due course he was acquitted of the
charge that he and his followers had stirred up trouble
in the North, and on 25th October 1660 obtained his
release.

One more recital of Fox travelling under duress
before we take leave of men and manners upon the
Road. A few years later he was again arrested at
Swarthmoor and on a similar charge. But the charge
failed, whereupon the Justices resorted to the usual
expedient and put to him the oath of Supremacy and
Allegiance, and, on his refusal to swear—oaths he
held were sinful—committed him to Lancaster jail.

A few years later, still a prisoner, he was sent, by order of the King and Council, to Scarborough Castle. Ailing from long imprisonment in a smoky, scarce habitable, chamber, he was haled away by the Under-Sheriff and some bailiffs who, upon his demand to see their warrant and his protests against the illegality of the proceedings, showed him their swords. As they hurried him through the streets—he knew not whither—he told them, amidst all the townspeople, that he had received from them neither civility, humanity, nor christianity. Very weak and hardly able to sit on horseback, his clothes reeking of smoke so that they were loathsome to him, he was carried towards Bentham, a 'wicked gaoler' whipping the horse from time to time to make him skip and leap, and then derisively asking 'how doe you Mr. ffox'. Though they missed their way they came at length to Bentham, fourteen miles distant. They were met there by a marshal and a company of troopers ; and by many of the county gentry and numbers of the common people who had assembled to stare at the famous prisoner. Taken to an inn while the guard pressed horses and raised the Hundred bailiff and the constables to accompany him on his further journey, Fox obtained permission to rest his weak and weary limbs on a bed. They passed on to Giggleswick which they reached that night, where a fresh set of constables were set to guard him, men with clogs who sat drinking and talking in his room all night so that he could get little rest. As they travelled onward next day several Friends came to see him upon the road and in the street of a market town through which they passed. He asked the soldiers whither they were taking him. Some said that he was to be sent beyond sea while others declared he was bound for Teignmouth Castle. All expressed fear that he might be rescued out of their hands—Friends were many in the North. They arrived at York on the following day, where the marshal put him into a great room, and where 'most part of two troopes' came to see him and were 'very loveinge' after he had spoken to them. So too was the Governor of York, Lord Frescheville, who visited him the same evening. He was sent to Scarborough two days later, with no more than four or five soldiers, 'very civill men' who carried themselves 'very loveingely' towards him. At Malton, where they baited, he was permitted to speak with Friends who came to visit him. On arriving at Scarborough he was taken to the inn for the night. The next day he made acquaintance with his new prison house, Scarborough Castle, where he suffered eighteen months' confinement before release came.

IX

TRAVELLERS AND TRAVELLING

'. . . if all persons, both ladies, much more Gentlemen, would spend some of their tyme in Journeys to visit their native Land, and be curious to Inform themselves and make observations . . . it would . . . fform such an Idea of England, add much to its Glory and Esteem in our minds and cure the evil Itch of overvalueing fforeign parts : at least ffurnish them with an Equivalent to entertain strangers when amongst us. Or inform them when abroad of their native Country, which has been a Reproach to the English, ignorance and being strangers to themselves.'

Thus wrote Mrs. Fiennes more than two hundred years ago. The advice is still profitable, the reproach not altogether undeserved. The English people have ever been wont to value foreign scenes, though not foreign ways, above those of their own varied and wonderful little country.

If there is now little excuse for ignorance there was, as we have already seen, good reason why the inhabitants of seventeenth-century England should make their journeys as few and short as business, health, and social intercourse permitted. It was rare for persons to seek change of scene in sustained travel. John Evelyn, on his return from his extended foreign travels, made, it is true, acquaintance with the English countryside in two fairly extensive tours ; but, though he lived to a long and hearty old age, he never again felt or answered the call of the open road. Pepys, during the eight years comprised by his diary, ventured on but one expedition of discovery : to Salisbury, Bath, and Bristol. For the rest he was content with the change of scene and interest that his business trips

THE CLIFFS AT DOVER

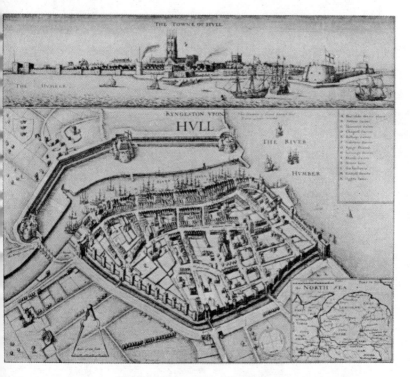

VIEW AND PLAN OF HULL

From engravings by Hollar

gave him, together with an occasional visit to the old family home at Brampton in Huntingdonshire.

The labouring people knew little beyond their own immediate neighbourhood.   Farmers and yeomen rarely left their homesteads except to go to market. Even among the gentry there were many who went no farther than the county town, the centre of local interest and gaiety.   Conversely, the inhabitants of the more remote districts were quite unaccustomed to meeting strangers.   With what suspicion they treated those who ventured into their midst will be set forth later.

Few were the spirits, foreign and native, who took upon themselves the role of explorers ; their daring was restricted for the most part to some half-dozen counties. Indeed, of all the writers of travel memoirs of this period none but Mrs. Celia Fiennes could claim know-ledge of every English shire from Land's End to Liddisdale.   Foreigners who visited these shores had little of the stuff of explorers within them.   Custom demanded acquaintance with the capital and the two universities.   Probably a visit was paid to the court wherever it happened to be ;   Nonsuch, Theobalds, Greenwich, Oatlands, Hampton Court, or Windsor. Beyond sights such as these, and the domestic beauty of the landscape, there was little to detain them in a country noted for its humid climate, boorish inhabi-tants, and inelegant speech.

But, as the unaccustomed eyes of foreigners saw and noted much that native writers passed by without com-ment, we may accord them precedence, and will through their eyes first make acquaintance with this England to which we too are strangers.   To avoid the tedious-ness of covering the same ground many times, one single tour, generalizing impressions and experiences, must stand for all.

One visitor having adventured upon the crossing, amid what dangers and difficulties we have already

seen, disembarks at Dover. Having viewed the Castle
—stepping in fear over the rotten ' planchers ' of the
floors—he procures a horse at the post-house and sets
out for Canterbury. No sooner is he in the saddle and
started, than he is followed by all the boys of the
neighbourhood, hooting and crying—enough to
frighten the horse—'a Mounser, a Mounser', until,
their annoyance increasing as they see the butt of their
remarks outpacing them, they fall to calling out
' French dogs, French dogs ', a little pleasantary he
takes not ill, for the rabble in other countries enjoy
hurling offensive names at the unoffending heads of
foreigners—has he not been taken, or mistaken, in
the Low Countries for a Frenchman and dubbed
Mushroom ? With such greetings at every considerable village on his route, he passes over hill and dale,
noting as he goes how curiously the fields are inter-
sected by hedges. If he has started late in the day he
spends the night at Canterbury. Here next morning
his attention will be attracted by the lowliness of the
English houses, the projecting windows of the ground
floor scarcely higher than a man's waist ; above, the
higher stories project out beyond one another to give
light and space to the upper rooms and some degree of
air, the upper casements, unlike those on the street
level, being made to open in the middle. When he
has visited the Cathedral, the College, and the Castle,
he again takes post and, enjoying the sight of the cherry
gardens which cover so much of this Kentish country,
travels to Sittingbourne where he once more changes
horses.[1] He has already seen on his way from Dover
more than one hill-top beacon. He now sees other
evidence of preparedness for war—or robbers, or
possibly both ; long poles, about a mile distant from
one another, on the tops of which are ' little kettles '
to contain fire; beneath, small huts to shelter those

[1] See Note O, p. 332.

whose business it is to attend to them.[1]   Later, he will
see them in other parts of England.   He passes
through Chatham and Rochester ; the way is paved,
and almost continuously bordered with low, thatched
houses.   Crossing over Rochester Bridge, raised high
above the Medway with a six-foot balustrade to prevent
persons falling over in the night—one of the finest
bridges in England—he reaches Gravesend, ' where
the king keeps ships of war, and some old hulls of
gallies taken from Spain by Queen Elizabeth '.   He
alights here to take boat for London.   He makes some
purchases while awaiting the tide, acquiring not only
the woollen stockings or riding cloak he needs in this
cold, uncertain climate, but a handful of tokens or
' fardins ' as they are not infrequently called, small
change issued by local tradesmen and legal tender only
in the neighbourhood of issue.   Later he will learn
wisdom and insist upon receiving some of the small
silver coins as change.   Towards evening he embarks
and is rowed Londonwards.   If the moon be full,
he will see clearly the prospect on either hand ; the
infinite number of ships, the shipyards, the many
villages, the castles and palaces, the workshops and
cottages, which border the river banks in curious
medley.   Or perhaps it is no more than dusk.   As he
approaches the city his ear is greeted by the ringing
of many church bells.   This is a favourite exercise and
amusement with the young folk of London.   He lands
at the steps beside Somerset House, and hiring
a couple of porters to carry his trunk between them,
walks to the neighbourhood of Covent Garden, or
' le Commun Jardin ' as he may perhaps call it, where

---

[1] It is Jorevin who describes these signal-posts. The description roughly
tallies with the beacons delineated in Ogilby's road books, but there were,
at the most, only six of these on the road between London and Dover—
Ogilby shows no more than five—and on this, the chief route to the
Channel ports, they were more numerous than elsewhere, as reference to
Ogilby demonstrates.

he has engaged lodgings with a compatriot. It is only rare, venturesome natures that, for gain of knowledge, will seek native society.

If he is young and has some knowledge of English he will do well to con *The Art of Living in London,* wherein he will find guidance how he may avoid the harpies and tricksters who prey upon his like. Of guide-books there are few. But, if his visit occurs towards the close of the century, he will find information of a somewhat arbitrary kind, it is true, in Chamberlayne's *Angliae Notitiae* (1669), and a more comprehensive survey of London in De Laune's *The Present State of London* (1681) concerning the metropolis. Moreover, there are many little books of voyages in French and German which will tell him something of the life, sights, and scenery of England, not to mention Camden's and Blome's large, descriptive works, each styled *Britannia,* and the many maps and atlases that have appeared since Saxton in the previous century undertook the delineation of the kingdom. Best of all for his guidance will be Ogilby's *Britannia,* first published in 1675, an invaluable compilation for those upon the road, but at present only to be obtained in folio, and therefore not adapted to wayside study.[1] However he is now settled for some days or weeks in the metropolis and has a mind to taste its pleasures.

There is much to do and much to see ; the Tower lions and the Tower armoury—the great sword and armour of William the Conqueror, and the armour of his jester, with horns affixed to the casque ; the tombs at Westminster Abbey ; Westminster Hall—the roof of which, says the biographer of his highness the Duke of Stettin, ' suffers no spiders or venomous

---

[1] *Itinerarium Angliae,* almost a facsimile of the *Britannia,* was published the same year. There were road-books of smaller size, the information of which was usually arranged in tabulated form. See *The Road-Books and Itineraries of Great Britain, 1570 to 1850,* by Sir Herbert G. Fordham, 1924.

creatures '—Whitehall ; Paul's, old, in ruins, or in course of re-erection ; the Royal Exchange, and all the fine shops—scarcely to be equalled in any other city of the world, declares M. Sorbière, a writer not over tender to English susceptibilities. London Stone he must needs visit, or he will be told, according to the old adage, that he has not seen London, together with much lore about its origin : that it has grown there spontaneously, or that William the Conqueror set it up in token of victory. Of course he goes to London Bridge, for it is one of the wonders of the world. Indeed, he has to go there twice before he can tell aught of its rarities ; for, the first time, as he stands gazing at the Northern gateway, he finds himself mobbed and jeered at by the loiterers there gathered, and has perforce to retire. Nor is it until he finds native escort that he dares to return. The London populace is incorrigibly rude. They will laugh at the strange and unfamiliar attire of the attendants of a foreign ambassador, mock at the representatives of an unpopular power, overturn the coach of another yet more unpopular, and mob the Queen herself, if either she, her religion, or her country of origin raises their ire.

Tired of the sights of London—and perhaps of the insolence and want of manners of the London street-folk—he can go down river to Chatham to visit the fleet, or, stopping short at Woolwich, join the throng of nobles, gentlemen, and citizens, who have flocked to see a newly launched man-of-war. A fitting end to the day will be a stroll in Moorfields, the citizens' recreation ground, with its jugglers and Merry Andrews to divert the weary mind.

That he visits the playhouses is as certain as that he patronizes prize-fights between fencing-masters, cock-fights, and bull and bear-baitings—' a fine amusement ' this according to the Duke of Stettin's biographer— unless, that is to say, he is so luckless as to visit London during the Puritan régime, when all amusements are under ban. If such is the case then the ring in Hyde Park—' Ay-parte ' or ' Ey-parc ' will be his nearest approximation to its rightful name—will be shorn if not of beauty—' the English ladies are very handsome and . . . they know it very well ' says Jorevin—at least of much interest. Yet he may come upon such a scene as the Lord Protector himself driving his coach-and-six with such furious lashing of the whip that the horses run away, flinging the great man from off the coach-box upon the pole. Likewise, the attraction of St. James's Park and the Mall will be heightened if there is a possibility of seeing the Merry Monarch at play in the Mall or feeding his ducks beside the canal ; his graver, less facile, brother strolling without ceremony thereabouts—distinguished from his attendants only by his blue garter—saluting all those who stop to look at him. The Park, moreover, can show not only the gay plumes of Kings and courtiers but also a menagerie of strange beasts and birds. Here also can be seen a telescope for the use of the scientifically-minded sovereign.

Should he feel so inclined our foreign visitor can intrude into Whitehall and watch Royalty plying knife and fork. Though royalty is sacrosanct, little or no restraint is placed upon the curiosity of the vulgar. It is possible, therefore, for him to make excursions to the various royal homes within reach of London. A pleasant outing is that by river to Wolsey's old palace of Hampton Court, and back by way of the fair Surrey lanes to Southwark. Neither the petulant cries of the poor prisoners in the Southwark jails, nor the rotting heads on London Bridge lessen, much less spoil, his appreciation of a lovely spring or summer's day. Such sights and sounds are common to every country, and has he not, coming from Dover, passed without a shudder under more than one gibbet, each with a hideous burden cased in chains swinging and creaking in the wind ?   A woman in the stocks under ' a little shed made of wood ' will excite his curiosity ; a poor wretch at the cart's tail, being flogged from Newgate to Tyburn, will raise perhaps a momentary feeling of compassion, as he walks from Holborn to Cheapside to procure money for his further journey from one of the goldsmith-bankers who there do business.

The following day, hiring a nag, he sets forward to Oxford.   There he finds a free meadow set aside for the grazing of travellers' horses, and there, under guidance of a college professor, perhaps chance-met in the Physic Garden, he visits all that is worthy of notice, the College Halls and Chapels, the Library, and—if his visit is made during the last three or four decades of the century—the new-built Sheldonian Theatre.   It is in Oxford too, maybe, that he is enabled, through the good offices of his innkeeper-host, to watch the funeral ceremonies of a ' my Lord ' ; the oration at the house of the defunct, extolling his virtues, his qualities, his titles of nobility, and those of his whole family ; the drinking by those assembled from a vessel, placed upon the coffin, to the health of the deceased ; the passing through the streets to the church, the corners of the pall held by four of the dead man's relatives, the other participants carrying boughs and lighted torches ; the service within ; and, finally, the committal, with the boughs thrown upon the coffin, the earth overspread and the torches extinguished therein.

So far his travelling has been easy ; the roads well defined, the persons who have catered to his wants—the postmaster, hackney-man, innkeeper, and the like—accustomed to the habits and requirements of foreigners.   Now, passing onwards to Bristol, Worcester, or Coventry, he loses his way ; once, twice, he is in doubt as to a turning ; he fails to make his hostess understand his meaning. Then it is that Latin comes to his aid. In Latin, the fellow-traveller he meets at the cross-roads puts him on his way ; in Latin the parson, hastily summoned by the landlord of the ' Stag ' or the ' Angel ', finds out his requirements, and settles him for the night ; and in the same universal medium a ' late commander in the low countries ', summoned in like fashion, broaches conversation, though, to delude the good hostess, with the air of speaking French.

A braggart, doubtless, this gentleman, like others of his race who had chanced to set foot on foreign soil. M. Jorevin—we now take leave of our representative foreigner for one who has travelled more extensively— knew this self-vaunting type. A young clockmaker who had worked in the galleries of the Louvre and had thereby learnt some French, fell into conversation with Jorevin upon the quayside at Holyhead, while they were awaiting embarkation for Ireland. The subject he broached was the skill and valour of Englishmen. He feared no two Frenchmen, he said, a provocative remark that Jorevin was unwise enough openly to resent. ' It would not be . . . a man of your sort that could terrify me sword in hand ', he exclaimed ; whereupon the young fool drew his sword and crying ' defend yourself ' sprang forward. Jorevin drew back, the other fell in his lunge, exposing himself to the Frenchman who gave him a thrust in the arm and would have killed him, so he confesses, had not other intending passengers come up and prevented him from doing other than break his antagonist's sword upon a neighbouring rock. It was fortunate for Jorevin that he had witnesses to his inoffensive attitude, for, as a foreigner, it would probably have gone ill with him had the crowd arrived later, to find perhaps the clockmaker mortally wounded.

If the foreigner had good reason to beware of getting entangled in disputes, it was even more incumbent upon him to avoid giving rise to suspicions—though his mere presence, except on the more usual routes, was cause for suspicion in itself.

To Halifax came in March 1679 some 'lusty' foreigners dressed in loose garments whom no one could understand. Some said they were Jews, others Persians. Although they were 'full of money' it was long before any in the town would lodge them. To a neighbouring village a few weeks later came another stranger in black clothes lined with fur. Happily for him he had an interpreter who could put the villagers at their ease. He was an Italian bound for Halifax 'pretending to goe to Dr. Hooke' as Heywood cautiously puts it, adding 'what became of them I know not'. Even at Oxford, three Germans who came afoot into the town and inquired for lodgings were taken by the rabble for Frenchmen come to fire the town. Only after they had been examined by the Mayor and proved innocent travellers, did their captors suffer them to be released.

Happily, Jorevin, with whom we now complete our tour, escaped more lightly. At Stowmarket, on his way South from Scotland, he met a young man, a friend of the people with whom he was lodging. This youth having entertained Jorevin 'with several pleasant discourses', proceeded to ask him whence he came and of what country he was, well knowing, as Jorevin explains, by his manner of speaking English that he was a foreigner, and, by his clothes, that he was a Frenchman. He followed it up by expressing astonishment that Jorevin should travel the country alone. Upon this he took his leave, and as Jorevin subsequently became aware, went straightway and gave notice to some townsmen that there was a stranger in the place and that it would not be improper

to know on what designs he came to England by a way
not usually frequented by passengers. Jorevin had
finished supper but a short time when the young man
returned and entered his chamber, followed by the
parson and his curate. The former, speaking in Latin,
announced that he had come on behalf of the townsfolk to know who he was and what business brought
him among them. Jorevin replied that he had come
to England to see the court, and London, ' so much in
reputation at Paris ', also the universities, and that he
was on his way to Holland by way of the Harwich
packet-boat. This answer assuaged their fears, and
feeling, probably, that they now owed an explanation
to the stranger, they told him that they had been
' jealous ' (fearful) of the French in England ever since
it was suspected that they had set fire to the city of
London. The incident was thus ended, and all that
was necessary to be done was to pay for the two or
three pots of beer which had been consumed during
the parley—though who paid does not appear—for,
as Jorevin adds, ' no kind of business is transacted
in England without the intervention of pots of beer '.
He might have added ' and tobacco also ', so addicted
were Englishmen and Englishwomen to pipe smoking;
in the taverns, at home, and—in the West—even at
school, where the proper management of the pipe
entered into the daily curriculum. His English misadventures were ended. He went unmolested through
the peaceful Suffolk country ; through ' Olmeso '
(Woolnen ?), ' Claine ' (Cleydon), ' Niden ' (Needham),
and Ipswich, and so by river to Harwich, which, as
he discovered while awaiting the return of the packet,
was situated in the ' most agreeable ' country in
England. Thence he crossed to Holland ; with a
goodly residue of English crowns, we fear, despite the
searchers, for he adds, as a last injunction to the
intending traveller and reader, that ' English money

will not pass current in Holland, unless to a great loss in the exchange.'

Of English travellers who set out to discover their native country some half-dozen have left record of their adventures and impressions.   First of these in point of time was John Taylor, the water poet, who during the course of thirty-five years made eight different expeditions by land and sea in and about Great Britain.   Whatever love of adventure and curiosity stirred within him, he had also the definite object in view of obtaining material for the sale of pamphlets ; it was a journalistic enterprise, in fact, according to the tastes and limitations of the era.   His first venture in 1618 was a ' Pennyles Pilgrimage ' from London to Edinburgh ;   an exploit which attracted so much attention that he performed it with considerable ease, thanks to the good-hearted knights, squires, innkeepers and other folk dwelling beside the Western route to Scotland, who gave generous hospitality to himself, his man, and his baggage-horse; though of what his baggage consisted it is hard to imagine, for he tells us that his horse shifted shoes twice—at Sutton Coldfield and at Manchester—to his one change of shirt.   Nevertheless, it was afterwards said that he disregarded his undertaking to carry and spend no money.   He had twice to make lodging by the roadside, at Dunsmoor Heath and at Stone ; and once saw the beer that had been ordered for him consumed by the wondering rustics who had been attracted thither to watch his progress.   At most places there were persons ready to do him service though it were but to guide him over the Westmorland Fells.   And the beer flowed freely all along the route, especially for the first fifteen or twenty miles from London.   Happily, as we learn from a subsequent tour, the London and South Country beer, though given in large measure, had not the potency of the liquor in the North, where

' it would fox a dry Traveller, before he had half
quencht his thirst ', or his arrival in Edinburgh might
have been longer delayed.   Some country-house visits
to the Scottish nobility and gentry followed, and then
the return journey was made in the same kindly way
until he reached Islington, where his friends had
assembled to pay tribute to his prowess in convivial
tankards.

Exploits of this description—to digress for a while—
were very popular alike with gentry and commonalty, before Puritan ascendancy overwhelmed Merry
England.   In 1600 Kemp, the famous comedian,
danced Morris-fashion from London to Norwich,
accompanied by his tabourer, Thomas Slye, his
servant, William Bee, and George Sprat as overseer.
' A Nine Days Wonder ' it was called, a modest
estimate, for it took him a month to cover the distance ;
and all that time crowds lined the route as he passed,
sometimes to his discomfiture, by getting in the way
and hindering his progress, which was none too easy
at the best, so thick was the mud and so deep the holes.
Some followed him for long miles—fifty people
accompanied him out of Brentwood though he stole
away early.   Others, of greater daring, undertook to
tread a mile or two with him.   One young fellow, ever
at his heels, stuck fast in a broad plash of water and
had to be rescued by his comrades.   In Norfolk he had
to suffer alike bad roads and parties of villagers,
twenty, forty, or a hundred strong, who gathered on
the route, crying that the fairest way was through
their village or the nearest and best road to the right
or the left.   His entry into Norwich—his State or
rather Terpsichorean entry—was delayed some days
to enable ' divers Knights and Gentlemen, together
with their wives and children, who had been many
days before deceived with expectation ' of his coming, to
assemble and watch his progress into town, a feat that

WILLIAM KEMPE.

the original Performer of Dogberry in Much ado about Nothing.

From a Wooden cut Prefixed to Kempes Nine Daies Wonder. 4to. 1600.

From a woodcut of 1600

would have been wellnigh impossible but for the
whifflers who made way for him through the crowd
which 'pressed so mightily' upon him. Had great
Elizabeth herself deigned to honour once more the
capital of the Eastern Counties, her reception could
scarcely have evoked more enthusiasm. The buskins
he had worn were deposited in the Norwich Guildhall,
placed 'equally divided, nailed on the wall '.

In 1622 Taylor undertook a sea voyage to York,
of which mention has already been made. With two
companions he set out in a four-year-old wherry,
furnished with wine, beer, bread, meat, sails, anchor,
cables, sculls, oars, card and compass, lanthorn,
candle, tinder-box and match. It was a rough voyage,
interrupted and almost terminated by the suspicions
of the good folk of Cromer. But it might have ended
in yet more disastrous fashion, for the trio were
ignorant of the tides and shoals of the Wash. Nor
were they free of hindrances when they turned inland.
Entering the Fosse Dyke—' Forcedyke Flood ' Taylor
calls it—connecting the River Witham at Lincoln
with the swift, North-flowing Trent, they found that
monument to Roman skill in a neglected and impassable
state. As a consequence they made eight miles hard
going in nine hours. After such toil the good cheer at
Hull and the more solemn entertainment at Bishops-
thorpe must have been doubly welcome to the Thames-
side watermen. A year later he embarked in a wherry
for Salisbury. This proved a yet more stormy passage,
though it accomplished its purpose by demonstrating
the possibilities of water communication between
Christchurch and Salisbury.

Sixteen years passed before he again ventured
forth. This time he set out upon a ten weeks' ride
through the Midland and Northern Counties. He
went first to Leicester where his brother kept the
' Blue Boar ', and to Nottingham where the poor

' doe dwell in vaults, holes, or caves, which are cut and digged out of (or within) the Rocke ' ; and to the Peak Country. Thence, passing East and North by Hull, the ' most defensible Town in the Kingdom ', he reached Cawood Castle where he dined with the Archbishop. He spent the next night in an alehouse in company with two drovers of hogs going to Leeds market, and a tinker ' who made pretty Musique with his *Banbury* Kettle-drum '. He passed next to Leeds which he describes as being for its size one of the most populous towns in England, the inhabitants amounting to about twelve thousand souls. From Halifax, where he saw the famous guillotine, he rode by ways ' past comparison or amending ' over the ' lofty Mountaine called *Blackstone Edge* ' to Chester ; whence he turned Southward to Leicester, and home to London, having accomplished six hundred and forty-five miles—' of sundry measures and sizes '—in the space of ten weeks.

Ten years later—ten years of change in thought and aspect—he went afoot and on horseback to see ' The Wonders of the West ' ; the ' little pritty City of *Bathe* '—a Bath lacking as yet the impress of Beau Nash and John Woods—Wells, its cathedral spoiled and defaced ; Glastonbury, shorn by the soldiery of its famous hawthorn but with another growing in its stead. Then came Barnstaple, St. Michael's Mount, the Land's End, where he cut his name four inches deep in a small patch of earth among the rocks, and whence he saw two royalist privateers waiting off the Scilly Isles, which were still held for the King, to attack passing shipping—a second Algiers some called it. He passed homeward through Plymouth, which was ' too full of suspitions ' to invite sojourn, though he stayed long enough to wish health and liberty to Colonel William Legge who was held prisoner in the Guildhall—Taylor was a royalist, as became a

King's waterman—so by Wilton to Salisbury, where
entry into the cathedral was refused except upon
payment of money, and finally to London : five
hundred and forty-six miles in eight weeks and a half—
six of which were spent in travel—by ' a youth of
threescore and ten, with a lame leg and a halfe '.   A
good record indeed.   The lame leg, as we learn subsequently when he consults an Italian physician or
mountebank, had been stricken at Oxford, nine years
previously, by a ' Blast of lightning and Thunder, or
Planet stroke ' ;   an affliction which the doctor by his
medicine hoped to cure.

It was three years later that he made his next circuit.
This was up by the Western Midlands and back
through the maritime provinces of Wales; a tour which
demonstrates in striking fashion the ravages caused
by the Civil War.   At Lichfield he found the cathedral
in ' sad confusion ' ;   at Flint the castle almost buried
in its own ruins, the town spoiled and with few trades-
people and not one alehouse, so that he was fain to
seek a private lodging.   A mile out from Carnarvon,
in which town he had spent five hours, he was recalled
by a trooper to be examined by the governor, Colonel
Mason.   This proved a fortunate delay.   When the
governor knew his name and business he gave him
entertainment for the night and furnished him next
day with a guide, and ' something else ' to bear his
charges for one week's travel.   The pride which
refuses financial assistance is a modern growth.   The
honest waterman gladly accepted and recorded dona-
tions towards his travelling expenses, even from the
Italian physician at Chester—no wonder he scorned
to call him mountebank—who not only gave him free
treatment, on the introduction of a friend, but paid his
night's charges at the ' Feathers ' Inn.   He found
Harlech ' almost inhabitable '.   It had ' neither hay,
grass, oats, or any relief for a horse ' ;   a lack of com-

modities not peculiar either to the time or place, for in many upland and isolated districts scarcity of fodder added to travellers' difficulties. At Barmouth, whither he next journeyed, he was constrained to employ a couple of boys at a groat apiece to go out and cut grass for his nag ; a sorry mount at best if we may believe the punning description with which he starts this travel tour. Carmarthen proved 'one of the plentifullest towns' that he ever set foot in, and cheap moreover, with butter at twopence halfpenny or threepence a pound, beef at a penny halfpenny a pound, oysters a penny a hundred, eggs twelve a penny, pears six a penny, a salmon two and half feet long for twelvepence, and nothing scarce but tobacco pipes ; a contrast to Pembroke where some houses were standing, some down, and many without inhabitants. So by the 'well strech'd Welch Mountainous Miles' he journeyed to Puritan England, with its strictly kept Sabbath days, wholly different from those of Wales, where 'the lawful and laudable games of trap, cat, stool-ball, and rackets, &c.' were still played by the young folk in the churchyards after service ; a sight to gladden his old eyes. It was his last vision of 'Merrie England', or rather 'Merrie Wales', for he did not live to see the return of the second Charles and all the delirious merry-making which ensued.

One more journey he made, a very little journey to 'Sussex by the sea' and Kent, where, at Romney and Hythe, he just missed sight and sound of a fight between the English fleet and Van Tromp's forces. However, at the 'Star' Inn at Rye, a loyal rhyme painted on a cloth rejoiced his heart.

> No flower so fresh, but frost may it deface
> None sits so fast, but hee may lose his place,
> Tis Concord keeps a Realme in Stable stay
> But Discord brings all Kingdomes to decay.

No subject ought (for any kinde of Cause)
Resist his Prince, but yeeld him to the Lawes
Sure God is just, whose stroake, delayed long
Doth light at last, with paine more sharp and strong
Time never was, nor ne'ere I thinke shall be,
That Truth (unshent) might speake, in all things free.

Nearly twenty years before this date, four other travellers had been on pilgrimage through England. One, Sir William Brereton, Baronet, of Handforth, Cheshire—who later became a well-known Parliamentary commander—had journeyed through the Northern and Western shires in passing to Scotland and returning from Ireland. The other adventurers, three gentlemen of the Military Company of Norwich, with the *noms de guerre* of ' a *Captain*, a *Lieutenant* and an *Ancient* ', had made a survey of ' 26. famous Shires . . . 15. fayre, and strong Cittyes . . . 40. neat and ancient Corporations . . . and . . . 13. ancient rich and magnificent Cathedralls ' ; in all eight hundred miles of extent. It is the ' Lieutenant ' who takes upon himself the task of scribe. As he has a lively, vivid, and intimate style, disclosing as well the men and manners of the time as the adventures of the jolly, care-free trio, his tale is more adapted to exposition than the somewhat dignified, prosy, and objective discourse of the Cheshire baronet. Therefore the military shall ' carry on ', to use an expression that, had the lieutenant known it, he would indubitably have used and cherished.

From Norwich they made a tour of England, North, West, South, East, and North again, missing only the extreme west and southern seaboard counties. Travelling on their own horses they accomplished on an average thirty to forty miles a day, as a rule by alternate long and short journeys : a leisurely pace that enabled them to devote some time to the castles and cathedrals on their route, and gave opportunity for convivial

intercourse with innkeepers and townsfolk. Indeed
the generous display of hospitality and the curious
mixture of freedom and formality in intercourse are
the features which most strike the modern reader of
this little book. Now the Dean of Durham, their
compatriot, bade them welcome to his ' large and
sumptuous Table ', plied them with fat venison, sweet
salmon and other good cheer, and would have had
them stay a week if they had been so minded. Then
the Lord William Howard of Naworth, their country-
man also, feasted them at Corby Castle with 'live roe'
venison, and a good store of wine, suffering them not
' to speake uncover'd, nor stand up ', as duty required,
but seating them near him at the board, and himself
accompanying them through the garden to the river,
whence one of his gentlemen saw them safely over the
' dangerous Fells ' to Greystoke Castle, another
possession of the Howard family. Nor was it only
the masters who made the trio welcome with good
cheer. At Eccleshall Castle, near Stafford, whither
they had gone sightseeing while baiting their horses,
they were given, after they had viewed the chief
rooms, excellent glasses of wine. At the Bishop's
Palace, Wells, having been shown over by one of the
bishop's gentlemen, they were taken into the ' 8 square
Buttry ', and tasted ' exceeding good Wine, and
strong Beere '. They were entertained in like fashion
at the neighbouring deanery, and, again some time
later, in the butteries and cellars of the halls and
colleges at Oxford. At Wigan the ' noble, boone
Parson, another honest Gentleman, and Mr. Organist '
accosted them in the market place as they were returning from Morning Service—they were strict church-
men—and invited them to a draught of 'Wiggin Ale';
' better Ale and better Company ' no traveller could
have desired. Then, having had their morning
draughts, they went to Mr. Organist's house to hear

his domestic organs and viols and join in song until
they partook of breakfast in company, after which,
when they were ready horsed for Chester, the parson
bestowed upon each of them a piece of ' Canall Plate '—
that is plates or other utensils made of Cannel coal
extracted in the neighbourhood and capable of taking
a fine polish.   At Chester, roused unwillingly from their
' sweet sleep ' by the city waits—they grudged their
rest rather than their money—they attended service
at the cathedral, and, having ' marcht the rounds of
the City on the walles, two Miles about ' under
guidance of their host, they viewed the city gates and
the ' rare waterworks ', like those of London ; after
which they paid the mayor a visit at his own house,
until he was called away by his brethren to the Pent-
house—Mansion house—to which he invited their
attendance.   There they watched the formalities of
making two citizens freemen.   The candidates first
appeared with helmets on their heads and halberts
in their hands, and took oath before the mayor that
they would have those weapons always ready for the
defence of the King and the city.   They were then
relieved of the military symbols, and were sworn free
members of the city.   A pottle of wine and sugar
ended the meeting as far as the travellers were concerned, for embracing the brethren ' Kindly ' they
departed upon their further travels.

The feelings of good fellowship evinced towards
strangers by sophisticated dwellers of towns contrasted
with the suspicions felt and expressed by the inhabitants of the more remote towns and villages, where
a strange face was rarely seen.   Allusion has already
been made to this characteristic of primitive and
isolated communities.   We have seen innocent
travellers taken up by the Watch, and foreigners
catechized and imprisoned until proved innocent by
constituted authority.   We read of Taylor being mis-

taken by the villagers of Blisland in Cornwall for
a process- or writ-server—unpopular members of
officialdom—and nearly beaten before he could explain
his presence among them ; of strangers, a century
and more later, being greeted with ducks (stones) or
set at with dogs when they made their appearance in
a village. It is said that Camden the topographer,
hardy traveller as he was, approached the benighted
Lancashire folk in 1607 ' with a kind of dread ' though
determined to run the hazard of the attempt, ' trusting
in the Divine assistance '. To range the little-fre-
quented ways, themselves often uninviting to man and
beast, must have called for no small degree of courage
in pleasure-travellers. Indeed in the Border Counties
of the North there was nothing to attract the travellers
whose sole object was to see the country. The country
abounded with ' dismal high precipices ', ' great
rocks ', ' black, moorish ground ', and ' hideous,
hanging hills ', that with ' the murmuring noyse of
those great waters, would make a man think he was
in another world '—perhaps like children seventeenth-
century travellers enjoyed the notion of fear. The
ways were not only steep and stony and loose, boggy
and miry, but narrow, intricate, and winding, so that
such lowlanders as the three of Norwich feared them
as seamen fear the Bay of Biscay, expecting at every
step their nags to fall with them into the bordering
deeps. The natives, if not actively inquisitive or
hostile, were sullen and discourteous ; at least they
seemed so to the above venturous trio, though it may
be that the language difficulty accounted in some part
for the apparent indifference of the Fell folk to the
welfare of these strangers.

' . . . we could not understand them,' says the Lieutenant,
' neither would [could ?] they understand us, that had we not
happily lighted on a good old Man (having lost our way in
this dayes travell upon the Fells) wee had beene . . . laid up

irrecoverably, without help, or hopes : for we had as much adoe, although with his directions to get off safely. . . . It was a hundred to one that wee should so escape.

That a gentlewoman should have braved such discomforts and perils in remote places with no more than a couple of men servants is testimony to a stout heart, a sound constitution, and more than a touch of the ' wanderlust ' without which none ever set forth upon the open road.

Mrs. Celia Fiennes—for with her, saving a few digressions, we may complete our panorama of seventeenth-century travel—accomplished during the last decade of the century some three thousand miles of travel, almost entirely on horseback. This wide and comprehensive survey entitles us to regard her as the forerunner of the modern woman explorer, as the discoverer of an England little known to her contemporaries and less known to us ; where women sit at their spinning-wheels in the village streets and knit in groups under the hedgerows ; where pack-horses bring the cloth from cottage looms to the fulling-mills in town, whence it is carried to the market place for disposal ; an England where travel can be leisurely and travellers can divert the tedium of the way with coursing hares or shooting goslings, with small fear of reproof from outraged ownership or from guilty or time-obsessed consciences ; [1] an England scarcely

---

[1] Mrs. Fiennes relates that while riding beside Ullswater through a forest or park ' where was deer skipping about and haires ', she had, by the means of a good greyhound, ' a little Course, but ' she adds, ' we being strangers could not so fast pursue it in the grounds full of hillocks and ffurse and soe she escaped us.' As the Earl of Orrery, the Very Rev. Rowland Davies, and his brother, were proceeding to Chester to cross to Ireland, they stopped outside Tarporley while the Earl and Davies's brother shot twelve goslings. This occasioned, as Davies tells us, their riding through Tarporley without stopping—though neither geese nor goslings appear to have been protected by law, the townsfolk probably regarded the wild fowl in their vicinity as their own preserve.   Game laws were strict in regard to pheasants, partridges, hares, conies, and deer.   But, if one may judge from the number of Acts passed under Elizabeth and during the seventeenth

more populous than modern London but as remote and as ignorant as the European Russia of to-day.

Writing in a colloquial and intimate style, she notes with a woman's keen eye, with a curiosity as universal as that of Pepys, and a naïvete few even of her contemporaries can equal—though it was an age of childlike curiosity and credulity—all that passes before her, the aspect of town and country, the forms of transport in use and the various manners and customs to be found in different localities, as a result of immunity from the levelling intercourse of travel ; she notes it all in a vivid and colloquial style that ignores grammar, spelling, and conventional punctuation, but is not proof against the insidious French fashion of ' discovering a prospect ', and some other alien expressions, strangely exotic in the homely framework of her diction.

She writes sometimes of the aspect of the country— the borders of Devon are ' fruitful Country's for Corn, graseing, much for inclosures ' ; the Rochdale to Manchester country is ' all enclosed with Quicksetts Cut smoothe and as Even on fine Green Bancks, and as well kept as for a Garden '. Her notes form a faithful record of rich and barren soils, of the condition of the roads which resulted therefrom ; of the curiosities of agriculture, and of other works of man. She has no eye for the colours and the contours of the landscape or the beauties lent to verdure and sky by atmospheric and seasonal effects. Perhaps it is as well, for their treatment requires a pen more skilled than hers. Phrases such as ' high stony hills ', ' low moorish ground ', ' deep enclosed country ' might indeed be taken as synonomous with the varying kinds

century, it was impossible to suppress ' the diverse disorderly persons ' who poached game, frequently at night, carrying their spoil to market towns to be sold. Possibly the travelling gentry considered that the property qualification, entitling those holding freehold or leasehold land to shoot game, rendered them immune from prosecution.

of bad roads if it were not that she dilates with more particularity on the ' causeys full of holes ', the ' stony precipices ', and the ' sad deep lanes ' which were, for the most part the nation's lines of communication.

Her attention is frequently drawn to the position and aspect of the country houses of the gentry—in Devon ' one Can ... rarely see houses ... they allwayes are placed in holes '. Alighting from her horse, she visits some mansion of lord or squire—admittance was rarely denied—and notes with true feminine zest and detail the exact manner of its laying out ; as well the servants' bedrooms, the backstairs, and the bathroom—where it existed—as the chambers of ceremony ; the design of its formal gardens, the fish-ponds and fountains, the orchards of apples, pears, cherries, and the Carolina gooseberries, and may be the ' great Wildernesse ', and the park ' where the deer do sport '.

For the towns she has not only a keen but critical eye. The streets must be clean and well pitched ; the houses must be in the ' new London mode '—a style increasingly popular since the Great Fire—if not she will speak of them with a certain measure of disdain. Nottingham is the neatest town she has seen—this is early in her days of travel—' built of stone and delicate ', with ' Large and long Streetes much like London, and the houses Lofty and well built '. The streets of Newcastle-on-Tyne are likewise ' broad and handsome, and very well pitch'd, and many of them wth very ffine Cunduits of water in Each allwayes running into a large stone Cistern for Every bodyes use. . . . Their shops are good and are of Distinct trades, not selling many things in one shop as is the Custom in most Country towns and Cittys '. The traffic is noteworthy for the ' Little sort of Dung potts ' used, and for the ' abundance of Little Carriages wth a yoke of oxen and a pair of horses together, wch is to Convey the Coales from the pitts to the Barges on the river ' ; no ship ' above 2 or 300 tun Can Come up quite to the Key '. At Scarborough she has already seen ' 70 sails of shipps pass the point ' which, she supposes, are colliers and their convoys transporting coal to London. Some eighty years earlier Foscarini, Venetian Ambassador in England, had counted nine-eight ships ' with tops ' in the port of Newcastle, and had been told there were ' more than as many again further down '. At Bristol he had found forty-three vessels ' with tops ', besides ' ten of seven or eight hundred tons, and other smaller ones in the part nearest the sea '.

This great city likewise has a great trade in coal. Near Kingswood on the way to Bath, where the coal is hewn, Mrs. Fiennes tells us that ' a great many horses ' are to be met with ' passing and returning Loaden wth Coales ' for which twelvepence a horse-load of two bushels is given. In this great city of Bristol ' there are signs to many houses that are not Publick houses just as it is in London ' ; the houses are ' pretty high, most of timber work, the streetes . . . narrow and something Darkish, because the roomes on the upper storys are more jutting out '.

Colchester is less up-to-date ; yet it is in the midst of a busy and populous countryside. Between Dunmow and Colchester ' you pass but halfe a mile Ere one Comes to two or 3 houses all along the road '. ' Their buildings are of timber of Loame and Lathes and much tileing ; the fashion of the Country runs much in Long Roofes and great Cantilivers and peakes '. Most of their buildings are old ' Except a few houses builded by some Quakers, that are brick and of the London mode '. Nevertheless, she considers the town ' Looks Like a thriveing place by the substantiall houses and well pitched streetes wch are broad Enough for two Coaches to go a breast, besides a pitch'd walke on Either side by the houses secured by stumps of wood, and is Convenient for 3 to walke together '. Colchester is, of course, the centre of the woollen baize or bays industry, and the low ground surrounding the town is used for the process of bleaching this material, as at Norwich it is used to like purpose for the woollen stuffs.

Some towns are noteworthy rather as centres of gentility, of local fashion, and of gaiety than as seats of industry. Many of the lesser gentry live in these all the year, and neighbouring landowners come to them for the winter months, when the country is more or less isolated and local fodder perhaps scarce. At Shrewsbury ' there are abundance of people of Quality . . . more than in any town Except Nottingham '. Here ' are noe fine houses but there are many Large old houses that are Convenient and stately '—praise indeed—and here in a garden ' Every Wednesday most of the town the Ladyes and Gentlemen walk there as in St. James' parke '. On many occasions they must give, unconsciously, examples of correct and incorrect deportment to the young gentlewomen of the ' very good schoole . . . for Learning work and behaviour and musick ', which is situated in this ancient border town. At Bedford, too, there are many gentlefolk though, here again, they live in ' such old houses '. Possibly they lack the aesthetic susceptibilities of Mrs. Fiennes, or, possibly, the amenities of the situation make up for the old-fashioned aspect of the town. There is the fine bowling-green with its seats and summer houses, to which the country gentry resort, especially on market days ; there are the many little pleasure boats, chained to the river banks when not in use ; and the supply of live fish, pike, perch, tench, &c., which are kept in baskets or trunks of perforated wood attached to the riverside gardens, a boon to a country town many miles from the sea.

With a diligent curiosity that would do credit to
a disciple of Baedeker she makes pilgrimage to the
chief sights of every town she visits : the cathedral
or church, the almshouse and the school, if it is of
sufficient importance as a seat of learning. She has
neither reverence for age nor eye for the beauty of
decay. The new classic form enshrines her ideal.
Yet some of the cathedrals do call forth her admiration,
though it is in terms of ' curious ', ' neat ', ' large ',
' lofty ', and, more rarely ' magnificient ', that she
dispenses praise. On Winchester she is indeed severe.
The Cathedrall ', she says, ' is one of the biggest
in England and is to be admired for its Largeness, not
its neatness or Curiosity . . . ' It must however be
remembered, in justice to Mrs. Fiennes, that these
edifices, which had endured through generations of
strife and neglect, were not so well preserved or
reverently cared for as they are to-day. To give an
extreme instance. Lichfield—in ' sad confusion ' in
1652 as Taylor has already told us—required the
utmost efforts of its Bishop, Hackett, to restore it.
' No gentleman lodged, or scarce baited in the city ',
says the Hon. Roger North, ' to whom he did not pay
his respects by way of visit, which ended in plausible
entreaties for some assistance towards rescuing his
distressed church from ruin.'

Keener, and perhaps more genuine, is her interest
in local manufactures ; again typical of her time. She
rarely misses an opportunity in the towns and villages
which she traverses of obtaining knowledge of the
industries pursued, and of gaining insight into the
methods employed. Thus at Exeter she watches the
processes of dyeing serges in vats, yellow, black, blue,
green, and scarlet.

At Canterbury she visits the silk-weaving looms of
the French refugees, and sees the making of several
fine flowered silks. She is also initiated into the making

of brown paper from pounded rags. She inquires at Bedford and at Malton, Yorkshire, into the infant woollen and linen industries respectively established in those towns ; rather, it would seem, like village industries, the one in the room above the market house, the other in the gatehouse and outbuildings of a ruined mansion. At Castleton Bridge in Yorkshire she makes acquaintance with the blowing and annealing of white glass, and at Northwich, in Cheshire, describes the getting of rock salt and the boiling of it in tidal waters. The mining of iron, coal, copper, and tin all find mention in her pages.

Of Derbyshire mining she writes: ' They make their mines at the Entrance like a Well and so till they Come to the Coale, then they digg all the Ground about where there is Coale and set pillars to support it, and so brings it to the well where by a basket Like a hand barrow by Cords they putt it up—so they Let down and up the miners with a Cord '. In the tin-mining district of Cornwall she sees

' at Least 20 mines all in sight wch employs a Great many people at work almost night and day, but Constantly all and Every day including the Lords day wch they are forced to [do to] prevent their mines being overflowed wth water. More than 1000 men are taken up about them, few mines but had then almost 20 men and boys attending it either down in the mines digging and Carrying the oare to the Little Bucket wch Conveys it up, or Else others are Draineing the water and Looking to the Engines that are draineing it, and those above are attending the drawing up the oare in a sort of windlass as is to a Well. Two men keeps turning bringing up one and Letting down another, they are much Like the Leather Buckets they use in London to put out Fire, wch hang up in Churches and Great mens halls.'

Of the new water-engines used in draining the mines, she says: ' They do five tymes more good than the mills they use to turn wth horses, but then they are much more Chargeable '.

To an inquiring nature such as Mrs. Fiennes's it is a congenial pursuit to investigate the customs and characteristics of the folk in whose midst she sojourns. Host or hostess are not infrequently the source from which she gleans information on this and other points. In Cornwall her palate is tickled with its first taste of ' west Country Tarts ' ; ' an apple pye wth a Custard all on the top ' and clouted cream, ' the most acceptable entertainment that Could be made me '. Some time previously her eye has been attracted by the ' West Country rockets ' : no comestible this, but a garment worn by the women of the three Western shires ; ' a Large mantle doubled together of a sort of serge ' or ' linsywolsey and a deep fringe or ffag at the Lower end . . . some to their feete, some only just below the wast ', in the summer white, and in the winter red. At Penzance she finds that the fires are of turf, furze, or fern, ' the only ffewell to dress a joynt of meat and broth ' for lack of wood and coal thereabouts, and scarcity of shipping round the Land's End since the war. At Truro she makes acquaintance with a curious kind of stepping-stones giving passage across the ditches, which ' are the ffences and Guards of their Grounds one from another '. They are ' severall stones fixed aCross and so are Like a Grate or Large Steps over a Ditch that is full of mudd or water, and over this just in the middle is a Great stone fixed side wayes wch is the style to be Clambered over '. ' . . .they are ', she adds, ' very troublesome and dangerous for strangers and Children.' At Gascoyn [Garstang] near Lancaster, she meets with clap bread, which is brought her in ' a great Basket such as one uses to undress Children with '. She describes them as thin wafers made of oatmeal and ' as big as Pancakes and drye that they Easily breake into shivers '—the Northern shires had no wheat save what was supplied from the South. Near Peterborough she sees cakes of

cow-dung drying on the cottage walls for use as fuel;
another indication, if any be needed, of the expense
and difficulty of transporting bulky commodities such
as coal and wood.   Ray, the naturalist, observed in
neighbouring Lincolnshire a more comely decoration
to the walls, house-leeks being grown, he knows
not why, on the clay corners and ridges of the thatch-
roofed cottages.

Curiously enough the games, processions, feasts,
and other observances of annual or more frequent
usage, find little place in Mrs. Fiennes's lively pages.
It is true she speaks of a Holy Thursday procession
at Leicester and describes at some length the Green
Bower Feast at Lichfield.   Of the latter she writes :

'The Bailiff and Sheriff assist at the cerimony of dressing
up Baby's wth garlands of flowers and Carry it in procession
through all the streetes, and then assemble themselves at the
Market place and so go . . . to a hill beyond the town where is
a Large Bower made wth greens, in wch they have their feast.
Many lesser Bowers they make about for Conveniency of the
Whole Company and for selling fruite Sweetemeetes and
Ginger bread wch is a Chief Entertainment.'

Before passing on we will take a few other peeps at
old-time customs.   There are the hurling-matches of
Cornwall, described by Ray.   This is a ball game—or
rather two different games of ball called In-hurling
and Out-hurling—played parish *versus* parish against
the church wall, after due proclamation has been made
by the town crier carrying a silver-plated ball.   There
are the Easter Monday sports at Clark Bridge near
Halifax of stool-ball and other games, enjoyed by
hundreds, young and old, in the churchyard, on the
green and all along the town, to the indignation of the
Rev. Oliver Heywood who records it.   There is
Plough Monday at Yarmouth when the boys of the
place go round singing at every house and receive
reward in the shape of food and money.   Prettiest

custom of all is that of the beating of the bounds, or
water frolic, also to be seen at Yarmouth. The town
bailiffs in their wherries with drums beating and
colours flying, followed by twenty boats or more carrying other borough officers, youths in white ' grenadier '
caps, victuals for the subsequent feast, and those
unofficial elements who are not afraid of the ' press ',
advance in two processions up the Rivers Waveney and
Yare. The first party go as far as St. Olave's, or
St. Thule's Bridge, where proclamation is made calling
upon those with grievances to come forward and be
heard ; while the second is similarly engaged upon
the sister stream. Then each partakes of an alfresco
dinner, and so back to Breydon, where amid firing of
guns, huzzas, and the drinking of healths, the two
parties meet. In the evening return is made to Yarmouth, the whole company attending the town bailiffs
to their homes before dispersing.

Not a word has Mrs. Fiennes to say of those mock
ceremonies to which the passing wayfarer was asked
to submit ; a species of toll upon his purse as well as
a survival from past ages, but one which still pleased
the somewhat childlike mentality of the seventeenth-
century traveller. We may therefore briefly set forth
two popular observances of which record has come
down.

The Highgate Oath was a burlesque ceremony of
unknown origin and long practice.[1] Each traveller,
upon his first visit, as he alighted at the inn on the top
of Highgate Hill—perhaps he had walked up to ease
the coach-horses, or had alighted for the fun of the
thing—had an oath administered to him upon a pair of
horns which were mounted upon a long pole. He

---

[1] ' The custom ', writes Lysons, ' of imposing a burlesque nugatory oath
on all strangers, upon their first visit to Highgate, is well known : how or
when it originated I have not been able to learn : a pair of horns, upon
which the oath is administered, is kept at every public-house.' Vol. ii,
p. 441, 2nd edition.

swore never to eat brown bread while he could get white—rye bread was the usual diet among the labouring classes—never to drink small beer while he could get strong, and never to kiss the maid while he could kiss the mistress, unless he liked the other best; whereupon he was admitted to the freedom of Highgate—at that time a village of considerable importance on the Holyhead road as the meeting-place of three alternative routes out of London.

At Robin Hood's Well in Sherwood Forest there was a form of initiation or investiture—accounts differ—having some imaginary connexion with the famous outlaw whose habitat it was said to have been. The ceremony is described as follows by the Rev. James Brome, who, as travel tutor to the two sons of an ' Eminent Merchant ', made several extensive tours in England towards the close of the century.

' Being placed in the Chair [an ancient one, said to have belonged to the outlaw] we had a Cap, which they say was his, very formally put upon our Heads, and having perform'd the usual Ceremonies befitting so great a Solemnity, we receiv'd the freedom of the Chair, and were incorporated into the Society of that Renowned Brotherhood.'

Whether in the course of three-quarters of a century the ceremony had suffered distortion of meaning, or whether, as is most probable, the Lieutenant of Norwich before mentioned and his comrades lacked knowledge of the ' Renowned Brotherhood '—they were certainly in too much of a hurry to wait for the ' charge ', though not for the cup of ale which preceded it—the trio of military men were most decidedly under the impression that, for a fee of fourpence each, they had received the honour of knighthood!   According to Evelyn, who from want of knowledge or disdain makes no mention of the ceremony, the chair was a stone one and had an iron ladle chained to it for taking up water from the ' crystal spring '.

Whatever the views, political and religious, of travellers in this century, whatever their pursuits and inclinations, they one and all had nothing but the most intense and wondering interest in and admiration for the caves, the standing stones and ' moving ' hills, the wells of strange properties and all the other phenomena, real and imagined, with which nature and legend had dowered the land. It was the spirit of the Renaissance working within them, the resurgence of intellectual curiosity and inquiry no less than the quickening of the imaginative faculties ; a spirit that led as well to the founding of the Royal Society and the varied and sometimes curious experiments carried out before its members, as to *The Faerie Queene* and the great literature that followed ; that prompted Harvey's discovery and the researches of Sydenham as surely as it produced Inigo Jones and Wren and the great masterpiece of St. Paul's.

No traveller visited Derbyshire but he straightway went to see the Seven Wonders of the Peak ; or, at least the three of most renown : Eldon Hole, Poole's Hole, and the Devil's Arse. Young Edward Browne described the first as ' a pit [of] such vast depth, that the greatest ingines and the boldest fellows that could bee found to goe down never find any bottome ' ; Brome said it was reputed to be a bottomless abyss. It struck terror into some of Browne's party to hear the noise of the stones which they threw down it, so long after they had left their hands. Mrs. Fiennes was more impressed by a further element of mystery ' . . . its reported ', she writes, ' that severall Attempts have been made to ffence the whole round wth a stone Wall as the manner of the fences are all over that Country, but yet it has been all in vaine. What they built up in the day would be pull'd down in the night and so its vaine to trye the securing it round from any falling in—this the people tell

us '. Fortunately the cattle had ' a sort of instinct
in Nature ' that withheld them from its vicinity.
Not so one ' wretched villain ' who, Browne tells
us, confessed at the gallows that he had robbed a
gentleman and thrown him and his horse into its
depths.

Poole's Hole, ' a hollow Cave under a high Rock ',
as Browne describes it, was so called, says Mrs.
Fiennes, ' from a man of that name that was a Robber
and use to secure himself in that place like a house,
and so the Country people imagined he made it, but ',
she adds, ' some think it was dug to find mines or
marble or Chrystal . . .' Poole's Chamber with his
stone table and bed were shown to visitors, together
with many other wonders of stalagmite and stalactite
creation, including the ' Queen of Scots' Pillar ', at
which point that unfortunate Queen, it is said, and
certainly most other sightseers, turned back. ' Wee
brake of a piece of this pillar ', writes Edward Browne,
' and brought it away with us.' On leaving the cavern
' a company of damsells '—says young Browne (' some
poor Women ', says the elderly Brome)—were wont
to meet visitors, ' very cleanly dreast, having each of
them a little dish of water full of sweet hearbs which
they held out to us to wash our hands, which wee had
dirty and bedaubed with the slime within this hole,
which done and wee being somewhat taken with this
pretty custome, did the more freely immerge our
recompences for this odde kinde of civility '. At the
Devil's Arse the people who attended upon visitors,
lighting the way with candle and lanthorn, actually
lived in a cave, in poor little houses built of stone or
clay—accounts differ—' and thatch'd Like Little
Styes '. In one, a little bigger than the rest there had
lived, some years before Mrs. Fiennes's visit, a gentleman and his wife ' worth above 100£ a year wᶜʰ he
left to his brother Chooseing rather Like a hermite

to Live in this sorry Cell '. A true tale, for Mr. Middleton, who was one of the party visiting the cave at the
same time as Mrs. Fiennes, had actually ' dined ' with
the couple on carrots and herbs.   The other wonders
of the Peak were some marble stones which ' by their
orderly disposition into several Rows ', seemed ' rather
to have been the contrivance of Art, than of Nature ' ;
a well that ebbed and flowed, ceasing ' its miraculous
motions but on Great raines ' ;   the hot well at Buxton ;
and a hill called Mamtour or Mam-tor, near Castleton,
with a cliff face—Mrs. Fiennes likened it to a hayrick
cut in half—down which sand kept trickling, especially
when there was the least wind, no uncommon thing in
that country, making it so dangerous to ascend that
none ever attempted it.

In the Mendips there was Wokey Hole, ' the most
admirable piece of Nature's Workmanship in our
English Nation '—the wonderful Cheddar caves lay
unknown and unexplored—with its simulated churches,
cellars, butteries, kitchens, halls, and all the glittering
weird shapes and forms to enchant the eyes of him
who trod its stony ways for a furlong or two.   An
echo ' making a Melody more sweet than ordinary '
enticed ' Gentlemen and Ladies in those Parts to
bring Musick and Dance ' in a special dancing-room ;
while, in another compartment, a table formed out
of the rock naturally suggested itself as a place in
which to drink wine, though it meant carrying the
bottles for ' near half a Mile under ground '.   A day's
journey away and there was another curiosity of
nature, the St. Vincent's Rocks near Bristol with a hot
spring gliding between them into the river below,
much resorted to by persons for the purposes both of
washing and drinking.   It was a favourite sight with
the seventeenth-century tourist—had there been a
' Baedeker ' in those days it would have been double-
starred—who descended ' neere 200 slippry steps '

by a steep rocky and winding way ; and then, his capacity for wonder spent, climbed up again, to turn pioneer and dig and delve for Bristol or Bastard diamonds—bright, sparkling stones, looking as if they were polished and irregularly cut.

To the many wells of strange character and curious properties the traveller made his way, whether it were merely to look and wonder, as at the commercially useless bone-wells, pitch-wells, and burning-wells, or to bathe and be refreshed as at the medicinal springs, which had come to be the panacea for many of the ills whose cure baffled the skill of the medical profession. But let us, before considering the many and various spas—so named in imitation of the Belgian Spa—allude to one or two other wonders of nature pleasing to the all-curious seventeenth-century mind. Such was the earth at Apsley in Bedfordshire, which turned alderwood into stone if it were left within the ground seven years—the sceptic would have long to wait—such the Devil's Bolts near Harrogate, three stones of a pyramidal shape said to have been shot by that active gentleman, but on what account does not appear. There was Knaresborough, with its three rarities, St. Robert's Chapel—a vaulted hermitage hewn out of the rock—a dropping well which covered wood with stony bark, and the medicinal springs. There was Stonehenge, 'one of the wonders of England', says Mrs. Fiennes ; 'as prodigious as any tales I ever heard of them', says Pepys, who adds, ' God knows what there use was ' ; and at which Evelyn struck with a hammer but could break no fragment. There was also Marckley Hill in Herefordshire which had, on the 7th February 1571 at about six at night ' moved with a roaring noise from the place where it stood, and by seven the next morning had gone about 200 Foot, and so continued its Travels for 3 days together, to the great Horror and Astonish-

ment of all the Neighbouring Inhabitants, whereupon
Kynaston Chapel, Trees, Hedges and Sheep Folds
fell down, and which adds much to the Wonder two
High Ways were turned about 300 Foot from their
former Paths . . . Pasturage being left in the place
of Tillage, and this in the place of Pasturage '.   Last,
but by no means least, we must note the effigy of the
' native of Groenland ' at the Trinity House of Hull, to
which travellers repaired for mere sight of him in
his ' coat of Skins . . . in his right hand, a pair of wooden
oars . . . in his left a dart, with which he strikes fish;
on his forehead a thing like a trencher which serves
as a *bonne-grace* to fence his eyes from the sun, and it
may be too, from the dashing of the water.   Behind . . .
a bladder or skinbag, in which we suppose he bestowed
the fish he caught ' ;   though some said, ' it was
a bladder full of oil, with which he used to allure the
fish to him '.   This unfortunate Eskimo, known as
' the wild man ' or ' the bonny boate man ', had been
taken in 1613 by Andrew Barker of Hull, and refusing
to eat or speak—much good it would have done him
had he attempted to speak with his captors—' died
with hunger and sullenness in the space of three days ',
and was buried in an alien land without kayak or
weapons to help him in further travels beyond the
grave.

A score or so of medicinal springs, scattered in many
counties, North, South, East, and West, ministered to
the health of the nation.   Of these Mrs. Fiennes
visited, as bather or sightseer, some ten or twelve.
No portion of her travel tour comes more clearly before
the reader than her description of the society gathered,
the daily life pursued, in these newly rising communities.   On no other subject does she display the
same air of assured knowledge as on the constituents
and uses of the various mineral waters and the means
taken for their replenishment.   Let us therefore again

seek her guidance in this final peep into the realms of
seventeenth-century travel.

Of some of the spas she visits the fame has long since
departed ; in some the germ of decay was even then
visible.   At Alford in Somersetshire there was ' no
good accomodation for people of fashion, the Country
people being a Clownish rude people '.   Therefore
its excellent spring of alum water ' good for all sharpe
Humers ' was not so frequented as formerly, except
by those of the neighbourhood who came or sent
thither to fetch water for the brewing of beer.   Canterbury spring suffered, most likely, from proximity to
the more excellent Wells near Tonbridge.   Moreover
there was some diversity of opinion concerning its
powers of healing.   A gentleman lodging in the same
house as Mrs. Fiennes ' Complained of a numbness
in his Limbs after drinking it sometyme '.   And
Mrs. Fiennes herself was more impressed with the
' fine walks and seates and places for the Musick '
than with the water, which had an unpleasant taste and
slow action.   ' . . . I like no spring ', she says, ' that
rises not quick and runs off apace[;] that must have
most spirit and good off the minerall it Comes from '.
Of Barnet likewise, populous and popular because of
its nearness to London, she has little good to say.

' . . . its a Large place and the houses are made Commodious
to Entertain the Company that Comes to drink the water,
wch Certainly if they be at the paines to go once and see would
have but Little stomach to drink them. The well is a Large
place walled in 8 square . . . and over it is Lattices of wood
round to Looke down into it and so Covered like a house
above ; below are staires down to a doore to go in to dip the
water there. I stood at the Lowest step above the water to
Look into it, its full of Leaves and Dirt and Every tyme they
dip it troubles the water, not but what they take up and let
stand—Looks Clear but I could not taste it.'

Pepys was less wise, it would seem, when he visited
the place in July 1664.   He ' drunk three glasses, and

walked, and come back and drunk two more ; and so ', he continues, ' we rode home, round by Kingsland, Hackney, and Mile End, till we were quite weary ; and not being well I betimes to bed'. These injudicious glasses probably induced alike the night sweat and the night fears which followed—a scare of burglars which had no other origin than the attempts of the dog, shut out of doors, to gain admittance.

Bath, of age-long repute, and Tunbridge Wells, a mushroom growth since Henrietta Maria encamped beside its spring, both found favour in Mrs. Fiennes's eyes. The latter place had excellent, quick-rising springs ; commodious buildings two or three miles around for lodging visitors ; a market plentifully supplied at cheap rate by the surrounding country, and with fish from Rye and Deal. It had also shops ' full of all sorts of toys, silver China, milliners and all sorts of Curious wooden ware wch this place is noted for ' ; while for amusements there were ' two Large Coffee houses for tea, Chocolate &c., and two Roomes for the Lottery and hazard board'. There was a paved, covered walk for wet weather—doubtless the Pantiles—and there were other walks of mixed sand and clay for dry weather; together with such conveniences as a daily post from London during the season, stage-coaches five days a week from London to neighbouring Tonbridge, a daily coach to ' the Wells ' during the season for eight shillings apiece, and a service of carriers twice a week.

Bath had its drawbacks : it was difficult of approach —' 5 mile down a very steep hill and stony, a mile from the town scarce any passing and there descends a little Current of water continually from the rocks '— it had many indifferent houses—though ' severall good houses built for Lodgings that are new and adorned, and good furniture '—it had a low, unpleasant climate. Nevertheless, Bath had two inestimable advantages, five magnificent baths and an excellent system of management.   The Cross bath

' in the middle has seates round it for the Gentlemen to sitt, and round the walls are Arches wth seates for the Ladyes, all stone, and the seate is stone and if you thinke the seate is too Low they raise it with a Coushon as they call it, another Stone, but indeed the water bears you up that the seate seemes as easy as a down Coushon.   Before the Arch the Ladyes use to have laced toilet hung up on the top of the Arch and so to shelter their heads even to the water if they please.   You Generally sit up to the Neck in water, this Cross bath is much the Coolest and is used mostly in the heate of summer ; there are Gallery's round the top that the Company that does not Bathe that day walkes in and lookes over in the bath on their acquaintance and company—there are such a number of Guides to each bath of women to waite on the ladyes, and of men to waite on the Gentlemen, and they keepe their due distance.   There is a serjeant belonging to the baths that all the bathing tyme walkes in galleryes and takes notice order is observed and punishes the rude, and most people of fashion sends to him when they begin to bathe, then he takes particular Care of them and Complements you every morning wth deserves its reward at the end of the Season.   When you would walk about the bath I use to have a woman guide or two to Lead me for the water is so strong it will quickly tumble you down, and then you have 2 of the men guides goes at a distance about the bath to Cleare the way '—doubtless, of the certificated ' impotent poor '.

Space fails for her descriptions of the King's and Queen's baths, the latter so-called from James I's Queen who visited it in 1615.   Frightened in the King's bath by a flame like a candle which rose to the top and spread in a large circle, she took herself to the new bath, although assured by the physicians that the apparition was due to natural causes.   That something, however, may be seen of the frequenters of Bath other than the ' Quality ' with which Mrs. Fiennes so largely concerns herself, we append the description given by the ' Lieutenant ' of Norwich two generations earlier.

'There met wee', he writes, 'all kinde of Persons, of all shapes and formes, of all Degrees, of all Countryes, and of all Diseases, of both Sexes : for to see young, and Old, rich, and poore ; blind, and lame ; diseas'd, and sound ; English and French ; men, and Women ; Boyes and Girles, one with another, peepe up in their Caps, and appeare so nakedly, and fearefully, in their uncouth, naked Postures, would a little astonish and put one in mind of the Resurrection.'

Fortunately for the susceptibilities of Mrs. Fiennes, *les convenances* of the newly arising, polite society had, some time before her visits, decreed the wearing of garments of fine, yellow canvas.

How great was the faith in the curative powers of mineral waters, how impelling the force of fashion, the defective arrangements at some of the best-known spas abundantly testify. At Buxton good accommodation was lacking.

'The house thats Call'd Buxton Hall wch belongs to the Duke of Devonshire its where the warme bath is and the well, its the Largest house in the place tho' not very good ; they are all Entertaining houses and its by way of an ordinary. . . . You pay not for y^r bed roome and truely the other is so unreasonable a price and the Lodgings so bad, 2 beds in a Roome, some 3 beds and 4 in one roome, so that if you have not Company Enough of your own to fill a Room they will be ready to put others into the same Chamber, and sometymes they are so Crowded that three must Lye in a bed. Few people stay above two or three nights its so Inconvenient. We staid two nights by reason one of our Company was ill, but it was sore against our Wills for there is no peace nor quiet with one Company and another going into the bath or coming out ; that makes so many strive to be in this house because the bath is in it. Its about 40 feet Long', she continues, 'and about 20 or 30 ffoote broad being almost square. There is 10 or 12 springs that bubble up that are a Little warme, its not so warm as milke from the Cow, and not a quick spring, so that its not Capable of being Cleansed after Everybody has been in. Its warme Enough just to Open the pores of ones body, but not to Cause sweat, . . . Its Cover'd over the top, but not Ceiled and there is an open place in the middle like a Tunnell w^{ch}

pours the Cold down on the head, it would in my thoughts be better if it were Exposed all to the aire and sunn. There is a pave^{mt} of Stone on one side at the brim to walke on, with benches of Stone to Sitt on. You must have a guide that Swims with you, you may Stand in some place and hold by a Chaine and the water is not above y^r Neck, but in other parts very deep and strong it will turn you down.'

At Epsom the spring itself was at fault. Doubtless this was the reason of its being covered over with timber and ' so darke you Can scarce Look down into it. . . . Its not a quick spring ', she continues, ' and very often is dranke drye, and to make up the defficiency the people do often carry water from Common wells to fill this in a morning ; this they have been found out in which makes the water weake and of Little opperation unless you Can have it first from the well before they Can have put in any other '. Nor were the surroundings inviting.

' There is a walk of trees by it, but not very pleasant, there is a house built in which the well is and that is paved with brick to walke in in the wet weather, and where people have Carrawayes sweetemeates and tea etc., but it Look'd so dark and unpleasant more Like a Dungeon, that I would not Chuse to drinke it there, and most people drinke it at home.'

Buildings and lodgings, however, were good, the latter with gardens at the back, and with ' great curiosityes ' in cut hedges and pollarded trees, ' almost before all doores '. So too were the diversions, the coffee, dancing and gaming houses ; the shops for sweetmeats and fruits ; the ' raceing of boys or Rabbets or Piggs ' on a Monday morning ; the evening meetings on the upper green, with bowling for gentlemen, and walking for ladies ; and also the lower green ' much neater greener and warmer ', with its large room with hazard boards. But, says Mrs. Fiennes,

' the Greatest pleasure of Emson [a variant of Epsom] is Either Banstead Downs where is good aire and good rideing for Coaches and horses, with a pleasant view of the Country,

or Else Box Hill which is 6 or 7 miles off . . . Cover'd with box
. . . and . . . other wood . . . Cutt in Long private walks very
shady and pleasant, and this is a great diversion to the Company
and would be more ffrequented if nearer Epsom town.'

Yet, but for the tyranny of fashion, the company
had no need to go so far for outdoor amusement.

' On the hill where is the race posts ', she adds a few pages
later, ' they have made a ring as in Hide Parke, and they Come
in Coaches and drive round, but it is only Lords day nights
and some nights. There has been 40 coaches and six which
are the Gentlemen in the country round, and 20 and 2 horses.
The Company in the town Epshum shall be Clutter'd wth
Company from Saturday to Tuesday and then they many
times goe, being so neare London, so come againe on more
Satturdays.'

Testimony, indeed, to the time-honoured adage,
' There is nothing new under the sun '.

NOTES

A (see page 60)

J. E. Thorold Rogers, in the *History of Agriculture and Prices*, vol. vi, gives the following prices for saddle-horses.

	£	s.	d.
1611–12. Grey ambling gelding for Provost, King's Coll. Cambridge	18	0	0
1614–15. Gelding for President, Christ Ch. Coll., Oxford	15	0	0
1625–26. Warden's gelding, All Souls, Oxford . .	15	15	0
1627–28. President's horse, Magd. Coll., Oxford .	20	0	0
1630–31. Gelding for President, Christ Ch. Coll., Oxford	12	0	0
1630–31. Horse for President, Christ Ch. Coll., Oxford	15	0	0
1635–36. Horse for President, Christ Ch. Coll., Oxford	18	0	0
1647–48. Two nags with one saddle, bridle, and furniture, Christ Ch. Coll., Oxford . .	22	4	0
1657–58. Warden's horse, Christ Ch. Coll., Oxford .	17	10	0

These were without doubt all fine, picked animals. Prices mentioned as having been paid for horses whose use is unspecified are much lower; from a few pounds upwards. Sumpter-horses fetched about ten pounds (1613–14 Cambridge, 1636–7 Oxford).

B (see page 73)

In the *History of Agriculture and Prices* the prices paid for coaches and chariots are given as follows :

	£	s.	d.
1634. New coach, King's Coll., Cambridge . .	42	15	4
1663. New carriage, Provost, King's Coll., Cambridge .	40	0	0
1666. New glass coach, two harnesses and curtains, New Coll., Oxford	38	5	0
1684. New coach, King's Coll., Cambridge . .	22	0	0
1687. Chariot, Cuckfield, Sussex . . .	28	0	0
1689. New carriage, King's Coll., Cambridge . .	52	1	0
Coach wheels were renewed for the following sums :			
1631. Pair coach wheels, King's Coll., Cambridge .	1	4	0
1637. New coach wheel, King's Coll., Cambridge .	1	2	0
1667. Four coach wheels, Yotes Court, Kent . .	1	10	0
1685. Set of coach wheels, London . . .	4	10	0

C (see page 76)

The following is the list of prices paid for coach-horses given in the *History of Agriculture and Prices*.

		£	s.	d.
1620.	Two bay coach-horses, King's Coll., Cambridge	18	6	8
1636–7.	Two dapple-grey coach-horses, King's Coll., Cambridge	16	12	6
1638–9.	Young coach-horse, King's Coll., Cambridge .	14	11	0
1660–1.	Carriage-horse, King's Coll., Cambridge .	19	5	0
1667–8.	Carriage-horse, King's Coll., Cambridge .	15	0	0
1667–8.	Carriage-horse, King's Coll., Cambridge .	17	15	0
1668–9.	Coach-horse, King's Coll., Cambridge . .	9	0	0
1670–1.	Carriage-horse, King's Coll., Cambridge .	15	0	0
1671–2.	Four-year-old coach-horse, Yotes Court .	13	0	0
1672–3.	Black coach-gelding, Yotes Court .	10	15	0
1673–4.	Two coach-horses, King's Coll., Cambridge .	20	0	0
1674–5.	Coach-horse, King's Coll., Cambridge . .	15	0	0
1681–2.	Coach-horse, King's Coll., Cambridge . .	13	5	0
1686–7.	Two coach-geldings, Cuckfield . . .	14	10	0
1686–7.	Coach-gelding, Cuckfield . . .	10	0	0
1692–3.	Coach-horse, Eton	16	0	0
1698–9.	Pair coach-horses, Harting, Sussex . .	43	0	0

D (see page 91)

The following list, culled from the *History of Agriculture and Prices*, shows some of the prices paid for trunks and other receptacles for luggage.

1603. Cloak bag, 5s. 6d.
1616. Trunk, 10s.
1617. Cloak bag, 6s.
1618. Trunk, 8s.
1636. Portmantle, 10s.
1642. Trunk, 6s. 4d.

1648. Portmantle, 7s.
1655. Little trunk, 9s. 6d.
1657. New portmantle, 7s.
1661. Sealskin trunk, 15s.
1662. New portmantle, 10s.

Sir George Chaworth, prior to his departure on an embassy to Spain, bought two trunks, one at eighteen shillings, and one at nine shillings. *Losely Manuscripts*, ed. by Alfred J. Kempe, p. 430.

E (see page 129)

'Common Innes are appointed for travellers and wayfaring men. ... And therefore if any Inne-keeper shal suffer persons inhabiting in the same towne, or any other persons (contrary to the statute) to be usually tippling in his house : such an Inne-keeper may be accompted as well an Alehouse-keeper, as an Innekeeper, & may be bound by Recogn[isances] with suerties, for the keeping of good order, as Alehouse-keepers are : and so Judge *Warbeton* delivered it in his charge at Cambridge Assises, *Ann. Dom.* 1613. Or else it seemeth they may be committed As Alehouse-keepers without Licence. Also it hath been agreed for Law, That such Innes as have bin erected since the Statute of 5 *Ed.* 6 *cap* 25 [for binding alehouse keepers by recognisance] and were not Innes before, ought to have Licence ; & that such Inne-keepers are to be bound by Recognisance with suerties for keeping of good orders, as Alehouse-keepers are.' *The Countrey Justice*, Michael Dalton, 1618, p. 26.

The Hertfordshire Justices published, in 1596–7, ' Articles which all alehouse keepers and vittlers hereafter following are with their sureties bound to observe and keep uppon the forfeeture of their several recognizannce : 1. Firste that everye of them be continually furnished as well with convenyent lodginge as allsoe with good and holsome vitualls fitt to serve all suche as uppon honeste occasions shall repayre unto his house. 2. Item that none of them doe lodge any person or persons but suche as he will answere for. 3. Item if knowledge doe come to the towne of any robbery committed then everye one of them shall declare to the Connstables the names, apparrell, and, if he can, the dwelling place allsoe of all such persons as dydd lodge in his house two daies before or two daies after suche robbery commyted.' Other items declare against unlawful games, eating and drinking in time of Divine Service on Sundays or holidays ; against dressing meat in Lent and at other prohibited times ; against allowing persons dwelling in the same town as the alehouse keeper, except such as have necessary business with him, to drink and tipple in the house ; against suffering persons other than lodgers to tarry in the house after nine o'clock from Easter to Michaelmas, and after eight o'clock in the winter; against selling ale or beer above the regulated prices. Lastly, it was ordained ' that none of them shall buye any goodes of any wayfaringe man or passenger, or others, that shall bring the same to their howses to sell, but shall firste before he shall buy then make the constable or some officer acquainted therewith, whereby if any suspition may be conceaved that the same goods were stolne the partie and the said goods may be staid '. Then followed the names of certain publicans of the towns and villages of Hertfordshire and their sureties. Some years later a fresh set of orders (this time emanating from the Privy Council) was issued.

F (see page 134)

An ordinary was the equivalent to the modern *table d'hote* (the word is still used in small country towns, especially on market days). It was commonly served in taverns and inns about midday, and was ' composed of a variety of dishes in season, well drest, with all other accommodation fit'; Cotton's *Compleat Gamester* as given in Wheatley's *Pepysiana*. Prices varied considerably. On the 4th July 1663 Pepys and Creed, ' coming late ' to the ' King's Head ' ordinary at Charing Cross, dined very well at the second table for twelve pence each. On another occasion, at the same tavern, Pepys spent a like sum, obtaining a veal chop, bread, cheese, and beer. At the famous Pontac's, celebrated in verse and prose by Dryden, Defoe, and Swift, the charge in 1690 was three shillings, according to the *Journal* of the Very Rev. R. Davies. This gentleman spent as little as sixpence for a dinner at the ' Black Eagle ' (Bride Lane ?) and as much as two shillings and sixpence at the ' Blue Posts ' (Haymarket or Holborn). In the country Brereton commonly spent sixpence or eightpence on his dinners. Taverns, coffeehouses—introduced in the mid-century—and Rhenish-wine-houses were great centres of conviviality, and much time was spent in them drinking, smoking, and gaming, to the impoverishment of many a gallant, and the profit of landlords and their more predatory guests.

G (see page 162)

' They take them [the condemned] five and twenty at a time, every month, besides sudden and extraordinary executions in the course of the week, on a large cart like a high scaffold. They go along quite jollily, holding their sprigs of rosemary and singing songs, accompanied by their friends and a multitude of people. On reaching the gallows one of the party acts as spokesman, saying fifty words or so. Then the music, which they had learnt at their leisure in the prisons, being repeated, the executioner hastens the business, and beginning at one end, fastens each man's halter to the gibbet. They are so closely packed that they touch each other with their hands tied in front of them, wrist to wrist, so as to leave them the option of taking off their hats and saluting the bystanders. One careless fellow availed himself of this facility to shade his face from the sun. Finally, the executioner having come down from the scaffold, has the whip applied to the cart horses, and thus the culprits remain dangling in the air precisely like a bunch of fat thrushes. They are hard to die of themselves and unless their own relations or friends pulled their feet or pelted them with brickbats in the breast as they do, it would fare badly with them. The proceeding is really barbarous and strikes those who witness it with horror.' Horatio Busino, Chaplain of Pietro Contarini, Venetian Ambassador in London, 1618, *Venetian State Papers*, vol. 1617-19.

H (see page 192)

The following licence to travel was granted pursuant to the Act of 1649-50, wherein it was ordained that applicants before receiving authorization should take an engagement of being true and faithful to the Commonwealth without King or House of Lords. The licensee was in this case an old gentleman of eighty years of age.

' Whereas John Willoughby, of Peyhembrey, in the county of

Devon, Esq., beinge desirous to visitte his children and kindred, and
to live sometyme with them, for which end he hath petitioned for
a Licence to Travell, in obedience to an Acte of Parliament in that
behalfe made, bearing date the 26ᵗʰ of February 1649. By virtue of
which Acte (he haveing taken the engagement before us) wee doe give
him libberty to travell to Tolland and Sellworthy, both in Somersett-
sheire, and to Seaton and Axmouth in Devon, and to retourne againe
within seaven monethes after the date hereof, soe as in the meane tyme
he acte nothing to the prejudice of the State. Hereunto wee subscribe
our hands and seales, the 25th day of March 1651 (1652).

> Wllm Fry
> Tho Drake
> Ro. Duke
> John Tyrlinge

' Indorsed : My Lycence to Travell, and mencioning my ingage-
ments.' From *The Trevelyan Papers*, Part III, Camden Soc., No. 105
p. 273.

I (see page 198)

Stoppage of intercourse between neighbouring towns gave rise
sometimes to dissension. An indignant letter was sent, in 1633, from
Beverley to Hull, upon the stopping of Beverley people at the gates of
Hull, as a result of a false report that a fresh outbreak of Plague had
occurred at Beverley. The town was safe and in good condition, said
the writer, the people in the Pest House about to be set at liberty, and
the house to be cleansed. Four years later the tables were turned.
Beverley closed its gates against Hull. The Corporation of Beverley
forbade any concourse of people to assemble in the town, and also the
entry of any goods or persons from Hull, upon pain of five pounds
forfeiture for each offence. Inhabitants of Beverley were forbidden
to resort to Hull except upon licence from the Mayor and two
Governors, penalty for transgression being ten shillings for every
offence. Any inhabitant of Beverley who entertained an inhabitant
of Hull without a certificate from the Mayor of Hull approved by
the Mayor of Beverley and two governors of the town was liable to
a penalty of five pounds. See *Bygone England*, by William Andrews,
F.R.H.S., 1892, pp. 28–30.

J (see page 226)

' The Right to Purveyance or Pre-emption as it was called, was
a prerogative enjoyed by the Crown, of buying up provisions and other
necessaries for the use of the Royal Household at an appraised valuation,
in preference to all other purchasers, and even without the owner's
consent.' John Nichols, *The Progresses of King James the First*,
vol. i, p. x.

'The prerogative of purveyance included, besides the right of pre-emption of victuals, the compulsory use of horses and carts and even the enforcement of personal labour.   In the midst of ploughing or harvest the husbandman was liable to be called on to work and to lend his horses for the service of the court. . . .' W. Stubbs, *Constitutional History of England*, vol. ii, pp. 538–9, ed. 1877.

This ancient feudal right, which was not legally abolished until the restoration of the Monarchy in 1660, was a heavy tax upon the country-side, and, moreover, a constant subject of complaint owing to the abuses indulged in by the royal purveyors.   The assessed value of goods was always far below market value.   Some purveyors abated payment by exacting poundage; that is withholding twelvepence in the pound on what they had agreed to pay.   Some exacted double poundage, first when the price was fixed, and, subsequently, when payment was made.   Others warned more carts than were necessary, and then granted exemptions on receipt of payment.   There were some who took ten times the quantity of goods needed and sold the overplus.   Often when the cattle which had been conscribed reached their destination, abatement of price was made by purveyors on account of the impover-ished state in which they arrived after their journey.   At times pur-veyors even went so far as to withhold the whole sum of money that was owing to their enforced caterers.   Goods and carts were seized on the highways, contrary to law, or taken by night instead of by day as was ordained.

To avoid all these abuses a custom (of an intermittent character) arose during the later years of Elizabeth for counties to make composi-tion at fixed rates in lieu of service.   The arrangement apparently extended only to purveyance for the King's own residences, or standing houses, and did not take account of provisions required for the King's Progresses.   See *Quarter Sessions from Elizabeth to Anne, chiefly of the County of Devon*, p. 9.   In 1605 abuses reached such a height that the Commons determined to make petition to the King for abolition of the odious imposition.   Sir Francis Bacon was deputed to be spokes-man and made an impressive appeal.   'If it be not', he said, 'the most heinous abuse, yet it is the most common and general abuse of all others in the Kingdom.'   Although the traffic was not abolished, it is probable that grievances were redressed.   But it was only for a time.   In 1621 some 'cartakers' (purveyors) were committed to prison for mis-appropriation.   A year later schemes were under consideration for the prevention of abuses.   How little compassion the prodigal James had for his oppressed subjects is shown by an incident related in Aikin's *Memoirs of the Court of James I.*   One day when the King was hunting at Royston, a hound was discovered to have a paper tied about his neck, with the following prescription; 'Good Mr. Jowler, we pray you speak to the king (for he hears you every day, and so he doth not us) that it will please his majesty to go back to London: for else the country will be undone : all our provision is spent already, and we are not able to entertain him longer.' The King took the strangely presented petition as a jest and did not relieve the neighbourhood of his unwelcome presence.

K (see page 244)

When Lord Guilford went on the Northern circuit, he was invited to see the coal mines and salt works ' with the wonders that belonged to them '. He and his party were taken by the magistrates down to Tynemouth Castle in a barge, the equipment of which was ' very stately '. Ahead ' sat a four or five drone bagpipe ', and astern a trumpeter. Arrived at Tynemouth they saw the making of salt, then had supper in the open air, upon an island near the town, where good appetites, and provisions, charming scenery, the ' merry stories of the Scots ', and the strange tales related by some of the Newcastle Aldermen of their ' coal-works ', made the evening pass agreeably. Next day the party dined with Sir Ralph Delaval at Seaton Delaval, where they saw his salt pans, and the harbour he had made for the export of his coal and salt. On the way South from Lancaster ' his lordship took all the advantage he could of seeing great towns and places of Note '. Where the distances between any two assize towns were great, it was customary for the Judges and their train to rest at some country mansion ; usually, it would appear, at the same mansion year after year. In the Camden Miscellany, vol. 4, an account is given, for the years 1596–1601, of the expenses of the Judges riding the Western and Oxford circuits. The charges were borne partly by the Exchequer and partly by the Judges themselves. Among the items we note rewards to messengers for the bringing of presents, alms for the poor, and payment for the drying of boots ; the last a recurring item, even during summer circuits.

L (see page 253)

Bull-baiting, like bear-baiting and cock-fighting, was a popular pastime. Strutt, writing in the earlier part of last century, believed that there still remained in some market towns the rings to which the animals were attached. Such sport, he added, rarely ended without some sort of riot or confusion. In London the baiting of bulls, bears, and horses was forbidden in the streets. In Somersetshire, at the January Quarter Sessions, 1607–8, order was made ' that all Bulbaytings, Bearebaytings, Churchales, Clerkeales, Woodwardsales, Bidales, and all kindes of such like ales whatsoever ' were to be suppressed throughout the county, and that an order made by the Lord Chief Justice and other Justices of the Peace of the County was to be ' fully renewed, confirmed, and established '.

This same year Thomas Nethellyng confessed at Quarter Sessions that ' he keepeth three fighting bulls, with which he travelleth to such watches and other places as he is hired ; and saith since Easter he hath been at Ilton, two days at Baker's Churchale, and had for his Bull's fighting there 13*s*. 4*d*. ; and at Ilchester with John Bowden at a watch which he kept ; and at Gregory Stoke with one Trystram Bale, who kept a watch, and had there 9*s*. He was likewise at Meere in Wiltes, where he stayed two days with his Bulls and had xx*s*. for his pains ; and was likewise at Sturminster in Dorset at Rasedown watch, where he stayed two days and had xx*s*. for his pains ; and was also at Sherborne Churchale with his bull, and stayed there one day, and had for his bull's fighting x*s*.' As a result of this ample confession he was whipped, or, in the words of the Sessions Roll ' Flagell. and relax.'. No further indictments are recorded until 1656, when information was lodged with the Justices of two more bull-baitings.

M (see page 259)

' Theoretically every person had one parish, and one only, in which he or she had a settlement and a right to parish relief. In practice it was often difficult to decide which parish had the duty of relief, and disputes gave rise to endless litigation. From this point of view eighteenth-century England was like a chessboard of parishes, on which the poor were moved about like pawns. The foundation of the various laws on the subject was an Act passed in Charles II's reign (13 and 14 Charles II, c. 12) in 1662. Before this Act each parish had, it is true, the duty of relieving its own impotent poor and of policing its own vagrants, and the infirm and aged were enjoined by law to betake themselves to their place of settlement, which might be their birthplace, or the place where they had lived for three years, but, as a rule, "a poor family might, without the fear of being sent back by the parish officers, go where they choose, for better wages, or more certain employment ". [Note.—Ruggles, *Annals of Agriculture*, vol. xiv, p. 205.] This Act of 1662 abridged their liberty, and, in place of the old vagueness, established a new and elaborate system. The Act was declared to be necessary in the preamble, because " by reason of some defects in the law, poor people are not restrained from going from one parish to another, and therefore do endeavour to settle themselves in those parishes where there is the best stock, the largest commons or wastes to build cottages, and the most woods for them to burn and destroy ; and when they have consumed it, then to another parish, and at last become rogues and vagabonds ; to the great discouragement of parishes to provide stock, when it is liable to be devoured by strangers ". By the Act any new-comer, within forty days of arrival, could be ejected from a parish by an order from the magistrates, upon complaint from the parish officers, and removed to the parish where he or she was last legally settled. If, however, the new-comer settled in a tenement of the yearly value of £10, or could give security for the discharge of the parish to the magistrates' satisfaction, he was exempt from this provision.' T. L. Hammond and Barbara Hammond, *The Village Labourer*, 1760–1832, pp. 88–9.

But the Act neither stopped contention nor fraud. Three more Acts were passed during the further course of the seventeenth century with this object in view, without avail. ' Of all the appeals ' to Quarter Sessions, write S. and B. Webb,' four fifths—we hazard the estimate— were those instituted by one parish against another, in the incessant litigation as to the settlement and the removal of the ever-increasing army of paupers '. *The Parish and the County*, p. 420, note.

N (see page 268)

Licences had to be renewed annually as appears from an announcement in the *London Gazette* of 14–17th April 1684 : ' All Persons concerned, are hereby desired to take notice of and suppress all Mountebanks, Rope Dancers, Ballad-Singers, &c., that have not a License from the Master of his Majesties Revels (which for this present year are all Printed with Black Letters, and the King's Arms in Red) and particularly Samuel Ratherford and . . . Irich, mountebanks, and William Bevell and Richard Oldworth ; and all those that have Licenses with Red and Black Letters, are to come to the Office to change them for Licenses as they are now altered.'

The following forged licence, purporting to have been issued by Sir Henry Herbert, Master of the Revels, was the subject of an indictment in 1630 at the Worcestershire Quarter Sessions. The omissions are due to its imperfect state. ' To all Mayors Sheriffs Justices of the Peace Bayliffs Con[stables] and all other His Majestey's officers true liege men and subjects and every of them greeting know ye that whereas the King's Most Excellent Majestie hath granted unto the Master . . . Commission under the Great Seal of England giving thereby charge with full power and authority to the Master of the Revells and his deputy for the orde[ring] . . . and putting down of all Plays Players and Playmakers as of all other Shewes whatsoever in all places within his Majesty's Realm of England as well wi[thin] as without I have by these presents licensed and authorised *John Jones Anne* his wife *Richard Payne Richard Jones* and their assistants to set forth and shew . . . motion with divers stories in it also tumbling vaulting sleight of hand and other such like feats of activity requiring you and every of you in . . . suffer and permit the said *John Jones* and *Ann* his wife *Richard Payne Richard Jones* and their assistants quietly to pass together with their said shews with . . . trumpets as they or any of them shall think fitting for the same from time to time and at all times without any lett or molestation . . . places of jurisdiction Townes Corporate Cities or Boroughs whatsoever within the Realm of England they behaving themselves ho[nestly] . . . laws of the Realm . . . on the Sabboth day or in the time of Divine Service you affording them your . . .' *Worcestershire County Records*, p. 470.

O (see page 282)

Three changes of horse were customary on this route; vide the expenses of Major Richard Ferrier who set out for the Continent in 1687.

		£	s.	d.
April 6.	For a coat	1	15	6
	For a sword	1	0	0
8.	For my passage to Gravesend	0	2	0
	For horse-hire to Sittenborn	0	5	9
9.	For charges at Sittenborn	0	2	4
	For horse-hire to Canterbury	0	4	8
10.	For charges at Canterbury	0	7	6
11.	For hors-hire to Dover	0	4	3
12.	For charges at Dover	0	7	0
	For passage to Callice	0	8	6
	For carriage of cloaths and boat	0	2	6
		5	0	0

APPENDIX I

THE seventeenth-century point of view in regard to the sanctity of private property is exemplified by the following anecdote, related by Ellwood in his autobiography. The story has the further advantage of demonstrating wayside manners.

He writes :

' My Father being then in the Commission of the Peace, and going to a Petty Sessions at Watlington, I waited on him thither. And when we came near the Town, the Coachman seeing a nearer and easier Way (than the common Road) through a Corn-field, and that it was wide enough for the Wheels to run, without endamaging the Corn, turned down there. Which being observed by an Husbandman, who was at plow not far off, he ran to us, and stopping the Coach, poured forth a Mouthful of Complaints, in none of the best Language, for driving over the Corn. My Father mildly answered him, That if there was an Offence committed, he must rather impute it to his Servant, than himself ; since he neither directed him to drive that Way, nor knew which Way he drove. Yet added, that he was going to such an Inn at the Town ; whither if he came, he would make him full Satisfaction for whatsoever Damage he had sustained thereby. And so on we went, the Man venting his Discontent, as he went back, in angry Accents. At the Town, upon Enquiry, we understood that it was a Way often used, and without Damage, being broad enough ; but that it was not the common Road, which yet lay not far from it, and was also good enough ; wherefore my Father bid his Man drive home that Way.

' It was late in the Evening when we returned, and very dark ; and this quarrelsome Man, who had troubled himself and us in the Morning, having gotten another lusty Fellow, like himself, to assist him, way-lay'd us in the Night, expecting we would return the same Way we came. But when they found we did not, but took the common Way, they angry that they were disappointed, and loth to lose their Purpose (which was to put an Abuse upon us) coasted over to us in the dark, and laying hold on the Horses Bridles, stopt them from going on. My Father asking his Man, what the Reason was that he went not on, was answered, That there were two Men at the Horses Heads, who held them back, and would not suffer them to go forward. Whereupon my Father opening the Boot, stept out, and I followed close at his Heels. Going up to the Place where the Men stood, he demanded of them the Reason of this Assault. They said, We were upon the Corn. We knew, by the Routs, we were not on the Corn, but in the common Way, and told them so. But they told us, They were resolved they would not let us go on any farther but would make us go back again. My Father endeavoured, by gentle Reasoning, to perswade them to forbear, and not run themselves farther into the Danger of the Law, which they were run too far into already ; but they rather derided him for it. Seeing therefore fair Means would not work upon them, he spake more roughly to them, charging them to deliver their Clubs (for each of them had a great Club in his Hand, somewhat like those which are called Quarter-Staves). They thereupon, laughing, told him They did not bring them thither for that End. Thereupon my Father, turning his Head to me, said, Tom, disarm them . . . Wherefore stepping boldly forward, to lay hold on the Staff of him that was nearest to me, I said, Sirrah, deliver your Weapon. He thereupon raised his Club, which was big enough to have knockt down an Ox, intending no doubt to have knockt me down with it, as probably he would have done, had not I, in the Twinkling of an Eye, whipt out my Rapier and made a Pass upon him. I could not have failed running of him through up to the Hilt, had he stood his Ground ; but the suddain and unexpected Sight of my bright Blade, glittering in the dark Night, did so amaze and terrify the Man, that slipping aside, he avoided my Thrust ; and letting his staff sink, betook himself to his Heels for safety, which his Companion seeing, fled also. I followed the former as fast as I could, but Timor addidit Alas, Fear gave him Wings, and made him swiftly fly ; so that although I was accounted very nimble, yet the farther we ran, the more Ground he gain'd on me, so that I could not overtake him. . . . Mean while the Coachman, who had sufficiently the Outside of a Man, excus'd himself from intermedling, under Pretence that he durst not leave his Horses, and so left me to shift for myself. And I was gone so far beyond my Knowledge, that I understood not which Way I was to go, till by hollowing, and being hollowed to again, I was directed where to find my Company.

' We had easy Means to have found out who these Men were (the principal of them having been in the Day-time at the Inn, and both quarrelled with the Coachman, and threatned to be even with him when he went back ;) but since they came

off no better in their Attempt, my Father thought it better not
to know them, than to oblige himself to a Prosecution of them.'

For some time after this (until his conversion to the Quaker
faith), Ellwood never went upon 'those publick Services'
without a loaded pistol in his pocket.

APPENDIX II

In *Much Ado about Nothing* Shakespeare parodies the proceedings of the Watch. The exaggeration, however, seems so
slight, the description, in the main, so little removed from
truth, that an extract of the relevant scene may well amplify
our picture of the Watch.

Act III, Scene iii.

Enter Dogbery and his Compartner with the Watch.

Dog. Are you good men and true?

Verges. Yea, or else it were pitty but they should suffer
salvation body and soule.

Dog. Nay, that were a punishment too good for them, if
they should have any allegeance in them, being chosen for the
Princes watch.

Verges. Well, give them their charge, neighbour Dogbery.

Dogbery. First, who thinke you the most desartlesse man to
be Constable?

Watch 1. Hugh Ote-cake sir, or George Sea-cole, for they
can write and reade.

Dogbery. Come hither neighbor Sea-coale. God hath blest
you with a good name: to be a welfavoured man, is the gift
of Fortune; but to write and reade, comes by nature.

Watch 2. Both which maister Constable.

Dogbery. You have: I knew it would be your answer:
wel, for your favour sir, why give God thanks, and make no
boast of it, and for your writing and reading, let that appeere
when there is no need of such vanity, you are thought heere to
be the most senslesse and fit man for the Constable of the
watch; therefore bear you the lanthorne: this is your charge:
You shall comprehend all vagrom men, you are to bidde any
man stand, in the Princes name.

Watch 2. How if a will not stand?

Dogbery. Why then, take no note of him, but let him goe,
and presently call the rest of the watch together, and thanke
god you are ridde of a knave.

Verges. If he wil not stand when he is bidden, he is none of the Princes subjects.

Dogbery. True, and they are to meddle with none but the Princes subjects : you shall also make no noise in the streetes : for, for the watch to babble and talke, is most tollerable, and not to be indured.

Watch. We will rather sleepe than talke, we know what belongs to a watch.

Dogbery. Why, you speak like an antient and most quiet watchman, for I cannot see how sleeping should offend : onely have a care that your billes bee not stolne : well, you are to cal at al the alehouses, and bid those that are drunke get them to bed.

Watch. How if they will not ?

Dogbery. Why then let them alone til they are sober, if they make you not then the better answer, you may say they are not the men you tooke them for.

Watch. Well sir.

Dogbery. If you meete a thiefe, you may suspect him, by vertue of your office, to be no true man : and for such kind of men, the less you meddle or make with them, why, the more is for your honesty.

Watch. If we know him to be a thiefe, shall we not lay hands on him ?

Dogbery. Truely, by your office you may, but I thinke they that touch pitch will be defilde : the most peaceable way for you, if you doe take a thiefe, is to let him shew himselfe what he is, and steale out of your companie.

Verges. You have beene alwayes called a mercifull manne, partner.

Dog. Truely, I would not hang a dogge by my will, much more a man who hath anie honestie in him.

Verges. If you heare a child crie in the night you must call to the nurse, and bid her stil it.

Watch. How if the nurse be asleepe, and will not hear us ?

Dog. Why then depart in peace, and let the child wake her with crying, for the ewe that will not heare her lamb when it baes, will never answer a calfe when he bleates.

Verges. Tis very true.

Dog. The end of this is the charge : you, constable are to present the princes owne person, if you meete the prince in the night, you may stay him.

Verges. Nay, birlady that I think a cannot.

Dog. Five shillings to one on't with any man that knowes the statutes, he may stay him, mary, not without the prince be willing, for indeed the watch ought to offend no man, and it is an offence to stay a man against his will.

Verges. Birlady I thinke it be so.

Dog. Ha, ah, ha, wel masters, good night, and there be any matter of weight chaunces, call up me, keepe your fellowes counsailes and your owne, and good night, Come, neighbour.

Watch. Well masters, we heare our charge, let us goe sitte here uppon the church bench till twoo, and then all to bed. . . .

APPENDIX III

How many things were needed by a gentleman traveller the following rude verses demonstrate—verses which the Rev. W. W. Skeat describes as the worst extant in the English language. They belong to Master Fitzherbert's *Book of Husbandry* (1534) and are therefore not strictly relevant to seventeenth-century travel.

' A lesson made in Englisshe verses, to teache a gentylmans servant, to saye at every tyme whan he taketh his horse, for his remembraunce that he shall not forget his gere in his inne behynde hym.

> Purse, dagger, cloke, nyght-cap, kerchef, shoyng-horne, and shoes.
> Spere, male, hode, halter, sadelclothe, spores, hatte, with thy horse-combe.
> Bowe, arrowes, sworde, bukler, horne, leisshe, gloves, stringe, and thy bracer.
> Penne, paper, inke, parchmente, reedwaxe, pommes, bokes, thou remember.
> Penknyfe, combe, thimble, nedle, threde, poynte, leste that thy gurthe breake.
> Bodkyn, knyfe, lyngel, gyve thy horse meate, se he be showed well.
> Make mery, synge and thou can ; take hede to thy gere, that thou lose none.'

> Reedwaxe, Sealing wax.
> Pommes, Pumice.
> Poynte, A tagged lace.
> Lyngel, Shoemaker's thread.

SOME BOOKS CONSULTED

Aikin, Lucy. *Memoirs of the Court of James I,* vol. i, 1822.
Aubrey, John. *Brief Lives,* ed. by A. Clark, 2 vols., 1898.
Bassompierre. *Mémoires du Maréchal,* Nouvelle Collection de Mémoires pour servir a l'histoire de France, J. F. Michaud et J. J. F. Poujoulat, S. 11, T. 6, 1850.
Bates, E. S. *Touring in 1600,* 1911.
Bibliotheca Lindesiana, vol. v, *Tudor and Stuart Proclamations,* 1910.
Birch, T. *History of the Royal Society of London,* vol. ii, 1756–7.
—— *The Court and Times of James I,* ed. R. F. Williams, 2 vols., 1848.
Blackstone, William. *Commentaries on the Laws of England,* Bk. I, ed. 1765.
Blencowe, R. W. Extracts from the Journal and Account Book of the Rev. Giles Moore, 1655–79, Sussex Archaeol. Soc. Coll., vol. i, 1848.
—— Extracts from the Diary of a Sussex Tradesman of a Hundred Years ago, 1754–65, Sussex Archaeol. Soc. Coll., vol. xi, 1859.
—— *The Paucity of High Roads in Sussex,* Sussex Archaeol. Soc. Coll., vol. xvi, 1864.
Blome, R. *Britannia,* 1673.
Bohun, Edmund. *The Justice of the Peace,* 1693.
Bramston, Sir John. *Autobiography of,* Camden Soc., No. 32.
Brereton, Sir William. *Travels in Holland, the United Provinces, England, Scotland, and Ireland,* Chetham Soc., No. 1.
Brome, James. *Travels over England, Scotland, and Wales,* 1700.
Brown, Rawdon. Diaries and Dispatches of the Venetian Embassy at the Court of King James I, *Quarterly Review,* July 1857.
Browne, Sir Thomas. *Works of,* vol. i, ed. 1836.
Bund, J. W. Willis. *Worcestershire County Records, 1591–1643,* Worcestershire Record Soc., 1900.
Burrell, Timothy. *Journal of,* Sussex Archaeol. Soc. Coll., vol. iii.
Burton, Thomas, M.P. *Diary of,* 1656–9, vol. i, 1828.
Calendars of State Papers, Domestic.
Camden, William. *Britannia,* Trans. 1610, 1695, 1789.
Cartwright, Thomas, D.D. *Diary of,* Camden Soc., No. 22.
Challoner, Richard, D.D. *Memoirs of Missionary Priests,* vol. ii, 1843.
Chamberlayne, Edward. *Angliae Notitia, or the Present State of England,* eds. 1669, 1687.
Clarendon, Edward Hyde, Earl of. *The Life of,* 3 vols., Oxford ed. 1827.
Clarendon, Henry Hyde, Earl of. *Correspondence, with Diary from 1687–1690,* 2 vols., ed. S. W. Singer, 1828.

Clavel, John. *Recantation of an ill ledde Life*, 1628.
Clowes, William Laird. *The Royal Navy*, vol. ii, 1898.
Coach and Sedan pleasantly disputing for Place and Precedence, the Brewer's Cart being moderator, signed Mis-amaxius, 1636.
Cooper, Elizabeth. *The Life and Letters of the Lady Arabella Stuart*, vol. ii, 1866.
Cotton, Charles. Epistle to John Bradshaw, Esq.; Chalmers, *The Works of the English Poets*, vol. vi.
Coulon, Louis. *Le Fidèle Conducteur pour le Voyage d'Angleterre*, 1654.
Cowper, The Earl of. MSS. of the *Coke MSS.*, Hist. MSS. Comm., 12th Report, App., 2 vols.
Cox, J. Charles. *Three Centuries of Derbyshire Annals*, 2 vols.
Creighton, Charles. *A History of Epidemics in Britain*, ed. 1891.
C[resset], J[ohn]. *A copy of a Printed Letter from J. C., to a Postmaster in the Country, with directions for the management of his design for putting down stage coaches* . . . 1672.
—— *A copy of a Letter in answer to J. C.*, 1672.
—— *Stage Coaches Vindicated, or Certain animadversions upon several papers written by J. C.*, 1672.
Cunningham, Peter. *Handbook for London*, vol. ii.
Cunningham, William. *Growth of English Industry and Commerce*, vols. i and ii.
Dalton, Michael. *The Countrey Justice*, 1618.
Davenant, William. *Declamations at Rutland House, Works*, 1673.
Davies, Rowland, V. Rev. *Journal* of, Camden Soc., No. 68.
Defoe, Daniel. *An Essay upon Several Projects*, 1697, *Works*, vol. iii, ed. 1840.
—— *A Tour of Great Britain*, 1724, 3 vols.
—— *Journal of the Plague Year*, 1665, 1754.
Dekker, Thomas. *A Knight's Conjuring done in earnest : Discovered in Jest*, Percy Soc.
De Laune, Thomas. *Angliae Metropolis, or the Present State of London*, eds. 1681, 1690.
D'Ewes, Sir Simmonds. *Autobiography and Corr. of*, 2 vols., 1845.
—— *College Life in the Time of James I, Illus. by the Diary of*, 1851.
Dictionary of National Biography. Col. Thos. Blount; James Butler, 1st D. of Ormonde; Sir John Coventry; Sir John Fenwick; Charles Gerard, 2nd Brn Brandon and E. of Macclesfield; Dr. Robert Hooke; Charles Paulet, 1st D. of Bolton and M. of Winchester; Charles Talbot, D. of Shrewsbury; Lady Arabella Stuart; Barbara Villiers, Duchess of Cleveland.
Dugdale, Sir William. *Life and Diary and Corr. of*, ed. 1827.
Du Vall, M. *Memoirs of*, Harl. Misc., vol. iii, 1809.
Earle, John, D.D. Microcosmography, ed. 1897.
Egerton. *The Papers, Public and Private*, Camden Soc., No. 12, 1840.
Ellis, Henry. *Original Letters Illust. of English History*, S. 1, vol. iii.

Ellis, Henry. *Original Letters of Eminent Literary Men of the 16th, 17th, and 18th Centuries*, Camden Soc., No. 6.

Ellwood, Thomas. *History of the Life of . . . by his own hand*, 1765.

Evelyn, John. *Diary* of, ed. William Bray, Everyman ed.

—— A Character of England, *Misc. Works*, 1825, and Harl. Misc., vol. x, 1813.

Falkland, The Lady (Elizabeth Cary). Her *Life*. Also *Memoirs of Father Slingsby*, 1861.

Fell, Sarah. *The Household Account Book of, 1673–8*, ed. N. Penney, 1920.

Ferriet, Richard, Major. *Journal* of, Camden Misc., No. 9.

Fiennes, Celia. *Through England on a Side Saddle in the time of William and Mary*, 1888. Edited by the Hon. Mrs. Griffiths.

Firth, C. H. *Cromwell's Army*, 1902.

Firth, C. H. and R. S. Rait. *Acts and Ordinances of the Interregnum*, 3 vols., 1911.

Fox, George. The *Journal* of, ed. by N. Penney, 1911.

Gardiner, S. R. *History of England, 1603–42*, vols. i and v, 1863, 1875.

Gemilli-Careri, John, Dr. *Travels through Europe, A Coll. of Voyages and Travels*, (A.) and J. Churchill, vol. iv, 1745.

Gilbey, Walter, Sir. *The Harness Horse*, 1898.

—— *The Great Horse*, 1899.

—— *Horses, Past and Present*, 1900.

—— *Early Carriages and Roads*, 1903.

Gonzales, Don Manoel. *Voyages of, Coll. of Voyages*, John Pinkerton, vol. ii, 1730.

Grammont, Count de.—*Memoirs* of, trans., ed. by Sir Walter Scott, 1846 [T. Blount].

Grand Concern (The) of England Explained ; in several proposals offered to the Consideration of Parliament. London, 1673, and Harl. Misc., No. 8.

Grey, Antichell. *Debates of the House of Commons*, Coll. by, 1667–94, vol. i, 1769.

Halkett, Lady Anne. The *Autobiography* of, Camden Soc., N.S., No. 13.

Hamilton, A. H. A. *Quarter Sessions from Queen Elizabeth to Queen Anne*, 1878.

Hammond, J. L. and B. *The Village Labourer, 1760–1832*, 1922.

Harbin, Rev. E. H. Bates. Quarter Sessions Records for the County of Somerset, *Som. Record Soc.*, Nos. 23, 24, 28.

Hardy, W. J. *Hertford County Records*, Notes and Extracts from the Sessions Rolls, 1581–1698, vol. i.

Harley, The Lady Brilliana. The *Letters* of, Camden Soc., No. 58.

Harper, C. G. *Stage Coach and Mail in Days of Yore*, vol. i, 1903.

—— *The Newmarket, Bury, Thetford, and Cromer Roads*, 1904.

—— *Half Hours with the Highwaymen*, 2 vols., 1908.

Harrison, William. *Desc. of England in Shakespeare's Youth :* the second and third books of his *Desc. of Britaine,* ed. by F. J. Furnivall. Also Part 4, containing a description of the locks and weirs on the Thames in Shakespeare's time.

Hatton. *Corr. of the Family of,* 1601–1704, Camden Soc., N.S., Nos. 22, 23.

Head, Richard, and F. Kirkman. *The English Rogue,* in the *Life of Meriton Latroon,* 1665, R.P. 1874.

Herbert of Cherbury, Lord. *Life* of, by himself, ed. 1830.

Heylyn, Peter, D.D. *Hist. and Misc. Tracts* of, and *Life,* by G. Vernon, 1681.

Heywood, Oliver, Rev. *Autobiography, Diaries, Anecdotes, and Event Books, 1630–1702,* ed. by J. Horsfall Turner, 4 vols, 1872–85.

Hind, Capt. J. *Life* of, *Hist. and Biog. Tracts,* George Smeeton, vol. ii, 1820.

Holloway, William. *History and Antiquities of Rye,* 1847.

Howard, Sir Robert. *The Committee,* 1735.

Howard, Lord William. *Selections from the Household Books of Howard of Naworth,* Surtees Soc., No. 68.

Howell, James. *Epistoloe Ho-Elianae,* ed. 1890.

—— *Instructions for forreine Travel,* 1642, ed. by Edward Arber.

Howitt, William. *The Rural Life in England,* vol. i, 1838.

Humpherus, Henry. *History of the Origin and Progress of the Company of Watermen and Lightermen of the R. Thames,* vol. i, 1887.

Hutchinson, Lucy. *Memoirs of the Life of Col. Hutchinson,* ed. 1906.

Jeaffreson, J. C. *Middlesex County Records,* 4 vols., 1888–92.

Johnson, Capt. Charles. *Lives of the Highwaymen,* 1734.

Jorevin, M. *Desc. of England and Ireland in the 17th Century, The Antiquarian Repertory,* Francis Grose, 1809.

Josselin, Rev. Ralph. *Diary* of, 1616–83, ed. for Roy. Hist. Soc. by E. Hockliffe, 1908.

Joyce, Herbert. *Hist. of the Post Office,* 1893.

Kemp, W. *A Nine Days' Wonder, in a dance from London to Norwich,* 1600, *An English Garner,* Edward Arber, vol. ii, 1903.

King, Gregory. *Natural and Political Observations and Conclusions upon the State and Condition of England,* 1696, ed. by George Chalmers, 1804.

Lambard, William. *The Duty and Office of Constables,* 1677.

Lee, W. L. Melville. *A Hist. of Police in England,* 1901.

Leigh, Edward. *A Diatribe of Travel,* 1671, Harl. Misc., No. 10.

Le Neve. *Cal. of Corr. relating to the Family of Oliver Le Neve of Witchingham, Norfolk,* 1675–1743, ed. by Francis Rye, 1895.

Leonard, E. M. *Early Hist. of English Poor Relief,* 1900.

Lewin, William. *Her Majesty's Mails,* 1864.

Lilly, William, *Life* of, by himself, 1774.

Littleton, E. *Proposals for Maintaining and Repairing the Highways*, 1692 (B.M.).

London Gazette, The, vol. 1682–5.

Loseley. *The . . . Manuscripts*, ed. by A. J. Kempe, 1835.

Lower, M. A. *Sir William Springett and the Springett Family*, Sussex Archaeol. Soc. Coll., vol. xx.

Luttrell, Narcissus. *A Brief Hist. Relation of State Affairs from Sept. 1678 to April 1714*, 6 vols., 1857.

Lysons, Daniel. *The Environs of London*, vol. ii, ed. 1811.

Macaulay, T. B. *Hist. of England from the Accession of James II*, vol. i.

Mace, Thomas. *Profit, Convenience, and Pleasure to the Whole Nation (Highways of England)*, 1675.

Magalotti, Lorenzo. *Travels of Cosmo, Grand Duke of Tuscany, through England, 1668–9*, 1821.

Maitland, William, *Hist. of London*, vol. i, 1756.

Markland, J. H. Some Remarks on the early use of Carriages in England, *Archaeologia*, No. 20.

Martindale, Adam. *Life of*, Chetham Soc., No. 4.

Mather, William. *Of Repairing and Mending the Highways*, 1696 (B.M.).

Meriton, George. *A Guide for Constables, Churchwardens, Overseers of the Poor*, 1669.

Misson, H. *Memoirs and Observations in his Travels over England*, trans. by Mr. Ozell, 1719, from original French of 1697.

Morris, J. *The Troubles of our Catholic forefathers as related by themselves*, 1872–3.

Morrison, Alfred. *Coll. of Letters* comp. by A. Thibadeau, *Cat. of the Coll. of Autograph Letters and Hist. Documents formed between 1865 and 1882 by A. M.*, vol. iii.

Moryson, Fynes. *An Itinerary*, 4 vols., reprint of 1617 ed., 1907–8.

Newcome, Henry, Rev. *Diary of*, Chetham Soc., No. 18.

—— *Autobiography of*, ed. by R. Parkinson, D.D., Chetham Soc., Nos. 26–7.

Nichols, John. *The Progresses, Processions . . . of Queen Elizabeth*, vol. i, 1823.

—— *The Progresses, Processions . . . of King James the First*, 4 vols., 1828.

North, Roger, The Hon. *The Lives of Baron Guilford . . . together with the Autobiog. of the Author*, ed. by A. Jessop, D.D., 3 vols., 1890.

Norwich. *Extracts from the Court Books of the City of, 1668–88*, ed. by Walter Rye.

Notes and Queries. S. 1, vols. i and vii ; S. 2, vol. x.

Ogilby, John. *Britannia*, 1675.

—— *Itinerarium Angliae*, 1675.

Ogilby, John. *The Traveller's Guide,* 1699.

Overbury, Thomas, Sir. *Characters, Misc. Works,* ed. by E. F. Rimbault, 1856.

Pennant, Thomas. *Some Account of London,* 1813.

Pepys, Samuel. *Diary* of, ed. by Lord Braybrooke.

Planché, J. R. *Cyclopaedia of Costume,* vol. i, 1876.

Plot, Dr. Robert. *The Natural History of Oxfordshire,* 1677.

Post Office, An Hist. Summary, 1911.

Prideaux, Humphrey. *Letters of, to John Ellis,* Camden Soc., N.S., No. 15.

Privy Council Acts, N.S., 1600–1, 1613–14.

Proclamations, Books of.

Proctor, Thomas. . . . *Concerning the mending of High-ways, as also Waters and Iron-works,* 1610.

Prothero, Rowland E. *The Pioneers and Progress of English Farming,* 1888.

Pryme, Abraham de la. The *Diary* of, Surtees Soc., No. 54.

Radcliffe, Sir George. *Life and Corr.* of, ed. by T. D. Whitaker, 1810.

Rawdon, Marmaduke. The *Life* of, Camden Soc., No. 85.

Ray, John. *Memorials of* (including Itineraries of travel), Ray Soc., 1846.

Relation (A) of a Short Survey of 26 Counties, 1634, ed. by L. G. Wickham Legg, 1904.

Reresby, Sir John. *Memoirs* of, 1634–89, ed. by J. J. Cartwright, M.A., 1875.

Roberts, George. *The Social Hist. of the People of the S. Counties of England,* 1856.

Rogers, J. E. Thorold. *The History of Agriculture and Prices,* vols. v and vi, 1887.

—— *The Economic Interpretation of History,* vol. i, 1905.

Rye, W. B. *England as seen by Foreigners in the days of Elizabeth and James I,* 1865.

Rymer. *Foedera,* Syllabus in English, vol. ii.

Serre, M. de la. *Hist. of the Entry of Mary de Medicis . . . into England,* 1638, trans. 1639, *Antiquarian Repertory,* Francis Grose, vol. iv.

Sheppard, William. *The Office and Duties of Constables,* 1641.

Skippon, Philip. *An Account of a Journey made through Part of the Low Countries, Germany, Italy, and France, A Coll. of Voyages and Travels,* (A.) and J. Churchill, vol. vi, 1746.

Slingsby, Sir. Henry. *Diary* of, 1638–48, ed. by D. Parsons, 1836.

Smiles, Samuel. *Lives of the Engineers,* vol. i, 1861.

Smith, Capt. Alex. *A complete Hist. of the Lives of the Highwaymen,* 3 vols., 1719.

Sorbière, Samuel. *A Voyage to England,* 1667, trans. 1709.

Spence, Joseph. *Anecdotes, Observations and Characters of books and Men,* 1820.

Statutes of the Realm.   Edw. I to Will. III.

Stettin-Pomerania, Philip Julius, Duke of. *Diary of a Journey through England in the Year 1602*, trans. of the Roy. Hist. Soc., N.S., vol. vi, 1892.

Strauss, Ralph. *Carriages and Coaches*, 1912.

Strickland, Agnes. *Lives of the Queens of England*, vol. viii, 1845.

Strutt, Joseph. *The Sports and Pastimes of the People of England*, 1838.

Stubbs, William. *The Constitutional Hist. of England*, vol. ii, 1877.

Sydney, the Hon. Henry. *Diary of the Times of Charles II*, ed. by R. W. Blencowe, vol. ii,

Sydney, W. C. *Social Life in England from the Restoration to the Revolution, 1660–90*, 1892.

Taswell, William, D.D. *Autobiog. and Anecdotes of*, 1651–82, Camden Misc., No. 2.

Taunton, E. L. *Hist. of the Jesuits in England, 1580–1773*, vol. i, 1901.

Taylor, John (the Water Poet). *The Wonderfull Yeare*, 1603 ; *Phoenix Britannicus*, J. Morgan, 1732.

—— Spencer Society, *Works*.

Thacker, F. S. *The Thames Highway : a history of inland navigation*, 1914.

Thomson, Richard. *Chronicles of old London Bridge*, 1827.

Thoresby, Ralph. *Diary* of, 1677–1724, 2 vols.

Thornton, Alice. *Autobiog.* of, Surtees Soc., No. 62.

Traill, H. D. *Social England*, vol. iv, 1895.

Trevelyan, G. M. *England under the Stuarts* (*Hist. of Eng.*, ed. by C. W. C. Oman), 1904.

Trevelyan Papers, Part iii, Camden Soc., No. 105.

Trotter, Eleanor. *17th Century Life in a Country Parish*, 1919.

'Turbervil, Hodge' (Colonel Hewson ?). *Walk, Knaves, Walk, Phoenix Britannicus*, J. Morgan, 1732.

Turner, C. J. Ribton. *Hist. of Vagrants and Vagrancy*, 1889.

Turner, Rev. E. *High Roads in Sussex at the end of the 17th and commencement of the 18th Centuries*, Sussex Archaeol. Soc. Coll., No. 19.

—— *Domestic Habits and mode of Life of a Sussex gent in the 17th and early part of the 18th Centuries*, Sussex Archaeol. Soc. Coll., No. 23.

Unwin, G. *Industrial Organisation in the 16th and 17th Centuries*.

Vanbrugh, Sir John. *The Provok'd Husband, or a Journey to London* ; *Plays*, vol. ii, 1759.

Venetian State Papers, 1603–7, 1613–15, 1615–17, 1617–19.

Verney. *Memoirs of the Family of*, 4 vols., 1892–99.

—— *Hist. MSS. Rep.*, App. to Rep. 7.

Walmysley, T. *The Expenses of the Judges of Assize Riding the Western and Oxford Circuits, 1596–1601*, Camden Misc., No. 4.

Walton, Isaak, and Charles Cotton. *The Compleat Angler*, 1808.

Webb, Maria. *The Fells of Swarthmoor Hall and their Friends*, 1865.

Webb, S. and B. *English Local Government: The Parish and the County*, 1906; *The Story of the King's Highway*, 1913.

Wheatley, H. B. *London Past and Present*, 3 vols, 1891.

—— *The Story of London*, Medieval Town Series.

—— *Pepysiana*, 1899.

Whitelocke, Balstrode. *Memorials of the English Affairs . . .*, 1732. Edited by Arthur, Earl of Anglesea.

[Williams, John, alias T. Machet]. *The Confession of Four Highway-Men*.

Winwood, Ralph. *Memorials of Affairs of State*, vol. iii, 1725.

Wood, Anthony. *The Life and Times of*, 1632–95, coll. by A. Clark, 5 vols., Oxford Hist. Soc., 1904.

Wotton, Henry, Sir. *Reliquiae Wottonianae, Life and Letters*, 1685.

Wyntours. *The Wyntours of Huddington and the Gunpowder Plot*, Birmingham and Midland Institute, Archaeol. Sect., trans., vol. xxx, 1904.

Young, Arthur. *A Six Weeks' Tour through the Southern Counties of England and Wales*, 1772.

MAPS

Bartholomew, J. G. *The Survey Atlas of England and Wales*, Sect. 7, p. 18.

Hollar, W. *The Kingdom of England and Principality of Wales*, 1664.

London Topographical Society: reproductions of maps of London.

Speed, J. *The Atlas of England and Wales*, 1608.

INDEX

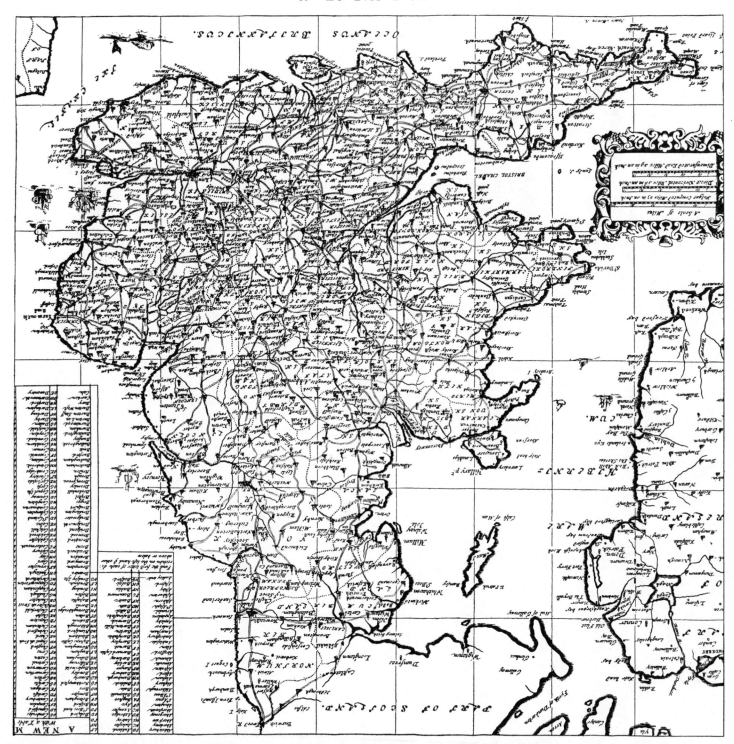

DATE DUE

2/3			
GAYLORD			PRINTED IN U.S.A.